China has already become the world's third largest economic power, and it currently presents enormous business opportunities. Yet there is still a dearth of information in the West about how Chinese firms are run.

In this invaluable book, Professor Child addresses this lack, examining management in China in all its different aspects. He covers the development of Chinese management during the period of economic reform in a number of areas including enterprise leadership, decision making, the management of marketing and purchasing transactions, the work roles of senior managers, personnel practices and reward systems. The experience of foreign firms entering joint ventures with Chinese enterprises is also reviewed in detail. The book provides a comprehensive and up-to-date survey of the subject, written on the basis of field work and direct contacts which the author has with Chinese enterprises.

Cambridge Studies in Management 23

Management in China during the age of reform

Cambridge Studies in Management   23

Formerly Management and Industrial Relations series

Editors
WILLIAM BROWN, *University of Cambridge*
ANTHONY HOPWOOD, *London School of Economics*
and PAUL WILLMAN, *London Business School*

The series focuses on the human and organizational aspects of management. It covers the areas of organization theory and behaviour, strategy and business policy, the organizational and social aspects of accounting, personnel and human resource management, industrial relations and industrial sociology.

The series aims for high standards of scholarship and seeks to publish the best among original theoretical and empirical research; innovative contributions to advancing understanding in the area; and books which synthesize and/or review the best of current research, and aims to make the work published in specialist journals more widely accessible.

The books are intended for an international audience among specialists in universities and business schools, undergraduate, graduate and MBA students, and also for a wider readership among business practitioners and trade unionists.

For a list of titles in this series, see end of book

Management in China during the age of reform

John Child

The Judge Institute of Management Studies
University of Cambridge

PUBLISHED BY THE PRESS SYNDICATE OF THE UNIVERSITY OF CAMBRIDGE
The Pitt Building, Trumpington Street, Cambridge CB2 1RP, United Kingdom

CAMBRIDGE UNIVERSITY PRESS
The Edinburgh Building, CambridgeCB2 2RU, United Kingdom
40 West 20th Street, New York, NY 10011–4211, USA
10 Stamford Road, Oakleigh, Melbourne 3166, Australia

First published 1994
First paperback edition published 1996

Printed in the United Kingdom at the University Press, Cambridge

Typeset in Times 10/12 pt

*A catalogue record for this book is available from
the British Library*

Library of Congress cataloguing in publication data

Child, John. 1940–
Management in China in the age of reform / John Child.
    p.   cm. – (Cambridge studies in management: 23)
Includes bibliographical references.
ISBN 0 521 42005 9
1. Management – China. 2. Joint ventures – China – Management.
3. China – Economic conditions – 1976– I. Title. II. Series.
HD70.C5C4516   1994
658'.00951 – dc20   93–41565   CIP

ISBN 0 521 42005 9 hardback
ISBN 0 521 57466 8 paperback

Contents

Part III   Joint ventures in China

Contents

Preface to the paperback edition

The publication of this paperback edition of *Management in China During the Age of Reform* affords an opportunity to update the reader on relevant developments since the book first appeared in 1994. This preface begins by recording salient economic developments in China which have taken place since then. It notes key events in the state-owned sector of industry on which much of the book concentrates, and concludes with a synopsis of developments in the foreign-funded sector. Although new events follow one another rapidly in China, the underlying economic and political structures and systems which mark out the country's unique character as an environment for management have not changed dramatically. I therefore believe that the analysis offered in the following chapters remains valid and useful.

China's economy has continued to develop rapidly during the 1990s, in terms of its growth, participation in world trade and investment in resources. It is now, without question, one of the world's major economic powers with a GDP which by 1995 ranked third behind those of the USA and Japan. It is estimated that, with a continuation of present trends, China will have become the world's largest economy by the year 2005.

In the first half of the 1990s, China attained a rate of economic growth that averaged 10.1 per cent despite a slow-down during 1990 and 1991. This level of economic growth has surpassed that of any other significant economy in the world. By 1994, China ranked first in the physical scale of production of many raw materials such as coal, cement, cotton and cereals, though its per capita output of agricultural and industrial goods was generally still far below that of the norm for developed countries. The structure of Chinese industry remains heavily weighted towards primary and secondary industry, with an as yet underdeveloped tertiary sector. Some 60 per cent of the country's total labour force is engaged in agriculture, while the large secondary sector accounting for almost half of the country's output value is still relatively inefficient.

A number of manufacturing industries have, nevertheless, become internationally competitive. This is especially true for industries, such as electrical products, which have attracted considerable foreign investment, and the newer technologies and methods of management which accompany it. These areas of production have also benefited from a rapidly expanding domestic market. China is, for instance, anticipated to become the world's largest market for personal computers by 1998. The so-called 'Open Door Policy' has been reflected in a rapid growth of China's international trade. This increased annually by 19.7 per cent from 1991 to 1994, greatly exceeding the world average growth rate of 4.5 per cent in the same period. China ranked 11th among the world's trading nations in 1995. With the exception of 1993, it has run a positive overseas trade balance during the 1990s to date, and had built up its foreign reserves to $US 75.4 billion by the end of 1995. This positive balance is, however, threatened by a high rate of inflation and double-digit growth. Enterprises with foreign investment are playing a major role in the increase of foreign trade. Such enterprises in 1995 accounted for 39.1 per cent of the national combined total of imports and exports. Although these foreign-funded firms have until now recorded a higher value of imports than exports, the gap is rapidly closing. During 1995, for instance, the value of their exports grew by 35 per cent, while the value of imports they accounted for rose by only 19 per cent.

Through considerable investment during the 1990s, China has endeavoured to sustain high growth and an improvement in socio-economic quality. In 1994, the proportion of GDP going to investment was 36 per cent, which is approaching twice the figure for many developed countries. About 10 per cent of this investment was supplied by foreign companies, including those owned by Overseas Chinese. Foreign capital-funding has been the most rapidly growing component of investment in China. It is easily the largest recipient of foreign direct investment among developing countries, and in 1995 stood second only to the USA as a global destination for FDI. Other indicators of improving socio-economic conditions include a rising literacy rate for adults, which at 73 per cent in 1992 was above the world median, a large and growing body of trained scientists and technologists, and an average life expectancy which at 69 years comes close to that of developed countries. Despite these improvements, however, China still lags behind developed countries in certain key respects such as the quality of its infrastructure and the share of its GDP going into research and development. The reform of its state-owned industries remains a particularly urgent need, requiring injections both of capital and of superior management.

As indicated above, foreign-funded firms are making a significant contribution to China's development. By the end of 1995, 259,379 projects involving negotiated funds of $US 395 billion had been approved, with some $US 135 billion actually being deployed. The 120,000 foreign-funded enterprises in operation by the end of 1995 employed 16 million people and accounted for over 13 per cent of China's national output value. Many of them are important sources of technology transfer and new management expertise.

Foreign-funded firms also contributed 10 per cent of China's total tax revenue in 1995, a rise of 60 per cent over the previous year. By end-1994, the largest sources of foreign investment in China in order of magnitude, following Hong Kong and Macau (through which much re-investment is channeled back into China), were Taiwan, the USA, Japan, Singapore and the UK.

Since 1992, there has been a steady increase in the number of transnational corporations investing in China, coming mainly from the 'Triad' of the USA, Japan and the European Union. Most of the projects funded by transnationals are relatively large scale and capital intensive. They bring advanced technology, high-level management expertise and a long-term strategic orientation. This category of foreign direct investment has primarily fed the development of the electronics and machinery sectors, and infrastructural projects. The Chinese partners are in the main state-owned enterprises, the revitalization of which has been a major objective of the Chinese economic reform, as this book describes in some detail.

State-owned enterprises in 1994 contributed approximately 34 per cent of China's gross industrial output by value, but were by that time accounting for under 7 per cent of the country's industrial growth and hence were playing only a minor role in driving China's economic development. It is, however, not easy to obtain either a comprehensive or a balanced view of the condition of state-owned enterprises. This is partly because there are quite wide variations in their economic health and vitality, and partly because their inefficiencies and losses have often been exaggerated by factors such as the communal burden they are expected to carry and misleading accounting systems which result in the understatement of book profits.

While some state-owned enterprises had improved their position, through rationalization, mergers and the exploitation of export opportunities, the majority were still in trouble. Their low efficiency was reflected in falling profits, rising losses, increasing indebtedness and a shortage of funds. Many of them face increasing competition from joint ventures with foreign companies and wholly-owned foreign subsidiaries. The inability of state enterprises to pay each other for goods and services continued to increase during 1995, according to a survey of some 300,000 businesses across China (Walker 1996a). This so-called 'triangular debt' also draws the banks into making unproductive loans and distorts the whole financial system.

During 1994 a series of new reforms was promulgated for the banking, taxation, foreign trade, enterprise and social security systems. These measures were to a large extent intended to reduce the financial burdens on state enterprises and improve their competitiveness. They heralded a unified tax system for domestic enterprises designed to ease the incidence of tax falling on state enterprises, a progressive separation of welfare and other non-productive activities from enterprises, and an increased application of the 1986 bankruptcy law. According to the State Tax Administration, the overall tax burden on companies did in fact fall by about 20 per cent in 1995.

Additional capital has been raised by some prominent state-owned enterprises through the issue of shares on the Shanghai, Shenzhen and Hong Kong stock markets. The performance of these shares has, however, been lukewarm at best. Problems of disclosure and indifferent management continue to present risks for portfolio investors. There has been discussion of experimenting with wholesale privatization, though the official watchword has continued to be that China will remain a socialist market economy.

A development of the social security system was also envisaged in order to provide a safety net for employees who would be displaced by downsizing and rationalization among state enterprises. Its introduction has, in practice, been very slow and this has contributed greatly to the delay in the implementation of further enterprise reform, particularly in view of the authorities' marked desire not to provoke social unrest. As it is, China already admits to an unemployment level of 3 per cent, and the true figure is probably closer to 10 per cent.

By the second half of 1995, it had become apparent that enterprise reform was proceeding only slowly. The implementation of bankruptcies among state-owned enterprises, originally scheduled to begin in that year, was postponed to await the establishment of appropriate social security arrangements to provide for displaced employees. Radical solutions such as privatization were no longer being seriously considered, although the conversion of state enterprises into joint stock companies through the formation of joint ventures with foreign-investing partners continued to be encouraged. Improvements are now expected to come from within the system in its largely existing form, and this places the onus on achieving better enterprise management. As an article in the official *People's Daily*, 26 October 1995, put it, 'it is the management system that is not in keeping with the market economy'. To emphasize this view, the *People's Daily* of 11 December 1995 took the unusual step of announcing that seven heads of state-owned enterprises in the north-eastern industrial city of Shenyang had been dismissed for bad management. As Chapter 9 describes, the central government has several times used Shenyang as a standard-bearer in its drive towards further economic reform. It was, for example, in 1986 the first city to permit the bankruptcy of a state-owned enterprise.

Employment and human resource management is one area of enterprise reform in which experimentation has continued. The so-called 'Three Systems Reforms' (*san gaige*) have concerned employment contracts, payment systems and social insurance. The introduction of contracts for employees was an important feature of the labour market reforms introduced in the second half of the 1980s. It signalled that lifetime employment could no longer be taken for granted and introduced limited-period contracts for newly recruited workers. By 1994, 26 per cent of staff and workers in state-owned enterprises were employed as contract workers (*hetong gong*), a proportion that had risen steadily over the previous ten years. The percentage of contract workers in collective enterprises was somewhat less at 20 per cent, while the figure for other firms (including foreign-funded ones) stood at almost 46 per cent (State Statistical Bureau 1995: Table 4-11). The contract system offered enterprises a growing opportunity to plan employment and secure additional flexibility in employment policy, as well as exerting some pressure for employees to perform adequately.

Reformed reward systems now stress material benefits. A 'post-plus-skills' formula was introduced by the government in 1992, whereby the basic salary is supposed to be determined by the responsibility of the post, plus technical skills acquired, with a bonus added for achievement of performance targets. The social insurance reform is intended to compensate for the progressive loss of the 'cradle-to-grave' protection which Chinese workers had enjoyed since the 1950s, and which has become a serious burden for state enterprises in particular. With the 1994 Labour Law, implemented in early 1995, fully legitimizing redundancies for the first time, unemployment insurance now assumes a critical role in covering a percentage of former earnings plus welfare benefits and pensions.

As with all the new laws and regulations under China's economic reform programme, it has taken time for new provisions to be implemented. In addition, they are typically subject to a large measure of local re-interpretation. Warner (1996) investigated the specific implementation of the employment reforms in ten enterprises located in Beijing and China's North-East during 1993. He found considerable variation in the extent to which the new provisions had been implemented, with the proportion of workers on contracts ranging between 10 and 100 per cent, and with the post-plus-skills payment system operating in only six of the enterprises. As already noted, it is also taking longer than anticipated to implement the new social security arrangements.

The management policies being encouraged in the present phase of enterprise reform are illustrated by state enterprises that have been officially selected as models worthy of emulation. One such is the Handan Iron and Steel Works, located some 300 km south of Beijing (Walker 1996b). Before 1990 when it began to introduce reforms, Handan was a loss-making enterprise. In that year, net profit was 1 million Yuan and net assets 580 million Yuan. By 1995, profits had climbed to 709 million Yuan and net assets stood at 4.6 billion Yuan. One of the first changes was to introduce accounting standards which valued the real cost of producing a ton of steel and set production targets based on market prices. The workers' bonus system was revised so that, instead of being paid extra whatever their contribution, workers are rewarded according to how well they achieve targets and contain costs. A strong market orientation has been injected into the firm, together with a determination not to incur the bad debts which were a concomitant of the regime of transacting on the basis of traditional ties and old relationships. Handan's policy is now not to ship any product until a contract is signed or payment received.

China's recent economic performance has been remarkably successful and, despite interludes due to inexperience in macro-economic regulation and political upheaval, the country's programme of economic reform has moved forward at a reasonably steady pace. This is not to say that there are no substantial problems remaining. As well as the inherited problem of the state enterprises, others are the concomitant of economic development itself. Any visitor to China in recent years cannot but be aware that a major environmental problem has emerged, and that corruption and lawlessness have become almost endemic in certain parts of the country. While the infrastructure has improved enormously during the past ten years, especially in telecommunications and internal air travel, power supplies and provision for the internal transportation of goods still trail the growth in demand for such services.

These problems are clearly pressing, but there is one issue which threatens to divide the country itself. It stems from the fact that the market forces given increasing rein under the economic reform have, since the mid-1980s, increased inequalities both between regions and between urban and rural areas. Given the natural economic advantages of the coastal provinces, which have attracted the lion's share of foreign investment, the gap in per capita income between them and the inland regions is likely to grow. Government policy-makers are acutely aware of these and other problems, which have been exacerbated by a combination of rapid growth and the progressive liberaliz-ation of market forces.

The Chinese authorities are keen for investment by foreign companies to play a role in resolving some of these difficulties. With this in mind, they have now more clearly distinguished between those industries, commercial activities and regions in which foreign investment is to be encouraged, or at least permitted, and those in which it is to be restricted or banned altogether. They continue to welcome inward foreign direct investment, but are determined to steer it towards priority sectors and the disadvantaged inland regions.

In June 1995, the central government published its *Interim Provisions on Guidance for Foreign Investment and the Industrial Catalog Guiding Foreign Investment*. The Interim Provisions apply to projects involving Sino–foreign joint ventures, co-operative ventures, and wholly-foreign-owned projects, together with all other types of project involving foreign funding. These projects are divided into four categories, in which foreign investment will be, respectively, encouraged, permitted, restricted or prohibited.

Projects in which foreign investment is encouraged are those contributing to agricultural development; those providing new and advanced technology, or assisting the conservation of energy and raw materials, or the production of scarce equipment and materials; projects which contribute to exports; projects which assist environmental policies on renewable resources and pollution; and projects which direct investment to the inland central and western regions. The *Industrial Catalog* lists in detail the industries in which foreign investment is encouraged, under the following broad categories: agriculture and related industries, advanced products in textiles and other light industries, transportation, post and telecommunications, coal, power generation, certain ferrous and nonferrous metals products, selected petroleum, petrochemical, chemical and mechanical engineering ('machine building') products, advanced electronics products, certain sophisticated building materials, most pharmaceutical products, space and aviation products, special-purpose shipbuilding, new technology industries and certain high-technology services. While foreign investment in transportation, postal and telecommunications products and technologies is encouraged, investment in the operation of facilities in those areas is prohibited. Foreign investment is to be restricted in industries which are already satisfying domestic demand, are subject to overall State planning, involve the exploitation of rare mineral resources, or are monopolistic in nature.

Excise duty and tax adjustments have led to some concern among foreign investors. The Chinese authorities decided late in 1995 to abolish tax exemptions on the import of machinery and equipment by foreign-funded enterprises, as from 1 April 1996. This removed an advantage that foreign-funded firms had enjoyed over domestic enterprises, and meant that foreign ventures requiring sophisticated imported plant and equipment would have to pay a 40 per cent duty plus 17 per cent VAT on them. Although the removal of the exemption is being phased over two years for larger projects with a total investment of $30 million or more, foreign companies complained widely that this was a further illustration of the Chinese government's tendency to change the rules of the game unpredictably. For example, the chief representative in Beijing of the semi-official Japan External Trade Organization (JETRO) was reported as saying that sudden changes in the law and a lack of transparency in their application are major worries for Japanese companies: 'Almost every day they announce new laws . . . but very often we have trouble interpreting them' (Walker and Ridding 1996). Previously, in late 1993, China's State Council published new tax regulations which included the standardization of taxation policies governing domestically and foreign-funded enterprises. Two years later, this provision had still not been implemented, though an official intention to do so 'gradually' continued to be expressed (*Beijing Review*, 18 March 1996: 4).

This general tightening of policies toward foreign-funded firms raises the question of whether the time is approaching when China will no longer rely so much on foreign investment. The long-term aim appears to be one of establishing internationally competitive indigenous industries under Chinese control. This can be seen, for example, in the Automotive Industrial Policy formulated in 1994 and expressed in the *2010 Long-Term Target for National Economic and Social Development* published in March 1996. The policy envisages continued support from foreign investment in the medium term, in order to build up a modern production capacity and basic R&D capabilities by the year 2000, but then a move towards a self-supporting and internationally competitive automotive industry by the year 2010.

The authorities have made it quite clear that they only intend to offer preferential treatment to foreign investors who suit its industrial policies and can contribute to its development needs. There also has to be uncertainty in the long run as to the degree of managerial control which China will permit foreign parent companies and other investors to exercise over their subsidiaries and joint ventures. This could frustrate the preference of foreign investors, particularly multinational corporations, to increase their equity share and degree of active management control over joint ventures with Chinese partners. The intention is partly to compensate for the limitations of Chinese management and partly to integrate such ventures more closely both with their other China operations and with their international organizations (Meier et al. 1995).

Many of the multinational companies operating several joint ventures or subsidiaries have responded to the authorities' recent willingness to approve investment holding companies, when they can meet the minimum criteria of having at least $10 million in existing investment and a commitment to another $30 million. There are both financial and managerial benefits to establishing a holding company. On the financial side, it can act as a foreign currency swap centre for subsidiary companies; it has the potential to provide debt financing and to ensure a more efficient circulation of capital. On the managerial side, a holding company can act as an agent for the sales of its China subsidiaries and hence generate synergies in marketing and distribution. It may also help to promote some rationalization in procurement and production.

Generally speaking, the Chinese authorities regard foreign direct investment as playing a positive role through the provision of capital investment, as a vehicle for technology transfer, a contributor to management development and domestic market development, as a source of exports and import substitution, and in assisting state enterprises. On the other hand, they have been concerned about a number of negative features associated with foreign investment, such as the competitive effect of foreign brand names on local products, the greater interest that joint ventures are perceived to have in the domestic market than in exporting, the laying off of older Chinese employees when local enterprises form joint ventures with foreign partners, and smuggling and other illegal practices, especially in joint ventures with Overseas Chinese partners.

Surveys indicate that the majority of foreign investors find China a profitable investment environment, with good longer-term prospects. Nevertheless, many continue to face formidable difficulties in managing their ventures in China, according to investigations conducted by the author and his colleagues in recent years. The changes in government laws and regulations, plus the vagaries of their interpretation at the local level, are a major headache for most foreign managers in China. Logistical problems also continue, including poor infrastructure and services, low-quality suppliers and an insufficiency of market information. Bad debts and rising costs are other frequently mentioned concerns.

Companies in the consumer goods sector, marketing international brands, face the problem of counterfeiting and copyright piracy. While this has received most attention in connection with compact disks and computer software, the CEO of one large American soap and toiletries corporation told me recently that he considered it to be the most serious problem his company faces in China today. The authorities have taken some steps to reduce the problem – for example, it had registered some 460,000 trademarks by the end of 1994 – but enforcement at the local level continues to be variable.

Human resource issues also present a significant challenge. Problems of relationships between Chinese and foreign personnel are often mentioned. Indeed, the major frustration experienced by Chinese joint-venture managers concerns the behaviour of their foreign colleagues and how this can sour the relationship between them. For example, many expressed the view that foreign managers were arrogant and insensitive, and failed either to understand the Chinese environment or to consult them about this and other matters. Such problems can normally be overcome if efforts are made to create trust, improve inter-personal communication and encourage shared decision-making. A less tractable problem is the shortage of competent local managers available to the rapidly growing numbers of Sino–foreign joint ventures and foreign subsidiaries. This has brought to the fore issues of motivation and human resource development, against a backcloth of extreme labour mobility between companies which are bidding for good Chinese managers with high salaries and other benefits.

These issues point to the dynamic of the contact between traditional and foreign approaches to management which China's Open Door Policy and economic internationalization have brought about (Child and Lu 1996). This is particularly evident in joint ventures, where ways have to be found of reconciling the two. Although it reflects certain cultural influences, the traditional Chinese approach was largely shaped under the pre-reform centrally-planned economy. As following chapters describe in detail, most Chinese enterprises until the mid-1980s operated within a command system under which planning quotas for inputs and outputs were imposed on them. As a consequence, managers had to involve themselves closely with the higher governmental officials upon whom they were dependent, giving rise to a system of personal rather than formalized relations and roles. They were generally political appointees. Chinese managers had to meet physical performance targets and their decisions had to take account of multiple criteria which derived from social and political considerations as well as economic requirements. By contrast, the approach to management which has developed in the market economy emphasizes competence for the job, devolved strategy-formulation, formalized organizational procedures, and financial performance criteria. During the early period of internationalization, there were many accounts of conflict between these two approaches when most Chinese joint venture partners were still subject to strong direct governmental influence. Even today, it remain a major challenge to integrate the two traditions to the mutual benefit of both.

China, then, offers one of the most important contexts for business and management in the world today. Understanding it presents a daunting practical and intellectual challenge, but one that cannot be put aside. It is this book's aim to contribute to the task.

John Child
Cambridge, May 1996

References

Beijing Review 1996. Will China Reduce the Use of Foreign Capital? 39/12, 18–24 March: 4.

Child, J. and Lu Yuan. 1996. Introduction: China and International Enterprise. In J. Child and Lu Yuan (eds.) *Management Issues in China: International Enterprises*. London: Routledge.

State Statistical Bureau. 1995. *China Statistical Yearbook 1995*. Beijing.

Meier, J., Perez, J. and Woetzel, J.R. 1995. Solving the Puzzle: MNCs in China. *The McKinsey Quarterly*, 1995/2: 20–33.

Walker, T. 1996a. China 'on Track for Growth and Inflation Goals'. *Financial Times*, 7 March: 6.

Walker, T. 1996b. Chinese Enterprises Sent to Market. *Financial Times*, 3 May: 5.

Walker, T. and Ridding, J. 1996. Far Less of an Easy Ride. *Financial Times*, 10 May: 21.

Warner, M. 1996. Human Resources in the People's Republic of China: The 'Three Systems' Reforms. *Human Resource Management Journal*, 6: 30–41.

1   Introduction

This book is concerned with the management of enterprises in China. Its setting is the world's largest country which is in the midst of a momentous programme of economic reform. The reform is leading to what one commentator thought could be 'the greatest economic miracle ever' (*The Economist* 1992a: 58) and is generating an unprecedented level of interest on the part of foreign investors.

China is now one of a mere handful of socialist countries left in the world, in company with Cuba, North Korea and Vietnam. Not only is it a giant among these but it is rapidly becoming a colossus on the world's economic stage as well. The conjunction of socialism and swift economic development lends China a special interest. Its state socialism gives rise to an amalgam of economic and political institutions which mould the country's system of industrial governance and which determine the criteria for managerial decisions and actions. At the same time, its economic development has been markedly hastened in the past fifteen years by policies aimed at decentralizing that system of governance, introducing market forces, and opening up trade and investment relations with the rest of the world. It is now generally agreed that China's system of industrial governance must continue to reform away from its original state socialist model if the pace of its economic development is to be sustained.

This is also tacitly accepted by those in China who have pushed forward the country's programme of economic reform since its inauguration in December 1978. The changes already accomplished and their consequences for business and management in that country are considerable. The severe retrenchment initiated in the Autumn of 1988 after the economy overheated, and the tightening of political control over enterprise management following the June 1989 Tiananmen Square incident, now appear to be relatively short-term deviations from the longer-term path of economic reform.

Much has been written on China's economic reform and its future prospects (e.g. Tidrick and Chen 1987; Nolan and Dong 1990; Hussain 1992; Fan and Nolan 1994). The reform has been directed towards applying market forces to economic transactions, the controlled opening of the Chinese economy to foreign investment and trade, and the decentralization of economic administration from central government down to provinces and large municipalities. Within the broad frame of these developments, the reformers have intended to transform factories into enterprises and to charge their managements with responsibility for their performance, permitting them an accordingly greater autonomy over enterprise policy and other areas of decision making. While it has experienced problems, many of which still remain, the Chinese economic reform has been remarkably successful. It is today held up as an alternative to the all-at-once, root-and-branch 'big bang' approach to post-socialist economic reform which many Western advisors have advocated for Eastern Europe. The Chinese model is one of reform by incremental and experimental innovation, with the state retaining a major role in the overall regulation of the economy and probably a significant stake in the ownership of industrial property as well.

China is therefore a test case for socialist and post-socialist economic reform, and indeed for economic development in general. It also provides a challenging application for competing theories on management and organization, all of which derive from Western experience. Different perspectives purport to throw light on the nature and sources of interpretations and practices in and around organizations, variously adopting culture, institutions, political ideology, economic rationality and industrialization as their main theoretical points of reference. Investigations of Chinese management promise not only to provide information of direct relevance to those who are active in that economy, but also to illuminate the relevance of Western thinking on management.

The title of this book expresses its basic objective: to further our understanding of Chinese management during the age of reform. More precisely, the book concentrates on developments in the management of state-owned enterprises following the decision in 1984 to apply the reform to such enterprises on a national scale. The book's main justification lies in the fact that there is still a dearth of information available on what the Chinese economic reforms have actually meant on the ground – at the level of managing enterprises. Little is known, for example, about the extent to which managers have been allowed to assume authority over business and organizational decisions, or how freely they have been permitted to engage in market transactions. There is equally the question of whether they are sufficiently trained and experienced to assume such new responsibilities. Another important matter requiring clarification concerns the contribution to Chinese management development that is being made by foreign direct investment through Sino-foreign joint ventures.

Much has been said and written about the intentions of the reform at the enterprise level, both by foreign authors (e.g. Warner 1987) and in Chinese sources such as articles in the official English-language weekly *Beijing Review*. Many papers have been written by non-Chinese authors on the basis of quick, one-off and generally superficial studies which concentrate on one aspect of

Chinese management attitudes or experience. These reports often employ a questionnaire-based methodology, the validity of which is particularly suspect in this context (Shenkar 1991 contains several such examples). These studies may be stimulating in terms of their propositions, and collectively wide ranging in the issues they address, but are rarely informative in terms of their results. Many articles have also been written on the reform by Chinese authors. Some of these present useful case-study material, but they do not usually permit the reader to assess the quality of the sources of their information (e.g. He Wei and Wei Jie 1992). It is also rather rare for them to present a broader comparative picture. There are a few studies, or collections of papers, which are not so limited in their methodology, depth or comparative coverage, although at the time of writing (1993) they are no longer up-to-date in their material (e.g. Walder 1986; Laaksonen 1988; Child and Lockett 1990; Campbell, Plasschaert and Brown 1991; Jackson 1992).

This book focuses on management within Chinese enterprises, particularly state-owned enterprises, and in joint ventures with foreign partners most of which also involve state-owned enterprises on the Chinese side. Rather unusually, it is able to draw upon information which the writer obtained directly from such enterprises working in collaboration with Chinese colleagues. Moreover, much of this information was collected at two points in time during the economic reform process, firstly in 1985 when the reform had been newly extended to urban industrial enterprises throughout China and then between 1988 and 1990. Close contact was maintained with the enterprises in the intervening years. During this four/five year period the reform had deepened.[1] It is therefore possible to provide some indications of how the intentions of the reformers have been practically implemented across a variety of areas including enterprise leadership, decision making, the management of transactions, the role of senior management, personnel practices, reward systems, and the management of joint ventures. While the chapters to follow draw upon this original research as much as possible, they also refer to relevant investigations which others have conducted in order to extend the collective knowledge base and to compare findings.

The greater part of the writer's research in China was concentrated on six state-owned enterprises in Beijing. The China–European Community Management Institute (CEMI), where he worked part-time from 1985 to 1988 and full-time in 1989 and 1990, had developed close and continuing relations with these enterprises through extensive project work conducted by Master of Business Administration (MBA) students, and by means of executive courses and consultancy. This core group of six enterprises with which CEMI started to collaborate in 1985 subsequently grew to eleven, and comparative information is available on some topics for this larger group. Table 1.1 provides a profile of the six core enterprises as of 1985 and 1989/90.

Table 1.1. *Profile of six Beijing enterprises, 1985 and 1989/90*

		Total employment		Official size category	
Enterprise*	Date of foundation	Oct 1985	End 1989	1985	1990
Audio	1955	848	850	small	medium
Audio-visual	1973	2,200	2,820	medium	large
Automotive	1966	3,883	5,620	medium	large
Electrical					
Switchgear	1955	718	630	small	medium
Heavy electrical	1956	1,869	1,905	medium	medium
Pharmaceutical	1973	957	913	small	medium

* Pseudonym to indicate product area but disguise identity.

These enterprises had been introduced to CEMI on the basis of their management's interest in working with an institute which was a repository of Western ideas and knowledge. They were headed by reform-minded directors. While the six enterprises varied in size and product area, none of them represented the category of extremely large, state-owned firm which is found in basic industries such as chemicals, iron and steel and petrochemicals. It should also be recalled that these are all state-owned enterprises, and do not represent the rapidly growing collective and private sectors of Chinese industry. In short, the six firms cannot be taken as typical of Chinese enterprises, or even of state-owned firms.

Nevertheless, much of the micro-level thrust of the reform has been directed at 're-vitalizing' state-owned enterprises and, in this respect, the Beijing firms provide test cases for an evaluation of its progress. The small and selective nature of our main sample is also a limitation imposed by the wish to conduct intensive research within each enterprise. Nevertheless, for some purposes (such as the study of individual earnings) the unit of analysis changes and the sample sizes increase substantially. The size limits of the sample do not anyway prevent its constituent firms from being used as focal points for understanding the economic reform and the process of its implementation over time. Indeed, as was argued earlier, the present need is for non-superficial studies of Chinese enterprises and their management, and intensive engagement with the six firms offers an important opportunity in this respect.

Certain sections of this book also draw upon studies conducted in thirty-four joint ventures between Chinese state enterprises and foreign equity partners from Europe, Hong Kong, Japan and the United States. In these studies, Chinese and European colleagues conducted interviews with the senior Chinese and foreign managers to explore the way the joint venture was being managed, changes that had been introduced and problems experienced. Reference will also be made to a number of other studies which have also been made on Sino-foreign joint ventures.

The book divides into four parts. Part I sets out some key elements in the context of Chinese management. Following this introduction, chapter 2 discusses three factors which together have an important bearing on management in China, namely the country's position as an industrializing and modernizing economy, its system of industrial governance and its culture. Chapter 3 concentrates on the development of the economic reform, including the restructuring of economic management and the opening up of the economy.

Part II contains seven chapters, each of which addresses a different aspect of managing the Chinese enterprise and how this has been changing under the reform. Chapter 4 considers the question of enterprise leadership, particularly the relationship between enterprise directors and party secretaries who represent respectively the administrative and political lines of authority which permeate all Chinese public organizations. Chapter 5 examines the extent to which the reform has led to the decentralization of decision making to enterprises and whether it has also encouraged a greater delegation of decision making responsibility within them. This assessment is made by reference to decisions on a wide range of issues. Chapter 6 focuses on the process whereby decisions are reached in our sample of Chinese state enterprises: a total of sixty decisions are used to draw comparisons across different categories of decision issue and also between early and later stages in the reform.

Chapter 7 presents information from several sources on how input and output transactions are managed in China. This provides some indication of the extent to which Chinese managers are now able to carry out transactions themselves through market relations rather than being subjected to the administrative control of higher authorities. Chapter 8 considers the still very limited evidence we have on how senior Chinese managers carry out their jobs, and whether this appears to differ markedly from patterns that have been noted in Western countries. Chapter 9 turns to that area of policy and practice which in Western parlance is normally identified as human resource management, a concept which remains foreign to China despite some significant developments in activities such as training. Chapter 10 draws upon the writer's research into the structure of earnings for various categories of Chinese managers and employees. It also examines whether there has been a shift under the reform from a configuration of traditional influences on earnings to the use of criteria to reflect levels of responsibility and performance as advocated by the reformers.

Part III turns to joint ventures in China. These are regarded by the governmental authorities as extremely important channels for inward investment and its corollaries of modern technology, high standards of management and the development of an exporting capability. Chapter 11 concentrates on the establishment of joint ventures in China, including a brief review of the legal framework governing them, questions of complementarity between the partners, and the process of negotiating their formation. Chapters 12 and 13 then examine the management of Sino-foreign joint ventures. Chapter 12 focuses on the key issue of control, including conflicts between partners which both occasion and arise from the question of control; it also reviews the problems which foreign managers have experienced in China. Chapter 13 focuses on the more dynamic properties of the Sino-foreign business relationship including changes which have resulted from foreign involvement and the process of adjustment between the partners.

Each of the above chapters contains a short concluding section on its particular theme. Part IV which contains chapter 14 endeavours to stand back from the detail in order to address three issues. First, the extent to which mainland China has developed a business system, in which firms have become economic actors relating with one another through markets. Second, the kind of analytical framework by which the character of Chinese enterprise management, operating within this context, may be better understood. Third, how well Western 'tools' for making sense of management and organization can be applied to China and what comments can be offered on Western perspectives from a knowledge of Chinese management.

Some of the material in this book has previously appeared in other forms. Chapter 4 derives from Child and Xu (1991) and chapter 5 from Child and Lu (1990). A part of chapter 10 draws on Child (1990b) and a part of chapter 14 on Child (1990a). Reference is also made at relevant points to other publications on China by the author and his colleagues.

This book builds upon many hundreds of hours of original research which it would have been completely impossible to have accomplished without the help of many friends and colleagues in China and elsewhere. A particularly large debt of gratitude is owed to Dr Lu Yuan, my former student and now colleague at the University of Cambridge. He worked with me on many of the investigations reported here and his own research into decision making in Chinese enterprises is of a path-breaking nature. His research is summarized in chapter 6 and will be published shortly. Special mention must be made of Yan Ping who has always been generous in giving her time, knowledge and encouragement to my activities since we first conducted fieldwork together in Spring 1986. She has become a good friend and colleague. I have also benefited from working with Xu Xinzhong, who studied with me for his MBA, during which time we were able to conduct the investigation into the managerial role of party secretaries reported in chapter 4. Dr Chen Derong has contributed a great deal towards developing my insight into the Chinese system and into the Chinese people themselves. The same is true of the friends I have made through the academic link between my former university, Aston, and the People's University of

China, which was funded by the British Council and the Chinese State Education Commission. Here I should mention Professors Shi Liming, Fu Hanfang, Wang Xinming and Zhu Fudong. In recent years, Professor Chen Zhicheng of the Beijing University of Science and Technology has offered me both insight and personal support for which I am most grateful. Many of the larger-scale studies reported in this book relied on the fieldwork of several cohorts of Chinese MBA students at CEMI. In this connection, I should like to repeat a point made elsewhere, because it highlights the methodological importance of the contribution the students have made:

A foreigner faces obvious difficulties in securing valid information within Chinese enterprises. Quite apart from the problem of language and meaning, there is also the tendency to provide a mere gloss to someone who is a double outsider – neither of the enterprise nor of the country. The virtue of working with mature, industrially experienced indigenous students lies in their ability to approach more closely to the real situation prevailing within enterprises and to gain the confidence of respondents. . .[The students] had built up an extensive network of informants and had generated goodwill through the practical assistance [previous] projects had afforded. (Child 1990b: 233)

The staff at CEMI, including Jan Bourgonjon the recent Director, were always forthcoming in offering me assistance, both in the four years from 1985 when I was a teacher and then visitor at the Institute and during 1989 and 1990 when I served as its Dean and Director. Professor Max Boisot, my predecessor in that appointment, has worked with unfailing patience to sharpen my analytical appreciation of Chinese mysteries and has offered a particularly insightful critique of my writings. I have also gained considerably from the insight and experience of friends who appreciated the importance of Chinese management and organization many years ago and who pioneered research into the subject – especially Dr Martin Lockett and Professor Malcolm Warner.

Last, but only in chronological time, colleagues and staff in the Judge Institute of Management Studies at the University of Cambridge have been extraordinarily tolerant while I concentrated on completing this book. I am sure that they were as relieved to see it finished as I was. Several of my immediate colleagues in the Centre for International Management gave generously of their time to read and comment on a previous draft, especially Professors Suzana Rodrigues and Malcolm Warner, Sally Heavens and Roland Villinger. Sally Heavens carried out a considerable amount of copy editing, for which I am especially grateful. My secretary, Samantha Cover, offered particularly trenchant comments on the book's readability and later worked womanfully to reproduce several of its more complex diagrams.

Part I

The context of management in China

2 Economy and system

This chapter looks at three key features of the context for managing enterprises in China. These are the country's status as an industrializing and modernizing economy, its system of industrial governance, and its culture. Each is first described so as to set the scene and then its implications for Chinese management and organization are discussed. In this way, the chapter lays a foundation for understanding Chinese management in terms of its main contextual fundamentals. The subsequent chapter then reviews the major change of recent times that has occurred within this context, namely the economic reform programme.

An industrializing and modernizing economy

Economic overview

Although China is still a developing country, with a per capita national income in 1992 of US$367, it has already become a major economic power.[1] It is the world's largest agricultural producer and among the eight largest industrial producers. It is the world's third largest economy, calculated on a purchasing power parity basis. China's industrial development was led historically by the textile industry which remains a significant force, but other industries have developed rapidly, often with the help of foreign capital and know-how. China has, for example, become the world's third largest shipbuilder and the fourth largest steel producer. It is also the third largest producer of beer in the world, put under the table only by the United States and Germany.

This significant industrial presence stems from the combination of a huge population, a relatively high share of national income attributable to industry, and rapid economic growth.[2] China's population in 1992 was 1.175 billion. Figure 2.1 shows the uneven distribution of that population and per capita national income, with the latter being clearly differentiated between coastal and inland provinces. The labour force in 1992 totalled 594 million. While approximately 60 per cent of employed persons are still engaged in agricultural and related work, with only some 17 per cent in industry, industrial activity contributed 50.6 per cent of national income in 1992 and agriculture only 28.6 per cent. In addition, commercial activities contributed 9.2 per cent, construction 6.7 per cent and transport 4.9 per cent.

Figure 2.1 China: provinces, population and per capita income, 1990. *Source:* 'A Survey of China: When China Wakes', *The Economist*, 28 Nov. 1992.

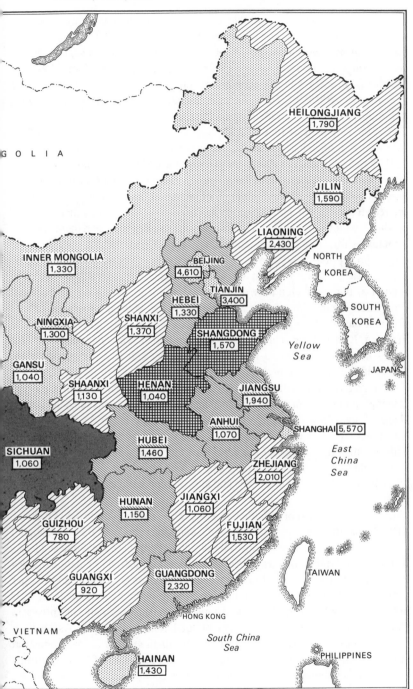

HEILONGJIANG
1,790

JILIN
1,590

LIAONING
2,430

NORTH
KOREA

SOUTH
KOREA

JAPAN

G O L I A

INNER MONGOLIA
1,330

BEIJING
4,610

TIANJIN
3,400

HEBEI
1,330

SHANXI
1,370

SHANGDONG
1,570

Yellow
Sea

NINGXIA
1,300

GANSU
1,040

SHAANXI
1,130

HENAN
1,040

JIANGSU
1,940

SHANGHAI 5,570

ANHUI
1,070

HUBEI
1,460

SICHUAN
1,060

ZHEJIANG
2,010

East
China
Sea

HUNAN
1,150

JIANGXI
1,060

GUIZHOU
780

FUJIAN
1,530

GUANGXI
920

GUANGDONG
2,320

TAIWAN

HONG KONG

VIETNAM

South China
Sea

PHILIPPINES

HAINAN
1,430

The country's recent growth has been impressive, though as we note later, not without problems. In the fourteen years following 1978, China's economy recorded an average annual growth rate in real terms of almost 9 per cent, which was its longest period of high and relatively stable expansion since 1949. This means that in 1994, China's economy is four times larger than it was in 1978 (*The Economist* 1992b). The value of industrial output has grown since 1978 at approximately twice the rate of agricultural output value.

The development of foreign trade has been another marked feature of the recent period. As a share of national income, foreign trade rose from 10 per cent in 1978 to 32 per cent in 1990. In these terms, the Chinese economy has become more open than those of India and Brazil, and it now ranks 11th among the world's trading powers. An indication of industrial development is the fact that the recent growth of China's exports has been driven mainly by manufactured products, which now account for some two-thirds of exports, and there has been a relative shift away from raw materials. Textiles and clothing contribute the largest proportion of export value, though exports of higher technology products, such as electrical goods, have been rising rapidly. The livelihood of a large section of the population now depends directly or indirectly on international trade and foreign investment, especially in the coastal provinces. These provinces have a total population of almost 200 million, roughly equal to that of Japan, Korea, Taiwan and Hong Kong combined. They have turned themselves into labour-intensive manufacturing bases and have developed close links with international markets.

China's industrial economy is now a diversified one with a significant representation in most branches. The production of textiles contributes the largest share of industrial output by value (11.5 per cent in 1991), followed by 'machinery' (9.0 per cent), chemicals (7.4 per cent), iron and steel (7.0 per cent) and food manufacturing (6.7 per cent). The electrical sector as a whole is also substantial (7.6 per cent), including a large (and rapidly growing) contribution from the manufacture of electronic and telecommunications equipment (3.5 per cent).

In 1991, China had approximately 808,000 industrial enterprises. Of these, 419,000 had the status of 'independent accounting units' and they contributed 78.2 per cent of total gross industrial output. According to the Chinese classification of enterprise size based on asset value, the industrial population divides into relatively few large and medium-size enterprises (1 per cent and 2.3 per cent of the total respectively), and an overwhelming number of small firms. If one includes village and household units as well, then small enterprises in China account for over 50 per cent of total industrial output. As Hussain (1990:5) comments, this weight of small firms distinguishes China's industrial structure both from those in the former planned economies of Eastern Europe and the Soviet Union and from those of market economies.

This size distribution of firms is important because in China the size of firms has been connected with their ownership and the extent of their integration into the planning system. Larger firms are generally state owned. In formal terms they are owned by the whole people though, as we note later in this chapter, the property rights attaching to them are complex and far from clear cut. Those enterprises which continue to have to produce part of their output according to the state plan are normally in the largest size bracket. Small enterprises were never effectively incorporated into the planning system and now coincide with the non-planned sector which today also includes many medium-size and some large firms. Therefore the scope of output planning in China depends not only on government reform policy but also on the relative growth rates of small enterprises *vis-à-vis* large ones.

The ownership of enterprises has become more diverse during the period of economic reform. In terms of output, the pre-1978 economy was dominated by state-owned enterprises. Since then the collective sector, comprising enterprises owned by communities or their own employees, has grown dramatically and a new dynamic sector of individual and private enterprises has also prospered (albeit temporarily set back by ideologically inspired policies following the Tiananmen Square incident of 4 June 1989). Foreign ownership has also been permitted, primarily in the form of equity joint ventures though since 1988 the number of wholly owned subsidiaries has increased rapidly.

Between 1978 and 1992 the proportion of industrial output contributed by state-owned enterprises dropped from 80 per cent to 48 per cent. The collective sector grew according to the same measure from 19.8 per cent to 38 per cent (including township and village collectives: 13.0 per cent) and the individual/private sector grew from 0.2 per cent to 6.7 per cent. Companies with foreign investment accounted for over 5 per cent of industrial output in 1992. The growth of the non-state sector within the economy as a whole has in effect amounted to a process of de-nationalization without privatization (Qian and Xu 1993).

The state-owned sector remains the largest by some margin in spite of its relative decline. State-owned enterprises are heavily represented in the extractive and heavy industries, and also in areas of strategic importance such as energy and defence-related production. Much of the rapid growth in other sectors has been concentrated in consumer industries such as textiles and in services such as hotels and restaurants.

As well as being generally larger in scale than those under other forms of ownership, state-owned enterprises also harbour a relatively large part of the underemployment that exists within Chinese industry. Estimates are that at least one-fifth of the workers in state industrial enterprises, which is some 20 million, are unproductively employed. It is not surprising therefore that the share of industrial employment accounted for by these firms is considerably higher than their relative contribution to output value. At the end of 1990, employees in state-owned urban industrial enterprises made up 68.3 per cent of total urban industrial enterprise employment, with collective enterprises taking up only 29.0 per cent of the same total. State-owned enterprises have tended to be the dinosaurs of Chinese industry and the main thrust of the economic reform towards industry has been directed primarily towards their revitalization.

Another point to note is that ownership status, size of enterprise, branch of industry and regional location are not independent of each other in China. The heavier sectors of industry producing energy supplies, basic materials and mechanically-engineered products are generally comprised of large state-owned enterprises, some of which have now entered joint ventures with foreign partners (as is the case with most state automobile producers). Areas of strategic importance such as aircraft, defence and transportation equipment are also under state ownership. The larger, more capital-intensive state enterprises tend to be concentrated in the North of China. Many of these were developed with Soviet assistance during the 1950s and adopted the Soviet system of concentrating authority into the hands of factory directors.

Smaller, lighter industry tends to be concentrated in the coastal areas south of the Yangtze River. China's textile industry for instance grew up in and around Shanghai and adopted a more collective mode of work organization. Southern China is predominantly characterized by labour-intensive production which in the beginning was often based on traditional craft products such as toys, but which today has a strength in more advanced products such as light electronics. Some heavy industry is also to be found in inland provinces such as Sichuan, where it was often established for reasons of national security rather than economics.

Collective and private enterprises are spread over a wide area of China and these include so-called township and village enterprises which have grown in small towns and villages as rural reform has released large numbers of agricultural workers. These patterns of differentiation within the Chinese industrial economy have to be borne in mind when reading this book, which draws heavily on investigations in one location – Beijing – and only into state enterprises. Its data on foreign joint ventures are rather more widely based, though even then the writer's research is intensive rather than extensive in coverage for reasons outlined in the previous chapter.

Detailed information on the total population of foreign-funded enterprises in China is not readily available, but there is no doubt about their significance in recent years as a vehicle for importing both investment and know-how. The inflow of foreign direct investment from capitalist countries has increased from virtually zero in 1978 to US$221 billion in terms of negotiated funds and US$60 billion in utilized direct investment by the end of 1993. Over 50,000 foreign-funded enterprises had gone into operation, employing more than

5 million Chinese workers. The majority of these were equity joint ventures, which accounted for 39.6 per cent of all foreign investment in China at the end of 1991.

In short, state-owned enterprises are still the dominant ownership type, and also constitute the sector widely recognized to be in most need of improvement. Enterprises with foreign management, especially ventures with Chinese state firms, possess a special potential for accelerating China's development. This book therefore focuses on these two types of economic unit, in parts II and III respectively.

Implications of industrialization

Economists and sociologists have long debated the implications of industrialization for the organization of economy and society (Kumar 1978). Industrialization signifies here the mechanization and the rational organization of productive activity, not just in manufacturing but in any or all the sectors of the economy (Moore 1962). The debate remains inconclusive over the large question of whether industrial societies have eventually to adopt similar economic, social and even political systems in order to be competitive and effective, an issue revived by recent developments in Eastern Europe. On the one side is the argument that industrialism has a 'logic' which stems largely from its use of science and technology (cf. Aron 1967) and which requires the 'modernization' of a society's competences and institutional practices for its successful realization (cf. Harbison and Myers 1959; Kerr et al. 1960). This implies a convergence between industrial societies in these characteristics. Critical of this view are those who point out that different countries, including those of East Asia, have successfully adopted contrasting models of organizing an industrial society (cf. Whitley 1994) and who could therefore argue that the logic of industrialism has limited rather than overwhelming social and organizational implications.

Clark Kerr, a long-time exponent of the thesis that the logic of industrialism will lead to convergence between economic and social systems, subsequently modified his position to allow for a tension between opposing forces bearing on this issue. In so doing, he nevertheless held to the view that the process of modernizing economies and opening them to international competition creates a drive towards a convergence between countries around the most effective way of organizing such economies:

The forces most strongly at work [for convergence] are the drive for modernization, the intensity of competition among nations, the existence of common human needs and expectations, and the advent of common practical problems with common solutions. The main barriers to convergence are inertia, inefficiencies, resource constraints, and the holding power of any antagonistic preindustrial beliefs. (Kerr 1983: 86)

China is now striving to achieve modernization, and is encouraging a degree of competition both internally and through opening up to foreign trade. It shares human needs and practical problems with other nations. The implication of Kerr's argument is that it will therefore be obliged to adopt forms of economic management and organization comparable to those which have assisted the successful modernization of other nations. Indeed, this is part of the rationale expressed by Chinese leaders for inviting foreign companies to participate in the modernization process, although they do also talk about adapting these to suit China's situation. The thesis that industrialization is a compelling social force therefore draws attention to certain features which, it claims, are liable to accompany the process of modernization on which China is now engaged.

Although there are differences of emphasis among exponents of the industrialization thesis, there is wide agreement on the core features of the process. These are an increasingly complex division of labour and skills, the development of the factory system of production and subsequently of large formal organizations, the extensive commercialization of goods and services and their exchange through the market, a growing scope and density of communications, and an educational and training system capable of filling positions within the evolving occupational structure. The sophistication required to manage these more complex organizations and transactional arrangements will clearly grow in step with them. Professional management is therefore also identified as a requisite for industrialization. Additionally, to provide the engine of growth and hence the wherewithal to invest in further modernization, the dynamic force of entrepreneurship and a striving for achievement and betterment among the population at large need to be encouraged (cf. Burns 1969; Feldman and Moore 1969).

Central to this thesis is the view that successful industrialization requires resources to be allocated and managed on the basis of rational decision criteria. This means that the character of economic management should differ from that in traditional or non-industrial society. Weber (1964) believed that management based upon and operating through legal-rational authority was of this rational type and enjoyed a superiority in basing its actions upon technical knowledge and modern methods without the sources of inefficiency, such as nepotism, corruption or narrow ideologies, which accompanied traditional or charismatic authority systems.

In the case of China, the argument from a logic of industrialization implies the need for policy initiatives in several key areas which are listed below. We shall note in chapter 3 that policy makers have indeed paid considerable attention to these factors since the initiation of the economic reform. The reform itself is officially linked to the goal of modernization, though a major point of discussion concerns how far this modernization can be achieved through institutions and practices which retain 'Chinese characteristics'. The notion of Chinese characteristics in this context can signify the recognition of the society's strong link with its past; it can also signify the political intention to pursue modernization within a framework of socialist objectives and institutions. This recalls the fact that industrialization has now been attained in ways that diverge from the earliest 'Western' examples, most notably involving a more directive and interventionist role of the state.

The conclusions for China from applying the logic of industrialism are that it needs to:

1   introduce rational systematic methods of managing complex organizations;
2   train people in the necessary technical and managerial competences;
3   grant sufficient autonomy to those in charge of enterprises for them to exercise entrepreneurship at least to the extent of formulating and pursuing their own business plans;
4   encourage the development of systems to motivate people at work;
5   create efficient means for the exchange of goods, services, information and other communications, so that markets can function efficiently.

This list implies that China as a developing country will have to overcome a set of opposite characteristics, namely a lack of management systems, limited levels of technical and managerial competence, restricted enterprise autonomy, underdeveloped motivation systems and limited and/or inefficient market transactions. It is arguable that some of these characteristics are also underpinned in China by the system of state socialist industrial governance and the continuing strength of traditional culture. The economic reform tacitly accepts that both the system of industrial governance and traditional culture present obstacles to effective modernization. Their implications for management are now reviewed in turn.

The system of industrial governance

Ownership and property rights under Chinese socialism

China remains officially a political and economic system based on socialist ownership. Following 'the socialist road' is one of the regime's four Cardinal Principles and the country's Constitution declares that all the means of production are publicly owned. Jiang Xiaoming (1992) points out, however, there is a substantial difference between the Western concept of ownership, together with the property rights attaching to it, and that conventionally followed in China. The Chinese concept of ownership (*suoyouzhi*) is appreciably more ambiguous and is a political and ideological consideration rather than an economic and legal one. The term *suoyouzhi*, when used in China, implies an overall system of governance based on the ideological principles of socialism, such that all the means of production are ultimately a public asset and that the state acts as the custodian of this public ownership.

A fundamental problem with public ownership is that of identifying any specific owners to whom the managers of industrial assets should be accountable. Who actually owns Chinese 'state-owned' enterprises is a particularly vexed question which has not been resolved, but which is extremely germane to proposals now being discussed for issuing shares in these enterprises to members of the public and/or to employees, or even privatizing them entirely. While the owners of collective enterprises are defined more precisely as all the people who belong to them, the situation remains confused since there is a wide range of *de facto* positions in regard to their property rights. For some collectives these approximate to the position of a state enterprise, while at the other extreme some can more or less function as private firms. Many state-owned enterprises and most collectives are heavily dependent upon the goodwill and sanction of local governments, which in this way are significant holders of industrial property rights (Granick 1990).

A key element in the Chinese economic reform has been the aspiration to separate the functions and officials of government from those of enterprise management. Government, indeed 'the state', in China includes both administrative and political (party) wings. So while confusion remains over the question of industrial ownership, the reform has in important ways proceeded to modify the property rights attaching to the management of industrial assets. These changes under the reform are detailed in the next chapter and provide some parallel to the so-called 'divorce of ownership from control' in Western economies (cf. Berle and Means 1932). The distinction between property rights and ownership is a critical one to make with regard to the Chinese system of industrial governance and changes occurring in it under the reform.

Property rights refer to the right to determine the use of assets, to dispose of them, and to decide on the distribution of the income stream they produce including its re-investment. In Western societies the sanctity of private property is deeply rooted; property rights normally attach to private ownership and they are safeguarded by law. This contrasts markedly with the Chinese notion of *suoyouzhi* which implies that in the final resort property is held only on the sanction of the ruling authority. However, since this principle is extremely general and vague, it has not interfered with the pragmatic ground-level redistribution of industrial property rights under the economic reform. The long-standing decoupling of property rights from ownership in China has, in fact, permitted the reform of industrial governance through amending property rights to take place under a socialist regime in which ownership remains nominally unchanged.

Before considering the reform itself and its main provisions, a description of the main features of the Chinese industrial governance system is required, together with the general implications these have for the management of enterprises (particularly state-owned ones). The impact of the reform on this system and its attendant property rights is then discussed in chapter 3.

The structure of industrial governance

Although policies of overall economic management have altered considerably in China over the past forty years, there has been rather less change in the structure of urban industrial governance. As with all systems of state socialism, the government and the party are inextricably linked – both constitute 'the state'. State socialist societies are above all political economies. The structure of China's industrial governance therefore contains two parallel hierarchies, that of administration and that of the party.

The essentials of the administrative structure were laid down in the early 1950s on the pattern of the centralized Soviet model. It locates the enterprise within a matrix comprising two administrative lines leading down to two categories of bureau which relate with state-owned enterprises. Party organs parallel and are embedded in each unit of the structure, which is outlined in figure 2.2.

At the apex of the matrix are the National People's Congress which makes laws and issues the country's principal regulations, the State Council which approves the more important regulations governing enterprises, and the State Planning Commission which formulates such industrial regulations and can itself issue the more minor or specific ones. There are also national ministries, both for industrial categories and for specialized functions such as taxation. Within this set of national bodies, Lieberthal and Oksenberg (1988) in their studies of energy policy making have discerned four tiers: 'the top 25 to 35 leaders; the personal staffs, leadership groups, research centers, and institutes that link the leaders to the bureaucracies; the supra-ministerial commissions which co-ordinate policy; and line ministries. Energy decisions can be made at any of these levels, with considerable consequence for the range of considerations that are taken into account.' (pp. 27–8)

Below the central government there are local government administrations at the municipal and provincial level. Cities not enjoying provincial status have their own administrative bureaux of lesser rank. At this level, the local industrial bureau (today often renamed an industrial 'corporation') has a particularly close relationship with the enterprise. Its involvement can extend to any aspect of the latter's work and operation and includes the significant powers to appoint directors and to approve contracts specifying enterprise performance targets. Such a relationship approximates more to that of a holding company than of a multidivisional corporate group. This is because the bureau generally fails to develop any strategic rationale itself, which is usually left to the enter-

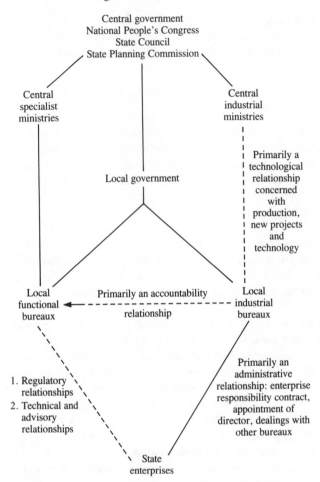

Figure 2.2 The higher administrative structure of state enterprises. *Source:* Child and Lu 1990: figure 1.

prise. Local industrial bureaux have a reporting line to the relevant industrial ministry, but (unlike the former USSR) their main line of accountability is to the local government. This is the first hierarchical administrative line.

The second administrative line is a functional one and divides at the local authority level into two types of bureau: one regulatory and the other technical-cum-advisory. Local regulatory bureaux, colloquially known by the Chinese as 'the Mothers-in-Law', have the right of direct intervention in enterprises over matters within their particular purview. Different bureaux specialize in tax, auditing, industrial and commercial issues (regulation of sales and distribution channels), pricing, investment finance (through the local bank), power supplies, personnel matters (personnel regulations and keeping cadres' files) and workers' employment. While these bureaux have their own lines to equivalent specialist national ministries, such as the central treasury, their strongest channel of accountability has, under the devolution of administrative powers, become that to the local government. The technical-cum-advisory bureaux do not have the right to initiate direct interaction or negotiation with enterprises. They perform support functions concerning, *inter alia*, technology development (the research institutes) and system reform.

In parallel with this system of administrative governance is one of political governance through the hierarchical structures of the Communist Party of China (CPC). Chapter 4 notes how the powers and direct managerial involvement of the CPC have waxed and waned at different times since the 1949 Revolution and examines the recent position in some detail.

The party continues to have a formal role within the enterprise to promote ideological awareness and to 'guarantee and supervise' the implementation of government and party policies. This role embraces the organization of party activities inside the enterprise, the communication of information on policies and the approved 'line', and the monitoring of employees – especially managers. A key issue in China has been how best the party can fulfil this role, and this remains a live question so far as the relationship between enterprise party officials and management is concerned. Most managers are members of the party, and political loyalty is an important factor in the promotion of personnel.

Chinese trade unions are ideologically regarded as 'mass organizations of the working class led by the party'. There are fifteen industry unions, which at the end of 1987 had over 93 million members accounting for 89.7 per cent of the country's total workers in urban state enterprises. The top council of these unions, the All-China Federation of Trade Unions (ACFTU), has departments dealing with the economy, finance and accounts, international issues, organization, propaganda, safety, wages, and women's needs. Below it are federations or councils which duplicate these functions at regional, provincial and municipal levels; there are also industry unions organized in a similar form at these levels and down to that of the enterprise (Ng 1984; O'Leary 1992). Trade unions are not mandatory in firms with foreign involvement, such as joint ventures. However, 92 per cent of foreign or foreign-participating firms in the Shenzhen Special Economic Zone were said in 1987 to have trade unions operating (Nyaw 1991) and it is likely that they are present in the majority of such firms.

Within the enterprise, as well as providing the executive arm and secretariat for workers' congresses (Workers' and Staff Representative Congresses), the union's other formal roles are to assist management make a success of running the enterprise and expanding its productive forces, to defend the legitimate rights and interests of staff and workers, and to assist management in carrying out government decrees concerning workers' interests and welfare. In practice, the union movement has continued to be subordinate to the authority of the party which has regarded it as a potentially rival political force, and which it clearly became during the protest movement of Spring 1989. In the words of one commentator union activities have 'been constrained by party authority into forms of practice which have severely compromised its ability to represent the industrial concerns of workers' (O'Leary 1992: 371).

At the local level there are other institutionalized interests which bear upon the activities of management. The responsibilities of managers in the PRC extend beyond economic effectiveness into the area of social provision for employees, in terms of a wide range of welfare and other benefits and payments. Within the enterprise, the workers' congress enjoys rights to comment on managerial policy from the standpoint of its members' interests and to be consulted on matters such as the proposed dismissal of an employee. The enterprise is also obliged by local government bureaux and agencies to support the local community, in ways ranging from the funding of community projects to the provision of street cleaning,

The hierarchical lines from administration and party create vertical dependencies for enterprise management, although (as we note later) these are to a significant extent counterbalanced by the dependencies of external organs on the success of the enterprise for tax revenues, incomes, contributions to the community and so forth. Under the former planning system, managers were obligated to their higher administrative authorities for the fulfilment of quotas and targets, while they relied upon them to arrange the supply of necessary scarce resources. These authorities also continue to control senior managerial appointments and they can significantly influence the allocation of managers' personal rewards.

Under the current responsibility system, managers are responsible to the authorities for meeting agreed profit and investment targets, and for contributing tax revenues from profits. On the political side, managers are accountable to party officials and committees for ideologically acceptable conduct. Enterprise managers also depend on co-operation from workers for the fulfilment of economic goals. Most workers enjoy job security as well as a privileged ideological legitimacy as members of the proletariat. They are therefore in a strong position to withhold such co-operation. Moreover, they can readily voice their dissatisfaction through the workers' council or its officials in the trade union (both of which come under the leadership of the party) and in this way bring further pressure to bear upon management. The way that enterprise management is lodged within this system of dependencies is portrayed in figure 2.3.

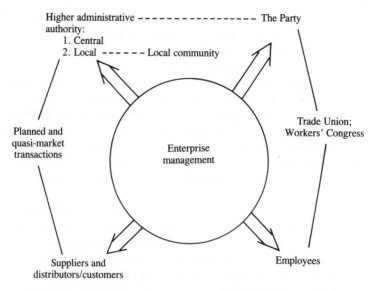

Figure 2.3 Location of Chinese enterprise management within a system of dependencies.

Walder (1986) has analysed the extension of these relationships into the factory itself by reference to the concept of 'communist neo-traditionalism'. In using this term he does not intend to imply that the features in question are not 'modern' and betray a continuing influence of traditional culture, but rather to point out their affinity with the characteristics associated in Western social science with traditionalism, namely dependence, deference and particularism (p. 10). In fact, Walder concludes that such features are primarily the product of the way state socialism is organized rather than of specifically national traditions:

After my field experience, when I read about other institutions in China and other communist societies, I frequently detected the same underlying themes of dependence and vertical loyalties, even though the authors often did not draw attention to them. I gradually came to view the patterns of authority I had studied in state-owned Chinese factories as sharing certain generic features with other communist institutions, and I came to understand these generic features as the outcome, albeit unintended, of basic features of the organization of established Leninist parties and of central planning. (pp. xiv–xv)

Implications of the industrial governance system

The management of Chinese enterprises is located within a network of interlocking relationships (Henley and Nyaw 1986). Walder (1989) points to the constraining nature of these relationships in describing four 'facts of life' in the world of the Chinese managers of state enterprises and many larger collective firms as well. The first is the continued importance of vertical relationships with the government bureaucracy, the co-operation of which can still considerably influence management's ability to secure prosperity for its enterprise. The second is that 'the enterprise is a political coalition' in which managers continue to require the support of other enterprise officers, particularly the party secretary. The third is that 'the enterprise is a socio-political community' with managers being judged on social criteria by both the party and trade union. The fourth concerns the continuing importance of non-market exchange relationships, particularly in the area of securing shortage supplies and trade credit.

Clearly, each of these conditions impinges on the locus and criteria of industrial decision making. In combination they pose fundamental contradictions for enterprise directors who are expected to reconcile economic with ideological criteria and to embody the interests both of the state (through their contractual responsibility to the administrative hierarchy) and of the enterprise as a corporate social group (Yang 1989).

The institutional context of the management process in China must in large degree be understood as a dynamic system of interdependency relationships, especially between levels in the governance structure. It is a system of power, but one in which there is the potential for actors and their agencies (including managers and their enterprises) to intervene in decisions from different levels and points in the system. The dominant dependency is that of the enterprise upon higher authorities, but it is not a one-way relationship. As Montias (1988) points out, centrally planned economies that have evolved from the original Stalinist model are all characterized by bargaining between system levels.

Clegg's (1989) work on power captures some important essentials of the Chinese situation. He argues for an extension of the analysis of power beyond a concentration on its causality to a consideration of its use in the light of strategy, necessity and the organizational framework within which the parties are located. This leads him to a representation of the 'circuits of power' in which what he terms 'agencies' are the source of rules and obligatory procedures for social relations. In the PRC, the term would apply to governmental regulatory bodies. The rules and procedures establish rights of access to resources and to their disposition. Agencies are potentially in tension with the operational units which they are endeavouring to control but upon which they at the same time depend. Through developing their own rationales of production and discipline, the operational units deploy what Clegg calls 'facilitative' power which itself empowers and modifies the social relations upon which agencies are constituted. Clegg's analysis thus depicts mutual dependencies and dynamic processes of action within recursive circuits of power. Within these circuits there are 'obligatory passage points' at which the parties concerned attempt to fix expectations and rights in stable representations of necessity and normality.

The responsibility systems introduced under the economic reform programme have been intended to shift the balance of power and initiative from higher administrative agencies to operational units and within such units from the party towards management. As with any realignment of powers, considerable resistance could be expected, particularly regarding the system's obligatory passage points. The structures of central planning and hierarchical administrative control have been solidly laid down, or 'sedimented' in Clegg and Dunkerley's terms (1980), and are not easily removed. These structures constitute accretions of power over enterprise management with respect to both operational and personal resources. Operational resources include finance, information, access to markets through control over approved product lists, and assistance in the supply of materials, power and local services. Personal resources include senior managerial appointments and salaries. The functionaries running the sub-hierarchies within the system will be unwilling to forego benefits that accrue from these powers of patronage, and which include opportunities to benefit from corruption. The bodies which previously enjoyed institutionalized powers over enterprises, namely the governmental administrative hierarchy and enterprise party committees, may be expected to strive to retain those powers, compensating for formalized changes through reliance on non-formalized strategic personal connections through which the enterprise can be either assisted or sanctioned.

Opposition to the reform might also be expected from the workforce and local community insofar as its implementation through labour rationalization and the introduction of differential performance-based payment schemes threatens respectively job security and the terms of reward previously struck with management (the 'effort-bargain' as Behrend 1957 called it). Moreover, many enterprise managers will be reluctant to acquire the new perspectives and learn the new behaviours and techniques required to put their greater autonomy to fruitful use under more competitive conditions which pose a greater risk of failure and fewer possibilities of being rescued from it.

Further problems arise because the infrastructure of macro-economic regulation is not yet sufficiently developed in China to support the decentralization of responsibility for economic performance to enterprises. For example, until prices are freed from subsidies and administrative control, it is extremely difficult to assess enterprise performance objectively, and decentralization through arms-length accountability depends upon the availability of reliable performance measures. The absence of valid price indicators creates a problem for the economic evaluation of investment which is likely to permit the intrusion of other criteria such as the personal influence of bidders with funding agencies. Because of the underdevelopment of mechanisms for indirect regulation of the economy, the autonomy formally extended to enterprises is liable to be retracted by the central authorities in responding to economic or political crises, as happened in the latter part of 1985 and to a much greater extent after September 1988.

Chinese culture

Main characteristics of Chinese culture

Although the history of China has been marked by periodic political upheavals of a violent kind, its majority Han people have experienced the longest span of homogeneous cultural development of any society in the world. Chinese culture and tradition is therefore particularly deep-rooted and before the present century it was largely undisturbed by foreign influence. It is a strong attribute of Chinese society, of which the members remain very self-conscious. As Fairbank has put it (1987:367), 'the influence of China's long past is ever-present in the environment, the language, the folklore, and the practices of government, business and interpersonal relations'. Other writers have also emphasized the influence of China's culture on the way that its organizations are managed (e.g. Pye 1985; ECAM 1986; Lockett 1988; Redding 1990).

There are in practice many difficulties in defining 'culture' and also in assuming that it is equally shared by all the members of a nation-state. Kroeber and Kluckhohn (1952) cited 164 definitions of culture which taken together encompass a whole range of components: knowledge, values, preferences, habits and customs, traditional practices and behaviour, implements and artifacts. Keesing (1974) made a useful distinction within this range between 'ideational systems' and 'adaptive systems'. The former are those sets of ideas, shared symbols and meanings which are transmitted intergenerationally and which can be expected to mould work attitudes, expectations and behaviours through the process of socialization. The latter are the institutional arrangements which express a society's values in relation to the needs of its members to cope with the environment.

In the PRC since 1949, many of the society's institutions, such as its educational system and its system of industrial governance, have been given a strong political character both to reflect the new political ideology and with the intention of using institutions as instruments for bringing their members' values into line with the ideology. If political ideology becomes established in people's minds and is handed on by them to the succeeding generation, then one could consider that it has become part of the culture. This has probably not happened to a great extent in China. Redding (1990) contrasts the persistence of traditional Chinese culture with 'the communist veneer of the People's

Republic' (p. 41), and quotes the confidential comment of an elderly professor in Guangzhou that 'the thing you must remember about China is that for the past thirty years we have all been acting'. Assuming this to be correct, we prefer to treat Chinese political ideology as an aspect of the institutions of political economy rather than as an indigenous part of the culture. The following discussion will therefore concentrate on the ideational aspects of Chinese culture which may be expected to have some bearing upon managerial behaviour and practice.

Fairbank has commented that in China 'regional differences are too great to be homogenized under a unitary state' (1987: 363). In so large and diverse a country as China, a further complication arises in the use of the term 'culture' since, while the population may generally share the core elements of a common culture, they will also exhibit contrasts in attitudes and behaviours. Such contrasts are often remarked between northern and southern China, which at certain times have been divided politically and which have not even had a common spoken language. Northerners, for example, are said to be more formalistic and less entrepreneurial and to reflect the ethos of the bureaucratic Bei Jing ('northern capital').

Various authorities on Chinese culture put forward somewhat different lists of key elements which are likely to have a particular bearing on management. There is, however, wide agreement on the following, which derive primarily from Confucianism. As Shenkar and Ronen (1987a) state:

The culture of traditional China encompasses diverse and competing philosophies, including Taoism, Buddism, Legalism and a host of local 'little traditions'. Nevertheless, Confucianism is most clearly defined as the foundation of China's great cultural tradition, and Confucian values still provide the basis for the norms of Chinese interpersonal behavior. (p. 266)

The Confucian tradition has a concern for the correct and well-mannered conduct of one's duties, based on a sound respect for the social conventions of a patrimonial system. It stresses order, hierarchy, quality of relationships and obligation to social collectivities, especially the family (Smith 1974; Waley 1938). Age is respected, particularly in the case of male heads of family, while education is also valued as the means to achieving a better social status which reflects well on the family.

Lockett (1988) identifies four cultural values which he argues have particular relevance for management in China:
1 respect for age and hierarchy;
2 orientation towards groups;
3 the preservation of 'face';
4 the importance of relationships.

Principles such as harmony (Shenkar and Ronen 1987a) and the superiority of moral over legalistic control of behaviour (Boisot and Child 1988) are also culturally significant in China and relate closely to the features in Lockett's list.

It is widely agreed that the Chinese respect age, authority and hierarchy. This stems from the Confucian concept of *li* (rite, propriety) which plays an important role in maintaining a person's position in the social hierarchy. As Needham (1980: 284) has argued, this ancient concept proved more suitable than any other for the traditional bureaucratic system in Chinese society. The tradition it embodies favours organizational hierarchy and centralized decision making.

In Chinese tradition, the extended family is the basic social unit, which encourages the development of a strong collective and group orientation. Within the bounds of the family or clan, its members are expected to maintain harmonious relationships. The family's moral judgement, especially as expressed by the father, provides the standard for approved behaviour. These same features also characterize in a somewhat diluted form the individual's attachment to other groups. They direct people's loyalties towards their family and work groups, and to the specific standards these apply, rather than to broader social entities.

'Face' is essentially the recognition by others of a person's social standing and position. There are two Chinese concepts of face, *lien* and *mianzi*. Whereas *mianzi* stands for prestige and personal success, *lien* stands for the confidence which others have in one's moral character. Losing *lien* can incapacitate a Chinese person as a member of his or her community (Bond and Hwang 1986). The Chinese attach importance to the views others hold of them far more than most other cultures. Any form of idiosyncratic behaviour carries the risk of losing face and is culturally inhibited in China. The preservation of face connects with group identity since there is a strong expectation that any conflicts within the group will remain private; if publicized, the group as a whole is demeaned.

The fourth particularly significant concept in Chinese culture is *guanxi*, which refers to the quality of a personal relationship outside an individual's immediate family. Thus, when a petitioner asks a resource allocator to disburse a social benefit under his control, the latter will first consider the *guanxi* between them and then adopt appropriate rules of social exchange. Persons who have *guanxi* usually have at least one fundamental characteristic in common such as birthplace, lineage or surname, or they share a significant experience such as attending the same school, working together or belonging to the same organization (Jacobs 1979).

Implications of Chinese culture

To date, there have been fewer studies into the effects of traditional Chinese cultural attributes on management in the PRC than on their relevance for non-mainland business and management (e.g. Redding 1990). It is nevertheless reasonable to assume that these cultural characteristics will reinforce the hierarchical and conformist attributes of the top-down command structure that China's economy has acquired under socialism. For they lead to a high value being placed on social control, virtually as an end in itself.

The specific attributes of traditional culture can cause problems for the improvement and reform of Chinese management. Respect for age can inhibit an acceptance of the younger, qualified managers whom the exponents of economic reform wish to see appointed to lead the re-invigoration and modernization of Chinese industry (cf. CPC 1984: 32–3). Despite a major investment in training (discussed in chapter 9), there remains a shortage of professional and technical skills among managers, many of whom have stayed in their positions for a long time. The cultural respect for age and hierarchical position makes it difficult to resolve the problem, since it inhibits any challenge to older managers (Lockett 1988).

Chinese organizations face major problems of collaboration and communication of a horizontal kind between different departments. Identities and loyalties are vertical in direction, and reflect the high respect that Chinese people have for their own hierarchies. The problem is further exacerbated by group orientation. This tends to be most strongly directed towards the immediate working group and its leadership, which is the workplace equivalent of the family. Here is a clear case where the vertical loyalties built into the command system are likely to be reinforced by the culture.

A strong orientation towards the group can have further consequences. It may undermine attempts to separate party from managerial functions which were previously undertaken by one senior group within the enterprise. It tends to unite with the preference for egalitarianism and present difficulties for the development of individual responsibility and for rewarding performance on an individual basis. A belief in egalitarianism has been encouraged in China both by tradition (especially in peasant society) and by the leftist strand of socialist ideology. Unwillingness among Chinese managers to assume personal responsibility is a frequently expressed concern of foreign partners in joint ventures. It is the product of a centralized hierarchical system, evident in former command economies such as Hungary (Markoczy 1990), and one which the Chinese cultural environment is likely to reinforce.

Individual initiative and the evaluation of personal performance can be severely discouraged by the significance attached to face, as are frank contributions to discussions or problem solving. The preservation of face will be reinforced by the value attached to preserving harmony; conflict usually ends with a loss of face for one party, and sometimes both.

A preference for an implicit and moral basis for business dealings rather than a formal legal footing means that the viability of dealings rests upon trust between the parties. Within business relations, the norm of reciprocity applies with the expectation that one favour will eventually be repaid with another. Mutual favours are performed and 'strings pulled' on the basis of the *guanxi* between people, both within and across organizations. As Lockett (1988: 489) has stated:

In Chinese organizations continuing relationships are of great importance, in part based on family and other ties, such as clan, shared surname, home village, region, education or other shared experience . . . In business, relationships are important as contracts are often not strictly specified in legal terms but rely on trust between the parties. (Lockett 1988: 489)

When there are shortages of supplies, the cultivation and use of *guanxi* by enterprise managers can make the difference between continuity and disruption of production. On the other hand, the use of relationships to 'go through the back door', as the Chinese put it, can undermine the credibility of formal systems and distort the allocation of resources according to economic or strategic criteria.

There is a wider implication of the fact that Chinese tradition favours the implicit structuring rather than precise formalization of social relations (ECAM 1986). For if a preference for ambiguity is carried into the rules and regulations governing the implementation of economic reforms, then the latitude for re-negotiating and even negating them will be enhanced. Weber (1968) concluded from Western experience that the codification and routinization of laws and economic rules are two necessary conditions for firms to be able to exercise autonomy. In other words, the rules of the game applied to relations between enterprises and external parties, especially government, have to be codified with respect to matters of law and financial obligation. Secondly, government must apply the rules in a routine manner – in other words consistently and predictably – so that the managers of enterprises can use their autonomy to plan ahead.

When laws and regulations are poorly codified, as is often the case in China, *ad hoc* obligations are liable to be imposed upon enterprise managements by local, essentially patriarchal, agencies which may inhibit them from concentrating on economic objectives and also from entering into wider market transactions (Blecher 1989). Here, then, is another example of how behaviour encouraged by the structure of industrial governance is likely to be reinforced by its cultural milieu.

Conclusion

The main characteristics of the Chinese economy and system posited by the three perspectives of industrialization, system of industrial governance (state socialism) and culture, are summarized in table 2.1 which is adapted from Lu

(1991). It is evident from this tabulation that the characteristics of Chinese culture and tradition are more compatible with the system of state socialism than either of them are with the attributes claimed for successful industrialization. Boisot (1990) argues, in a rather similar vein, that the Chinese are not yet attuned to a 'Schumpeterian' kind of learning process based on disequilibrium models of innovation and opportunity; both their culture and governance system are more attuned to an equilibrium model.

This observation leads to the proposition that, inheriting a culture with strong feudalistic origins, China provides a favourable context for the social acceptance of the paternalistic public bureaucracy system that has characterized state socialism. Both the culture and the system emphasize unified leadership and authority, collectivism, mutual dependence, moral incentive and conformity of thought. These characteristics sharply contrast with the pluralism of ownership, competition, individualistic entrepreneurship, economic incentive and innovation, which have generally been associated with successful Western industrialization. Although Walder (1986) does not attach much weight to the impact of traditional Chinese culture, except to admit that the recent system of industrial authority 'represents the integration of patrimonial rule with modern bureaucratic form' (p. 251), our suggestion that this culture provides fertile ground for the acceptance of patrimonial bureaucracy is not inconsistent with his empirical observations.

Some further implications arise from this comment. First, if in China both the culture and the system lead to similar managerial characteristics, it is important to discover whether one of these contextual factors is the more potent influence. Potency here refers to both the strength and the embeddedness of the influence. The combination of two comparisons would throw useful light on this issue: (1) between countries with similar systems but contrasting cultures, and (2) between countries with the same cultures but different systems. These comparisons should indicate whether management, and indeed particular features of management, are moulded primarily by culture or system. A lead into this kind of investigation was provided by Shenkar and Ronen's (1989) comparative study of the 'work goals' expressed by Chinese managers in the PRC and other Chinese communities, which pointed to differences of priority in those areas where one could expect system contrasts to have a direct bearing.

Secondly, although it is conceivable that a socio-political ideology such as Marxism-Leninism can in time become an internalized culture for successive generations of people, the evidently limited appeal of such ideologies in socialist and formerly socialist countries makes it more plausible to suggest that traditional cultures have helped the acceptance of communist neo-traditionalism rather than that communism/state socialism has itself had a significant cultural impact. This means that the historical process has been one in which culture led to system. Once the system with its authoritarian grip was

Table 2.1. *A comparative summary of characteristics posited by the perspectives of industrialization, industrial governance system and culture applied to China*

Type of characteristic	Perspective		
	Industrialization	Industrial governance (state socialism)	Culture
1. Economic and socio-political governance	separated	unified political and economic governance	unified authority of leadership and senior kinship roles
2. Dominant mode of authority	rational bureaucracy	one-party leadership	traditional (official and family) status position
3. Economic management	market economy	central planning	local networks but with official intervention (especially in crises)
4. Ownership	diverse ownership	state monopoly of ownership	imperial/feudal ownership dominant
5. Control over enterprise management	ownership separate from management	state control	family control
6. Economic elites	professional managerial elites	political appointees	government officials and major property owners
7. Decision mode	entrepreneurial	collective	family/collective
8. Dominant ethos	innovation	conformity	conservatism
9. Socially approved motivation	economic	political	pursuit of traditional values (especially regarding relationships)

Source: adapted from Lu (1991).

in place, it could then contribute itself towards shaping observable patterns of organizational behaviour.

Thirdly, whether it is culture or system that is the more powerful force shaping Chinese organizational behaviour, both tend to work against the success of an economic reform. Within a centralized system, reforms that are introduced on a top-down basis will, of course, carry some weight, but their implementation relies on the instrumentality of intermediate institutions and their acceptability at those levels. The successful implementation of changes at the enterprise level in turn depends on sympathetic developments in external institutions, such as the introduction of more liberal rules of the economic game. The attempt to modernize Chinese management and the factors which frustrate this are themes running through the following chapters.

3 Economic reform and opening to the outside world

In spite of the post-Tiananmen political reaction which gave rise to a renewed emphasis on holding fast to 'socialism with Chinese characteristics', the country's leaders continued to assert their commitment to 'firmly pushing forward reform and opening to the outside world' (CPC 1990). Early in 1992 Deng Xiaoping inaugurated a campaign to initiate a deeper and more innovative phase of economic reform. At the time of writing (1993) it is clear that reform is very much back on the agenda. Many provinces, especially the southern coastal ones, have continued to take the initiative in pursuing further reform and foreign economic relations, and the conservative politicians have failed to slow this momentum or to put forward a concrete alternative programme.

This chapter examines the main provisions of the economic reform and the associated policy of opening economic relations to the outside world. The reform has involved major changes in the Chinese system of industrial governance, some of which were foreshadowed in earlier periods. The first section summarizes these earlier phases of industrial governance from the beginning of the Communist government in 1949 to the onset of reform in 1978. The economic reform programme itself is then discussed, with particular attention to the changes in economic management. The third section identifies the key dimensions of change in China's industrial governance; these dimensions indicate policy options on which there are still differences of opinion within the country. The final section describes measures that have been taken to open the economy to the outside world.

Phases of Chinese industrial governance up to the reform

The system of industrial governance in China has passed through four main phases since 1949, prior to that of economic reform which has now become the most durable phase of all. Each phase involved a different degree of centralization and control in the relationships between government and enterprise, as well as a different emphasis between ideological/moral and economic/material principles. The systems of leadership within enterprises which accompanied these phases will be examined more closely in chapter 4.

1953–1956 Central planning

Following the transformation to socialist ownership in the early 1950s, a centralized planning system was established along Stalinist Soviet lines. China's first Five Year Plan was launched in 1953. Key components of the system were a highly centralized mode of command planning, a hierarchical enterprise management system, and an elaborate structure of individual material incentives in industry (Riskin 1987). Plans were passed down to production units through provincial and municipal planning authorities. Larger factories in the priority heavy industrial sectors normally had executive authority concentrated in the hands of their directors. Worker participation was limited to worker representative congresses which were chaired by the trade union secretary and concerned with welfare matters. This so-called 'one director [or 'one man'] management system' was adopted as the official norm in 1953. Material incentives were increased in coverage so that by 1954 over 40 per cent of the industrial labour force was on piece-rate bonus systems. A significant differential was also built into the wage system during this period.

1957–1961 Decentralization and the Great Leap Forward

The Soviet-derived system contributed to substantial advances in heavy industrial output during the 1950s and the framework of its planning structure remains in place today. It was, nevertheless, incongruous with Chinese revolutionary ideology and with existing industrial traditions of collective leadership. It relied, moreover, upon the availability of technically trained managers which China did not possess at the time, a constraint which also spoke for broadening the base of contributions to decision making (Andors 1977; Littler 1985).

From 1957 to 1961 in particular, moral encouragement was given primacy over material incentives. The coverage of bonus payments to industrial workers was reduced, while managers and technical staff were now excluded from receiving a bonus. Factory directors were made responsible to party committees. During these years of the 'Great Leap Forward', the watchword was 'politics in command' and there was a strong shift towards a collectivist and ideological emphasis in economic management.

In November 1957, the State Council announced decisions on the administrative decentralization of industry. Control over the great majority of light industrial enterprises passed from central to provincial governments, along with heavy industrial enterprises other than large ones in strategic sectors. At the same time, the number of mandatory targets imposed on enterprise directors was reduced from twelve to four: production quantities, total employment, total payment bill and total profit (Riskin 1987).

1962–1965 The period of readjustment

There were sharp declines in agricultural output in 1959, 1960 and 1961 leading to widespread famine, while the output of both light and heavy industry also declined significantly in 1961. This crisis led to a phase of 'readjustment' (Riskin 1987) in industrial governance marked by a strengthening of central planning and a reconsolidation of executive managerial authority. Factory directors were accorded more responsibility over enterprise operations, although their decisions were now more closely guided by the centre than before. Factory hierarchies were reinforced and functionally divided roles elaborated. The party was distanced from the everyday operations of the factory, though it continued to play a major role in the co-ordination of factory planning. A minor relaxation in centralization was introduced in 1964.

Although workers were now discouraged from sharing directly in managerial tasks, the responsibilities of the workers' congress were in 1961 extended from matters of welfare and the achievement of planned targets to include the discussion and resolution of all issues within the enterprise touching on workers' interests. There was a re-establishment of individual material incentives for industrial workers after 1961.

1966–1976 The Cultural Revolution

The third phase of economic management was in turn terminated abruptly by the onset of the Cultural Revolution in 1966, though subsequently restored ten years later. The Cultural Revolution put politics and ideology more firmly in command than they had ever been. Hierarchical management was abolished in favour of factory revolutionary committees which were intended to introduce direct worker participation in discussions of factory policy. Piece wages and bonuses were sharply reduced or eliminated altogether. Competitive, individual and material incentive was rejected in favour of co-operative, collective and moral incentive (Prybyla 1976).

While the motives behind the Cultural Revolution remain a matter of debate, it is apparent that Mao Zedong chafed at the limitations placed on his personal leadership both as a reaction to the Great Leap Forward and with the development of a bureaucratic economic administration which transformed his charismatic leadership into one of planning and control routines. Mao's strategy referred back to that developed during the anti-Japanese and civil wars in the revolutionary bases in Yan'an and elsewhere. This mobilized a mass nationwide movement combining direct workers' control guided by ideologically primed local party leaders with loyalty to a charismatic, rather than bureaucratic, central leadership. The Cultural Revolution was *inter alia* intended to discredit and remove the layers of administration and industrial management which intervened between the working class and its leader. Lockett's (1985) study of the Beijing General Knitwear Mill, officially regarded as a model factory during the Cultural Revolution, suggests, however, that radical changes to previously established managerial structures and reductions in white-collar numbers were in practice short-lived.

With Mao's death and the fall of the 'Gang of Four' in 1976, the Cultural Revolution was brought to an end. For a while the third phase of economic management was restored before the decision of the Third Plenum of the party Central Committee in December 1978 to embark on a major programme of reform in the Chinese economy. This programme of reform, interacting with inherited structural and behavioural characteristics, has shaped the present pattern of enterprise management in China.

The economic reform programme

The intention to undertake economic structure reform, as it is officially known, was announced at the Third Plenum of the Eleventh Central Committee meeting of the Communist Party of China, held in December 1978. The new policy adopted as its guiding theme the 'Four Modernizations' of agriculture, industry, science and technology, and defence. It was both an immediate reaction to the shortcomings of the Cultural Revolution and a desire to transcend the limitations of the Soviet-style centralized system developed in the first half of the 1950s and largely restored at the beginning of the 1960s. It was based on a consensus that the economic failings of the Mao period had to be rectified.

Output per unit of capital invested had declined by a quarter from 1952 to 1978. On some assumptions, labour productivity had hardly improved at all over the same period (Riskin 1987). 'Overcentralized management, irrational investment decisions by bureaucrats, and poor labor motivation were the primary reasons for the failures in industry' (Walder 1989: 408). In 1978, the party leadership recognized that Maoist economic policy had failed to:

1 increase personal per capita income, as opposed to National Income, partly due to short-sighted population policies;
2 increase the stock of available technological knowledge, including the import of advanced technology from abroad;
3 reduce the inefficiency due to a lack of motivation and commitment among managers and workers (X-inefficiency);
4 improve allocation efficiency, namely the direction of resources to their best uses;
5 make use of comparative advantages in foreign trade as opposed to complementary trade restricted to filling gaps in domestic supply (Krug 1989: 22).

The Cultural Revolution was seen to have dissipated incentive and responsibility for economic performance through egalitarianism, the weakening of management, the general devaluation of expertise and the claim that ideological fervour and inspired leadership could substitute for technical knowledge. The mass mobilization of workers against the authority structures through which central direction operated had led to chaos and destructive factionalism. The xenophobia of the period had denied the country opportunities for inward investment and technology transfer. The older, Soviet-style system was not, however, regarded by the 1978 reformers as an appropriate model to which to return. For while it was acknowledged to have played a role in establishing a heavy industrial base in China's developing economy, it was now viewed as too rigid. Its heavy, centralized administrative approach confused the functions of government and enterprise, imposed undue uniformity and suppressed initiative, failed to adapt to market demand, and did not link rewards adequately to economic performance (Huang 1985).

There have been a number of complementary strands in the economic reform which, significantly, began by focusing on the provision of incentives to achieve an increase in agricultural production. In the industrial sphere, with which we are concerned, the aim has been to restructure economic management in order to invigorate and modernize enterprises. The opening of economic relations to the outside world (the so-called 'open-door policy') was seen as a further necessary change to promote the same objectives. Figure 3.1 sets out the key events which have occurred in the reform to date.

The reform has involved:

1 changing the distribution of property rights (in the sense of a right to use assets) away from the state through the de-collectivization of agriculture, the deregulation of the economy (including easing of the right to establish collective and private firms) and decentralization of much remaining regulation, and the easing of access by firms to the factors of production;
2 shifting from the hierarchical administrative regulation of economic transactions towards a system of market regulation guided by the state;
3 strengthening the management system within producing units through an enhancement of managerial competence and discretion;
4 improving incentives by linking remuneration and responsibility to performance through incentive payment schemes and responsibility systems.

The restructuring of economic management has centred on reforms to the management of state-owned enterprises. These were in essence intended to transform the basic economic organization from a production unit (factory) to a business enterprise. Hussain (1990:1) has identified three main periods in the process to date:

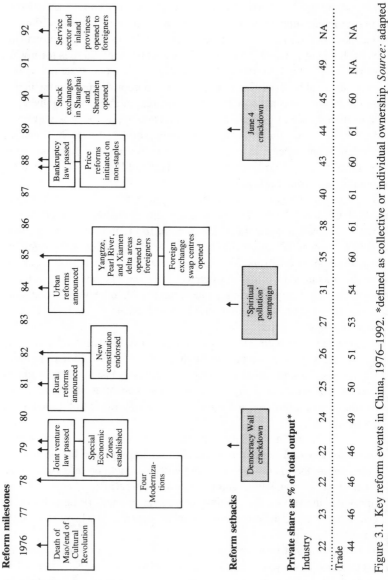

Figure 3.1 Key reform events in China, 1976–1992. *defined as collective or individual ownership. *Source*: adapted from Shaw and Woetzel 1992: exhibit 13.

1979–84 Permitting enterprises to produce outside the plan, to retain depreciation allowances and a portion of profits; a shift in the financing of working capital and investment from the government budget to enterprises' own funds and bank loans; discretion over the recruitment of workers and the introduction of performance-linked wage bonuses.

1984–86 Letting enterprises sell above-plan output at negotiated prices and to plan their output accordingly; new procedures for the appointment of enterprise directors; the replacement of remittances with profit taxes; a diversification of the sources of finance; leasing of small state-owned enterprises to managers.

1987– Formalization of the role of enterprise directors, their methods of appointment and criteria for the evaluation of their performance; the introduction of performance targets for directors (the system of management contracts); introduction of a bankruptcy law; formalization of the main provisions into the 1988 Enterprise Law.

Hussain notes that:

Broadly, the first phase consisted of granting financial and a measure of operational autonomy to enterprises within the context of the traditional output planning. It was only in the second phase that market transactions began to be allowed to co-exist with 'plan transactions' and influence the pattern of output. In the third phase the focus shifted to the links between enterprise management and economic administration, and to the ownership status of enterprises. (p. 1)

Two further phases have since occurred. The first was inaugurated by the central authorities in September 1988 and continued into 1990. This was an austerity programme of recentralization and economic readjustment which followed the diagnosis that the economy was 'overheating' by mid-1988. It reduced investment, partly through administrative directives and partly by cutting the money supply. The central government also re-extended the range of direct price controls and subsidies. Its programme succeeded in sharply reducing inflation and in turning a current account deficit into a surplus by 1990.

The latest phase commenced during the latter part of 1990, since when economic restrictions have been eased and the economic reform has proceeded along several fronts. By 1992 it was claimed that some 80 per cent of prices were being set by the market. Price subsidies on basic foods and energy were reduced. Experiments resumed into the issue of enterprise shares and more firms were declared bankrupt. The non-state-owned sector of industry again expanded rapidly. Foreign investment was being introduced at a record rate. By the middle of 1992, however, signs of overheating were re-appearing and it remains to be seen whether any new dampening of the economy will be accompanied by direct administrative restrictions on management although the measures introduced in July 1993 avoided this.

Returning to the beginning of the reform, the search began after 1979, through a series of experiments, for a new structure of economic management which would combine responsiveness to economic need (improved allocative efficiency) and incentive (improved X-efficiency) with the maintenance of overall central direction. The measures through which economic restructuring proceeded have been detailed by others (e.g. Perkins 1988) and only the key developments are mentioned here as a background to understanding the present-day situation. The reform proceeded incrementally rather than according to any grand design. It built upon certain precedents before 1978 and then developed according to a stepwise learning process.

The first reform experiments in agriculture and industry were instituted in Sichuan, the political base of reform leaders Deng Xiaoping and Zhao Ziyang. The agricultural reform was based on the household responsibility system whereby land is contracted to peasants, and on various incentive policies linked to permitting higher levels of commodity production for rural 'free markets'. The marginal rate of return to peasants from land available for private production was much higher than that from collective land, and the reform thus provided a major incentive to increase private output. After the freeing up of rural markets in 1979, all components of farm output grew more rapidly, especially cash crops and animal husbandry, and most dramatically rural industry founded on the basis of now-surplus labour and capital (Perkins 1988).

As has been continually stressed by the Chinese themselves, the task of reforming agriculture was inherently easier than that of reforming industry. Urban industrial reform is a more complex matter. It has developed through a longer process of trial and error which still continues. Key elements have been the decentralization of administrative powers to the provinces and municipalities, the development of market relations, the delegation of responsibility for performance to enterprise managers, and the encouragement of incentive systems.

By mid-1979, over 100 state-owned enterprises in Sichuan Province were authorized by the central government to assume new powers over production and marketing. A system allowing some retention of profit was introduced to create a link between enterprise performance and reward. There were new forms of investment financing, and opportunities for enterprises to use depreciation funds were improved. By the end of 1980, most provinces had initiated pilot experiments in enterprise management, including profit retention, covering a total of some 6,600 state enterprises.

In 1981 there was a recentralization of decision making with respect to the allocation of inputs and the distribution of products, especially in heavy industry which had suffered a 5 per cent decline in output that year. A drain on foreign exchange reserves led to the centrally imposed postponement or cancellation of many contracts for foreign equipment. The introduction of profit retention had also reduced state revenue. The government now decided to keep more direct administrative control over key allocative and distribution decisions, but at the same time to apply a form of the responsibility system which had been successful in the agricultural sector. This was intended to clarify responsibility for success and failure at all levels of the industrial hierarchy down to factory workers. It was complemented by a contract system allowing for direct inter-enterprise transactions. By the end of 1982, this reform was being tried out in over 3,000 state-owned firms.

Although government planning and control of state-owned industry were retained, the bureaucratic apparatus was streamlined at this time. The number of ministries and commissions was reduced from 98 to 52. The State Planning Commission and the State Economic Commission were given more direct responsibility for enterprise planning and control, but with many decision-making powers, including finance and investment, being delegated to provincial authorities. The local branches of foreign trade corporations were given wider powers to negotiate directly with overseas trade partners. In March 1982, selected cities were designated to pioneer urban economic restructuring, particularly to decentralize enterprise management and create conditions for more effective market transactions.

By 1984, while substantial progress had been made in a number of areas of reform, there were also some grounds for disappointment. Industrial/urban reforms lagged behind those in the rural sector, especially after the nationwide implementation of the Production Responsibility System in agriculture in 1983 (Byrd 1991). So a movement was initiated to 'deepen' urban reforms, focusing on the state-owned enterprise.

The State Council decided in May 1984 to expand the decision-making powers of state enterprises in ten areas: production planning, product marketing, pricing of products outside the State plan, materials purchasing, use of surplus funds, disposal of assets, organization, personnel management, payment systems, and affiliations between enterprises. In October 1984 a directive was issued increasing enterprise autonomy, releasing certain enterprises from central ministry control and permitting some prices to float. Enterprises could now charge market prices for production achieved in excess of the quotas allocated to them under the central plan. In February 1985, powers to plan their own technological development were devolved to state enterprises, while in September 1985 large and medium-size firms were also granted powers to pursue their own marketing policies.

The measures allowing enterprises more freedom to devise their own market and innovation policies were intended to improve allocative efficiency. Another key objective of economic reform was to improve incentives and the main instruments here were profit retention by enterprises and bonuses for workers. Prior to the reform, factories were essentially responsible for fulfilling production quotas, under a quota responsibility system, and they handed over any surplus funds to the state. Following experiments in profit retention, the government in 1983 began to substitute tax payments for profit remittances, with state enterprises paying a progressive profit tax of up to 55 per cent, supplemented by an adjustment tax levied on those which were deemed to have secured excess profits because of favourable pricing or other factors (Tidrick and Chen 1987). Retained profits could be used to pay bonuses and/or pay for new construction or renovation, which increased the incentive for profit maximization. This system was generalized in 1985 with 55 per cent becoming the uniform rate of state profit tax, but was then in turn replaced in 1987 by various 'Contractual Responsibility Systems'.

After the Cultural Revolution, the principle of 'to each according to his work' was revived and by 1979 about 90 per cent of industrial workers and staff were again receiving a bonus. Enterprises generally came to pay bonuses out of retained profits so providing in principle a link with overall performance. Initially bonuses were limited to 25 per cent of basic salary, but in 1984 this limitation was replaced by a progressive bonus tax as a more flexible control over the level of bonus payments (Tidrick and Chen 1987).

In 1984, lessons from the various reform experiments were drawn together in a key policy document intended to point the way to an extension of industrial reform across the whole country. This document was adopted in October 1984 by the Party Central Committee and entitled 'China's Economic Structure Reform'. It reaffirmed the 'pressing necessity' of the economic reform programme and it expounded a 'systematic' and 'all round' policy to be applied generally throughout the industrial sector. The document focused on the reform of enterprise management allied to a greater role for market forces and complementary reforms in the fiscal and pricing systems. Its main themes are now summarized (page numbers refer to the English version – CPC 1984).

Modernization was restated as the rationale for reform, the key to which lies in the 'invigoration' of urban industrial enterprises which then accounted for over 80 per cent of the state's tax revenue (pp. 8–9). The main requirement for injecting vitality into these enterprises was seen to be an extension of their decision-making powers so that they could respond to market forces and provide incentives. The major defects of the then existing economic structure were summarized as follows:

No clear distinction has been drawn between the functions of the government and those of the enterprise; barriers exist between different departments or between different regions; the state has exercised excessive and rigid control over enterprises; no adequate importance has been given to commodity production, the law of value and the regulatory role of the market; and there is absolute egalitarianism in distribution. This has resulted in enterprises lacking necessary decision making power and the practice of 'eating from the same big pot' prevailing in the relations of the enterprises to the state and in those of the workers and staff members to their enterprises. The enthusiasm, initiative and creativeness of enterprises and workers and staff members have, as a result, been seriously dampened and the socialist economy is bereft of much of the vitality it should possess. (pp. 5–6).

The new policy envisaged an extension of economic decentralization within a system of governmental planning in which the mandatory element would be reduced in favour of guidance plans and where control would be exercised through economic regulators rather than administrative fiat. Within this revised framework of state planning and control, enterprise management was now to take on significant new responsibilities (p. 10). These were:

1 to decide on the enterprise's operations and organization, including 'flexible and diversified forms';
2 to plan its production, supply and marketing in tune with market mechanisms;
3 to set prices within limits prescribed by the state;
4 to retain and budget certain funds;
5 to decide on recruitment, personnel and reward policies.

Enterprises would become 'independent and responsible for their own profit and loss and capable of transforming and developing themselves . . . [acting as] legal persons with certain rights and duties' (p. 11). Their directors would assume full responsibility for their performance under a unified management system. This is the so-called 'director responsibility system' which replaced the previous system of managerial responsibility to the enterprise party committee (and which the following chapter discusses in detail).

The policy document particularly stressed the need for local governments not to interfere in enterprise management or to create barriers to inter-enterprise contracting (p. 21). All government organs were enjoined to see their role as providing services to enterprises rather than treating them as their private dependencies (p. 23). They were also to 'eliminate such bureaucratic maladies as organisational overlapping, over-staffing, vague delimitations of functions and endless wrangling' which handicapped the effective operation of enterprises (p. 23). Within enterprises, managerial adherence to party principles and policies were, however, to be ensured by party organizations, while workers were to have the right to examine major decisions and articulate their interests through their own congresses and trade unions (p. 25). These policies were expressed in terms of establishing 'correct relationships' between enterprises and the state, and between enterprises and their members (p. 9).

A regulation approved in September 1985 by the State Council on 'Strengthening the Vitality of Large and Medium-Sized Enterprises' reiterated that enterprise plans should be drawn up with reference to market conditions and urged that 'enterprises should change from production oriented operation to production and marketing oriented operation' (*People's Daily*, 20 September 1985). The same regulation confirmed that the assumption of strategic powers by enterprises within the guidelines of state plans and policies should be formalized by a 'responsibility contract' between the enterprise director and higher authority.

The contractual responsibility systems introduced to most large and medium-sized state industrial enterprises during 1986–87 'at first sight display a bewildering variety and complexity' (Byrd 1991: 13). However, as Byrd shows, most or all systems have a common core of features and practices, while they differ from each other along identifiable dimensions. The common features are (1) the governance of relations between enterprise decision maker and supervisory agency by some form of explicit contract; (2) the entry of the enterprise director into the contract on behalf of the enterprise with an assumption of personal responsibility – a precondition for this contractual responsibility to work is that 'the director indeed has the requisite authority within the enterprise as well as *vis-à-vis* the supervisory agency' (Byrd 1991: 14); (3) some assumption of risk by the contractor, along with variability in his/her rewards, both linked to the performance of the enterprise; (4) contract terms that extend over several years.

The most common form of contractual responsibility system, which in late 1987 was chosen by the central government for rapid adoption in the bulk of state-owned enterprises, is the 'Contract Management Responsibility System' (CMRS). This has several variants, but in each case the contractual arrangement relates to the amount of profits an enterprise has to remit to the supervisory agency. Under 'double contracting ['the two guarantees'] and single link', the enterprise contracts to hand over an agreed amount of annual profit and tax for which it contracts; it is permitted to retain a proportion of any surplus it achieves above the contracted level. The second 'contracting' is that the enterprise guarantees to invest to increase asset values and develop technology by an agreed amount during the period of the contract. Increases in the enterprise's total salary fund are constrained to a maximum of 70 per cent of the increase in overall profit (this is the 'single link'). Targets were set in advance for the last four years of the Seventh Five Year Plan (1987–1990).

Other variants of the CMRS include (1) responsibility for an annual increase in profit remittance, (2) remittance of a fixed base amount of profit, with sharing above quota profits, (3) fixed profit remittance or loss targets, for low profit or loss-making enterprises, and (4) sectoral input–output responsibility systems involving targets for flows of resources and funds between sector ministries and the government.

The system is officially intended to place (governmental) ownership at arm's length to enterprise management, so allowing more decision-making space to the latter. In reality, however, that space is severely constrained by the fact that the system obliges enterprises to work to performance norms still largely determined by government bureaux in which considerable power continues to reside, norms which may not be compatible with the best developmental policy for the enterprise.

Enterprises were encouraged to make their own internal responsibility contracts with constituent departments and/or with external suppliers. The contracting principle was extended to cover employment in October 1986, abolishing life-tenure for newly recruited employees not enjoying the status of 'cadres' and making contract renewal conditional upon their performance and the needs of the enterprise. Fixed-term contracts for enterprise directors had been instituted by State Council directive in September 1984. To complement these measures to increase enterprise responsibility, the director responsibility system, which had been operating experimentally since 1984, was made the sole leadership system in September 1986. This enables directors to accept responsibility for the performance of their firms, as required by the contract responsibility system, by freeing them from the policy direction of local party committees.

The question of enterprise ownership has been a matter for considerable debate during the reform process. As chapter 2 noted, there has since 1978 been a steady rise in the proportion of industrial output contributed by collectively and privately owned firms which by virtue both of their ownership status and their generally smaller size are less subject to economic regulation by government agencies. The desire to reinvigorate state-owned firms, to clarify their managerial accountability and to draw China's high proportion of savings into productive use has also led to experiments in the public issue of corporate bonds. Some 25,000 smaller state enterprises have been leased to management which takes on full responsibility for their operation in a quasi-ownership mode in return for either a fixed sum or proportion of profit to the government. The range of ownership in Chinese industry has also been extended by encouraging foreign enterprises to flourish either as equity partners or more recently under wholly foreign ownership.

Throughout the reform years, attention was also given to strengthening a decentralized system of production by greatly increasing managerial and technical training. The 1984 reform policy document stated that:

Reform of our economic structure and the development of our national economy badly need a large contingent of managerial and administrative personnel, and especially managers, who are both knowledgeable in modern economics and technology . . . our present urgent task is to promote boldly thousands upon thousands of young and middle-aged managerial personnel and take steps to train them. (pp. 31–2).

Up to the Sino-Soviet split in 1960, training courses were taught by Soviet advisors and technicians – there were over 10,000 Soviet 'experts' in China at that time (Warner 1992: 4). The emphasis was on training production management in a system where the economic units were but factories producing to the central plan, and no distinction was made between the training of management and that of higher white-collar staff (cadres) generally.

Since 1979, considerable attention has been given to management training in its own right, with the State Economic Commission being empowered to implement a programme for this. It organized courses for the senior managers of large factories; it initiated training for high level technologists; and it ran programmes to bring specialist middle managers up-to-date. After the abolition of the SEC at the national level in March 1988, these responsibilities were assumed by the State Commission for Restructuring the Economic Systems. By 1988 the total number of persons studying management-related subjects (excluding correspondence and evening courses) approached 107,000, of which over 4,000 were postgraduates, 43,000 undergraduates and 60,000 in work. There were over 300 higher education institutions offering management training courses in China (Warner 1992). Despite these large-scale efforts in management education, and the complementary development of technical training (Hunter and Keehn 1985), China remains very short of personnel who can manage modern competitive enterprises and run sophisticated technologies.

Many of the provisions to restructure economic management were brought together in the 'Law Concerning Enterprises Owned by the Whole People' (i.e. state-owned enterprises) passed in April 1988, to take effect on 1 August. This law pulled together and codified items of reform policy that had first been announced some years previously. In China, the announcement of official policy can precede the issuing of detailed regulations by several years and, even then, the policy may not have been precisely formalized in its entirety. Detailed regulations were issued on largely financial matters such as cost calculations, investment, price constraints, disposal of assets and bonus levels.

However, policies to expand enterprise autonomy have not been precisely formulated, which continues to leave the determination of this matter to a process of negotiation between the enterprises and local bureaus. Despite the Enterprise Law and a few others like the Bankruptcy Law, the major instrument for overall control over enterprises remains the issuing of regulations from the State Council, the State Planning Commission, ministries and local authorities. Indeed, the centrally imposed austerity programme in the Autumn of 1988, coupled with a tightening of political control following June 1989, for a while placed many of the decentralizing provisions in abeyance in favour of renewed intervention by both government and local party organs.

Dimensions of change in China's industrial governance

The economic reform is often represented by the Chinese themselves as a major break with the past. In reality, its principles of decentralization, recognition of market forces and use of economic incentives played a role in previous initiatives on the way that the economic system was managed. As we have seen, there had been attempts to decentralize economic management in 1957, in 1964, and more extensively during the Cultural Revolution. The so-called 'responsibility system', under which a material incentive is provided to households, collectives and (since 1987) state enterprises by contracting with them to achieve specific economic targets and allowing them to keep all or part of the income from any surpluses gained from supplying the free market, was first tried in agriculture as early as 1953–4 and then used in various forms in different localities until the mid-1960s. The concept of the 'Four Modernizations' which is closely associated with the reform had been formally proposed by Zhou Enlai in 1964 and foreshadowed by Mao Zedong in 1957. Not only is there a continuity in the transfer of reform principles from agriculture to the industrial sector, but it can further be argued that earlier reform initiatives failed because of left-wing political intervention rather than as a result of their inherent deficiencies.

The phases of industrial governance in post-1949 China have thus involved movement along several dimensions which lend them their paradoxical quality of change alongside continuity. Several writers have identified underlying dimensions in terms of which this process can be analysed. Lee (1987) has argued for the significance of two such dimensions. The first concerns the balance between guiding principles. These can be characterized in simple terms as the principles of ideology and politics (a 'political' mode), on the one hand, and those of economic and technical necessity (a 'pragmatic' mode), on the other. This is the contrast between seeking truth from theory and seeking truth from facts, to extend Deng Xiaoping's famous aphorism. The second dimension concerns level within the system as a benchmark for the centralization or decentralization of economic decision making. Thus economic decentralization can be characterized as devolution through the key levels of (1) central government (the State), (2) local government and (3) the enterprise. Decentralization implies that economic initiative moves down the administrative hierarchy towards the enterprise.

There are some parallels between Lee's framework for analyzing Chinese industrial governance and those advanced respectively by Hackman (1989) in terms of 'delegation arrangements' and by Boisot and Child (1988) in terms of information characteristics. Hackman identifies level of decision making (centralized/decentralized) and level of formalization as two key dimensions. Boisot and Child single out information diffusion and codification.[1] As Child (1990a) has argued, these frameworks are comparable if one acknowledges that decentralization requires a diffusion of information, that codification is part and parcel of formalization, and that political ideology is likely to be relatively uncodified (expressed in terms of general precepts, sometimes little more than slogans) compared with the more specific techniques and rules of technical expertise and systematic management.

A conjunction of the three schemes – from Boisot/Child, Hackman and Lee – produces the four modes of economic governance shown in figure 3.2 and labelled A to D. All of them have been tried in China at various times since 1949.

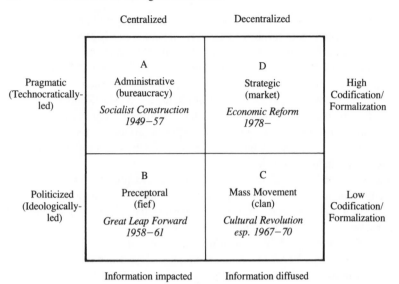

Figure 3.2 Framework for analysing changes in China's system of industrial governance since 1949.

Lee describes the pragmatic mode (Mode A) as 'administrative' when the policy process was centralized and top-down. The administrative approach was the first to be attempted after 1949 and was implemented through hierarchical bureaucratic channels. These channels were relatively formalized although they never attained the level of formalization manifest in the Soviet system on which they were largely modelled.

The centralized political mode (Mode B) is what Lee calls the 'preceptoral' approach. This was driven by the ideology of class struggle and socialist morality, and was manifested in the Great Leap Forward between 1958 and 1961. This mode of managing economic action relied on the generation of mass enthusiasm through oratory and example much more than on formal regulations and systems. The Great Leap Forward was led from the top – implemented through the mobilization of mass action inspired by charismatic leadership and usually organized by the party. In this system, party officials led both local communities and factories somewhat as personal fiefs.

Lee regards the political approach as having always been led from above in China. The Cultural Revolution, however, evolved for a while after 1967 into a state of decentralized political action in which the polity fragmented into a number of factions (clans). This approximated to Mode C.

Mode D approximates to Lee's strategic approach. This system of industrial governance permits decentralized economic action which is driven primarily by the market. By contrast to the bureaucratic central planning of Mode A (the other 'pragmatic' mode), the strategic approach is activated by specific economic realities and market preferences with implementation and accountability located primarily in the relationship between enterprise and local government. In these terms, the Chinese economic reform represents a major shift towards the strategic approach.

Taking the period from 1949 as a whole, China's system of industrial governance has moved from a relatively pragmatic, centrally planned approach, through two main politicized phases in which ideological considerations and the restructuring of economic relationships were given primacy, and on to even greater pragmatism under the reform. These phases were dominated respectively by the three schools of thought that Jackson (1992) identifies within what she calls the 'market-plan controversy'. The first is the planning approach favoured by the government during the 1950s. It was supported by many party members and bureaucrats who had absorbed the Soviet planning tradition. Jackson calls this group the centerists. The second group consists of those who are on the left wing of the party and who are committed to the eradication of capitalism; they have been particularly concerned with authority relations in the workplace. Their policies dominated during the Great Leap Forward (1958-61) and the Cultural Revolution (1966-76). The third school is that of reform, advocated by the right wing of the party. Their ideas held sway during the period of recovery after the Great Leap Forward (1962–5); they have been particularly influential through most of the 1980s and again since 1991.

The essence of the economic reform has been a restructured relationship between government, especially at central level, and economic units which have been transformed from factories into enterprises. The previous role of government was that of planner, both of the macro-economy and of many production units in the micro-economy as well. The planning regime did not draw a sharp distinction between economy and factory as units of governance because, in theory at least, the aggregation of economic units constituted the planned economy. This distinction is now more clearly made and identifies two roles for the government: the first as overall economic regulator and the second as contractual monitor of enterprise performance and development (especially in the state-owned sector). The government's former role as planner, and its present ones as market regulator and enterprise contractor, are identified in figure 3.3. The figure also summarizes the institutional linkages between government and enterprises which pertain under each role and the behaviour expected of management in each case.

The opening of economic relations to the outside world

The encouragement of economic relations with the outside world has progressed down two main paths. First, the stimulation of direct trading

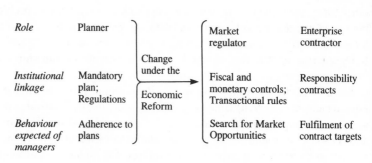

Figure 3.3 The change in industrial governance under the economic reform

relations. Second, measures to promote investment by foreign firms, especially in the so-called Open Cities and Special Economic Zones. Approximately 40 per cent of foreign investment pledged to China since 1979 has come through the formation of joint ventures.

China's foreign trade as a share of its national income rose from 10 per cent in 1978 to 32 per cent in 1990. By 1992, its total value of imports and exports placed China as the eleventh largest trading nation in the world. Its economic relations with the outside world have clearly opened up considerably under the economic reform, and it is now quite highly integrated into the world economy.

The Ministry of Foreign Economic Relations and Trade (MOFERT) was formed in March 1982 with a broad remit to encourage and supervise foreign economic relations in the broadest sense. According to Arthur Andersen (1993), its main areas of work include:

1   formulation and implementation of trade policies;
2   trade promotion;
3   regulation of trade (including import and export licences);
4   co-ordination, supervision and administration of the foreign economic relations and trade commissions of provincial and local bodies involved in trade and foreign investment;
5   negotiation and administration of aid as both recipient and donor;
6   regulation and promotion of foreign investment;
7   co-ordination of the import and export of appropriate technology in accordance with China's priorities for economic development;
8   marketing of contractual engineering services and labour services abroad and their operational supervision.

Under the former system of central planning, foreign trade was conducted on the basis of an overall plan with specific annual targets. The trade plan formed part of the central plan, and it was drawn up by MOFERT in consultation with the State Planning Commission. Under this system, MOFERT co-ordinated and supervised foreign trade through some twenty foreign trade corporations organized by industry. In the early 1980s, a series of reforms granted greater independence to the provinces to handle their own foreign trade. Local foreign trade companies were given the right to operate independently of their parents, while local foreign economic relations and trade commissions were given powers to issue import and export licences for a range of products and commodities. MOFERT's monopoly over foreign trade was also gradually eroded as the State Council authorized other import and export channels either through companies directly under its own supervision or through companies responsible to other ministries. Despite the re-imposition of central controls over imports and many key export commodities following the foreign exchange crisis of 1984, the trend was towards the decentralization of responsibility for foreign trade.

This was formalized under a new system announced in December 1987 which made the major import and export corporations autonomous from MOFERT and responsible for their own profits and losses. The intention was that they should become trading companies in the full sense rather than merely the governmental organs of trade administration. They were given the objective of generating profits from trading rather than simply gathering as much foreign exchange as possible without regard to profitability in the knowledge that losses would be subsidized. The same provisions authorized many new foreign trade corporations and allowed some large enterprises to deal directly with foreign businesses. A contract responsibility system was also introduced between units at different levels of the national trade corporations. Overall, these provisons were an attempt to apply the responsibility system to foreign trade and to stimulate its profitable expansion.

Inward investment has been encouraged by the provision of favourable fiscal regimes in selected geographical areas and by the reconstitution of industrial regulations to grant additional operating autonomy to joint ventures and foreign owned enterprises. Between 1979 and the end of 1992 there were 90,791 new foreign-funded projects in China, involving a total contractual investment of US$110 billion.[2]

The intention to create Special Economic Zones, with incentives for foreign investment, was announced in 1979. Shenzhen, Zhuhai, Shantou and Xiamen were designated as SEZs in 1980, and Hainan Island was added in 1988. Preferential teatment is granted to foreign investors in the SEZs with respect to tax incentives, flexible arrangements for land use with reductions available in charges, reduced welfare contributions, flexible arrangements for employing labour, and the possibility of preferential prices for raw materials and equipment. In April 1984 the government selected fourteen coastal cities, which were to be granted greater autonomy in economic policy making and allowed to offer special incentives to encourage foreign investment, including tax incentives. Each city would create a special district – an Economic and Technological Development Zone (ETDZ) – in which a particularly favourable economic regime would be created. Thus the ETDZs were to enjoy special rights to approve projects involving foreign investment. The fourteen coastal cities are (running north to south down the coast) Dalian, Qinhuangdao, Tianjin, Yantai, Qingdao, Lianyungang, Nantong, Shanghai, Ningbo, Wenzhou, Fuzhou, Guangzhou, Zhanjiang and Beihai.

In addition to the Special Economic Zones and the Coastal Cities, a range of other 'Open Economic Zones' were created during the second half of the 1980s, some by the central government and others by provincial and local authorities. These offer a variety of privileges and treatment for foreign investors. Three of these zones were established in 1985 and are now among the more developed – the Yangtze Delta, the Southern Fujian Delta and the Pearl River Delta. The incentives and special provisions available in the EZs are normally similar to those available in the fourteen coastal cities.

As indicated in the previous chapter, the equity joint venture has been a particularly important vehicle for the introduction of foreign investment into China under the open door policy. While all the activities undertaken by joint ventures are governed by Chinese laws, decrees and regulations, favourable treatment has been accorded to them through specific legislation in recognition of their special contribution and organizational form. The 'Law of the PRC on Chinese Foreign Joint Ventures', promulgated in August 1979, was the first of its kind. In October 1986, the State Council issued twenty-two 'Regulations Concerning Encouragement of Foreign Investment' which offer foreign-funded enterprises (including joint ventures) preferences and additional operational freedoms. In April 1990, an 'Amendment to the Law of the PRC on Joint Ventures using Chinese and Foreign Investment' was approved. Chinese law and regulations on joint ventures and other forms of foreign-funded enterprise are discussed at greater length in chapter 11.

Joint ventures are not only a channel for inward investment into China; they also provide the means for an import of technological knowledge and managerial skills. Yet, because they normally involve a degree of joint Sino-foreign management, they present particular challenges to the achievement of successful operational co-operation which are reviewed in part III. Indeed, much of the remainder of this book will be considering how the economic reform policies have been working out in practice especially at the level of enterprise management in the state-owned sector. The intention is both to provide the reader with some insight into the actual structures and processes of Chinese management today and, through so doing, to place the claims of the economic reform into a realistic context.

Conclusion

Although the Chinese economic reform is a bold and comprehensive undertaking, it is not a revolutionary so much as an evolutionary process. It displays continuity with the past, as well as breaking away from it.[3] As will become evident from reading the chapters which follow, official pronouncements on the reform give the impression of sometimes quite radical change and of its firm and steady implementation, while the reality at ground level displays considerable temporization with established norms, relationships and centres of power. This is not to deny the real progress of reform, but rather to indicate that its implementation is much more complex and less straightforward than the propaganda of its advocates admits.

A major reason for this is that the authorities are unwilling to take an extreme position on the policy dimensions underlying the oscillations in Chinese industrial governance since 1949. During the reform period they have tended towards a combination of decentralization and pragmatism, without entirely letting go of their opposite poles: centralism and politics. The institutional structures which reflect the latter remain in place and exercise some continuing influence. Industrial ministries and the State Planning Commission represent the continuity of centralism. The Communist Party of China, with its lines of authority extending into enterprises and their workplaces, represents a continuing role for political ideology and conformity. The economic reform has not yet been accompanied by any fundamental reform in either the administrative or the political arms of government, and the authorities have shown themselves to be particularly resistant to any erosion of the party's political leading role.

Partly because of the maintenance of these institutions, economic reform has not been achieved without considerable negotiation and struggle. This has from time to time surfaced, and it proceeds on a continuous basis behind the scenes, in the processes of economic decision making, in the patterns of managerial accountability, in appointments and other personnel policies. This, of course, recalls the point that it is particularly important to investigate the everyday realities of management in order to retain a balanced view of the reform.

The main provisions for economic reform in China have been twofold. First, central planning and control over resource allocation, pricing and distribution have been drawn back to permit the greater operation of market forces. Moreover, forms of non-state and foreign-funded enterprise have been allowed to develop and these have injected a powerful new competitive force into the economy. Second, new regulations and enactments have changed the formal provisions of industrial governance, as with the Director Responsibility and Contract Responsibility Systems, the 1988 Enterprise Law, and the regulations governing direct foreign investment. The leverage for reform, therefore, has come from changes to the system of industrial governance, albeit that these have been tempered by the determination to retain the means for ultimate political control over industry and its priorities.

The economic reformers are aware that changes to China's system of industrial governance are of themselves not enough to ensure success. As the previous chapter indicated, the infrastructural and human capital limitations of a developing country also have to be overcome, while some facets of the country's social and cultural legacy are also seen to stand in the way of policies aimed at weakening egalitarianism and other inhibitors of achievement orientation. The outstanding success of overseas Chinese business (Redding 1990) serves to remind us, however, that it is the combination of Chinese cultural mores with the institutional inheritance of state socialism rather than the culture itself which can be said to have inhibited economic development in the earlier years of the PRC.

Part II

Managing in Chinese enterprises

4   Leadership in the enterprise

A key issue throughout the forty years of the People's Republic of China has been which principle should guide the leadership of enterprises, especially those owned by the state 'on behalf of the whole people'.[1] Within the limits of the autonomy they are granted by higher authorities, the decision process in these enterprises has revolved primarily around the interlocking relationship between the director and party committee (especially the party secretary). The enterprise workers' congress, for which the enterprise trade union committee acts as an agent, has also to a varying extent enjoyed certain rights of approval over management policy. Under this system, management essentially stands for economic effectiveness, the party organization stands for the implementation of party and state policy according to correct ideological principles, while the workers' congress stands for the principle of 'democratic management'.

All three groups have a history of participation in enterprise leadership dating back to the second civil war of 1945–9. At that time, state enterprises in the revolutionary base area were led by a three-man team consisting of the factory director, party secretary and union committee chairman. This team addressed major production problems, and if the three members could not agree with each other, the director had the authority to make the decision (Zheng 1987). Since that time, many different models of enterprise leadership have been tried. At the time of writing, the issue has not been finally resolved, although the exigencies of modernization and industrial effectiveness point strongly towards the need for leadership by qualified and competent management.

This chapter examines leadership in Chinese state enterprises – the case of joint ventures is considered later in chapter 12. It begins by reviewing the main changes in the leadership system since 1949 which highlight the precedents and potentially conflicting principles that are still active in Chinese thinking today. The main shifts in enterprise leadership have been between the primacy of management and the party, reflecting shifts between economic and political criteria. Although from time to time granted significant formal powers over management, the workers' congress has not generally exercised as much influence as the other two groups. Chinese trade unions, which also carry out workplace functions on behalf of their members, have in practice been subordinated to party authority. Therefore, given that there is always an operational necessity for executive management, the issue of enterprise leadership in China has boiled down to the role of the party and its relationship to management.

Systems of enterprise leadership since 1949

In the first years of the PRC, factory management committees were established and operated in a manner similar to a management board in Western enterprises. They were chaired by the factory director, with a membership comprising managerial staff and an equal number of elected worker representatives. The director, as *ex officio* chairman, was answerable only to the secretary of the enterprise party committee. At the same time, it was decreed in 1950 that every state enterprise should establish a workers' congress as a consultative organ with the principal task of reviewing the enterprise's performance. The powers of the congress were, however, restricted by the requirement that all its resolutions had to be vetted and endorsed by the factory management committee before their ratification (Ng 1984). These mechanisms for democratic management did not on the whole establish strong roots. By the early 1950s, many factory management committees had become 'perfunctory' (Brugger 1976: 233), although workers' congresses normally persisted. Instead, the enterprise party committee tended to play an increasingly influential role. Since typically only between 10 and 13 per cent of the employees of an enterprise belong to the party (Laaksonen 1988), this committee was considerably less representative.

The First Five Year Plan was launched in 1953 and gave priority to the development of heavy industry with Soviet assistance. The Soviet model of enterprise leadership, the so-called 'one-man management' system, was introduced into larger factories in the heavy industries, predominantly in North-East China, and adopted as the official national norm. Under this system, the director was given unified authority over all activities within the factory, and took overall responsibility for fulfilling state plans and for factory production, finance and administration. The formal role of the enterprise party committee was confined to 'guaranteeing and supervising' (*baozheng he jiandu*) that the factory's operation and administration conformed to political policies. The party had responsibility for political and ideological matters, and for providing leadership over the trade union and youth league. However, the system claimed that politics must serve economics and it called for the party secretary to give total support to the director. Trade unions increasingly concentrated on enforcing labour discipline and regulations and on organizing campaigns to increase productivity (Hearn 1977). Factory trade unions formed part of the All-China Federation of Trade Unions (ACFTU) which functioned mainly as an umbrella organization. Lockett (1983) has outlined the key relationships under this system as in figure 4.1.

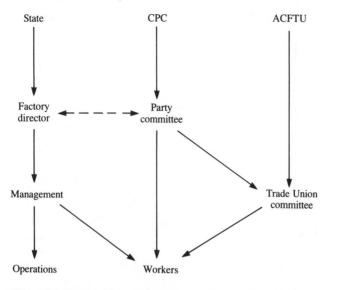

Figure 4.1 Key relationships under the 'One-man management system'. *Key:* → indicates an authority link, in the sense of hierarchical authority, election etc.; ↔ indicates reciprocal links of authority or influence; ←--→indicates similar links but of a weak or unclear kind; CPC=Communist Party of China; ACFTU=All-China Federation of Trade Unions. *Source:* adapted from Lockett 1983: figure 28.1

Under the one-man management system, the powers of the enterprise party committee were severely curtailed. Directors were responsible primarily to superordinate state bureaucracies and were able to ignore the views of party secretaries with relative impunity (Chamberlain 1987). The party committee was largely relegated to the sidelines and confined to the role of propagandist.

This Soviet model was incongruous with the revolutionary Yan'an tradition of mass mobilization, high ideological consciousness and the leading role of party activists. Moreover, systems of collective responsibility with some worker participation continued to exist outside heavy and large-scale industry, even in state enterprises and especially in East China. Thus a more participative alternative, sometimes called the 'Shanghai System', was available.

It was not surprising then that party cadres and workers expressed increasing dissatisfaction with the one-man management system. In 1956 it was announced at the Eighth CPC Congress that all enterprises must discard one-man management in favour of the 'Director Responsibility System under the Leadership of the Party' (DRSULP).

Under the DRSULP all major decisions for the enterprise were to be made collectively by the party committee. Everyday operations and administration

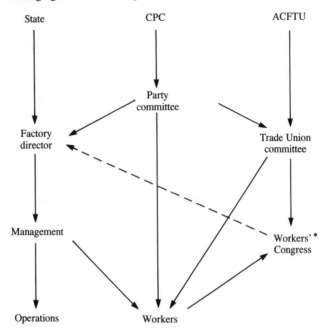

Figure 4.2 Key relationships under the 'director responsibility system under the leadership of the party'. *Key:* as for figure 4.1; *Workers' Congresses were active in the period 1956–7 but not in 1978–9. From 1979, Workers' Congresses were given certain democratic rights of supervision over the director's policies and plans, and also to elect managers. *Source:* adapted from Lockett 1983: figure 28.1

would be the responsibility of persons assigned to specific positions. The factory director was now an executor of party committee decisions with particular responsibility for production. The intention of this reform was to strengthen the role of the enterprise party committee, to democratize enterprise decision making by stressing collective leadership, and to combine efficient production and technical activities with political goals in order to introduce a stronger assertion of political considerations. The key relationships under the DRSULP are outlined in figure 4.2.

It was decided in 1957 to revitalize the workers' congress as an organ for mass participation in enterprise management and supervision, though this move was soon overtaken by the emphasis during the Great Leap Forward on the 'party secretary taking command'. Experiments in direct worker participation were tried in this period. These involved the participation of workers in managerial work and of managers in manual work, together with combinations of managers, technical staff and workers as project teams. Under this system, worker managers were elected by teams and confirmed by the party committee. The committee remained responsible for all important decisions and for the factory's conformity to the central plan.

The early 1960s have been described by Andors (1977: chapter 5) as a period of 'ambiguity' in enterprise leadership. The Great Leap Forward experiments were continued in some factories. In 1961 the 'Seventeen Industrial Regulations' were issued for state enterprises by the Party Central Committee. These reaffirmed that enterprises must implement a system of factory director responsibility, complemented by a workers' congress, with both coming under the leadership of the party committee. In general, however, managerial authority was reinforced and the influence of the party committee reduced although it remained the most important policy-making body in the enterprise. Workers' congresses regained some of their significance through the new regulations which extended their responsibilities to include the discussion and resolution of all issues within the enterprise touching on workers' interests, but in practice their influence appears to have been small (Lockett 1983).

During the first part of the Cultural Revolution, revolutionary committees took charge of work units, denying enterprise party committees participation in important decisions and marginalizing management as a function. Workers' congresses were also suspended. By 1972, however, party secretaries were normally back in command, controlling the revolutionary committee and the enterprise as a whole. Managerial hierarchies responsible to revolutionary committees were gradually restored in the early 1970s and trade union committees reintroduced.

The DRSULP was formally adopted again in 1978. The system was modified by regulations issued during 1982 and 1983. These recognized the need for adequate structures of management and placed the factory director in charge of enterprise administration. The director, however, still lacked the power to appoint managers and the party committee retained its leading role in all key areas of enterprise operations.

As Lockett and Littler (1983) have described in detail, it also became official policy after 1978 to reinstate workers' congresses and to encourage the election of managers, particularly those below, but not necessarily excluding, the director. Local union organization within the enterprise became merged with that of the workers' congress. Regulations issued in June 1981 envisaged that workers' congresses consisting of elected representatives of the workers and staff of an enterprise would take part in decision making in order to supervise management. The main powers of a workers' congress were to be: (1) to scrutinize the director's production plans and budgets; (2) to discuss and decide on the use of enterprise funds for welfare and bonus provisions; (3) to decide about proposed changes to the management structure, payment system or training provisions; and (5) to arrange the election of managers. The October 1984 decision on 'Economic Structure Reform' regarded workers' congresses and the enterprise trade union structure emanating from them as a democratic counterweight to the consolidation of managerial authority through

> examining and discussing major decisions to be taken by the enterprises, supervising administrative leadership and safeguarding the legitimate rights and interests of the workers and staff members. All of this expresses the status of the working people as masters of the enterprise. (CPC 1984: 25)

The workers' congress was therefore seen as providing a decentralization of checks and balances down to the level of the workforce to counterbalance the decentralization of decision-making powers under the enterprise reform. It had the potential to tip the balance of power between the enterprise director and the party (Jackson 1992). Workers' congresses have, however, generally met only a couple of times per year and their powers have in practice been exercised by enterprise trade unions which at first remained subordinate to the enterprise party committee. So rather than workers' congresses constituting an effective third force within Chinese enterprises and a check to management, the key power balance continued to be that between management and party officials. Even when enterprise trade unions and workers' congresses were removed from direct party control after September 1986, it will be seen that under the Director Responsibility System which was being implemented around the same time, directors were able to override opposition from enterprise management committees on which up to one third of the members were workers' congress representatives.

It had been possible in the relatively slow-growing and closed Chinese economy which prevailed up to 1978 to subordinate economic criteria to political principles, but this was to become increasingly difficult once the 'Four Modernizations' and the 'Open Door' were adopted as official policies. As economic reform proceeded after 1978 through experiments to enlarge the autonomy of enterprises and then to introduce various responsibility systems, the appropriateness of the DRSULP was increasingly questioned. As practised, the system was said to suffer a number of shortcomings (cf. Xiao 1986; Wang 1986; Zheng 1987):

1 the functions of party and management were blurred. In principle, the enterprise party committee made policy decisions and exercised general leadership, while the director assumed responsibility for everyday management activities. In practice, directors tended to seek the agreement of their party secretaries for anything they did, so causing their responsibility to become nominal. This meant that political instructions from the party tended to be regarded as administrative orders;

2 multiple leadership by higher-level organs (the party secretary reporting to higher party bodies, individual management functions reporting to

specialized government bureaux) presented enterprises with severe co-ordination problems;

3 meetings of the party committee could not cope with the pressure to become involved in the whole range of day-to-day management issues, and power quickly gravitated into the hands of the party secretary. The principle of collective leadership was thus abandoned in all but rhetoric (Chamberlain 1987);

4 the involvement of the party in everyday management business tended to undermine its core functions of pursuing ideological and political work and building the party organization;

5 the system was ill-suited to the new forms of partnership with foreign companies which it was now government policy to encourage. These required decisions to be made by joint operating committees or boards of directors in the case of joint ventures. Leadership through party committees on the Chinese side was difficult to reconcile with this mode.

Under the DRSULP, collective leadership tended to yield to the one-man management of party secretaries who were often not equipped to deal with the accompanying complexities. Economic considerations were subordinated to political principles both because that was the party's role and because its officials were normally not trained in enterprise management.

In 1980, and again at the end of 1983, Deng Xiaoping proposed that the DRSULP should gradually be replaced by the 'Director Responsibility System' (DRS). This system was discussed and formally adopted by the Sixth National People's Congress in May 1984. It was then implemented on a trial basis in selected enterprises in certain cities. The major policy document on 'China's Economic Structure Reform' adopted by the Party Central Committee in October 1984 (CPC 1984) affirmed the DRS with its basic principle that enterprise directors would assume full responsibility for the performance of their enterprises under a unified management system. With the passing in September 1986 of three sets of regulations governing the enterprise director, party committee and worker's congress (CPC 1986), the implementation of DRS moved beyond the experimental stage and was to be generally applied. By the end of 1987 it was claimed that more than 80 per cent of state-owned enterprises officially designated as large and medium size had adopted the system. The Enterprise Law passed in April 1988, to take effect on 1 August of that year, extended the DRS to all state enterprises.

The contractual responsibility systems introduced during 1986–7 singled out the enterprise director as the contract signatory and placed the responsibility for fulfilment of the contract terms on his shoulders.[2] A necessary precondition for these arrangements to work is that the director has the requisite authority within the enterprise as well as in relation to the supervising authority. Hence as Byrd (1991: 14) points out, 'all the contractual responsibility systems may well enhance the authority of the enterprise director, both internally and externally'. In this respect the DRS is consistent with the wider reform objective of clarifying and focusing responsibility for enterprise performance.

The director responsibility system

The policy document on 'China's Economic Structure Reform' adopted by the Party Central Committee in October 1984 called for 'a system of the director or manager assuming full responsibility' over enterprises (CPC 1984: 25). Under the DRS, the party committee no longer served as the leading organ of the enterprise. Instead, the director assumed a position of unified leadership, command and overall responsibility for the internal and external operations of the enterprise. As Zhao Ziyang put it in a speech of June 1986, 'the director should be the first figure in the enterprise; he occupies the central position and plays an essential role' (Zhao 1986). As the 'first figure', the director not only had the authority to direct operations, but also to determine internal organization and the making of all appointments. Moreover, under the contract responsibility system introduced from 1986 onwards, the director assumed responsibility for the business planning of the enterprise aimed at achieving, and if possible exceeding, the forward targets contracted with its supervising bureau. The key relationships under this system are depicted in figure 4.3.

The DRS meant that the director was no longer a mere executor of decisions made by the enterprise party committee. He was expected to submit proposals to the enterprise management committee, which in addition to the party secretary had up to one third of its members representing the enterprise workers' congress. Should, however, he meet with opposition from a majority on this committee, the director could insist on having the final word. He had the authority to decide on the appointment and dismissal of middle managers, though he had to seek the approval of the supervising bureau for higher appointments at the level of vice-director and 'chief' (engineer, accountant or economist). In the case of managerial appointments, the director was supposed to submit his proposals to the party committee for its opinion. Similarly, while he had the formal power of reward and punishment (including dismissal) of middle managers and more junior employees under the DRS, he was supposed to seek the opinion of the enterprise's trade union before acting upon that power.

The major responsibility allocated to the party committee and party secretary under the DRS was the exercise of political and ideological leadership. That is, to ensure that the director adhered to party and state policies and plans, to support the activities of mass organizations such as the trade union and youth league, to foster political and ideological education, and to strengthen the role of the party through the example set by party members as role models including actions to further achievement of the enterprise's economic goals. The party

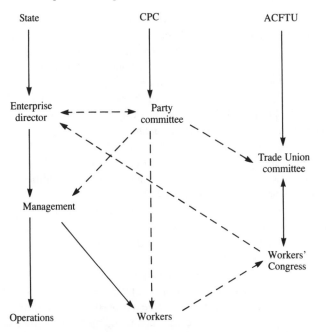

Figure 4.3 Key relationships under the 'director responsibility system'.
Key: as for figure 4.1.

committee no longer had a direct input into enterprise decision making and was instead expected to make suggestions and express opinions on important items, such as proposals from the director on personnel matters and on enterprise strategy and development.

The party committee nevertheless retained the responsibility to 'guarantee and supervise' the implementation of party and state policies within the enterprise. This was supposed to be realized by performing the following tasks: (1) to instruct party members and cadres about policies, regulations and laws, and in so doing to play an exemplary role; (2) to listen to the director's activity reports offering opinions and suggestions; (3) to strengthen control over discipline; (4) to enhance the life and self-awareness of the party's own organization; and (5) to monitor the performance of party and management cadres. In this way, the party and its secretary were seen to retain their core functions and indeed to have the opportunity now to give their undivided attention to them through a new division of labour which was officially taken to imply no relegation in the party secretary's status *vis-à-vis* the enterprise director. For instance, Peng Zheng, former President of the National People's Congress, maintained that 'to adopt the DRS is not to reduce the party's leadership nor to restore the one-man management system, but just to differentiate the functions of the party, management and workers' congress' (Peng 1984).

In practice, the laws and regulations bearing on the DRS were quite ambiguous about the role of the party secretary. Although the Enterprise Law of 1988 paid little attention to the party's position, it allocated responsibility to the director for the 'spiritual development' of the enterprise (which is primarily its ideological and political development) in a way that casts doubt on the party's influence in that sphere. For Article 45 of chapter 4 in that Law states that 'The director occupies the central position in the enterprise; he is fully responsible for the material and spiritual development of the enterprise'. This transfer to the director of the leading responsibility for ideological and political work was reiterated in a document issued by the CPC Central Committee at the time of the Law's publication in April 1988; this stated that 'after the separation of party and management, the director will be responsible for political and ideological work among employees, but this does not mean that the party committee may neglect this work' (CPC 1988).

The regulations on enterprise party organization issued on 15 September 1986 described the secretary's role as chairing the day-to-day work of the party committee, organizing the implementation of the committee's resolutions, complying with democratic centralism and party discipline, and doing his or her best towards the development of the party committee. There was supposed to be a new style of relationship between the director and party secretary with common objectives, a division of work, mutual support and close co-operation. The party secretary was expected to put aside a narrow power perspective in favour of taking the interest of the whole enterprise into account, and to support the director actively while at the same time carrying out the responsibility to 'guarantee and supervise' the implementation of party and state policies.

The problem of how to reconcile this last function with that of serving as a non-intrusive but concerned support for enterprise management was not addressed in official documents or statements. Indeed, these tended merely to reiterate the two diverse expectations that were placed upon the party. Thus Zhao Ziyang, reporting to the thirteenth National Congress of the CPC in his then role as party general secretary, expressed the hope that 'party organizations in enterprises should supervise the work done and ensure that it is accomplished. [However] instead of attempting to provide centralized leadership, they should support the directors and managers in their assumption of overall leadership' (Zhao 1987). Deng Xiaoping admitted that 'finding a solution to how the party should exercise leadership' is a 'key question' in China's reform which still remained to be solved (Deng 1987: 15,17).

The DRS clearly intended to remove enterprise party officials from direct responsibility for management and economic performance. This diluted the party's formal powers within enterprises and gave rise to the presumption that the influence of the party's leading official, its enterprise secretary, *vis-à-vis* the director would have diminished accordingly. Nevertheless, the DRS was described officially in terms of a redistribution of functions between director and the party organization rather than a change in their respective standing and, by extension, their power. Some commentators have in fact concluded that the party's power within the state enterprise was not in demise. Hunt and Gao (1990) for example suggested that 'whether or not it [the DRS] has seriously weakened the role of the party secretary still is doubtful, but it has opened the door wider to more expedient and pragmatic decision criteria' (p. 221). They pointed out that party secretaries now had more time to discipline party members within the enterprise and retained a variety of informal but substantial means of asserting influence either through their members or through resort to external power and pressure. Chamberlain (1987) maintained that even under the DRS, 'power continues to gravitate towards the enterprise party organization' (p. 650) because the party committee and its secretary continue to have three 'structural levers' at their disposal: their power to 'supervise' enterprise operations, their disciplinary authority over all party members including the director, and their continuing role in personnel management. Similarly, Walder (1989) identified four sources of power available to party secretaries: the right to be consulted on and formally to approve appointments the director wished to make to his own staff; the party's organized link to the workforce through its branches, the trade union and workers' congress; the party's ability to 'catch the ear' of the director's party and governmental superiors; and the party secretary's ability to offer help to the director should the former be well-connected at higher levels. Walder was writing on the basis of interviews conducted between 1984 and 1986 and he concluded that, in the majority of cases, the director 'would ignore or override the party secretary only at his peril' (p. 249).

The information employed by Chamberlain and Walder appears to precede the 1986 regulations on enterprise organization, after which the party's right to veto managerial appointments was diluted into one of just expressing an opinion, while enterprise trade unions and workers' congresses were removed from direct party control. Moreover, as we shall note, the party's internal enterprise organization also tended to contract. This points to the problem that available discussions of party–management relations in Chinese enterprises are not particularly up to date, nor are most of them based on direct enquiry within enterprises themselves. They tend to rely heavily upon reports and discussion from Chinese sources, the empirical basis for which is uncertain. With this in mind, it is interesting to note that what is possibly the only relevant, systematic and comparative survey within Chinese enterprises pointed to a fall in the influence of their party committees in decisions on strategy, general policy and working conditions even during the relatively early period of the economic reform, between 1980 and 1984 (Laaksonen 1988: 280–9).

There was, then, a need to clarify the leadership situation in Chinese enterprises and, in particular, whether the party's role in management did weaken or change, through direct investigation. We now report an early attempt to undertake such research in 1988, followed by an updating in the light first of the events of June 1989 and then of the recent revival of the reform initiative.

An investigation into enterprise leadership: scope and method

Evidence is drawn from two related studies (see Child and Xu 1991). The first was conducted by Xu Xinzhong in six enterprises located in Nantong, Jiangsu Province during August 1988. Nantong is situated just north of Shanghai and was at the forefront of economic reform – it was selected as one of the original fourteen coastal 'open cities' for foreign investment and one of the seventy 'experimental cities' in the reform. All six enterprises studied had adopted the Director Responsibility System (DRS) in 1984 as experimental sites. Although they were all located in the electrical industry, broadly defined, they differed in both size and products. The largest employed 1,560 persons and the smallest 260; their product specialties were condensers, electronic instruments, electric motors, radios, switchgear and welding machinery.

The second investigation was conducted by the author in six Beijing enterprises during September 1988 – these are the enterprises described in the introduction. These had adopted the DRS somewhat later, at various dates between 1985 and 1987. Four of the enterprises were in the electrical industry, producing audio, audio-visual, switchgear and heavy electrical goods, but they ranged quite widely in size. The two other firms produced pharmaceutical and automotive products. 'Automotive' will have to be excluded from much of the analysis because of its special circumstances: it had operated without any formal internal party organization since being reconstituted into a joint venture in May 1988.

The remaining eleven firms were heavily concentrated in the electrical industry and do not represent a cross-section of Chinese industry. The firms were nevertheless quite diverse in their products, types of markets and sizes. A common set of regulations define the DRS in state-owned enterprises and in this respect the firms investigated offer an opportunity to examine the way it affects the party's role across enterprises which differ in their operational characteristics and which are additionally sited in contrasting locations, with Nantong having a more innovative and experimental industrial tradition than Beijing. Should similar findings emerge from this varied background, there is a strong possibility that they may indicate a more general situation prevailing at the time within Chinese state enterprises.

The selection of firms to study was determined overwhelmingly by considerations of access and the quality of research co-operation offered. It is not common to conduct research of any depth within Chinese enterprises and their co-operation greatly depends on the quality of relationship that can be established with their staff. This is reflected in the investigatory procedures we adopted.

In Nantong, the investigation was undertaken through interviews and some informal observation. The interviews were guided by a checklist agreed beforehand between the two investigators for use in both locations, but were open-ended and exploratory in nature. Initial interviews were conducted with one or more middle managers, one of them normally being the head of the management office. The director and party secretary of each enterprise were then interviewed separately and privately. Xu's acceptability to his respondents was enhanced through several means. He obtained letters of introduction from the Nantong municipal government and its enterprise supervisory bureaux. He has close friends who serve in the middle management of three of the enterprises and succeeded also in securing helpful personal introductions to the directors from his other initial contacts in middle management. Informal observations served a confirmatory purpose and were made during interviews by noting, for example, how many managers and workers dropped in to seek instructions from the director or the party secretary during the interview. (In Chinese organizations it is usual for other staff to interrupt interviews for such matters; very few managers enjoy the 'protection' of outer secretarial offices.)

In Beijing, the author conducted separate interviews with each enterprise director and party secretary. The interviews with directors served to establish the scope of their decision-making powers under the DRS. The interviews with party secretaries contained questions on their roles, activities and staff resourcing. The author had already met the directors when carrying out research in the same enterprises three years previously, and through feedback of its findings had created the goodwill for this further study. Nevertheless, as a foreigner, he depended heavily upon the good offices of his colleagues at the China–EC Management Institute, Chen Derong and Lu Yuan, to reactivate his research relationship with the firms in 1988 and on Lu for interpretation during interviews.

The Beijing and Nantong investigations were conducted at almost the same point in time; they were planned together and both investigators remained in personal contact while in China. The common core of their questioning covered the following points:

1 how party secretaries perceived their role under the DRS;
2 the main activities carried out by the party secretaries;[3]
3 the composition of enterprise management and party committees;
4 the staffing of enterprise party offices;

Functions mentioned by party secretaries in 11 enterprises in response to the question: 'What are your main tasks as party secretary?' Each mention is indicated by a ✓

Function	Mentions by Enterprise										
	Nantong						Beijing				
	Condenser	Electronic instrument	Electro-motor	Radio	Switchgear	Welding machinery	Audio	Audio-visual	Electrical switchgear	Heavy electrical	Pharmaceutical
Ideological and political education	✓	✓	✓	✓	✓	✓	✓	✓	✓	✓	
Building party organization (meetings, membership)		✓	✓	✓	✓		✓			✓	✓
Supporting director's authority	✓	✓		✓	✓			✓	✓	✓	
Making proposals and suggestions to director	✓		✓	✓					✓	✓	
Monitoring performance of management							✓		✓		
Other:						Help resolve workers' living problems		Construct an enterprise culture			Enterprise development

Figure 4.4 Enterprise party secretaries' perceptions of their main functions.

5   the relative influence of the party secretary and the director in the management process. This was assessed more formally in the Beijing enterprises by reference to the making of specific decisions, while in the Nantong firms informants' perceptions were sought. In the Nantong enterprises, questions were also put on the perceived quality of the relationship between party secretary and director.

The role perceptions of party secretaries

Each party secretary was asked what he or she considered to be their main tasks. Virtually all the tasks they mentioned fall into the five categories listed in figure 4.4. Ten of the eleven party secretaries mentioned 'ideological and political education', primarily of party members within the enterprise but also with respect to giving a lead to its trade union and youth league. The party secretary for Pharmaceutical only mentioned ideological and political work obliquely in saying that she now delegated such work to lower-level branch officials within the factory. She claimed in fact to spend three-quarters or more of her time on production management, deputizing for the production vice-director.

When interviewees were questioned further on the content of ideological and political work, two main aspects were usually mentioned. One was the education of party members towards a better understanding of general party and state policies. The other was encouragement to party members to serve as 'role models' to other employees. This latter activity was several times linked explicitly to the formation of attitudes and behaviour which would assist the enterprise's productivity and/or support management's endeavours. In the Nantong electronic instrument enterprise, for example, the party secretary had initiated a campaign to encourage party members to make a greater contribution to new product development which she thought had been very successful.

The second most frequently mentioned task was the building and strengthening of the party's organization within the enterprise. This amounted to the organization of party meetings and attending to matters concerning membership.

Two other tasks, mentioned by seven and five party secretaries respectively, were (1) supporting the enterprise director's authority and use of executive powers and (2) making suggestions and proposals to the director or the management committee. These tasks are primarily concerned with assisting management. One occasion for the party secretary to make suggestions was when disagreement arose between the members of the management committee and he or she felt able to advance a compromise solution.

Only two party secretaries mentioned the monitoring of management as one of their functions. This may appear surprising in view of the commission given to the party to 'guarantee and supervise' the implementation of party and government policies within enterprises. The infrequent mention of this task could also betray an accommodation to the difficulties of carrying it out within the power structure prevailing within enterprises under the DRS, a possibility to which we return later.

The activities and resource base of party secretaries

The party secretaries were asked on which activities they spent most time at work. Their replies clearly indicate that the greater part of their working day was given over to assisting management, and in some cases directly carrying out managerial duties.

The DRS is intended to separate the role of the party within enterprises from that of their management. Party secretaries do nevertheless have some access to management discussions, at least those within the formal arena of the management committee, and many of them are long-standing members of the firm with previous senior management experience. This combination of access and experience may leave them well-placed to suggest solutions to disagreements which arise between managers, or indeed other employees. Other investigations have pointed to the saliency of inter-departmental conflicts within the structures that Chinese enterprises have inherited, in which there tends to be both a proliferation of departments and an unclear definition of their respective responsibilities (e.g. Lockett 1988). It is not surprising, therefore, that, in response to our question, seven of the party secretaries mentioned conflict resolution as their most time-consuming activity. The conflicts they helped to solve were particularly those between middle managers (department heads and workshop managers) though in some cases they also found themselves mediating between vice-directors.

Just as the Western role of co-ordinator generally benefits from a combination of relevant technical knowledge and inter-personal sensitivity (Child 1984), so several of the party secretaries alluded to the relevance of similar attributes in their roles as conflict-mediators. For example, the party secretary in Audio said that

My technical background helps to give me a common language in my relations with technicians and workers. It also helps me in solving conflicts between managers and generally to build a bridge from the party to management.

He also stressed the importance he now attached to knowledge of 'human resource management'. This was echoed by the party secretary in Switchgear who said that the activity on which she spent most time was co-ordinating department heads. While recognizing that this was officially part of the director's role, she was able to help resolve the managerial conflicts that were involved. She added: 'the most important competence I now require in my job is the ability to understand people, especially individual personality, so that I can access human relationships and so solve conflicts.'

Most of the party secretaries indicated that they spent more time than before out and about in the factories, now that their other duties had been reduced and they had fewer meetings to attend. Six of them mentioned a direct involvement in the improvement of shopfloor performance as an activity to which they gave a considerable amount of time. The secretary in Audio-visual, for example, said that he was assisting in the rationalization of work groups. By rationalization he meant that the work groups 'should make better use of their competences, materials and time'. He was concerned to stimulate competition between work groups in order to achieve higher performance. In carrying out this work, he claimed to focus on incentives, motivation and the behavioural aspects of human resource management. The party secretary in the Nantong electronic instrument enterprise, who was said to enjoy considerable respect from shopfloor workers because of her long experience, progression up from the ranks and technical training, spent much of her time dealing with production problems.

All the party secretaries indicated that more than half of their working time was given over to activities that in one way or another assisted management to achieve improvements in enterprise performance. They contrasted this with the pre-DRS situation when, despite the overall authority of the enterprise party committee, they (or their predecessors) would personally have spent more time on party activities rather than those of a more purely 'managerial' and non-political nature. It was generally reported that party meetings were held less frequently than in previous years and we were given the strong impression that they were taken less seriously. There had, in short, been a considerable shift from politics to economics in the time allocations of the party secretaries.

Several of the party secretaries said they now spent much of their time doing managerial work itself. We have already noted, for instance, that the party secretary in Pharmaceutical estimated she spent most of her time on production management. Of all the party secretaries interviewed, she appeared to have become the most absorbed into management as our note of her reply indicates:

The party secretary spends most of her time on two activities: (1) enterprise development and (2) management.

Enterprise development has an internal and an external aspect. Internally, the factory uses the quality circle concept learned from Japan. Her role here extends to human resource management and to working through the party to improve workers' attitudes towards production and towards the enterprise's objectives. Externally, her work on enterprise development means helping to run the factory's development planning system in respect of development feasibility studies and the consortium with other producers.

She estimates that 75/80 percent of her time is spent on production management matters. She deputizes for the vice-director of production when he is away. This is because she has considerable experience as a workshop manager and has also enjoyed the benefit of management training at the China Enterprise Management Association. The vice-director in any case spends most of his time on new developments. The party secretary and the vice-director together run the factory's internal production operations.

In the Nantong radio enterprise, the party secretary said he spent much of his time investigating and analysing new projects and reporting on these to the director. He had in fact a long and rich experience in the enterprise, having joined it back in 1969 and twice served as its director. The party secretary in Audio insisted on showing the writer the many analytical and educational charts which he had drawn up to assist the process of strategic decision making in which he took an active part. Indeed, much more space in his office was occupied by performance charts than by political literature, a fact to which he himself drew our attention.

The concentration of the party secretaries' *de facto* activities around direct support for management under the DRS was being echoed during the summer of 1988 in reports of discussions within government circles to the effect that they should become vice-directors in charge of 'administration'. This office normally covers canteen, housing, medical and welfare services, while its head also tends to act in a public relations role. One party secretary, in Audio-visual, had in fact already been appointed vice-director of administration by September 1988.

The tendency for party secretaries by summer 1988 to have concentrated their activities into the areas of conflict resolution, productivity improvement and advice to management, reflects the loss of previous responsibilities for personnel selection, discipline, ideological health of the enterprise and leadership of its trade union. The size of party organizations within the enterprises, and the range of their constituent units, had generally contracted over the previous three years in line with this adjustment under the DRS. Whereas before the introduction of the DRS, the enterprise party organization would typically be comprised of the secretary's office, a discipline office and a personnel office, with possibly propagation and organization offices as well, by 1988 this had normally shrunk to a party secretary's office only. Moreover, the number of intra-enterprise party branches had generally been reduced and in some cases previously full-time branch secretaries had been converted into part-time ones.

Table 4.1 provides details of the numbers of full-time party staff within the enterprises as of 1985 and 1988. It can be seen that the trend is generally downward, particularly in the Beijing firms which were in the process of adjusting to the introduction of the DRS between those dates. The Nantong enterprises had introduced the DRS in 1984 and had made their main cuts in party establishments during that year. The proportionate reduction in party staff appears to reflect the contraction in the party's role rather than whether the numbers employed by an enterprise had risen or fallen during the three year period. When expressed as a ratio of total numbers employed at the two points in time, which it is possible to do accurately for the Beijing firms, the decline in the party's human resource base appears particularly dramatic.

Influence of the party secretary in management

A comparison of the six Beijing enterprises between October 1985 and September 1988 revealed a concentration of decision making in the hands of their directors (Child and Lu 1990). While, on average, the directors were in 1985 personally taking just over twelve decisions from a list of forty-seven investigated, by mid-1988 they were taking somewhat over seventeen of these, including many of general policy significance. The main exception to this trend

Table 4.1. *Full-time party staff within the enterprises (1985 and 1988)*

| | Full-time party staff | | | |
| | Number | | Ratio to total employees | |
Enterprise	1985	1988	1985	1988
		Beijing		
Audio	8	2	1:106	1:445
Audio-visual	10	5	1:220	1:600
Electrical switchgear	9	4	1:80	1:174
Heavy electrical	15	8	1:125	1:225
Pharmaceutical	11	5	1:87	1:182
Automobile[1]	42	0	1:93	—
		Nantong[2]		
Condenser	5	4		
Electrical instrument	6	4		
Electromotor	5	3		
Radio	5	6		
Switchgear	4	4		
Welding machinery	3	3		

Notes:
[1] The automobile enterprise was converted to a joint venture in May 1988.
[2] Information on the ratio of full-time party staff to total employees was not available.
Source: Personal interviews.

was Automotive which in view of its large size had by 1988 developed a system of delegation within its management structure more than had the other firms. Of particular relevance was the fact that by 1988 none of the decisions investigated was reported to involve a significant input from the party committee or its secretary in his or her party role, not even managerial appointments on which the opinion of the party committee was supposed to be sought. On sensitive personnel issues such as dismissal of a worker or welfare provisions, management would consult with trade union officials representing the workers' congress rather than with party officials. The main source of constraint on the director's power appeared to arise from the enterprise's higher municipal authority rather than from the party. Under the contract management responsibility system in these enterprises (except Automotive), directors are formally responsible to the supervising municipal bureau and owe their appointments to it.

In the Nantong enterprises there was reported to have been a significant increase in the director's power over personnel matters following the adoption of the DRS. However, certain party secretaries were said to retain some influence in this area particularly if they enjoyed close relations with the supervising bureau and other local government organs such as the labour bureau. Moreover, action such as dismissal of a worker was said to be extremely difficult if the enterprise trade union did not accept the director's proposal. In other decision areas, directors now enjoyed the ability to propose action and normally to carry it through to implementation. Despite formal provisions for discussion with enterprise management committees and workers' congresses, these appeared in practice to be little more than a formality. Overall, the Nantong enterprise directors now enjoyed unified leadership, though with less power over personnel matters than in other areas of decision making. While their position varied from enterprise to enterprise according to local factors such as their personality, experience, expertise and connections with the supervisory bureau – and according to how the same factors characterized party secretaries and trade union chairpersons – it had strengthened in relation to that of the party's organs and officials.

Both of the party's key responsibilities under the DRS, to guarantee and supervise the implementation of party and state policy and to support managerial leadership, presuppose that the party secretary retains a significant degree of influence within the management decision-making process. The formal institutional provisions for exercising that influence are twofold: (1) the place given on every enterprise management committee to the party secretary, often accompanied by the trade union chairman and the secretary of the youth league, and (2) the inclusion of the director and one or more vice-directors on the party committee. In principle this gives the party access to deliberations on management policy and the means to call the director to account at meetings of the party committee. Real influence is, however, likely to require other supports, since decisions are often agreed away from formal arenas such as committees (as the literature of organizational behaviour richly illustrates – e.g. Pettigrew 1973). Moreover, the director is not obliged to accept the views of his management committee, and there may be little that party committees can do to force directors to account for their actions. In fact, although the directors of all the enterprises studied were party members, most did not report regularly to the party committee and one director had even lapsed in the payment of his party dues.

The Nantong investigation sought an assessment of each party secretary's influence in enterprise management from all those interviewed; in Beijing this assessment was obtained from interviews with party secretaries only and less directly from the examination of decision making described above. Based on this information, table 4.2 divides the enterprises very broadly between those in which party secretaries appeared no longer to enjoy any significant influence in the management process and those in which they seemed to retain some influence. The table also lists factors which appeared to contribute to that influence.

Although a precise assessment is not possible with the limited information

Table 4.2. *Assessment of party secretaries' influence in the management process and the sources of that influence*

Enterprises where the party secretary appeared to possess little influence in the management process	
Nantong	*Beijing*
Condenser	Electrical switchgear
Electro-motor	Heavy electrical
Welding machinery	Automotive (party organization absent)

Enterprises where the party secretary was said to enjoy some influence in the management process and the apparent sources of that influence

Enterprise	*Sources of influence*
	Nantong
Electronic instrument	• Technical background
	• Long experience in the enterprise
	• Previous appointment as director
	• Support from supervisory bureau
Radio	• Long experience in the enterprise
	• Previous appointment as director
	• Strong party team
Switchgear	• Ability to establish a good personal relationship with the director
	Beijing
Audio	• Technical knowledge, including management techniques
Audio-visual	• Knowledge of human resource management
	• Formal appointment as vice-director
Pharmaceutical	• Technical background (in production)
	• Long experience in the enterprise

at our disposal, it was clear that the influence enjoyed by party secretaries varied quite considerably. Relevant technical expertise, long-previous experience in the enterprise, sponsorship from the enterprise's supervisory bureau, and good personal relations with the director were factors which appeared to enhance their influence. Equally, similar influences bore on the power of directors, as in the radio enterprise where the director's limited length of service and experience reduced his power *vis-à-vis* the party secretary, but were to a degree offset by the strong support he received from the supervising bureau. Walder (1989) suggests the relevance of similar factors for determining the relative power of director and party secretary in each local situation: 'Much depends on the situation: who has been in the factory longer, their relative ages, their respective backing from above' (p. 248).

The factors identified provide for a combination of referent power, expert power and a kind of legitimate power deriving from supportive relationships (cf. French and Raven 1959). The referent power of party secretaries stems from their personal standing and, indeed, the example they are expected to offer looks to their influence being based precisely on the wish of others to emulate their lead. Secondly, technical expertise remains a scarce commodity in Chinese enterprises and party secretaries who possess it accrue influence in consequence. Thirdly, when party secretaries have previously held senior positions through which they appointed a considerable number of the enterprise's tenured middle managers, they thereby gain legitimate power from the support of an important managerial constituency. Similarly, personal support from the enterprise's supervisory bureau provides the party secretary with both additional legitimacy and a potential for exerting coercive power, and was said to be an important basis for the power enjoyed by the party secretary in the electronic instrument enterprise.

The case of the Nantong switchgear enterprise illustrates how personal skills can also affect the influence over management available to the party secretary, since this largely derived from his accommodation to a weak position. He recognized his relatively low level of independent power and therefore adopted a supporting role, carefully avoiding any confrontation with the director. He shared the same office with the director and two vice-directors, and grew in influence through his high level of acceptability which gave him direct access to informal top-level management discussions.

Consideration of two contrasting cases in which enterprise party secretaries enjoyed respectively low and high influence serves to illustrate the operation of the factors which have been identified. The party secretary in the Nantong welding machinery enterprise assisted the director by helping to resolve conflicts among middle managers and workers, and he also concerned himself for much of the time with welfare work chairing, for example, the firm's accommodation reform committee. His influence in relation to management was, however, weak and his party committee had little impact on the life of the enterprise, meeting as it did only once every three months. Inspection of the records of all meetings within this enterprise over the previous thirty months pointed to the minor nature of the party secretary's interventions. These were confined to offering interpretations of party and governmental policies, reporting on political and ideological work, and sometimes making concluding remarks aimed at finding a compromise between different opinions.

The director commented that 'the party secretary generally plays a minor role and has little influence'. The head of the enterprise office said that 'the party secretary has no funds and no power. His position might even be considered to be lower than that of the trade union chairman. It is not fair really.' The party secretary himself said that he did not know how best to carry out his role or indeed what his specific duties were. He thought that he did not have enough to do and was wasting his time. He went on: 'To guarantee and supervise are only hollow words. There are no criteria attached to them; there is no practical and proper way of implementing them. The central purpose of the director responsibility system is to reduce the party's leadership in enterprises.' This party secretary had been appointed in 1983 by the organization department of the CPC's Nantong city committee. He did not possess a high degree of technical expertise, nor did he enjoy a long-established career within the enterprise since he was appointed from another enterprise. There he had been in charge of the administration department which, together with his exclusion from the mainstream management process, probably helps to account for his concentration on welfare work. In other words, this party secretary did not possess any of the foundations for power and influence which we have identified and which are illustrated by the sharply contrasting case of the Nantong radio enterprise.

In the radio enterprise, the director consulted with the party secretary before making any decisions on major management issues. The latter deputized for the director in his absence, he investigated and reported to the director on new projects, and he took an active part in both management meetings and those of the enterprise's work committee. In this enterprise, the party committee retained effective leadership over both the trade union and the youth league, and the trade union chair was in fact filled by the deputy party secretary.

The enterprise director perceived that the party secretary 'had considerable power though not responsibility'. The deputy head of the enterprise office commented that 'the party secretary's power is due mainly to his personal abilities and to the support of other party members who look after the party's work'. This support enabled the secretary to spend most of his time on managerial activities. He perceived that his influence resulted from his qualifications and record of service. He had worked in the enterprise for twenty years and had held leading positions in it for over ten years, including its directorship twice. Many middle managers owed their promotion to him, so that over the years he had built up a network of personal relationships with them and they formed his supporting coalition. He enjoyed additional influence through the trade union and youth league. The relevance of technical expertise, long experience and the previous holding of respected positions in the enterprise as supports for personal power is apparent.

Nevertheless, although he provides an example of party influence which continued under the DRS to what is probably a fairly exceptional level, this party secretary was still aware of a diminution of his power and role under the new system and of difficulties in meeting his formal obligations. He commented that he did not have sufficient authority to 'supervise and guarantee' the implementation of party and state policies. He cited an example. When the chief accountant was drawing up the profit and loss sheets for July 1988, he asked the director for instructions. As a result, with the director's connivance, he modified the records in certain respects. The chief accountant was not a party member and could not therefore be questioned by the party committee. Since the director did not report to the committee regularly on his work, it could not pursue the matter through that means either.

Subsequent developments

The effectiveness of the Communist Party's ideological leadership, and indeed its very legitimacy, were severely questioned by the events of 1989. Following Tiananmen, the Fourth Plenary Session of the CPC Central Committee in June 1989 (CPC 1989a), and subsequent statements by party leaders (e.g. *Beijing Review* 1989a; 1989b) expressed a determination to rebuild the party's position, including the strengthening of its organization and influence within enterprises. For example, a discussion meeting in the Organization Department of the CPC held in July 1989 concluded that 'the party Committees in many enterprises have become sidelined . . . and no one is responsible for political and ideological work – the situation is very dangerous.' (CPC 1989b).

While it was recognized that the separation of party and managerial functions had made it more difficult to carry out the former, any reversal of this position had to be reconciled with the policy – re-affirmed after some initial hesitation – of maintaining the Enterprise Law and the contractual responsibility of directors for enterprise performance (cf. *China Enterprise Daily* 1989; Yuan 1990). As we noted above, the Enterprise Law had extended the DRS to all state enterprises.

The post-Tiananmen party role in enterprise leadership, and the party's relation to management, were conceptualized through a number of analogies. One depicted the management of staff respectively by the enterprise party organization and the director as two lines which stem from different perspectives but converge towards the same objectives (*China Enterprise Daily* 1990). Others spoke of 'two horses pulling the same enterprise cart' (Chen 1990) and 'the two hearts of the enterprise which must become one heart' (Yuan 1990). The standard official line was that the party secretary was now regarded as the 'core' of the enterprise and the director the 'centre'. Although these analogies were hardly precise, they nevertheless indicated clearly an official intention to reinstate the party in a leadership role and to redress its previous marginalization.

It was argued that party control should be enhanced along two lines – a greater involvement in management decisions and an increase in monitoring powers. In the first case, official sources recommended that directors should no longer have the power to make middle-level and senior personnel appointments without the approval of their enterprise party organizations. In the event of deadlock, the matter would be passed up to the supervising bureau for resolution. It was also stated that the party secretary had the right to propose business policy for the enterprise and to ask the supervisory bureau to arbitrate if there was a failure to agree with the director. In the second case, it was argued that the enterprise party organization should have power to criticize management, to warn a director who violates laws and regulations, and to take to court any director who refuses to heed the warning (*China Enterprise Daily* 1990).

A systematic picture of what these new policies meant in practice has not emerged; the subject became far too sensitive to investigate. Informal reports tallied with the examples from Sino-foreign joint ventures cited by Leung (1989). These illustrated the revival of political study groups, the granting to the party secretary of a veto over personnel appointments and promotions, and the joint involvement of the party secretary with general management in strategic decisions even to the point where party committee members sought to attend board meetings. Needless to say, these moves were strenuously resisted by most foreign managers.

The recent re-affirmation and strengthening of the economic reform will inevitably reverse the post-Tiananmen changes in enterprise leadership. The political backlash of 1989 and 1990 simply revived the problems of unclear and divided responsibility for which the DRSULP had been criticized and which managerial reform was intended to remove. Indeed, the contract responsibility system would be quite unworkable with divided responsibility. The suggestion that managers should again be appointed on the basis of political acceptability rather than competence was also particularly serious. It is significant therefore that by April 1992, the official line on enterprise leadership had been modified to the statement that 'the party's leadership is the core and the director takes responsibility'. While on the face of things this may appear to place enterprise directors in a position of responsibility without authority, in reality it amounts to an acknowledgement that they are again to assume the leading managerial role.

Conclusion

The official Chinese view has been that under the economic reform the changed role of the party in enterprise leadership amounted to a rationalization of its functions rather than a diminution of its powers. It was expected that in withdrawing from day-to-day management, the enterprise party organization would have more time to exercise overall supervision and to maintain a purview of the whole enterprise in the light of central policy intentions. As a result, the party would become more authoritative within its specialized framework of responsibilities. Some commentators, indeed, thought that the powers remaining to the party, such as that of discipline over its members, would make it difficult to transfer managerial responsibility to enterprise directors under the DRS.

Our evidence from 1988 indicates that the separation of functions between management and party was instrumental in reducing the latter's effective influence on enterprise decision making. Some of the party secretaries had limited access to the managerial decision process and to relevant information. All experienced problems in holding directors to account once the independence of the latter's actions became legitimized in terms of the overriding requirement to meet the targets contracted between the enterprise and its higher administrative authority. The increasing specificity of these economic targets, with the material prosperity of enterprise members now dependent on meeting them, inevitably gained precedence over the less precise and immaterial ideological goals of which the party is the guardian. A further indication of the dominance assumed by economic considerations lay in the way that the separation of functions between management and party with regard to decision powers was not reflected in the time distribution of the party secretaries' activities – they spent the bulk of their time on tasks related to achieving economic goals and even doing managerial work itself.

The shift towards a single line of managerial authority and responsibility under the DRS has been frequently discussed in terms of a separation of enterprise management from both government and party organs. In China, the latter institutions represent the 'whole people' who are in principle the owners of state enterprises. The withdrawal of government and party officials from managerial functions therefore has an affinity with the so-called 'divorce of ownership from control' which was held to characterize many large capitalist corporations, especially in the USA, before the advance of finance capitalism in recent decades (cf. Scott 1985). The concern expressed at the time by American writers like Berle and Means (1932) was that the development of management as a separate functional specialty, coupled with the dilution of shareholdings, reduced the ability of owners to ensure that managerial behaviour remained dedicated to the interest of ownership rather than to self-interest. *Inter alia*, the withdrawal of owners from a direct involvement in management was seen to reduce the resources of information, expertise and administrative support available to them for the purposes of maintaining control.

Chinese enterprise party secretaries complained in 1988 that they and their party committees were unable to 'guarantee and supervise' the behaviour of management to ensure that it conformed to the interest of the people, as owners, as expressed in official policies. The party committee had lost the status of a board to which management could be held accountable. The administrative resources available for party work were reduced. In some cases they had been moved towards the margins of the managerial decision process, acting more as conciliators rather than as initiators or ratifiers. While formal regulations had been issued on the enterprise role of the party, their constituent items were so vague as to be of little real support for the fulfilment of that role.

In other words, the re-alignment of party functions under the DRS did have a direct impact upon the influence of party secretaries through its consequences for resourcing, access to information, and formal decision rights. Here, as in other studies of organization, it was clear that the definition of function is not neutral with respect to power. Indeed, it appeared that those party secretaries who enjoyed a measure of influence in the management process did so because of their absorption into the functional ambit of management. The influence they enjoyed resulted from their technical expertise and previous senior managerial experience which gave them credibility and utility in the eyes of enterprise directors. They spent considerably more time on managerial activities than on party work, and it is questionable whether under these circumstances their influence could be effectively directed towards the evaluation and monitoring of management required by their formal duty to 'guarantee and supervise'.

Although our information derives from a relatively small sample, it leads us to conclude with some confidence that the political role assigned to the party was not being fully implemented. For this finding emerged consistently from all the enterprises we studied, despite their diverse characteristics. The influence enjoyed by party secretaries did vary but, as we have noted, this influence was largely founded upon, and directed towards, the contribution they could make to management rather than stemming from an independent monitoring role which guaranteed and supervised the implementation of political policies.

If it is official policy for the party to remain close to the 'core' of the enterprise under a director responsibility system, attention will perhaps be given to how this role can made into a constructive reality. One path is that which had developed by 1988 in the enterprises we studied, in which experienced party officials played a leading role in management, sometimes serving as the personnel wing of the management team. This would integrate them into management and offer access to the information at its command, but it might well compromise their ability to adopt an independent monitoring role. It also depends on party officials having the necessary degree of previous managerial or technical experience. Another path would be for party officials to concentrate on their 'guarantee and supervise' function in a role somewhat detached from everyday management. The problem here is that whatever formal rights of access to relevant information party officials were given, this might not in practice be forthcoming or they might not always have the expertise to use it to reach an informed judgement. Either way, the likely result is that they would become increasingly marginalized. Whichever industrial role is sought by the party, a great deal will rest on how much legitimacy party officials can continue to command in the eyes of workers and managers on both political and technical grounds.

5   Levels of decision making

It has been a central objective of China's economic reform programme to enlarge the decision-making role of enterprise management. Without so doing, it would be incongruous to allocate to managers responsibility for the performance of their organizations. The reform looked to increase managerial decision making through the introduction of two responsibility systems. The (enterprise) contract responsibility system involved decentralization from government bureaux to enterprises, in the sense of passing down to them the responsibility for attaining agreed targets and formulating appropriate business plans. The director responsibility system called for the director to assume full responsibility for operations and staffing within the enterprise, and this opened the way for delegation within an enterprise's management structure at its director's discretion.[1] The way the director responsibility system changed the respective roles of management and the party in leadership of state enterprises was examined in the previous chapter.

These responsibility systems were intended to shift the balance of power and initiative from higher administrative agencies to enterprises and within enterprises from the party towards management. In China, however, the links between policy intentions and their realization can be somewhat tenuous and long drawn out. The announcement of official policy can precede the issuing of detailed regulations by several years and, even then, the policy may not have been formalized in its entirety. Detailed regulations have been issued on largely financial matters such as cost calculation, investment, price constraints, disposal of assets and bonus levels. On the other hand, policy measures extending enterprise autonomy or concerning the relation between enterprise directors and party secretaries have not been precisely formulated, which leaves their determination to a process of accommodation between enterprises and local bureaux, in the first case, and between managers and party officials, in the second. Despite the Enterprise Law of 1988 and a few others such as the Bankruptcy Law, the major instrument for overall control over state enterprises remains the issuing of regulations from the State Council, the State Planning Commission, ministries and local authorities. These can be contradictory and unclear.

So while the economic reform has been moving towards the extension of managerial decision powers, the nature of the change has created areas of ambiguity which can be resolved only through local adjustment between management and other parties. It was suggested in chapter 2 that such adjustment will, in any case, be made necessary by the resistance of local supervisory bodies to withdrawal from their position of exercising direct control over enterprises which are their most important source of revenue. Nor is it *prima facie* evident that a shift from control by bureaux to that by the enterprise director will, in turn, encourage greater delegation within the management structure. Functional departments within enterprises previously secured a degree of autonomy by virtue of the support they could mobilize from their corresponding departments within the supervising industrial bureau/holding company. Under the new conditions, directors have more opportunities to centralize decisions to themselves, perhaps in the desire to secure a more unified approach, or because they may not trust the capabilities of subordinates, or simply due to the fact that they now bear a more exposed personal responsibility for their enterprise's performance.

It is important for these reasons to examine the extent to which the proclaimed intentions of the economic reform in regard to decentralization have actually been achieved in practice. Hitherto available studies of decision making in China have focused on large-scale investment projects falling within the purview of national planning, in which state commissions, ministries, the Bank of China and/or foreign funding agencies and provincial governments were the principal actors rather than the managers of individual enterprises (e.g. Lieberthal and Oksenberg 1988; Stewart and Yeung 1990). The evidence presented in this and the following chapter, although confined to a small number of state enterprises, does relate to a range of decisions on micro-level issues. It is also longitudinal in nature which offers the opportunity of detecting any changes that occurred during the implementation of the economic reform.

This chapter examines the level at which a wide spectrum of decisions was authorized, with particular reference to how far such authorization had been decentralized. Chapter 6 looks into the process by which decisions were reached in five of these areas. The two chapters draw upon the work of the author, Lu Yuan and their colleagues (Child 1987; Child and Lu 1990; 1992; Lu 1991; Lu and Heard 1995).

Levels of decision making

Evidence on the levels at which decisions were authorized, and how these had changed over time, was drawn from the six Beijing state enterprises described in the Introduction. During the three years between which they were studied

(1985 and 1988), the two largest enterprises had expanded considerably in sales and employment, and they had been officially 'promoted' from the medium to the large size category of state enterprises. Three other enterprises had been advanced to medium size, giving four in this category altogether. In 1985 this official size classification still carried important implications for an enterprise's upward reporting relationship, namely that those in the small category were subject to greater local economic control from the Beijing municipality's Economic Commission than were those in the medium and large categories.

Apart from Automotive, each enterprise had in 1986 or 1987 signed a 'Management Responsibility Contract' with a higher industrial authority. These contracts were respectively between:

Enterprise	Higher authority
Audio-visual	Beijing Municipal Electronics Industry Bureau
Heavy electrical	Beijing Municipal Machine Industry Management Bureau
Pharmaceutical	Beijing Medical Corporation
Audio	Beijing Municipal Electronics Industry Bureau
Electrical switchgear	Beijing Municipal Mechanical Industry Management Bureau

The responsibility contracts were signed with municipal industrial bureaux which would normally have a number of enterprises within their purview. The contract term was usually four years. The formal provisions of each contract were very similar, following the principle of 'Two Guarantees and Single Link'.

Automotive, by a considerable margin the largest of the six, had in May 1988 entered into a joint venture which placed it under less constraining regulations. Its management was now responsible to the joint venture's board of directors rather than to a governmental authority. Four of its senior managers sat on the board along with five representatives of the joint venture partners who also provided its chairman and vice-chairman. As a joint venture, Automotive is free to develop its own long-range plan and it was working on a five-year plan to run from 1988 to 1993. Another consequence of becoming a joint venture is that the enterprise now has the freedom to reduce the proportion of the output it produces on a quota agreed with two higher authorities (the state National Automobile Corporation and the Beijing Economic Commission). In 1985 this quota accounted for 70 per cent of its output and still as much as 67 per cent in 1988. Automotive's management intended to reduce this to only 40 per cent in 1989. While an enterprise can secure the raw materials for quota production at reduced cost, the price for that output is fixed at a below market level. As a result, the unit profitability of Automotive's non-quota output was some 60 per cent higher than that of its quota output.

Information was gathered at two points in time – October 1985 and September 1988 – about the extent of decentralization to the enterprises and delegation within them of forty-eight decisions. These decisions relate to the main areas of activity normally found in an enterprise, namely marketing, production and contingent functions, purchasing, finance and investment, organization, R&D, employment and personnel. A full list of these decisions is given in Appendix 5.1. Since only Automotive and Audio-visual still had some of their output allocated to an officially planned quota in 1988, the decision on pricing of products in the plan will not be used for comparative purposes, thus reducing the total effectively to forty-seven decisions.

The method of assessment used is based on that developed in the so-called 'Aston Programme' of organizational studies (Pugh and Hickson 1976). It particularly focuses on the extent to which decision powers are passed down a set of hierarchical levels, both within the enterprise and as between the enterprise and a higher authority and/or a governing board on which enterprise managers do not constitute a majority. Questioning was directed at establishing the lowest hierarchical role in which the incumbent could authorize action to be taken without this requiring further ratification.

Information on decision levels and other related issues was gathered directly from enterprises at both dates of study. The bulk of information for 1985 came from field investigations conducted with the aid of industrially experienced Chinese Master of Business Administration (MBA) students. Initially, the author visited each enterprise in September 1985 and interviewed its director and/or a vice-director accompanied by two European faculty colleagues working at the forerunner of what is now the China–European Community Management Institute (CEMI). Interpretation during these visits was provided by Chinese faculty colleagues. Teams of six MBA students per enterprise then collected detailed information during the following month on decisions as part of a wider investigation into management and work organization which the author directed.

Information for the follow-up study in 1988 was collected by the author and Lu Yuan during joint visits to each enterprise. In each one, interviews were held with the director, head of the management office, the party secretary and managers in charge of marketing, production, purchasing, engineering/technical, personnel, accounting and quality activities.

Enterprise autonomy

Table 5.1 shows the decisions for which authority was consistently withheld from some or all of the six enterprises. Several points are apparent about the situation in 1985. Decentralization was withheld primarily in certain areas, particularly the determination of investment levels, the size of the employment

Table 5.1. *Limits to enterprise decentralization 1985 and 1988 (decisions for which authority was withheld from some or all enterprises x=authority withheld Oct. 1985; φ=authority withheld Sept. 1988)*

Decision	A 85	A 88	B 85	B 88	C 85	C 88	D 85	D 88	E 85	E 88	F 85	F 88
Marketing												
Price of non-plan products[1]			x	2					x		x	3
Introduce new product		4						φ				
Type of market served	x											
Marketing territories	x											
Production and related												
Production plan		4										
Quality standards: inputs								φ				φ
Quality standards: outputs	x					φ		φ				φ
Purchasing procedure									x			
Investment and accounting												
Level of investment	x		x		x		x		x		x	
Choice of capital equipment			x									
Scope of costing system	x								x			
Personnel												
Recruiting workers									x			
Recruiting supervisors									x			
Recruiting managers			x		x		x		x		x	
Selection methods									x			
Size of total establishment	x		x		x		x		x		x	
Workers' basic salaries	x		x		x		x				x	
Cadres' basic salaries			x		x		x		x		x	
Dismiss worker					x				x			
Dismiss cadre			x		x				x			
Design of office systems		4										
Total of above decisions for which authority is withheld from the enterprise	7	3(0)	8	0	7	1	5	3	12	0	6	3

Notes:

[1] Excludes price of products in plan since this category does not now apply to all enterprises.

[2] Authority only to set prices for monochrome TVs, not colour sets.

[3] Approval of municipal price bureau still required for price increases, but this was more permissive in 1988; the bureau only suggested the appropriate margin of price increases.

[4] Approved by the joint-venture board, not by administrative bureau, and in this respect is devolved to the enterprise.

[5] Certain corrections have been made to the data for 1985 reported in Child (1987: table 2.3) in the light of further information since arising.

Source: Child and Lu 1990: table 2.

Key to Enterprises: A Automotive; B Audio-visual; C Heavy electrical; D Pharmaceutical; E Audio;   F Electrical switchgear establishment, the recruitment of managers, the level of basic salaries, and (in some cases) product prices. Decisions on internal organization, production and production-related activities, and most purchasing matters were already decentralized. Despite these regularities, however, the extent of decentralization to the enterprises was by no means uniform.

The nationwide application of the economic reform within Chinese state-owned industry was still at an early stage in 1985, and its progress in the six Beijing enterprises was clearly rather mixed so far as its central tenet of granting enterprises autonomy to make their own business decisions was concerned. The conclusion reached on the basis of contextual and specific knowledge of each enterprise in 1985 was that a combination of accountable regularities and purely *ad hoc* local factors were contributing to this variation. On the one hand,

Certain aspects of the distribution of decision powers among the Beijing enterprises hint at accountable regularities of a more general kind: for instance, that enterprises more strategically located in terms of their contribution to national plans for key products, such as the automotive company, will be granted less autonomy in respect of marketing policy. [Similarly, it might have been added, the lack of autonomy of Audiovisual to set prices for a highly sought-after mass consumer durable, colour televisions, in circumstances when government is battling against inflation]. This kind of inter-enterprise variation in responsibility is consistent with the official reform line that 'concrete forms of the responsibility system [should be] suited to their specific conditions' (CPC 1984:24) and expresses a clear contingency perspective. (Child 1987: 48)

On the other hand, the effects of local negotiated accommodation between bureau and enterprise were also evident:

It has become apparent, however, that the present state of economic reform at enterprise level cannot simply be ascribed either to official intentionality or to strategic and operational contingencies. Specific local factors are significant. Not least among these are the connectedness and disposition of key actors within the multiple power networks described by the enterprise's plural internal organs and its several higher authorities. There were several examples indicating how the operation of the director responsibility system was shaped by the situated power enjoyed by a single individual or by mutual accommodation between major actors . . . While reliable evidence is not available on the operation of such factors in relations between the enterprise and higher authorities, commentary in the Chinese press points to them having a key bearing on the autonomy that enterprise management is effectively able to secure. (ibid.)

The comparisons offered by table 5.1 indicate that within the range of decision areas surveyed, managements in all the enterprises had by the second half of 1988 secured a noticeable increase in autonomy and that the degree of variation in autonomy between them had reduced. The granting to management of authority to determine the level of investment for the enterprise up to a certain threshold, so long as it did not require foreign exchange, was a particularly important extension of autonomy which reflects the incorporation of investment targets within the new responsibility contracts. Individual investment projects still required external approval unless they were entirely self-funded and had no consequences for the community or environment. Another important area of increased autonomy was that of personnel policy in respect of recruitment, salaries and discipline. The total salary fund was also incorporated into the provisions of enterprise responsibility contracts. A third area in which, overall, enterprise autonomy had risen was that of marketing. Although inflation had become a particularly sensitive issue in China during the intervening three years, a further relaxing in external controls over product pricing was evident both through a move away from plan/quota production and through the reduction or abolition of such control over non-plan products where it had existed in 1985.

While, however, there were these extensions to management's right to authorize action in certain decision areas, the close examination of specific decision making processes reported in chapter 6 will indicate that in practice higher authorities could, and in large measure did, continue to control decision outcomes. They continued to enjoy effective influence over enterprises in this respect through the latter's dependence on them for the provision of information, endorsements and resources.

There were some areas in which enterprise autonomy diminished between 1985 and 1988, particularly on the matter of quality standards. Although certain conditions relating to product quality (and product improvement or new product development) are often written into responsibility contracts, the problem of raising product quality became so crucial for China's competitiveness that in certain industries external bodies began to exercise direct control over quality standards and procedures. In the case of Pharmaceutical, external control over quality matters had become particularly tight because of the medicinal nature of its products, and this was the reason why the introduction of new products by this enterprise had to be externally approved on medical grounds.

Another indicator of the increased scope for managerial initiative over the three years lies in the proportion of net profit left at their disposal after payment of tax (remittance of target profit in 1987). The introduction gave this statistic for the financial years 1984 and 1987, and it shows how in every case, bar one, the percentage of retained profit rose between the two dates. The figures suggest that whereas in 1985 a range of 15–20 per cent retention would not have been unusual, a range of 25–30 per cent was more often the case by 1987. Overall, then, the self-funding left in the hands and at the discretion of enterprises had risen proportionately as well as absolutely. Audio was the exception. Its poor profit performance in 1987 meant that although its director managed to negotiate a reduction in its profit target with the industrial bureau, the new target still result-ed in a reduction in the percentage of profit remaining to the enterprise. The perceptions of enterprise directors accorded with the conclusion that, overall, enterprise autonomy had increased. The main areas where they saw this increase were the following:

1 planning of the activities to be undertaken by the enterprise, particularly in respect of investment and marketing;
2 human resource management, especially hiring and firing, the allocation of people to jobs, and determination of the reward system;
3 the use of funds and capital, especially for new product development and new equipment;
4 disposal of unwanted assets.

When visiting the enterprises in September 1985, the author and his colleagues had asked each director to indicate the areas in which he or she wished to have greater autonomy. Campbell's (1987) analysis of the replies provides a reference against which it is possible to compare the responses to the same open-ended question made by the same directors three years later.

The result of this comparison (given in table 5.2) is consistent with our identification of the trend towards greater enterprise autonomy and the areas in which this is manifest. In 1985 the items which the directors mentioned most frequently as ones in which they desired greater autonomy concerned the recruitment and dismissal of workers, the setting of salary and bonus levels, the determination of product price levels, the use of financial surpluses and the selection of suppliers. In 1988 fewer items were mentioned overall. The most frequently cited ones concerned salary and bonus levels and the obligations placed upon their enterprises to perform and contribute financially to community functions. This second item had not been mentioned at all in 1985. Greater freedom to set price levels and to select suppliers were still mentioned by two directors, but other issues were mentioned by at most one director out of the six. Their previous frustration at lack of control over other personnel issues had largely evaporated, even though informal constraints were still imposed by local community agencies over the implementation of employment rationalization.

Delegation within enterprises

Comparison of the detailed profiles of the forty-seven decisions across the six enterprises between 1985 and 1988 enables conclusions to be drawn on the dis-tribution of delegated decision powers within those enterprises. The October 1984 policy document issued by the CPC's Central Committee on 'China's Economic Structure Reform' called for the creation of 'a mighty contingent of managerial and technical cadres for the socialist economy' (CPC 1984:33). It

Table 5.2. *Areas in which enterprise directors desired greater autonomy (six Beijing enterprises: October 1985 and September 1988)*

	Number of Mentions[1]	
Greater autonomy wanted to:	1985[2]	1988
Recruit and dismiss workers	5	1
Set salary/bonus levels	3	3
Set prices	3	2
Use financial surplus	2	—
Select suppliers	2	2
Determine type and quantity of products produced	1	—
Use foreign exchange they generate	1	—
Determine obligations to the local community	—	3
Determine innovation policy	—	1
Vary profit target	—	1
Undertake building work	—	1
Total	17	14

Notes:
[1] This is a count of the responses to an open-ended question put to enterprise directors: 'In what areas would you like greater autonomy?'
[2] *Source* for 1985 tabulation: Campbell (1987: table 4.2).
Source: Child and Lu 1990: table 3.

spelt out the areas over which qualified managers would assume responsibility, including production and operations, technological progress, economic planning, finance and accounting. In other words, the reformers envisaged not only the decentralization of authority to enterprises, but also the delegation of functional authority within the management structure. How far had the enterprises progressed down that road?

It was noted by Child (1987:37ff) that in 1985 the enterprises practised quite extensive delegation of production decisions and that indeed this had been the practice before the reform when Chinese enterprises had been essentially just factories oriented to fulfilling production plans expressed in terms of physical output targets. Comparison with studies in other capitalist countries suggested that decisions on the introduction of new products and type of market to serve also tended to be delegated somewhat further down management structures in the Chinese enterprises.

Table 5.3 lists the decision areas where the main changes were evident in delegation patterns between 1985 and 1988. By 1988, decisions on labour and personnel issues (though not organization), production and work allocation, purchasing and customer priority tended to be delegated further. For example, the selection and appointment of new workers was now typically decided by

Table 5.3. *Main changes in delegation within management (six Beijing enterprises: October 1985 to September 1988)*

Delegation within management had generally increased for:
1. labour and personnel issues (but not organization)
2. production and work allocation
3. purchasing
4. customer priority

Delegation within management had generally decreased for:
1. introduction of new products
2. finance and investment
3. design of office systems (including computing)

Source: Child and Lu 1990: table 4.

the heads of labour departments, namely functional managers, while the promotion of production workers to the position of workgroup leader (supervisor) was also often decided by the manager of a workshop. In 1985, these decisions had more often been confined to the level of vice-director, usually one level higher in the hierarchy. Decisions on the allocation of work to workers, on the machines and equipment to be used, and sometimes those on work methods, could now be taken by workgroup leaders whereas previously they were more often not delegated below the workshop manager at the next level up. In two enterprises, decisions on the choice of suppliers and on the procedure to be followed in making a purchase could be taken by buyers themselves which was previously never the case. Similarly, there were now more cases of decisions being taken about customer priority by salespeople themselves.

However, delegation tended to have been rescinded in certain other areas. This was particularly evident for the two strategic issues of new products and finance; and also for the design of office systems including the use of computers. Whereas decisions to introduce new products might previously have been left to the head of the engineering or technical function, now they tended to be in the hands of the enterprise director while, as table 5.1 indicated, in two companies approval had to be secured from a higher level still. The directors were also more often now the final deciders on non-budgeted expenditures and on the scope of the enterprise's costing systems. Given the decentralization of investment decisions down to them under the contract responsibility system, this meant that financial direction was by Autumn 1988 quite strongly concentrated in the hands of directors. Automotive was a partial exception to this conclusion, where the deputy director, who also headed the enterprise management department, could make some of the financial decisions. Probably because of its larger size and corporate status as a joint venture, this enterprise practised delegation within management to a greater overall extent than did the others.

Decisions on the design of office systems were now restricted to the enterprise director, and indeed had to be referred to the board in Automotive, whereas previously they had been delegated to below the director in four of the six enterprises. Having displayed sometimes appalling inefficiencies in the past, office organization and overheads were then receiving more critical attention in China including contentious attempts to shift a certain proportion of office workers into shopfloor jobs and even to declare them redundant. Office computers were also being introduced in larger numbers. For these reasons this decision area had come to assume greater importance.

As has already been noted, the patterns of delegation were not uniform across all the enterprises and we have only reported on those areas where trends were most singular. One method of capturing the whole picture of decentralization to each enterprise, as well as delegation within it, is to present the distribution of decisions by the lowest levels at which they could be taken. This is done graphically in figure 5.1.

The figure distinguishes five standardized hierarchical levels which, although derived from the Aston Programme's methodology, happen to coincide closely with the hierarchies in the Chinese state enterprises. The top level (level 5) is above the enterprise and would be a municipal bureau or a board which had a majority of non-executive directors. Level 4 is that of enterprise director or the enterprise management committee (in practice, the former was normally the final decision maker at this level). Level 3 comprises persons heading several departments such as vice-directors or chief engineers. Level 2 is the head of a single department, be this a production workshop or a specialized functional department; it may also be the head of a specific product group within a matrix structure. Level 1 is a workgroup leader or supervisor. Level 0 is an operative or a functional specialist such as a buyer or a salesperson.

What emerges clearly from this depiction of the data is that overall the main change in the distribution of decision making had come about in the relation between the enterprise and its director, without doubt prompted by the contract responsibility system. As noted earlier, a number of decisions previously taken above the enterprise were now decentralized to it. This decentralization had not, however, been matched by a corresponding net redistribution of decision making further down the management structure, with the singular exception of Automotive. The director of this enterprise was particularly conscious of the need to delegate, commenting that

during the previous three years authority has been distributed within the management hierarchy here, though not to the full extent necessary. It would be correct to say that delegation has been implemented for most managers and that those not competent to assume responsibility are now in a minority. In fact, during a recent rationalization we replaced 20 per cent of all managers as well as 30 per cent of all cadres [white-collar staff].

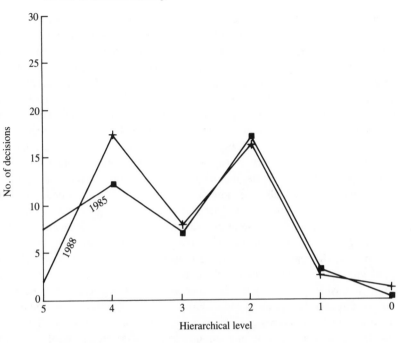

Figure 5.1 Distribution of decisions by hierarchical level (number of decisions from a total of 47 delegated to each of 5 hierarchical levels. Average for
6 Beijing enterprises October 1985 and September 1988). *Key to levels:*
5=above enterprise director (i.e. bureau or board with non-executive majority); 4=enterprise director or enterprise management committee; 3=head of
several departments (e.g. vice-director); 2=head of department, workshop or
functional area; 1=workgroup leader or supervisor; 0=operative or functional
specialist (e.g. buyer). *Source:* adapted from Child and Lu 1990: figure A1.

Another, less marked, exception to the lack of greater delegation below the
level of director was found in Audio, which had introduced a matrix system
with product managers at level 2 now exercising the responsibility of enhancing added value for their product groups and operating under the vice-director
for production in an integrative role *vis-à-vis* the various functional managers.
Decisions on matters bearing closely on the attainment of added value such as
the spread of markets served, the prioritizing of orders, production scheduling
and working of overtime were now delegated to the product managers.

Several of the directors interviewed complained about the excessive workload and attendant stress with which they were afflicted. They tended to take
the view that managers lower down were not yet ready to handle greater
responsibility, though they also attributed a degree of pressure to the continued

interference of community obligations with the concentration they could give to business matters, and the foisting onto their companies of arbitrary charges by local community bodies. They were also keenly conscious of the targets which had now formally been imposed on them under their newly signed responsibility contracts, and they appeared to fear that any loosening of their grip might jeopardize the attainment of those targets. These targets had, of course, been applied to operating conditions which remained highly uncertain so encouraging directors to engage in personally opportunistic behaviour and defensive tactics *vis-à-vis* their higher authority, which would also discourage delegation on their part (cf. Boisot and Xing 1992). Agency theory would, indeed, predict that the greater the risk borne by enterprise directors as 'agents' of their bureau 'principals', the more they will endeavour to consolidate control in their own hands, perceiving that this offers the best way to focus the collective effort onto meeting targets, avoiding mistakes and supporting any subterfuges they felt to be necessary in the process (cf. Eisenhardt 1989).

Whatever the reasons behind it, the failure appreciably to increase delegation within management to enable enterprise directors to concentrate on strategic business decisions has now become one of the major challenges in progressing the intentions of the economic reform. It places a premium on organizational development to introduce a culture and supporting mechanisms for delegated management and on the personal development of younger managers so that they can be better equipped to assume greater responsibility.

As Weber (1968) noted from Western experience, two necessary conditions for the exercise of autonomy by economic units are codification and routinization. The rules of the game applied to relations between enterprises and external parties, especially government, have to be codified particularly with respect to law and taxation. Secondly, government must apply the rules in a routine manner – in other words consistently and predictably – so that the managers of economic units can use their autonomy to plan ahead.

In the event of poor codification, mutual obligations are worked out on traditional or *ad hoc* lines and are subject to local reinterpretation. This creates localized practices and dependencies which are inimical to wider market transactions and the economies that follow from these. The routinization of rules guards against the possibility of an arbitrary exercise of power to which the managers of local units have to accommodate through inefficient practices such as opportunistic evasion, over-conformity and illicit payments.

China has by no means achieved an adequate, let alone comprehensive, level of codification in matters of legal rights and obligations or of taxation. As noted earlier, laws and regulations can be both vague and contradictory. This leaves them open to interpretation and amplification by local authorities. Power is consequently an active variable in the relations between enterprises and local bureaux in determining the conditions under which the former can carry on their business. Moreover, different bureaux use their powers *vis-à-vis* the enterprise in pursuit of different priorities.

In this situation the bureaux are liable to be seen to exercise their powers in a non-routinized and arbitrary manner. This explains why there were frequent complaints on the part of enterprise managements about 'administrative interference' (permitted by the lack of precise legal definitions of management rights) and 'arbitrary charges' levied locally on enterprises (permitted by the fact that the incidence of imposts is a negotiated matter). The order that governs the enterprise remains to a significant degree one which is negotiated rather than laid down with consistency or coherence. The open-endedness and uncertainty in this order is increased by the present confusion as to who actually owns the Chinese state enterprise. It is also exacerbated by the fact that central government still has the power to override certain key dimensions of economic autonomy such as pricing and does so in response to periodic crises.

We may consider some examples of how rights now officially decentralized to the enterprise are in practice subject to constraint and negotiation. Although enterprise managements now have the right to make decisions (and claim that they do) on managerial appointments, the size of their establishments and redundancies, and investment, these remain areas where local agencies often attempt to exert influence on the substance of such decisions. Moreover, the appointment of enterprise directors themselves remains in the hands of the industrial bureaux. Many cases have been reported of the removal of enterprise directors by industrial bureaux, with which of course they have a contract, and of attempts by the local personnel bureau to interfere in managerial appointments.

The lack of social welfare organizations able to accept responsibility for the care of redundant workers, who do not enjoy adequate unemployment benefit in China, can force management as the decision-making body to resort to subterfuges which effectively negate the decision to rationalize. The automotive enterprise, for example, was publicized as a pioneer in the rationalization of labour (which in conjunction with the labour contract system introduced in October 1986 became a prominent objective of the economic reform). While it did reduce the numbers on its books, the reality is that it tucked them away in a collective enterprise operating on the same site and performing services for the main enterprise under its protection. Management has not been able to relinquish the burden of supporting surplus labour even though it now has the right to determine that this surplus exists and who forms part of it. In order to activate this aspect of personnel policy, enterprise directors still need support from their bureau and/or ministry so that they can prevail against opposition from their employees, the enterprise trade union and the community on the basis that they are clearly carrying out official policy.

To take a third example, should an enterprise wish to fund investment through a bank loan, which is the normal source of external funding, it still effectively has to secure the approval of its industrial bureau since the local bank will in practice make this a condition of granting the loan.

The presence of constraints such as those illustrated forces enterprise management into a negotiating relationship with the public agencies in its local environment. Moreover, local charges and imposts are also subject to negotiation and arm-twisting. The Chinese central government has repeatedly stressed that the levying of arbitrary charges on enterprises is forbidden and that they have the right to turn down unreasonable charges for, say, educational support, street-cleaning, community medical services, transport and postal communications. In 1988 the government published special regulations to this effect.

However, we noted how this area of interference was a major complaint expressed by the directors of the Beijing enterprises when asked about areas in which they sought greater autonomy. A survey conducted among eighty-one enterprises in Hubei Province in 1988 indicated that the soliciting of additional financial contributions by local agencies was on the increase, often to finance projects which had been approved without funding (*Beijing Review* 1989c). The enterprises were in other words being regarded as a useful local cash-cow. Not only did these charges add up to a sizeable amount but dealing with the agencies concerned was seen to be a significant distraction from the task of managing a business. The reason why enterprises tend to come up with the money, despite having a right of refusal, lies in the power that can be exercised against them by the local administrative network. An unco-operative enterprise is liable to find its requests for investment funding turned down. Just as bad, it could find that the municipality has decided to undertake some prolonged road works which block its entrance or to carry out repairs which disrupt its power supply.

A final and economically very significant example of continuing dependence upon higher authority is seen with the problem of securing supplies. Particularly where some output remains on a planned basis at a controlled price, as is the case with both the automotive and audio-visual enterprises, the support of the industrial bureau can be vital in negotiations with the ministry to secure the enterprise's quota of inputs at the lower planned price level. This last example also points to the fact that the more that enterprises have come to rely on market transactions for their inputs and outputs, the more limited is the area of potential 'interference' from higher bureaux so long as they are able to fulfil their contract targets. For example, although its poor performance did compel the audio products enterprise to enter into re-negotiations with its industrial bureau during 1987/8, its recovery by the second half of 1988 had released it from any decision-making dependency on the bureau apart from the appointment of its director.

Over the period since 1984 when enterprise reform in the state-owned sector

began to be applied nationwide, the relationship between state enterprises and local authorities has changed from one in which the industrial bureau served as a controlling authority intervening directly, and often taking the initiative, in major areas of decision, to one in which that control has been transformed into the more arm's-length mechanism of the responsibility contract. Under the latter system the enterprise enjoys more formal autonomy and indeed has reduced its dependence on the industrial bureau despite the elements of this which remain.

However, the other side of the coin was that in the past the industrial bureau was able where necessary to protect an ailing enterprise from the pains of drastic adjustment. Now, since the industrial bureau must itelf meet certain targets for remitting taxation to the local government, it is constrained in the protection it can offer, even though when it has come to the test of bankruptcy municipalities have so far striven to sustain firms in recognition of the many externalities which they provide by way of education, housing and the like.

Moreover, what used to be regarded by enterprise managers as the 'one umbrella' protecting the enterprise from risk has now been transformed into 'the many gods' – a host of potentially interfering 'Mothers-in-Law'. In the previous situation the various specialized local bureaux did not enjoy direct access to enterprises – only the industrial bureau had this right. Under the newer system the coupling between industrial bureau and enterprise has been loosened with the shift to arm's-length control and responsibility. In principle this represents a positive step towards greater micro-economic autonomy. In practice, it tends to be seen as adding to the constraints upon enterprise autonomy because the legal basis for the 'Mothers-in-Law' has in fact not yet been codified and they can now impinge upon the enterprise directly with unclear limits to their authority. If, for example, the industrial bureau fails to meet its quota of taxation pooled from the enterprises with which it has profit contracts, then the local taxation bureau can go straight to the enterprises and attempt to extract some payment directly. The industrial bureau may still be able to offer some protection to its enterprises against interference by other agencies, but this is reported to be less than before. In short, the price of an enterprise's greater autonomy from a single controlling authority has become its engagement in negotiation with a range of more specialized local agencies.

It would be misleading, however, to interpret the exercise of powers and constraints as by any means a unidirectional process in which the enterprise is purely a subject party. Since local revenues, livelihoods and social welfare depend so heavily upon the economic success of enterprises, their managements have a substantial ground upon which to base their argument and from which to secure their objectives.

Secondly, and encouraged by some reform economists who see it as 'the third wave' in the reform and a move towards securing a better organization of production (*Beijing Review* 1988), an increasing number of enterprises have entered into horizontal associations ranging from informal liaison to cartels and even full-blown mergers. This horizontal integration may cut across local administrative boundaries as well as increasing the size of the new association or organization. Its attractions for management include the enhanced bargaining power that is afforded *viv-à-vis* local administrations. The heavy electrical products enterprise, for example, entered into association with fifteen similar producers across northern China and in 1988 held a three-day meeting during which there was agreement on the need for product price increases. This combination of producers prevailed upon the authorities to permit the increases. The audio products enterprise has also joined other producers of similar products to exchange information and to attempt a collective control of costs and prices.

We suggested earlier that the need to manage the boundary between their enterprises and higher authority very carefully under conditions of operational uncertainty in which they as agents bore most of the risk, inhibited directors from delegating decision making within the management structure. This reluctance to delegate is reinforced by cultural expectations. According to Chinese norms, it is typically the director who is expected to deal with the bureaux since they are considered to be organizations of higher status. The fact that the quality of its relationship with external bureaux can affect important strategic parameters for the enterprise is likely to deter deviation from those norms.

The progress of delegation within the enterprise is also constrained by the power asymmetries prevailing in areas of market transacting (see chapter 7). This was very clearly the case for transactions in obtaining supplies. Where supplies were readily available and were of a standard nature, it was noticeable that compared to three years previously the purchasing enterprises now contracted on the more impersonal or distant basis of letter and telephone, and that the transaction was often conducted by a buyer enjoying no managerial status. Where there was a shortage so that the suppliers enjoyed the greater power, the consequence was quite different. Suppliers in this position generally insisted on a senior ranking manager, such as the vice-director for production, dealing with them in person during which time they would have to be offered banquets and often other more substantial favours about which there was an understandable reluctance to go into detail! They would not respond to less direct communication and certainly not to a junior employee of lesser status. Sometimes the good offices with suppliers enjoyed by the industrial bureau or even the ministry were also elicited and again this had to be done by an enterprise manager of senior status. These relationships and accompanying perks were highly personalized and typically described in terms of 'establishing personal trust'. It was claimed that they would outweigh purely economic criteria determining to which enterprise a supplier would allocate priority.

In these ways again, the qualitative nature of external relationships effectively determined the delegation policy that could be pursued within the enterprise so far as managing purchasing was concerned. Powerful suppliers were not only able to extract more favourable material benefits from their transactions but also to decide priorities among customers according to the quality of the personal relationship they had cultivated with him, including the deference which their organizations displayed. Basically it is market failure which causes managers to rely on these informal and personalized methods which are reversions to the Chinese tradition of establishing an order based upon *guanxi*, trust relationships involving mutual reciprocity. Where enterprises such as the audio-visual company produced a product in high demand – colour TVs – but were constrained from allowing this to reflect in high prices, they capitalized on the position instead to establish favoured relationships. This particular enterprise issued coupons entitling their bearers to priority in securing a colour TV, a quite informal (if not illegal) practice which stood it in good stead with key officials in agencies such as the municipal bank.

Conclusion

The evidence presented in this chapter suggests that over the three years from 1985 to 1988 the managers of Chinese state enterprises secured additional autonomy to make investment, personnel and marketing decisions. This autonomy was, however, liable to be rescinded or offset by sudden changes in central government policy, while locally it was bounded by relational obligations which betray a combined influence of power dependencies and traditional mores within a very imperfect market context. In these circumstances it may be more correct to suggest that state enterprises have been accorded an increased measure of delegation rather than of decentralization in its full sense.

Official pronouncements on the Chinese reform claim an intention to move from a hierarchical to a market governance of economic transactions. The state at both central and local levels is to withdraw from the direction of enterprises through mandatory planning, and enterprises are instead to achieve the agreed targets specified in their responsibility contracts through their own direct engagement in market transactions both on the side of supply and of output. This provides the justification for enterprises to enjoy autonomy in the making of business decisions. The underlying rationale is one of efficiency: to promote the superior deployment, reproduction and accumulation of economic resources.

While improvements in efficiency have been achieved under the economic reform, and according to official Chinese figures at a rate that compares well with many other countries (State Council Research Office 1989), the devolution of economic authority from central government had not, in the case of state enterprises, been matched by a corresponding increase in the governance of economic transactions through the market mechanism. It has been argued elsewhere (Boisot and Child 1988), and borne out by the present evidence, that in circumstances which combine substantial market imperfection with continuing enterprise dependence on local authorities, the decision processes of state-owned enterprises continue to accord with more traditional patterns of Chinese organizational behaviour.

All six Beijing enterprises were still being treated by the city authority as an extension of its domain, particularly in its requiring them to perform what would in most countries be regarded as municipal functions. Even the automobile enterprise found that becoming a joint venture had not reduced this obligation, although dealing with it was now taking up much less of its director's time. Moreover, although the signing of responsibility contracts was formally supposed to place enterprises at an arm's-length relation to their bureaux, in practice the operation of these contracts had not removed the dependence of enterprises upon those bureaux in matters such as securing their good offices to obtain scarce supplies and to dispose of surplus labour. Moreover, the appointment of enterprise directors remained in their hands. Local economic areas are thus continuing to operate in many respects as fiefs with relations of hierarchical dependence in which informal contact and personal association count for a great deal.

It is difficult to explain this situation in terms of an efficiency argument. The persistence of hierarchical relations at the local level cannot be accounted for in terms of their greater benefit for economic efficiency, for as we have seen they are in many respects harmful to such efficiency. It is true that these hierarchical relations are sustained by a degree of continuing market failure, especially in the provision of market information and the availability of market choice, but at the same time firms such as the heavy electrical enterprise were having to use horizontal combination with competitors, itself an abrogation of pure market relations, in the attempt to wrest from local authorities the basic freedom of a market player to raise prices. This is an illustration of how the economic game is being played on a power basis.

The persistence of tradition appears to encourage the power dimension in Chinese economic relationships insofar as it ascribes value to status deference and other components of what the Chinese themselves call 'relationships of trust'. The care that enterprise managers took to cultivate these relationships and to honour those in a position of advantaged power was consistently apparent in dealings with key suppliers and with their industrial bureaux, behaviour which becomes evident when considering the process of decision making in the following chapter. This deference did not necessarily supplant the element of negotiation, or indeed a recognition that dependence was to a degree mutual, but it was clearly not in accord with the market process of transacting through an agreeement on price. In fact, it was claimed by several respondents that price would not determine the priority given to them by suppliers. Decisions to enter into economic transactions were being made according to personal criteria at least as much as on the basis of impersonal ones such as price.

Appendix 5.1 List of decisions or responsibilities investigated

Marketing
1. introducing a new product
2. the price of products: in the plan
3. the price of products: outside the plan
4. the type of market to supply (type of outlet, type of customer)
5. the geographical spread of sales (in China, exports, etc.)
6. the priority of different product orders and deliveries

Purchasing
7. the choice of suppliers of materials
8. the procedure for purchasing (e.g. whether to ask for several quotes, order quantities, terms of contract)

Production and work allocation
9. the overall production plan (annual) adopted
10. the scheduling of work (up to 1 month) against given plans
11. the allocation of work to be done among the available workers
12. which machines or equipment are to be used
13. the methods of work to be used (not including new expenditure)
14. when overtime will be worked

Quality control
15. what items will be inspected (including what %) – inward supplies
16. what items will be inspected (including what %) – completed products

Work study
17. which production operations will be studied (have industrial engineering applied)

Maintenance
18. the maintenance schedule or procedure

R&D
19. what research and development work will be done (i.e. how much and what priority)

Investing and accounting
20. the level of expenditure on new capital equipment
21. the type or make of new capital equipment
22. what will be costed: to which items will the costing system be applied
23. what unbudgeted money can be spent on capital items
24. what unbudgeted money can be spent on revenue/consumable items

Staffing
25. the numbers of workgroup leaders/supervisors
26. appointing workers from outside the factory
27. appointing supervisors from outside the factory
28. appointing managers from outside the factory
29. the size of the total workforce
30. the total numbers of managers above workgroup leader level
31. the promotion of production workers
32. the promotion of workgroup leaders/supervisors
33. the salaries of production workers
34. the salaries of cadres
35. the methods for selecting new workers and cadres

Discipline
36. dismiss a worker
37. dismiss or demote a supervisor or manager (cadre)

Training
38. the type of training offered

Welfare
39. what and how many welfare facilities are provided

Organisation structure
40. altering responsibilities/areas of work of non-production departments
41. altering responsibilities/areas of work of production departments
42. creating a new department
43. creating a new non-production job
44. creating a new production job

Office systems
45. the design of office systems (including the use of computers)

Representation of management
46. who is the most junior person who can deputise for the director in his absence

Who is the most junior person who can represent management in:

47. discussions with the party secretary
48. discussions with the trade union leader (or workers' congress leader)

6   The process of decision making

Judging by the accounts of senior managers in the six Beijing state enterprises, they could by 1988 authorize a wide range of business decisions themselves. But did this mean that they now enjoyed effective autonomy from administrative bodies? A close examination of the decision-making process in the same enterprises undertaken by Lu Yuan (1991) suggests an extremely qualified answer and this is reinforced by further findings from a retrospective study of investment decision making in both China and the UK (Lu and Heard 1995).[1]

Lu (1991) examined the process whereby decisions were reached in or around 1985, at the early stage of the decentralization reform, and then later on (mainly in 1988 and 1989) in five areas: investment, purchasing, product pricing, recruitment of labour, and organizational change. These were selected as areas in which the economic reform was intended to increase enterprise autonomy. Moreover, the first four decision areas involve relations with the enterprise environment and should therefore register any shift towards market transactions. Investment decisions involving the commitment of significant resources to major projects should be a particularly good indicator of how far Chinese state enterprises have come to enjoy substantial autonomy under the reform, since they act as economic and social policy signifiers and are therefore placed on the boundary between government planning and market forces as determinants of economic action within a social market economy. It was assumed that organizational change would be a concomitant both of increased managerial autonomy and of a greater adaptation to the market environment.

The categories of decision examined by Lu at the two points in time in each enterprise are listed in Appendix 6.1; within these five categories he investigated thirty decisions taken in 1988–9 and in or around 1985. For each decision, he investigated how the decision process had been initiated, how possible outcomes were developed and selected, who authorized the decision, and how the time sequence of the whole process could be characterized in terms of its duration and any interruptions. He also enquired about sources of information used in the decision process and the relations with higher governmental authorities that were involved.

The comparative China–UK study involved, on the China side, major investment decisions in three very large heavy industry enterprises (one general chemicals, one petro-chemicals and one iron and steel) initiated in 1983, 1984 and 1989. These decisions are also listed in Appendix 6.1 and it will be seen that the value of the investments was considerably greater than any of those studied in the six Beijing enterprises. The investigation covered similar ground to the earlier research.

This chapter reports the main findings of Lu's investigation which serve to indicate the extent of changes in the decision-making process over time, and reference is made to the second study where this can shed additional light.

Initiation

The investment decisions were evenly divided between the funding of process innovation and new product development. In both categories, and at both time periods, higher authorities (generally ministries or municipal bureaux) were the main initiators of the investment decision process. Initiatives from these authorities offered advantages to the enterprises chosen to implement them: a guarantee of funds and of market prospects. The market prospects stemmed from the fact that the products linked to the investment would secure a place on the ministry's approved list. When a project was formulated by a ministry, the most important consideration for the enterprise was therefore to seize the opportunity and bid for it. As a manager in Audio-visual said, it was a matter of 'get in first and think about other things later'. 'Other things' included whether the project was really justified in terms of the enterprise's business needs and/or could be implemented successfully.

The system of initiating investment in new projects therefore remained primarily funding-led rather than market-led, despite the professed intention of the reform to allow the market to guide enterprises (Zhao 1987). There was heavy administrative involvement even in the post-1985 cases of new product development, where the products were short-listed in the relevant ministries' new product development plans which identified their intended customers.

The three heavy industry enterprises each had large strategic or long-term planning departments and staff from these were the main initiators of proposals for investment. However, the proposal was only put forward once management had ascertained through 'mutual communication' with the higher authority's planning department that the authority agreed with the investment intention. In addition, a draft of the formal proposal was in each case submitted to the enterprise's administrative authority (respectively a ministry, municipal economic commission and provincial industrial bureau) which had to provide its initial approval before the draft went to other authorities for further approval and/or modification. Only after this process had been completed was a feasibility study started.

Compared with 1985, the purchasing managers in all six enterprises said that they were by 1988 more active in searching for buying opportunities both from sources under administrative control and from markets. They no longer relied primarily on an allocation of inputs under the quota system. Their initiative was encouraged by the acute shortages which had then developed. Nevertheless, industrial ministries and bueaux continued to play an important role in starting off the purchase decision process. This role arose from their provision of information about impending policy changes affecting relevant parameters (such as a restriction of imports or price increases), offers to supply from sources under their control, and their organization of trade fairs.

The granting of awards to, or official re-classification of, products by ministries had been the triggers for price increases in four of the enterprises in 1985; in the case of the Pharmaceutical and Audio enterprises, market changes acted as the triggers. The situation changed significantly in the later period, since higher authorities no longer played an important role in the initiation of pricing decisions. The main factor now triggering a decision to increase prices was internal cost pressures, articulated by the enterprises' financial departments. In the case of Audio, declining demand and rising stocks triggered a move to reduce prices.

Prior to the enterprise reform, the role of the municipal industrial and labour bureaux had been a proactive one with regard to recruitment. Each year the industrial bureau asked enterprises to submit their recruitment needs. It collated this information and passed it on to the labour bureau which decided on allocation quotas for each enterprise. Enterprises were obliged to accept recruits if the labour bureau insisted, even if they were in excess of what was required or were unsuitable. In three of the six decisions reached in 1985, the labour bureau actually initiated the recruitment process. Subsequently, the director responsibility system gave management some formal authority over labour management. By 1988/9, decisions to recruit new employees were initiated internally in response to assessments of need made by labour managers and the vice-director of personnel. These assessments depended on the enterprise's records of human resource profiles and task requirements, with the latter relating in part to its technology development plan. The introduction of contract responsibility systems also made an important difference because the way they linked increases in the salary and bonus fund to profit levels provided an incentive for economy in employment numbers so as to maximize per capita earnings.

Organizational changes, such as merging departments or establishing product divisions, were in both periods mostly initiated in response to the instructions or campaigns of local authorities. In the earlier period, instructions from the industrial bureau to implement the director responsibility system triggered decisions to reconfigure the management structure in four of the six enterprises. Automotive was selected by the local labour bureau as the experimental site for a new wage system. In only one case, Heavy Electrical, was its establishment of product divisions and profit centres initiated by its own management in the light of an expansion in market share and the need to improve internal co-ordination.

Similarly, all but one of the decisions to change organization made after 1985 were initiated by instructions from the local industrial bureau. They were responses to pressures from the Beijing government to rationalize the labour force, whereby ten local government bureaux in October 1988 published a regulation for 'Optimizing the Combination of Labour'. Enterprise managers were in fact reluctant to accept the need for these organizational changes which aimed at personnel redeployment and threatened the quality of their industrial relations, but they felt obliged to accept the Beijing government's requirements. The exception was Automotive which in 1987 initiated a reorganization of departments and employment contracts to accommodate to its formation of a joint venture, though the local government subsequently used the firm's experience as one of three models to propagate its own campaign.

Comparing the decisions as a whole over the 1985–8 period, market conditions appeared to become more important factors in initiating decisions on purchasing and pricing, but not necessarily for those on investment. Internal considerations of need and cost pressure became more important respectively for the initiation of recruitment and pricing decisions. Higher authorities continued to provide the main trigger, or at least the main hurdle, for initiating decisions on investment and organizational change. Their role in the initiation of decisions on recruitment and pricing noticeably declined.

Development and selection

Once an issue or possibility has been brought up for consideration, further work may be undertaken to examine its details; design or investigatory work may be carried out; some options may be closed off and preferred solutions identified. One cannot assume that all these activities necessarily take place but, as in Lu's study, it is possible to check whether they do. Certain decisions, for instance, may be so routine that these activities are not consciously gone through; in other cases they may all fall within the purview of a single person.

The investment decisions, being relatively major projects concerned with innovation, normally did involve some detailing or design work and a selection between options. Whereas the ministerial or bureau line authority over an enterprise was often the first to propose an investment project, and its initial agreement was essential for the project to proceed further, it was the evaluating functional bureaux which participated most in the detailing and selection of particular schemes – especially in the period after 1985. These bureaux had responsibility for matters such as foreign currency, electric power, labour supply, land usage, environmental impact, and technical standards. They retained powers to halt any project and an enterprise could be heavily dependent on them to provide access to resources or to the suppliers of resources. Enterprise managers were therefore obliged to alter the content of their proposals whenever one of these authorities requested it, regardless of how practical this was. Most of these bureaux had been established as an attempt to impose an external check on industrial decision making as it became more decentralized under the economic reform, and their officials were said to be particularly sensitive to the possibility that enterprise managers might attempt to ignore them.

Lu and Heard (1995) comment of the same process that enterprise managers had to gain the approval of every authority sequentially through intensive negotiation and persuasion. A major problem with this circuit was that the whole procedure could be stopped simply by one authority refusing its support. The need to secure approval from a large number of evaluating bureaux was a costly and time-consuming process and could impose a substantial burden on enterprises. Automotive, for instance, had to collate thirteen documents from evaluating bureaux into its feasibility study draft containing detailed comments on matters such as foreign exchange implications, environment, labour recruitment, source of funds and capital budgeting. One of Lu and Heard's large enterprises reported that over 200 official 'stamps' had been required for one investment project. The fact that face-to-face personal contact with key higher officials was particularly effective for gaining approval only added to the cost and time. The importance of having *guanxi* was emphasized and staff who possessed the right connections were selected to liaise with the various external agencies.

On the face of things, the bureaux and ministries appeared to set conditions for the approval of the investment projects while the enterprise mainly carried out routine detailing procedures and required modification. Although the relationship between higher authorities and the enterprise therefore looks to be substantially asymmetrical, managers were in practice able to secure some initiative by dint of their superior technical knowledge. Managers believed that bureau officials did not read their proposals carefully and had difficulty in understanding technical details.

Montias (1988) argues that within socialist systems that have evolved from the original Stalinist model, the possession by subordinates of more detailed information than their superior authorities gives them a bargaining advantage. This was true with respect to investment project details, but at the same time the enterprise depended in the first place on market and technical information supplied by the bureaux for the design and detailing of their projects. The extent to which they relied on higher authorities for such information hardly varied between the earlier and later sets of decisions.

There was very little need to undertake any detailing work in the case of purchasing decisions. In both time periods, purchasing managers generally relied on their experience to assess need, indicated by consumption and stock levels, in relation to the available opportunities to buy. They emphasized that a speedy decision was often essential in order to take advantage of favourable buying opportunities. The decisions were based upon known needs and were in that respect uncontroversial; the element of judgement entered in when it was a matter of deciding which purchasing opportunities to accept. In two enterprises – Audio-visual and Heavy Electrical – there was some prior design and detailing work in the case of specialized inputs such as integrated circuits. Where a selection had to be made between sources of supply or the quantity and/or quality of inputs, this was usually made by reference to the enterprise director who typically consulted with the chief accountant. The finance function was somewhat more involved in the post-1985 purchasing decisions than in previous ones, reflecting the greater attention now being paid to the enterprise's profit performance. Authorities outside the enterprise were not consulted at this stage at either period of time.

Some detailing work was carried out for pricing decisions, and there was little difference in how this was done between the 1985 and 1988 decisions. A cost-plus formula was normally used to estimate an acceptable profit margin before product prices were set, an approach which can be understood in the context then prevailing of limited sensitivity to the market, generally buoyant demand, and official judgement of enterprise performance in terms of profit level rather than profitability rate. Within the enterprise, the director or senior manager such as the chief accountant was always involved in discussing the proposed price change.

The opinion of higher authorities about proposed price increases was sought or second-guessed in cases where the products were socially or strategically important, as with colour TV sets and trucks, and where those authorities would eventually have to approve the increases. In such cases, the industrial bureau was consulted first and it had powers to permit or to delay the enterprise's intentions. For example, if the bureau gave a quality award to a product, this made it easier to increase its price. On the other hand, the bureau possessed sanctions such as cancelling a product's existing quality evaluation. Subsequently, an application to increase prices would have to receive the approval of the price bureau and there was an example from Automotive in 1985 where the price bureau insisted on a reduction in the proposed increase despite the fact that the industrial bureau was content with it.

The only development activity involved in recruitment decisions concerned the number of people to be hired and their future allocation to jobs, a task normally carried out by labour or personnel managers in all the cases studied. Development work on organizational change was usually carried out by line management, or the personnel department, under the supervision of a deputy director. Party secretaries took an active part at this stage, in both the 1985 and 1988 decisions, when the changes involved new managerial appointments. In the earlier decisions, managements maintained close contact with their industrial bureaux through which they reported on progress in developing proposals and received instructions in return. The industrial bureaux of Audio-visual and Automotive actively participated in the process of organizational design.

By 1988, it was normal that a draft proposal for organizational change would be sent to the enterprise's management committee for discussion. This meeting often only expressed a general opinion and left the matter for further detailed discussion among middle managers. During this further discussion, the draft would be modified several times. The process could go through several cycles of development and selection. The only instance of external intervention in the specifics of organizational change at this later date was in Audio-visual where management redesigned both the structure and labour system following instructions from the industrial bureau. The industrial bureaux were, however, actively involved in monitoring the progress of organizational changes which formed part of the municipally inspired rationalization programme mentioned previously.

Authorization

The investment decisions reached in 1985 or before were all finally authorized by the relevant industrial ministry, in the four cases where the ministry had provided some of the funding, or by the Beijing Planning Commission. Two of the decisions reached in the later period, involving new product development, were funded internally by the enterprises themselves and were authorized by their directors without the need for external approval. Other investment decisions required the approval of the State Planning Commission (two cases), the Municipal Planning Commission, or the Municipal Science and Technology Commission. The large heavy industry investments were approved in October 1985, October 1987 and August 1991 respectively, but all required the approval of central government: the State Council for the chemical projects and the Metallurgical Industry Ministry for the iron and steel project (construction of a local power station).

It appears that the possibility to fund investment internally had by the late 1980s given rise to a real possibility for decentralized decision making, especially on new product development which does not necessarily have the wider community impact of production investment. The realization of economic reform in this decision area therefore appears to depend on financial autonomy. Nevertheless, the local government continued to make this autonomy conditional through the sanctions which could ensue from the failure of one of its evaluating bureaux to approve the project.

The authorization of purchasing decisions was in all cases internal to the enterprise. In general, purchasing managers could decide on the priority and quantity of supplies, but approval was sought from the enterprise director when there was a shortage of working capital (which tended to be more acute in the later period).

All of the pricing decisions completed before 1985, except for pharmaceutical products, had required the authorization of one or more external authorities. The agreement of the industrial bureau was required in each of these cases, but the price bureau was involved only in one: the pricing of an audio electrical product. The approval of national industry ministries had to be obtained for increases in the prices of colour TV sets and trucks. Authorization from the ministry and the industrial bureau was still required for colour TV set prices in the later period, while the price bureau was involved in authorization of electric switchgear price increases. However, price increases studied in the other enterprises were authorized internally by senior management without the need to secure external approval.

In 1985, the municipal industrial bureau and in five cases the labour bureau had to authorize the enterprise's recruitment proposal, before allocating to the enterprise a quota within their employment plan. New employees could then be recruited according to that plan. None of the recruitment decisions taken in 1988 and 1989 required the authorization of higher authorities. While recruitment decisions had in some enterprises initially been delegated to labour managers, following the 1988 Beijing municipal campaign of labour rationalization, authorization in this area tended to be recentralized to the vice-director level.

Compared with the later decisions, the pattern of final approval of organizational change around 1985 reflected the fact that reform in this area was in a state of transition. It was less consistent, yet still more likely to be on a collective basis. In two cases, Audio-visual and Automotive, the industrial bureau took the final decision to approve a new organizational system, though in the second case the bureau also referred the matter to the enterprise workers' congress. While directors were now formally entitled to take this kind of decision within their enterprises, in four of the six cases the final outcome was referred to the party committee for approval. By 1988 the enterprise directors were authorizing similar decisions without formal reference to the party committee, but in three cases they did pass the decision to the workers' congress for consideration. Although the congresses studied the proposals, they only raised points concerning workers' welfare and benefits and did not challenge the essentials of the proposed changes which, it may be recalled, had been initiated at the behest of the municipal government.

Delays and interruptions

The control exercised by external authorities at all stages of the investment decision process considerably delayed the progress of projects to their final authorization. Internal discussion of projects normally took a matter of weeks; the securing of external approval could literally add years. The more recent projects in Audio-visual and Pharmaceutical each took over two years to achieve final approval, while those in Automotive and Audio each took four years.[2] By contrast, the two product development projects took far less time – around six months each. The earlier investment decisions were generally speedier, taking between one year and two years seven months. One reason for this was that China was at the time enjoying an officially approved investment boom, focused particularly on the import of foreign technology which was later more tightly controlled and discouraged.

Purchasing decisions at both periods of time took from about one week to six weeks to complete. There were no instances of delays or interruptions due to intervention from either inside or outside the enterprise. The longer duration of some decision processes, such as purchasing plastics from abroad (Audio-visual) or purchasing raw copper (Heavy Electrical), was due primarily to the additional information required before a choice could be made.

The process of deciding on product prices took longer. Those finalized in 1985 took between two weeks and three months; those completed at the later date took from just under one month to four months. Each instance of delay was due to the need to await external governmental approval of prices decided within the enterprise, which tended to take at least one month in the earlier period and about two weeks later on.

Recruitment decisions at both points in time tended to take between two and three months. In the earlier period, delays were usually due to the need to await labour bureau approval of the enterprise's intentions. In the later period they were due to a variety of factors, including waiting for information from the labour bureau on available graduates and the search for suitable recruits now that management enjoyed some discretion over who it hired.

The process of deciding on organizational change took from two-and-a-half to five-and-a-half months in the earlier period and from four to seven months later on. Although the earlier decision processes were more varied and more collective in nature, they were accelerated by the active involvement of party officials who provided ideological support aimed at convincing employees that the changes were necessary. This support helped to avoid the need for pilot projects which were set up during three of the later decision processes. Delay in the 1988 decision processes was also occasioned directly and indirectly by the involvement of the municipal authorities. The enterprises were to some extent constrained by the timetable of the municipal campaign, such as the

municipal government's organization of briefing meetings, training programmes and study of 'model' factories. Moreover, since this organizational
change had been imposed on the enterprises by the municipality, managers
were reluctant to accept it and certainly did not wish to push the change too fast
for fear of creating internal demotivation and disturbance. For these reasons,
some managements themselves delayed the initiation of, and development
work on, organizational change.

Most decisions took somewhat longer to reach in 1988 than in the earlier
period, with the main exception being recruitment. Delays were occasioned
primarily by the intervention of higher authorities and/or the need to secure
their approval or support. The nature of this intervention had become more
complex with the development of a wider range of functional bureaux,
substituting these multiple 'Gods' or 'Mothers-in-Law' for the previously
single 'God' of the industrial bureau. This intervention did not bear equally on
the five decision areas – it was most evident with decisions on investment,
organizational change and, to a lesser extent, pricing. Hence purchasing
decisions took by far the least time on average (0.33 months in 1985 and 0.71
months in 1988), while organizational change took half a year on average (5.6
months in 1985 and 6.7 months in 1988) and investment an average of around
two years (1.7 years in 1985 and 2.3 years in 1988).

Sources of information

One of the conditions for realizing the intention of the economic reform to
make Chinese enterprises more responsive to market forces is that their decisions should become better informed by the market. Such information would
have to be sufficiently focused onto the sector in which the enterprise actually
and/or potentially operates and it would have to be accurate and up to date.
There are serious doubts about the capacity of bureaucratic planning authorities to provide information of this relevance and quality.

Higher authorities, however, remained the most frequent source of information for decisions which the Beijing enterprises took on purchasing and investment, and they became somewhat more important sources of information
relevant to organizational change. The reasons for the continued reliance on
bureaucratic information sources have already emerged. In the case of
purchasing, industrial ministries or bureaux held valuable information about
sources of supply for scarce materials and other inputs; they also had advance
knowledge of impending policy changes which would, for example, affect the
availability of imported supplies. In the case of investment, key information
available only from governmental sources included indications of a new
government-inspired investment initiative, the likelihood of financial provision
for investment from public sources, and official attitudes towards inward

technology transfer. Higher authorities were important sources of information for organizational change in 1988 because this was brought about and monitored as part of an officially promoted rationalization campaign.

In this case and with investment decisions also, the higher authorities insisted on their inputs being taken into account by enterprise management. Thus the feasibility studies for several of the investment decisions were influenced, or even directed, by information coming from higher bureaux because the higher authorities would only be convinced by decisions which had taken such information or views into account. The Pharmaceutical company, for instance, based its investment plans on an output level for its major product of 500 million units because this was the level the local government wished to establish even though its own forecast based on market research (the one instance where this was used) indicated a figure of 300 million, which later turned out to be much more accurate.

On the other hand, there was some shift of emphasis towards the use of data secured directly from the market in the case of purchasing and pricing decisions. These decisions on input and output transactions did appear to have become more market-sensitive, though the dual pricing and supply system imposed a serious constraint on the extent to which it was economic to obtain some materials through the highly distorted 'free' market. However, information from the market was not collected on a systematic basis through, for example, surveys based on carefully designed sampling. Reliance was placed on personal contact, via personal relations with suppliers or via product salespersons. This accords with the importance attached to personal contacts in Chinese tradition; it also accords with the considerable scepticism expressed about market research in a context where sudden changes in government policy could render market research conclusions invalid, and with the unfamiliarity of Chinese managers with the technique. Nevertheless, the information that emanated from personal relations was often insufficiently specific for managers to make decisions and it was not always collated adequately within the enterprise. This indicates that the deficiency of many Chinese managers in technical knowledge and experience to collect, collate, analyse and disseminate relevant information systematically constrains the speed with which they can become sensitive to the market.

Relations with higher authorities

We have just seen how the higher authorities continued to exert a significant influence over organizational and investment decisions by virtue of their control of relevant information. They also maintained control over enterprises through the medium of regulations. These divided into public regulations which were announced by central or local government organs through the public media and internal regulations which were diffused only through internal administrative hierarchies. Regulations also differed widely in their degree of specificity, with internal ones generally being more focused and codified.

Regulations both provided the opportunity for more autonomous managerial action and at the same time constrained such action. The principle of decentralizing decision making under the economic reform was typically announced through rather general public regulations. However, many of the more specific internal regulations then set limits to that decentralization. Examples which arose in the decisions considered in this chapter included regulations specifying the grounds justifying price increases, and the procedure for evaluating the content of investment projects. Moreover, general public regulations were increasingly specified as they passed down the administrative chain, which gave ample scope for their re-definition by local authorities. Central government, such as the State Council, often issued a policy or regulation that had a low level of codification. The specific ministry concerned and the local government then typically issued a specific and more codified set of regulations. The regulations from central government were diffused through the public media, while ministry or local government regulations were diffused within their respective administrative hierarchies. This meant that general public regulations were not sufficient to guarantee the effective granting of decentralization to Chinese enterprises.

In fact, analysis of the five decision areas indicates the limited nature of decentralization that was achieved in the second half of the 1980s. The greatest shift towards decentralization occurred in the area of personnel recruitment, by which both the initiation and final authorization of such decisions had effectively come under the control of enterprise management. Management were taking more initiative in purchasing and pricing and had secured some decentralization in the approval of price changes and self-funded product development investment. But restrictions continued to be placed on pricing and the strategically key area of investment became even more hedged in by a series of bureaucratic hurdles.

Conclusion

There were consistent differences between the processes of decision making in the five areas at both points in time. Decisions on different matters contrasted relatively consistently in their levels of complexity, duration and the involvement of agencies external to the enterprise. Decisions on investment in new production facilities were highly centralized and controlled by the planning authorities. Their process was complex and lengthy, in which many actors from both inside and outside the enterprise were involved. At the other extreme, decisions on purchasing were taken entirely within the enterprise; the process was speedy and simple. Such decisions were made on the basis of the judgement of the specialists involved rather than in terms of impinging political or social interests.

Lu (1991) concludes that there were similarities between the different decision processes identified in his research and those found by investigators in other countries, particularly Hickson and colleagues (1986). This supports the view that the decision process is contingent to the issue under decision, even more than to the cultural or socio-political context. As Hickson et al. argue, 'the matter for decision matters most' (1986: 247).

The issue-contingent view would appear to gain further support from the similarities between the investment decision process evident in China and the conclusion drawn from various Western (chiefly American and British) studies that capital investment decisions are centralized, draw in numerous interests, and are consequently complex and lengthy (Lu and Heard 1995). Investment decision making appears to follow a similar process, despite the distinctiveness of the institutional contexts in which it is located. The format and procedures prescribed for investment decisions in China accorded with the principles of rational decision making, as they tend to do elsewhere. Investment represents the most important allocation of scarce economic resources in societies and therefore appeals to an inherent logic of rationality in terms of ensuring the most socially productive use of such resources.

It would be misleading, however, either to concentrate overmuch on the formal aspects of the decision process or indeed to overlook the features which distinguish the process in China from that in, say, the Anglo-Saxon countries. Chief among the differences is the involvement of public agencies in decisions which would normally be taken autonomously by company managers in Western countries, not just investment decisions but also those on product pricing and to some extent on organizational change. The active participation of government officials at one or more stages in the process of such decisions is also remarkable. In the case of investment decisions, the sequential round of securing approvals contrasted markedly with the process in equivalent British cases as did the personalized basis of connections with higher officials on which the speed and outcome of the approval process could depend.

The system of industrial governance in China is highly relevant to an explanation of such differences. First, China has an as yet ill-formed market economy in which prices do not necessarily provide a good guide to economic value. This makes it extremely difficult to use capital appraisal techniques to focus on criteria relating to the enterprise's own projected economic performance rather than those advanced by various external parties. The imperfections in input and output markets, and the limited scale of the labour market also sustain the dependencies of enterprises on government agencies for information and allocation. Secondly, China claims to be a socialist market economy which means, for state-owned enterprises at least, that ownership interests have a legitimacy to impose social as well as economic criteria onto the decision making process.

That very important part of the institutional context in China consisting of government agencies therefore impinges on the industrial decision making process both through the material dependencies enterprises continue to have on it and through the criteria of legitimacy that it imposes on them. Nevertheless, managers have to get decisions made that enable them to achieve their economic targets and here they resort to traditional modes of action, especially the use of informal networks of mutual assistance and favours, in the face of inadequacies both in the market and administrative governance of transactions (Boisot and Child 1988). In other words, managers' ways of making out within a problematic system of industrial governance are informed by another facet of the institutional context, namely the culturally embedded means for securing support and ensuring against adversity.

The previous chapter concluded that in terms of authorization levels, the managers of Chinese state enterprises had secured some additional autonomy to make investment, personnel and marketing decisions, but that this was a precarious autonomy. The present chapter's examination of the decision process qualifies this conclusion even more. It shows how enterprise managers still need either to secure the approval of higher authorities for their draft proposals, as in the case of production investment, or to second guess the reaction of interested bureaux which could create difficulties if unfavourable, as in the case of many pricing decisions. It is not simply the formal part played by government agencies in authorizing decisions that matters but the role they play at other stages of the process either as active participants or as players in the minds of the managers concerned.

The changes, then, which could be observed between 1985 and 1988/89 in the process of decision making were marginal ones. There were some changes in managerial behaviour in that managers were starting to take the initiative over seeking information and opportunities both within the arenas of the planning system and the market. This greater initiative was undoubtedly encouraged by the introduction of the contract responsibility system. It was also apparent that in areas of operational decision making, such as purchasing and labour recruitment, task requirements assumed more importance as initial stimuli and, where approval was decentralized to enterprises, managers set about acquiring more market information. However, the overall pattern of decision processes evident for the five areas investigated remained much the same.

Although under the director responsibility system authority within the enterprise was shifting during this period from the party to management, the continuing influence of external governmental agencies led to an emphasis on political expertise among managers rather than the professional expertise typically brought forth by industrialization in developed societies. The directors in all six Beijing enterprises had a strong political background and their technical knowledge was limited to production and engineering. The continued institutional significance of government authorities in the decision making system caused political criteria for organizational decisions and managerial career advancement to be retained despite the economic criteria embodied in management responsibility contracts.

Appendix 6.1 Categories of decision investigated by Lu (1991) and Lu and Heard (1995)

Lu (1991)

1. Purchasing inputs   e.g. purchasing steel sheets
2. Product pricing   e.g. increasing the price of a radio
3. Labour recruitment   e.g. recruiting university graduates
4. Organizational change   e.g. change from departmental to product group structure, involving the demise of seven departments
5. Investment   e.g. building of a new production line

Lu and Heard (1995) – Investment Decisions

	Decision		*Capital expenditure*
A.	Sino-oil	Ethylene plant renewal & expansion	2,800m Yuan
B.	Sino-chem	Caprolactam plant renewal & expansion	2,200m Yuan
C.	Sino-metal	Construction of a power station	20m Yuan

Input and output transactions

This chapter examines the ways in which Chinese enterprises secure their inputs and distribute their outputs. In Western terminology, these are the domains of purchasing and marketing, concepts which imply that enterprise managers engage actively in market transactions. Since the situation in China still involves some state enterprises in a mixture of market transacting and administered allocations, it is more appropriate to refer to input–output transactions rather than to imply *a priori* that these are accomplished entirely through the market.

The purchasing of inputs for production and the disposal of finished products are relatively routine, repetitive activities. They involve commodities which are often the easiest economic goods to transact through markets because of their standardization and physical mobility which are high compared with, for instance, land and labour. Inputs of materials and components are also rather specific to the production requirements of each enterprise, which will be known in detail to that enterprise's management and specialists rather than to higher administrative authorities. Similarly, managers are usually in the best position to appreciate the specific requirements of potential customers and how production can be designed and planned to meet these.

For these reasons, the Chinese authorities envisaged that decentralization in these areas would come at an early stage in the economic reform process. However, the concept of regulated markets allowed for the continued direct intervention of administrative bureaucracies in transactions on the grounds of strategic priority or the nation's economic health (as with directing scarce materials to 'key' industries or imposing import controls). Pricing is another area which government has been reluctant to evacuate in terms both of maintaining subsidies for social or strategic reasons and of controlling inflation, as in the two years following the overheating of the economy in Summer 1988.

Much of the bureaucratic structure of transactional control has in fact remained in place. The production of strategic goods is still partly governed by centrally planned quotas. Central and local government agencies retain some control over the distribution and pricing of key raw materials and they continue to play a role in regulating other input transactions. There has, indeed, been substantial resistance by government officials to the granting of transactional autonomy to the enterprises within their purview, even where this was sanctioned by the reform (Child and Lu 1990). All in all, administrative authorities remain active in the governance of Chinese economic transactions (cf. Blecher 1989).

After 1984, so-called 'dual track' pricing became widespread. Under this system, state-owned enterprises sold the goods produced under their state-allocated quota at a price also determined by the government. They were permitted to sell outputs above the quota level at higher prices, which in some cases were allowed to float within ranges that had been established in the early 1980s and in other cases corresponded to a true free-market level. Similarly, enterprises could purchase inputs in the plan at administered prices and access other sources at higher prices. Dual pricing took state enterprises partly into the market and so moved them towards conditions for encouraging greater efficiency and accountability. More recently, with inflation under control by 1990, the authorities have raised their administered prices for steel, pig iron, coal, rail and inland water transport, and unified dual prices for all cement production and a large proportion of transactions in metals. On the consumer side, prices of grain and cooking oil were raised sharply in May 1991 and subsidies were also cut on cotton, sugar, salt, public transport and other goods and services. By the end of 1991 only about half a dozen consumer products remained subject to state rationing (Long 1992). Nevertheless, the administrative machinery to control prices has been left in place in case there is a return of severe inflation.

In addition, the close alignment between politics and economics in China retains a role for socio-political criteria in economic transactions, and for the agencies that express such criteria. This means, as Walder (1989) points out, that enterprise managers cannot take transactional decisions guided purely by considerations of economic rationality. They have to take into account criteria of political and social acceptability which can inhibit their engagement in market transacting. They may be obliged, for example, to continue producing goods in-house in order to preserve enterprise employment even though the products could be secured with cost, quality or design advantages from an outside supplier. Local government agencies may exert pressure for purchasing and selling transactions to be directed to local firms, even when recourse to a wider market would again be to the economic advantage of the firm. Moreover, the conditions of shortage and the operation of a dual administered/market pricing system which have characterized China's transition from a centrally planned economy, mean that firms remain heavily dependent upon a hierarchical governance of transactions for materials supplies, with the added attraction of purchasing these at below market prices. The opportunities for arbitrage between the two price levels have not been lost upon higher government agencies which control or have access to supply channels. Enterprise managers have in many instances had to accept these practices and engage in informal private deals with officials both because this was sometimes the only basis for securing supplies and because their own re-appointment and career prospects depend heavily upon the sponsorship of such officials.

The ability of firms to enter into open-market transactions is also constrained by imperfections which are inherited from the pre-reform socialist economy and accentuated by China's relatively underdeveloped infrastructure. Solinger (1989) identifies three of these: limited market information, shortage, and a low level of product standardization. Market information is limited both by an underdeveloped information infrastructure and by its poor dissemination on the part of badly co-ordinated industrial and regional agencies of state administration. This sets obvious bounds to the choice of transactional partners and increases the risk of market transacting. Shortage, Kornai (1980) explains, has been endemic to socialist planned economies because of the forcing of growth and the inadequacies of planning itself. It increases the scope for opportunistic behaviour by market partners, such as reneging on contracts, and increases the risk of seeking supplies from the market. Shortage has also led to the tolerance of non-standardization of design and quality in a 'seller's market' and in China's case this has been accentuated by the lack of economic co-ordination. Firms have therefore found it difficult to obtain goods to the necessary standard by purchasing on the open market.

Market transacting in the 'pure' form of classical economics not only requires that full information is available about the choice of goods, their conditions of supply and their prices, but also that deals are made impersonally and impartially according to the dictates of economic rationality. This means that the high value granted in Chinese culture to trust-based relationships and to grounding economic exchange on the mutual confidence established through an often lengthy process of personal socializing is another potential inhibition to open-market transacting (cf. Boisot and Child 1988; Lockett 1988). Where bureaucratic co-ordination is rolled back to leave a still underdeveloped and imperfect market system, the basing of transactions upon such relationships could be a functional response to the risks of opportunism, but which itself paradoxically contributes to the maintenance of market imperfection.

Nee (1992) describes the range of institutionalized transactional arrangements in which firms engage in the China of the early 1990s, when analyzing how the range of industrial property rights and transaction governance structures combine to identify three types of firm. He calls these respectively 'non-marketized firms', 'marketized firms' and 'private firms'. Non-marketized firms 'depend on vertical ties to [state and municipal] redistributive agencies from which they receive resource transfers . . . Likewise, their output is directed to state and municipal agencies that redistribute it under the central plan' (p. 11). By contrast, the marketized firm is seen to operate primarily through market transactions which local government assists by providing valuable networks for access to supplies, capital and labour. Local governments, however, have less capacity to support unprofitable firms than do the central authorities. Private firms enjoy more formal autonomy from state intervention, but at the same time they have to rely upon performance in the market for their survival.

Present-day China therefore appears to be a context in which, despite the market orientation of the economic reform, the opportunities for market transacting are bounded by a combination of administrative, political, infrastructural and cultural constraints. The question arises as to how far in this mixed and complex situation firms exhibit transactional behaviour conforming to the predictions of economic analysis which assume the dominance of efficiency goals in a market system. An examination of transacting by Chinese firms should permit some commentary on the applicability to this context of explanations which have been derived from Western capitalism.

The chapter proceeds as follows. It first outlines the main categories of product identified in China and the channels through which they are normally distributed to and from enterprises. Evidence is then presented from case studies in state-owned enterprises on their management of input transactions. Taken together, this information helps to identify factors which distinguish between the use of different input and output transacting modes in Chinese industry.

Main product categories and their transaction channels

There are officially two categories of product in China, the planned product (*jihua nei chanpin*) and products outside the plan (*jihua wai chanpin*). The 'planned quota' (*jihua zhibiao*) is normally expressed in terms of a quantity of units of a specified product. The annual output of a planned product required from an enterprise is indicated by a plan quota which is issued by the planning authorities, including central or local planning commissions, central industrial ministries, and local industrial bureaux. These authorities also arrange transactions between enterprises. They order a certain amount of planned products from one enterprise, then allocate them to another enterprise. Both the supplier and recipient enterprises have no choice but to follow the instructions of the planning authorities. These transactions are valued in monetary terms, but at a level set by the planning bodies not by the market.

Enterprise managers have the authority to determine production levels, and sometimes prices and customer priority, for products outside the plan. This type of transaction becomes a bilateral exchange between supplier/producer and buyer/customer. The level of sales and price depends on the outcome of negotiation between the two partners. These sales are called 'self-determined sales' (*zixiao*). Previously the main products falling into this category were daily commodities and grocery products. After 1985, state-owned enterprises were delegated some autonomy to sell any production which exceeded the planned target. Such sales are also called 'self-determined sales', though the product (called 'the over-plan product') is controlled by the planning authorities. The prices of these products, choice of customers and distribution outlets remained subject to governmental regulations during the 1980s (Lu 1991: chapter 7).

The planned output quotas are matched by planned inputs allocated by the planning authorities. Products outside the plan do not enjoy an allocation of planned inputs in this way. Firms have to secure the inputs required for their production, such as raw materials, principally through market transactions involving direct purchases from suppliers. Those categories of input subject to planning, such as steel and non-ferrous metals, are often in short supply. It has been extremely difficult to purchase a planned product without the benefit of a planned quota because suppliers are required to fulfil the state plan first and only then permitted to sell any production exceeding the planned level. Purchasers have had to pay a much higher price for such supplies than those in the plan.

Within this system there are a number of different ways in which materials and products can be transacted. These are indicated by two sources which refer respectively to output and input transacting. The first is a set of investigations which the author and Chinese MBA students carried out in 1990 on the distribution channels and market conditions for five categories of product, which included industrial materials, domestic equipment and consumer products. The second source is a study which another group of MBA students conducted in 1988 on the input transactions of eleven state-owned enterprises located in Beijing. (The eleven enterprises are listed in Appendix 7.1 and they include the six core firms mentioned in previous chapters.)

These studies point to differences between the transaction channels characteristically used for industrial materials, for branded consumer goods, and for non-branded food products. They indicate the types of product transaction which were administered by governmental agencies, while at the same time showing how a considerable diversity of items are no longer transacted according to plan quotas and allocations. We examine the range of output distribution channels first and then turn to input transactions.

Output transactions

Different distribution channels and transacting modes are used for industrial materials, branded goods and non-branded consumables.

Industrial materials Chemicals provide an example of this category. Before 1980 only state-owned distribution agencies were allowed to conduct wholesale and retail transactions in chemicals. Ten years later, five other distribution channels had developed. The state-owned channel remained the single most important one and operated through five distribution enterprises: 1. *The China National Chemical Industry Supply and Marketing Corporation.* This has the duty to supply chemicals to other ministries and provinces according to state mandatory plans as well as to its own affiliated enterprises. It operates through eight regional branches which then sub-divide into provincial (municipal or regional) and prefectural (county) chemical industry supply and marketing companies. As well as implementing the state's allocation plans, the regional branches also undertake their own purchasing and selling operations. 2. *The China National Chemical and Light Industry Corporation.* This is a company affiliated to the Ministry of Materials, specializing in chemical materials listed in the state's mandatory plans and required by enterprises supplied under the Ministry's auspices. 3. *The China National Pharmaceutical Corporation.* The CNPC and its affiliated companies are organized into three tiers. There are six first-tier purchase and supply stations which come directly under the national CNPC and which are located in Beijing, Tianjin, Shanghai, Shenyang, Guangzhou and Chengdu. They purchase local pharmaceutical products and receive imported commodities. They allocate these goods to second-tier units over the whole of China as well as to some nearby third-tier units. They supply directly to some organizations such as large hospitals and a few large or specialist retail stores. They also hold a stock of medicines for unusual contingencies.

There are about 200 second-tier units which come directly under provincial pharmaceutical corporations. These replenish stocks from first-tier units and purchase local products. They allocate and transfer medicines to third-tier units and nearby retail stores. Areas are allocated to the second-tier units according to available physical distribution routes and not necessarily according to administrative boundaries. There are also some wholesale enterprises belonging to the pharmaceutical corporations of large municipalities which perform similar functions to the second-tier units.

Third-tier units come directly under prefecture pharmaceutical companies and are located in county towns. They acquire stocks from the second-tier units, purchase local products, and serve as wholesalers to supply and marketing co-operatives, retail shops, dispensaries and so forth. In larger cities, third-tier units take the form of wholesale stores and wholesale and retail shops. 4. *The China National Hardware Communication, Electrical Appliance and Chemicals Corporation.* Up to 1983, this corporation and its affiliates were also organized in three tiers as distribution channels for paints, coatings and similar chemicals. Since then, the central authorities have taken measures to decentralize transactions of such products. The six first-tier purchase and supply units were transferred to the cities and provinces where they were located and units at all levels were encouraged to organize trans-regional commodity supplies and to negotiate discount rates themselves. The decentralization has stimulated economic development and at the same time reduced the role of state-controlled distribution channels. For example, in Tianjin by the end of 1988, state-owned commercial chemical organizations accounted for only 5 per cent of the total number of commercial wholesalers and retailers. Collective organizations made up 12 per cent of the total and individually owned organizations 83 per cent. The share of state commercial organizations in turnover dropped from 71.6 per cent in 1978 to 48.6 percent in 1988; that of collectives rose from 28.4 per cent to 34 per cent and the share of individually owned organizations rose from zero to 17.4 per cent.

5. *The China National Agricultural Means of Production Corporation.* The main functions of this corporation are to receive agricultural materials, both produced in China and imported, and to allocate and transport them between provinces according to the overall state plan. It is also organized in three tiers, corresponding to the national, provincial and prefectural levels.

In addition to these state distribution companies, which are largely specialized according to different categories of chemicals, there are five other distribution channels for chemical products:

a supply and sales organizations belonging to the central government departments which are in charge of given industries;

b direct sales by chemicals producers: enterprises are allowed to sell all or part of their products directly to customers or industrial users;

c a variety of trading companies, set up jointly or solely by state or collectively owned distribution organizations, central or local government departments, or producer enterprises. These companies operate flexibly and actively, and have become a significant force in the industry;

d foreign trade firms: these, together with state-owned foreign trade corporations, are permitted to sell imported goods directly on the Chinese market at designated locations. In practice they distribute imports to all parts of China through different distribution channels;

e countless individual traders: these carry out transactions as retailers and there are also some individually owned wholesalers. Many are short of capital and often use their personal connections fraudulently to purchase deficient materials and resell them for a high profit.

Chemicals illustrate how in China industrial raw materials have in the past been allocated and distributed through state organizations, the infrastructure of which continues to play a major role. However, there has been a progressive decentralization to the local (provincial) level and a growth in transactions initiated by producers and trading companies which are not subject to direct administrative regulation and which can therefore be more responsive to market forces.

Branded goods Information was collected on the distribution of several types of branded goods: domestic gas water heaters, food, alcoholic spirits, bottled mineral water, and household chemicals. Chinese dwellings, even apartments in the cities, do not normally have a piped hot-water supply. Given the significant improvement of real incomes, the demand for domestic gas hot-water heaters has therefore been rising rapidly since they started to become available in significant numbers in 1983.

Because of their ties to a specific energy source and the issue of safety, the distribution of gas water heaters contrasts with the other branded goods just mentioned. There are three main distribution channels for the water heaters, namely, gas companies, wholesalers/retailers and direct purchase from the producing firm. According to central and local government regulations, only the gas companies or their authorized agencies are officially responsible for quality inspection, installation and control of the use of gas water heaters. To facilitate their control, the gas companies in some large cities have named 'designated' or 'recommended' heaters. Obtaining this product approval is an effective way for producers to access the market through the gas companies, especially in the large cities like Beijing, Shanghai and Tianjin where strict control is exercised. Wholesalers and retailers comprise another important distribution channel. The latter include larger department stores, hardware shops and various specialized gas appliance dealers. Despite the claim by most gas companies that they have the sole authorization for selling and installing gas water heaters, a large number of sets are sold through wholesalers and retailers, with the notable exception of Tianjin. Thirdly, many large employers purchase gas water heaters in batches directly from manufacturers as a form of welfare complementary to their provision of subsidized housing. Some of these employers, such as coal mines and oil fields, do not have to rely on gas companies for gas supply and are therefore free from their control.

Two main distribution channels are used by enterprises producing branded food (such as confectionery and soft drinks) and household chemical products (such as cosmetics, toothpaste and toiletries). The first is through state-owned merchandise companies and the second is through direct sales by manufacturers.

The state-owned channels comprise provincial and municipal companies for non-staple food, cigarettes, drinks and general merchandise, their subsidiaries and retail stores. For example, the state distribution system for mineral water in Beijing comprises the Beijing Sugar, Cigarette and Liquor Company as the first-stage wholesaler, then non-staple food companies in each city district as second-stage wholesalers, and then the retailers. This is the traditional channel which before the reform had a virtual monopsony position, purchasing almost

100 per cent of relevant merchandise from local manufacturers. The former system of level-by-level distribution has now become fractured, with distributors at different levels buying directly from manufacturers. Mandatory distribution relations have been replaced by sell-and-buy transactions by virtue of supply and purchase contracts. State-run wholesalers find themselves experiencing fierce competition. For example, the General Merchandise Distribution Stations of Guangzhou and Shanghai, two of the four 'level one' municipal wholesale stations, were by 1990 transacting only about 40 per cent of the total local sales volume of household manufactured goods. In Guangdong Province, by the same date, only 25 per cent of confectionery and biscuits, and 20 per cent of beverages, were distributed through state commercial channels. The rest was being distributed primarily by manufacturers themselves. Nevertheless, manufacturers do not necessarily seek to avoid state distributors entirely. For they are often prepared to take some of a manufacturer's stock when trade is slack and they also tend to provide a quick return of working capital. Moreover, the distinction between wholesaler and retailer is breaking down: some wholesalers have established retailing outlets while some retailers (such as department stores) engage in wholesaling.

There are today no restrictions on the direct marketing within China of branded consumer goods by manufacturers themselves, so long as they secure a licence from the relevant local authority. They can choose which goods are to be sold to which areas, what promotion to undertake and how payment is to be rendered. Soft drinks manufacturers, for example, can sell directly to hotels. However, state-owned enterprises still face restrictions on export marketing. For many years they had to export through specialized government export-trading companies. Under regulations issued by the State Council on 24 July 1992, state enterprises can now choose any foreign trade organization in China to import and export for them and they have the right to participate directly in negotiations with foreign businesses. By contrast, Sino-foreign joint ventures can export directly without having to go through a foreign trade organization.

Shaw and Woetzel (1992) comment on the new opportunities for sales and distribution that are opening up in China, allowing the state-controlled wholesaling system to be by-passed. They cite the case of electronic goods for which both joint ventures and Chinese enterprises can now establish proprietary sales and distribution channels that allow direct access to customers. The contrast they draw between the traditional and newer additional channels of domestic distribution is shown in figure 7.1.

There are six main channels for the direct sales of branded goods to the Chinese market:

1 *sales agents*: these include state wholesalers, friendship companies, large

Traditional channel

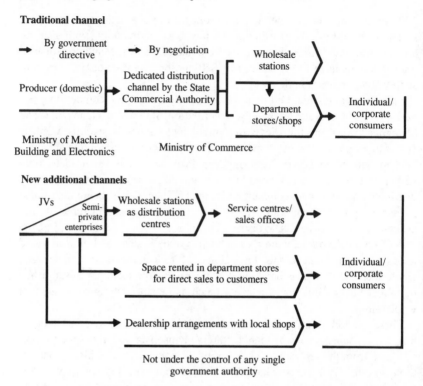

Figure 7.1 Domestic distribution channels for electronic goods in China.
Source: adapted from Shaw and Woetzel (1992): exhibit 12

hotels, stores and (sometimes) privately-owned shops. This channel is mainly used by food and beverage manufacturers such as Coca Cola and Pepsi Cola, the Far East Food Company of Shenzhen, Procter and Gamble of Guangzhou, and the Haikou Canned Food Company marketing natural coconut juice.

2 *regular major customers*: most significant manufacturers have established stable supply relations with some major customers such as department stores and factories (supplying these, for instance, with drinks during the summer).

3 *contractual sales*: this mode is popular among smaller enterprises which do not have the capacity to engage in market investigation and promotion. In Xiamen, for example, all of the good quality milk candy produced by the Sino-Singapore Nansheng Candy Factory is contracted to be sold to the Chinese partner's parent enterprise.

4 *spot contracts*: this type of contract is usually negotiated and signed at exhibitions organized by local government commercial bureaux.

5 *joint ownership of manufacturing and distribution organizations*: this is found among state-owned enterprises such as Shanghai Toothpaste and

Shanghai Household Chemicals.

6 *non-regular customers*: manufacturers also sell on an occasional basis to a
   range of wholesalers, retailers and (sometimes) end-users, mainly in order
   to secure flexibility in response to changing market conditions.

Comparisons between state-owned enterprises and joint ventures in the field
of branded consumer goods indicate that the former tend to make use of established state commercial channels, whereas joint ventures prefer to establish
their own sales forces and distribution channels. The dominant consideration in
the minds of state enterprise managements appears to be the desire to conserve
their limited promotion budgets and speed up the circulation of working capital. By contrast, the dominant consideration for joint venture managers appears
to be the preservation of their products' reputation against forgery or adulter-
ation and to be able to control their own product promotion directly.[1]

Non-branded consumer goods The distribution of vegetables and milk
provides two major examples within this category.

Before the economic reforms, the government controlled the production,
distribution and pricing of agricultural commodities, including vegetables.
Agricultural production was organized collectively and the government determined crop patterns by setting quotas for compulsory delivery to the State
Marketing Network. The aim was one of local self-sufficiency in grain and
vegetable production. Under the reform, the authorities have sought to end
the monopoly of the State Marketing Network and to encourage the diversification of distribution channels for vegetables. Private markets consisting of
small traders have been permitted to prosper. In addition to the growth of
such markets, there has been a large increase in the volume of direct sales
from peasants to urban residents. Privately-owned retail outlets have also
grown rapidly in number, some of them being former state-owned stores
which have been leased out to individuals on the basis of competitive bids.
Some large stores have been transformed into collective ownership or into co-
operatives. The larger stores remaining in state ownership have, nevertheless,
been granted financial and operational autonomy (Coady, Qiao and Hussain
1990).[2]

The distribution of milk is handled through two main channels. The first is
the State Farm Administration which normally supplies retail outlets in the
cities. These are today often private shops which sell fresh milk in plastic bags.
Shops selling soft drinks, and some catering outlets, also offer hot milk in the
cold seasons. The second channel consists of milk distribution depots run by
dairy companies which deliver fresh milk to subscribers.

While both vegetables and milk are today sold onto a competitive market in
China, as basic agricultural products they remain subject to national governmental regulations administered by state agencies which are still active. In par-

ticular, government subsidies and price controls have had a considerable effect on the production and consumption of milk, grain and vegetable cooking oil. The trend over the past few years has been for these subsidies to be reduced and for prices to be raised.

Input transactions

By 1988, planned quotas were only being applied to some 60 categories of goods, particularly basic raw materials such as steel and products considered to be of strategic importance like trucks. All of the eleven Beijing enterprises investigated were at that time securing their inputs of materials and components from several types of source. None relied entirely upon supplies from central or local government agencies, even of raw materials which were invariably the category of inputs in shortest supply on the market. Only five still had some of their input and output transactions organized on an official centrally planned quota basis: the audio-visual, automotive, boiler, heavy electrical and radiology machinery producers. The proportion of their inputs coming under a planned quota had diminished since 1985 – in the case of the two firms with the highest percentages, these had fallen from 80 per cent to 60 per cent (audio-visual) and from 75 per cent to 67 per cent (automotive). Planned quota supplies carry the disadvantage of a concomitant administered maximum price that can be charged for outputs in the plan, and this can substantially deflate unit profitability, especially for goods normally in high demand such as colour TV sets and trucks.

Although the reliance of firms on the central planning system for their inputs had declined by 1988, most remained heavily dependent on central or local governmental administrative agencies as suppliers or regulators of supply. They used the following six sources, the first five of which involved elements of co-ordination by higher administrative authorities:

1 Central government supply, through the State Material Supply Bureau or ministries such as the Ministry of Machine Building and Electronics. This source is supposed to provide a guaranteed supply for planned quota inputs and for other specified categories of production such as that destined for export. In trade fairs, which are usually organized twice a year, buyers transacted with sellers on the basis of officially stamped invoices. In practice, supplies available via the trade fairs did not always satisfy the quantities specified by quotas.

2 Supplies authorized by local authorities, such as the Beijing Planning Commission and the Beijing industrial bureaux which held supervisory authority over enterprises. These supplies were normally obtained through the Beijing Trade Centre, a state distributor. Local authorities also possessed powers to order supplies directly from firms, and some of these products

were used in exchange for supplies obtained from other local authorities.

3 Materials from other enterprises with which the firm enjoyed long-standing relationships and which formed a mutual-help club for dealing with shortages as well as for taking unwanted materials off each other's hands. Such exchanges were normally conducted under the supervision of the relevant local industrial bureau.

One method was for firms to participate in exchange meetings organized regularly (often weekly) by the bureau – so-called 'Material Trade-off Exchange Meetings' (*wuzi pingheng jiaoli hui*). This arrangement was a carry-over from the regular pre-reform co-ordinating meetings held between the bureau's subordinate factories. Another approach was to establish long-term transactional relations, often through the establishment of a consortium, which were closely supervised by the industrial bureau.

4 Suppliers of special materials such as silver who were regulated by the central government.

5 Imported raw materials. When these were needed on a regular basis and in large quantities, they were supplied by a central government foreign trade company; otherwise by a local import/export company.

6 Unregulated open market transactions.

Prices for all the categories of supply were administratively controlled except nos. 3 and 6, though (as noted below) firms could sometimes secure supplies at above administered prices from government sources through informal connections. They were lowest for material controlled by the central government – categories 1, 4 and 5. Prices charged by the local authority (category 2) tended to be about 10 per cent higher than in category 1. The prices of materials secured from the open market or bought from another enterprise ranged from between 40 per cent to 280 per cent (the latter being for some categories of steel) above the centrally administered price. This differential was tending to widen over time as shortages became more acute. There was a strong incentive therefore to obtain highly-priced materials from bureaucratically organized sources if a below-market price could be negotiated.

The channels for inputs and outputs suggest that the types of transaction in which Chinese state enterprises engage vary according to (1) the extent to which they are co-ordinated administratively rather than through markets and (2), when administered, whether this is by central or local government. Of the input sources just identified, numbers 1,2, 4 and 5 are administratively co-ordinated; number 3 is partly so, while number 6 involves market transactions. Central government agencies regulate transactions in the case of sources 1, 4 and 5, and local authorities regulate transactions from source 2 and sometimes 5.

Nee's (1992) classification of Chinese firms (state, collective and private) incorporates the same dimensions, but in the light of our information this understates the variety of transactional types which can be found among state enter-

Table 7.1. *Relative importance of input sources for six Beijing enterprises*

		Enterprise				
Source of inputs	Audio	Audio-visual	Auto-motive	Heavy electrical	Pharma-ceutical	Switch-gear
1. Central government	1	5	5	4	1	3
2. Local government	4	4	4	4	2	1
3. Other firms	4	3	4	3	3	3
4. Central government (special materials)	3	2	2	2	2	3
5. Regulated imports	2	2	1	3	2	2
6. Open market	2	1	1	1	5	2

Note:
Scoring: 5=dominant source (60 per cent+ of all inputs)
    4=major source, but under 50 per cent of total
    3=regular source, but not major
    2=minor source
    1=little (under 5 per cent of total) or none
Source: interviews with purchasing and other managers.

prises. He appears to assume that all state-owned enterprises rely primarily upon state-administered input–output transactions, and in so doing he understates the extent to which they engage in market exchange.

For instance, the relative importance of different input sources varied quite considerably among the six Beijing enterprises on which we have been focusing. Not only did some enterprises transact through the market but, on the other hand, even firms not entitled to planned supplies might secure these through the special relationships they had developed with administrative bodies. Table 7.1 provides an overall summary of the variation between the enterprises with reference to the six sources of inputs mentioned above.

The main channels of inputs for the audio-visual and automotive enterprises were their central ministries and to a lesser extent the local authority. They also traded some of their outputs directly with other firms in exchange for shortage raw materials or components. The audio-visual firm, for example, sold some colour TV sets to a TV tube firm in order to obtain its quota of tubes. The automotive enterprise sold between 15 per cent and 20 per cent of its annual output to a local authority distributor in order to secure supplies of steel from that local authority. The heavy electrical enterprise relied for about 40 per cent each of its supplies on its ministry and local authority. It enjoyed influence with them because it was one of the ministry's key transformer production bases and the only large transformer producer in Beijing.

The audio and switchgear firms did not possess the right to any planned quota inputs. In practice, however, they were able to secure some such supplies of steel and non-ferrous metals, albeit at prices above the administered level, through their relationships with the local industrial bureau and supplying companies respectively.

By contrast, the pharmaceutical enterprise required local agricultural inputs rather than any strategic raw materials, and it consequently engaged heavily in open-market transactions. It relied almost exclusively on the open market for the purchase of material such as royal jelly and raw honey from farms and bee product companies. Just 1 per cent of its supplies came from central authorities and little more through its local industrial bureau. Another 'food' producer – the winery which is one of the additional firms listed in Appendix 7.1 – also had little dependence on administered sources of supply. It secured its inputs of grapes and sugar through direct contracting with major suppliers and only supplemented these when necessary by purchasing from markets arranged annually by the local government. These two firms were exceptional in the extent of their market transacting. Most of the open-market transactions on the part of these and other firms were, nevertheless, conducted with long-established suppliers to whom they related on a basis of familiarity and trust.

The continued reliance of most firms on bureaucratically co-ordinated input sources appeared due to two main factors. The first was the strategic status of their input mix and their products. The second was a more general condition in 1988, namely the problems of shortage and inflation which became chronic in that boom year and which, at the time of writing (1993), are again recurring.

In China, basic raw materials such as oils, sheet steel, chemicals and timber are primarily supplied through central government channels and the state will usually have invested heavily in their extraction and processing. The state also tends to control the supplies of components which have to be imported in significant quantities, such as colour TV tubes until recently. Inputs of this kind are strategic for the state either as basic national (and often investment-hungry) resources or as drains upon hard currency reserves. To the extent that an enterprise such as the heavy electrical firm has a major requirement for such inputs, it will remain engaged in the system of bureaucratic transacting.

On the side of finished products, 'strategic' is defined by the authorities with reference to several criteria which extend to social as well as economic-cum-technological considerations. Among the five firms which were still subject to centrally planned quotas, these criteria referred to a product's key role in economic development (as with trucks, boilers and heavy electrical equipment), its export potential (as with colour TVs), its import incidence (as with TV tubes), its role in health and welfare programmes (as with medical radiology products), and its social sensitivity (as with the price of a much sought-after consumer durable such as colour TV sets). Consequently, the enterprises manufacturing these products continued to have a portion of their inputs and outputs governed directly by state bureaucratic co-ordination.

By contrast, transactions in product areas such as consumer pharmaceuticals and wine were left largely to market co-ordination. Neither their outputs nor their inputs are considered to be strategic in nature. Product prices were moderated by high levels of competition and producers purchased only a small proportion of their inputs from the state, if any.

In short, one factor determining the extent of bureaucratic governance over input transactions in China is the degree to which inputs and the production in which they are used are regarded as nationally strategic.

Secondly, supply shortages presented Chinese managements with a major headache in 1987–8 and manifested a serious market failure. Their incidence is indicated by the fact that while industrial growth in 1988 reached 20.7 per cent, total energy production rose by only 4.2 per cent, that of coal by 4.5 per cent and steel by 5.2. per cent (State Statistical Bureau 1989). The internal transportation infrastructure was also a bottleneck in the conveyance of supplies to where they were required. Official figures show an increase of only 5.1 per cent in the weight of cargo/km carried during 1988 despite the high level of general economic activity. Shortages were made worse by high levels of stockholding which were encouraged by the uncertainty of supplies and by the negative cost of tied-up capital when the inflation rate considerably exceeded the interest rate.

Conditions of chronic shortage and high inflation presented suppliers with many openings for opportunistic behaviour in the marketplace, through reneging on contracts or refusing to give assurances in respect of price, delivery and specification. Within China's underdeveloped legal system, it is difficult to enforce commercial contracts, especially with suppliers located in another administrative region. Bureaucratic agencies offered some prospect of further supplies either as direct sources or as organs which could bring some pressure to bear on behalf of the firms within their purview, thus in both ways reducing the risks of opportunism. Most of the firms were in 1988 therefore endeavouring to raise the proportion of their supplies obtained from bureaucratically administered sources.

Moreover, while all the firms claimed to be collecting more information on their own account than in 1985, they continued to rely mainly upon higher government authorities for relevant supply market information. This was even evident for a firm like the pharmaceutical enterprise which engaged heavily in open-market transactions. Its purchasing manager gave as the reason the less bounded nature of the information available to higher authorities:

The bureau understands more than we do. We have contact with only a small number of companies and farms. The bureau has a wider range of contacts because it used to act as the distributor of supplies between pharmaceutical factories before the economic reform . . . It also has a better idea of trends: what is going to come into short supply, where controls will be relaxed and so forth.

Many of the other firms set great store by information from central planning agencies, ministries and foreign trade companies. Such governmental agencies could give them an understanding of the general economic situation and a preview of likely new regulations having a bearing on input availabilities and prices. So while the shortage of many supplies led purchasing managers to undertake a more active search than three years earlier, both among government agencies and in the market, they continued to rely primarily upon the bureaucratic hierarchy for relevant information.

Despite the continued high involvement of bureaucratic agencies in input transacting, areas of more open-market transacting had also become established. In addition to agricultural inputs, many components, containers and consumable supplies were available without administrative restriction from a range of suppliers. The food firms obtained their supplies primarily from contracting directly with local farmers and processors. Other firms tended to use trade fairs or local markets for relatively standard non-customized items such as tape recorder magnetic heads and small electric motors. Although trade fairs and regional markets are often organized by local governments, some large enterprises had also begun to run their own purchasing trade fairs as a means of generating more of a market for this category of inputs. Open-market transacting tended to be used mainly for low-tech standardized inputs and for those whose quality could be readily assessed through personal inspection. The supply of such inputs does not present the purchasing firm with high risk: either their specifications do not have to be idiosyncratic to the purchaser's needs or it is easy to check on the required standards. Moreover, a choice of suppliers is available.

In cases, however, where the technical level and specificity of purchased components is high and it is difficult to secure supplies of reliable quality, as with X-ray tubes for incorporation into radiology machinery, purchasing firms sought to sign long-term contracts with a suitable supplier. On the basis of that long-term relationship, purchasers such as the audio-visual company were then prepared to invest expertise in aiding the supplier to meet the required standards. The importance of guaranteeing technical reliability through a close and continuing relationship was thought to more than offset the risk of foregoing alternative sources. Equally, the supplier gains longer-term security through this arrangement for his commitment to the production of outputs which enjoy only a specialized use. Insofar as the technical specifications of these inputs were likely to change quite frequently over time, longer-term collaboration also promised to remove some of the uncertainties of bounded technical rationality – of whether, for instance, suppliers could cope with these technical demands without close user-designer co-operation. Co-ordinated contracting of this kind, which incorporates elements of both market and hierarchical governance, therefore tended to be adopted where both purchaser and supplier engaged in idiosyncratic transactions and committed specific-use investments towards them.

The scope permitted to a market co-ordination of input transactions remains limited in China, though its incidence varies considerably between different areas of business. There is an essentially political decision to maintain bureaucratic control over strategic supplies and strategic producers. Firms themselves look to the agencies of government to reduce their exposure to opportunism and supply starvation in conditions of acute shortage, and they continue to rely heavily upon the administrative hierarchy for information relevant to their purchasing decisions. However, within the arenas of market co-ordination, the choice made by firms between discrete contracting and longer-term co-ordinated contracting appears to be consistent with the explanatory role offered by transaction cost economics (TCE) to the risks associated with bounded rationality and idiosyncrasy (Williamson 1975; 1985). Similarly, the desire to minimize the risks of opportunism appears to stimulate some retreat from exposure to the market as TCE would predict, though the chosen institutional refuge is peculiar to the Chinese social system.

Relational contracting

Williamson (1986: 105), following Macneil, has identified as 'relational contracting' those transactions in which the point of reference is the entire relationship between the parties as it has developed over time on the basis of familiarity and trust. Under this form of contracting, there is limited recourse to searching the wider market and transactions are co-ordinated through a social nexus.

Time and time again, managers in the Beijing enterprises insisted that in China the quality of the relationship between the transactors was more important than the price charged or any contractual condition. They maintained that this applied to Chinese exchange in general. This implies that economic relationships remain embedded in Chinese social norms even to the extent that the material and self-interested nature of the exchange is modified (cf. Granovetter 1985).

Many instances were related of how a firm's interest had suffered when it failed to cultivate a good relationship even though the other terms of the relationship were mutually acceptable. The automotive enterprise, for example, had at the beginning of 1987 signed a contract with a steel plant to supply thin steel plate specification B-112. In June of that year the steel plant informed the company that only thin steel plate B-110 was available, a similar type but of lower quality. In reality, type B-112 was available but the steel plant had sold the amount required to another truck manufacturer with which it had a longer-standing and closer relationship. Although the automotive enterprise was aware of what had happened, it felt unable to bring a suit against the steel plant for breach of contract since it depended upon it for future supplies and did not care to offend its management.

It was, of course, the advantageous exchange position enjoyed by the steel plant that afforded it the luxury of breaking its contract, and this point is indeed highlighted by the behaviour of the automotive enterprise itself in supply markets where it enjoyed a strong position. One of its senior managers stated that if the company double-purchased components to safeguard its production when supplies were short and then subsequently cancelled some of the contracts, this did not lead to any hard feeling because 'the relationship is more important than the contract'. The problem is that this is easy to claim from the vantage-point of a relatively dominant purchaser.

Similarly, while it was stated that the efficacy of even arm's-length transacting through a market depended upon the prior establishment of a personal relationship between the parties, it was also admitted in several interviews that even with this relationship in place, suppliers would probably respond to impersonal ordering only at a distance when the balance of market power lay with the purchaser.

Some qualification must therefore be attached to the claim, so frequently made by Chinese respondents and attributed by many of them to Chinese traditional norms, that relationship is the prime factor in ensuring the success of any transaction in China. While this assertion undoubtedly possesses some validity, if only because the parties themselves believe it, the salience of relationships appears also to be contingent upon other factors including asymmetrical market power or the possibilities of mutual benefit.

Having said this, there were benefits in the high-risk Chinese context of purchasing from suppliers with whom a long-term relationship had been cultivated. It reduced the likelihood of being supplied with sub-standard goods. Long-standing suppliers were more prepared to extend trade credit and to help out in an emergency. Relational contracting also reduced the risk of default on contracts where there was no guarantee that the provisions of the contract could be legally enforced, especially in other cities or provinces. It could reduce risk and provide a basis for mutual technical co-operation over the provision of specialized, high-technology inputs, as noted earlier. These are all positive transactional advantages under conditions of bounded rationality, information impactedness, product idiosyncrasy and potential opportunism.

Such benefits of relational contracting are consistent with Solinger's (1989) findings from Wuhan and with Walder's (1989) observations from interviews with enterprise managers. Solinger notes that many present long-term contracting relationships were set up by the pre-reform planning administration and she points out their continuing functions under the reform for coping with the contingencies of shortage, non-standardization and information deficiency. Thus, while relational contracting may accord with a culturally preferred mode of action in China, it also has advantages which are contingent to contemporary circumstances.[3]

Conclusion

The transition in China from a centrally planned to a regulated market system is only partly accomplished and has been interrupted at intervals due to alarms at the loss of economic control and reluctance to proceed too far with the dismantling of bureaucratic regulatory structures. As a result, China's economy is co-ordinated through a duality of bureaucratic and market modes.

Nee (1992) points out that the incidence of bureaucratic versus market transacting in China varies according to the property rights enjoyed by enterprises (their ownership status). The findings presented in this chapter point to a somewhat more complex picture in which the mode of transacting also varies according to a combination of strategic, technological and informational factors. Strategic factors include the official designation of some raw materials as being key to the economy and the social sensitivity attached to the price and supply of other commodities such as basic foodstuffs. Factors of a more technological nature include the extent to which the goods concerned have a specific use only and require special technological support, as opposed to having wide use and being of a more standard commodified nature. The scope and quality of information available to enterprise managers for making decisions on purchasing and marketing also condition their reliance on higher authorities. These technological and informational factors have a direct bearing upon transaction costs.

The duality of bureaucratic and market governance structures creates a context, combining institutionalized power and market forces, within which enterprises have to conduct their transactions. Power is institutionalized at both central and local government levels, carrying with it rights to regulate parameters such as prices and distribution channels. Administrative agencies are also heavily involved in the process of allocating the more strategic categories of supplies and products. The apparatus of bureaucratic co-ordination has beaten a fairly slow retreat from economic management, despite official enjoinders from time to time to do so. This is partly because of the vested interests which have been found in public bureaucracies to underpin resistance to change elsewhere in the world (cf. Warwick 1975; Biggart 1977), and partly because firms continue to rely upon the assistance of their superior administrative agencies to secure scarce supplies and to shield them in other ways against the risks and costs of market transacting. Market forces have therefore developed mainly in the interstices of state provision and in the less strategic areas of production, though since 1991 their progress has accelerated.

In those transactional areas where market co-ordination has developed, features identified by transaction cost economics, namely bounded rationality, asset specificity, idiosyncrasy and opportunism, did appear to identify in some degree the forms of transactional governance which were preferred. However, the possibilities open to state enterprises in China for choosing between alternative transactional structures according to the conditions postulated by Williamson depend on a number of other factors, all of which reflect considerations of institutional politics and power. The availability to firms of a choice in the first place depends on a political decision, namely the introduction of market relations that are free from governmental supply monopoly and/or mandatory regulations. It is the extent to which bureaucratic co-ordination has been drawn back that offers firms the choice between a market or a hierarchical governance of their transactions. This clearly emerged from a consideration of input transacting and a similar conclusion would emerge on the output side with respect, for instance, to the choice of distribution modes between disposal to a government agency and selling on the wider market. That kind of choice becomes available only when government agencies withdraw from the exclusive right to take a firm's outputs under a comprehensive system of planned quotas.

Considerations of power remain relevant even within spheres where market co-ordination has been established and where firms consequently have the freedom to secure materials and components from the external market. The distribution of market power established certain conditional limits on the transactional behaviour that could be sustained. Moreover, one party's superiority of market power enabled it to insist on the other accommodating to the relationship through processes of transacting which incurred clear inefficiencies for the latter. Even where there are no technical idiosyncrasies standing in the way of arm's-length ordering, the ability to do this efficiently via letter or electronic communication referring to a catalogue or other codified information appears in present-day China to depend largely on the market power of the purchaser. In other words, the necessary conditions for arm's-length market contracting – coded and diffused product information, efficient telecommunications – now exist for some areas of purchasing, but the sufficient condition for their use lies in the power to insist on this happening.

The significance of relational contracting in China was also noted, but again neither its incidence nor the different forms it takes can be accounted for solely in terms of economic rationality. In many cases it did provide for mutual economic benefit. It was, however, also often an arrangement institutionalized by the former central planning system and sustained by the powers which administrative agencies continued to enjoy over some categories of supply. In other cases, it was imposed by market dependency rather than chosen freely. In short, while a major shift towards the market has become clearly discernible since the launch of the economic reform, the state determines the speed and scope of moves towards market transacting. The Chinese authorities remain major participants in the governance of input and output transactions and the institutional legacy of the pre-reform planning system is apparent.

Appendix 7.1 *Enterprises where studies of input transacting were conducted*

(the six enterprises investigated directly by the author are highlighted in bold)

Enterprise	*Main products*
Audio	Tape recorders
Audio-visual	TV sets
Automotive	Trucks
Boiler	Industrial & power boilers
Electrical switchgear	Electrical switchgear for machine tools
Heavy electrical	Transformers, rectifiers, etc.
Low voltage electrical	Automatic controls, contact breakers, etc.
Marble	Natural & man-made marble products
Pharmaceutical	Chinese & Western medicines & tonics
Radiology machinery	X-ray equipment
Winery	Wine

8   The activities of senior managers

Chapter 2 set out three perspectives that illuminate the context in which the managers of Chinese enterprises are situated and the ways they are likely to operate in that context. The Chinese system of industrial governance locates managers within a network of constraining relationships. The character of Chinese culture indicates that managers are likely to cope with these constraints through certain modes of behaviour, which include building relationships for exchanging informal favours and maintaining harmony. The relative recency and particular mode of China's industrialization suggests that its managers may lack some of the systematic and formal techniques for running a business that are now well-established in the developed countries. In other words, these perspectives offer clues on what to expect about the work context of Chinese managers and their activities within that context.

The four 'facts of life' which Walder (1989) identified in the world of the Chinese manager derive primarily from the political and social system in which industry is located. Each presents the manager with a challenge. He or she has to cultivate vertical relationships, maintain a political coalition within the enterprise (especially with the party secretary), satisfy criteria which derive from the enterprise as a socio-political community, and develop non-market exchange relationships. On the political side, even under the director responsibility system the enterprise party committee and its secretary continue to perform a significant monitoring role and have to be consulted, particularly over personnel matters. Our examination of the decision-making process and the management of input–output transactions has confirmed that the vertical dependency of enterprise managers on higher authorities remains a salient factor, despite the decentralizing provisions of the economic reform. Enterprise directors, therefore, face pressures from above to adjust to the policies of higher administrative authorities and satisfy their contractual responsibilities to them; to a lesser degree they are also responsible to the party authorities. At the same time, they are under pressure from below to serve the interests of the members of the enterprise as a corporate social group. They are caught between the hammer and the anvil.

This predicament, and the pressures it imposes, is likely to oblige Chinese senior managers to direct more of their attention to hierarchical relations upward and downward than would be typical for their counterparts in other countries. This implies that the percentage of time and effort they spend on essentially administrative issues within bureaucratic structures will be relatively high as opposed to the time they devote to more commercial matters, particularly through communication with transaction partners in relevant markets, such as key customers, suppliers and finance-providers.

The cultural tradition within which they work leads to an expectation that managers will attempt to accommodate to the demands placed upon them through personal relations in which they endeavour to establish some tolerance based upon trust and negotiate in a relatively harmonious fashion some space within which to operate. This cultural preference is *inter alia* likely to be reflected in the use of informal rather than formal meetings. One would expect that the limited managerial training and experience of many Chinese executives will be reflected in a restricted and/or rather inefficient use of formal procedures, including those for the systematic conduct of meetings and planning of time. The combination of limited middle-management competence with a focusing of contractual responsibility upon enterprise directors is also likely to result in a reluctance on their part to delegate and a consequent top managerial overload, some indications of which were noted in chapter 5.

One would therefore expect that the particular circumstances of Chinese senior managers will lead their activities to differ in predictable ways from those of top managers in other countries. They will have a stronger vertical orientation, especially upwards to the industrial and other bureaus. They will deal with matters arising in a more personal and informal manner. They are likely to delegate less, and consequently to work longer hours. Their location within a close-knit, socio-political community will lead them to make less of a distinction temporally and socially between work and non-work life than in Western countries. This chapter considers the light which available evidence throws upon these propositions.

Sources of evidence

It is not easy to obtain access to top managers to study their daily activities in any country, and China is no exception. To the writer's knowledge, the study by Boisot and Xing (1991;1992) is the only one so far completed in which a researcher was able to observe and measure the activities of top Chinese managers directly. Other studies have relied on less direct and dependable sources of information, namely interviews (Stewart and Chong 1990; Chung 1990; Stewart 1992) or 'a survey', apparently by questionnaire (Hildebrandt and Liu 1988). They also offer a far less complete coverage of the managers' work activities.

For the Boisot and Xing study, Xing followed six directors of Chinese industrial enterprises with a stop watch for a period of six days each in 1987. All their
work-related activities were recorded and the recording took place from the
time the director arrived at the place of work in the morning until his departure
for home in the evening. Between these times, work off the enterprise's
premises was also recorded. The enterprises were located in Beijing and all
came from the mechanical construction sector. The firms differed, however, in
size and ownership status. Two were state-owned enterprises, two were
hybrid, i.e. a cross between state owned and collective' (p. 166) and the other
two were smaller collective firms. Apart from the fact that the burden of
managing a larger firm will be more onerous, size matters in China because it
puts managers more easily within reach of the supervisory bureaucracy and is
therefore likely to modify their behaviour. The Boisot–Xing study adopted a
research procedure modelled on Mintzberg's study of five American chief
executives (1973). This permits some comparison between the Chinese and
American cases, which must however remain tentative because of difficulties
in matching the two sets of managers by status, problems of establishing comparable categories of managerial activities in the two different contexts, and the
very small samples involved.

Stewart and Chong also intended to replicate Mintzberg's study, but their
differing methodologies do not permit a close comparison to be made. Twenty-
six senior executives from seventeen enterprises in the Chinese electronics
industry were interviewed. Of these enterprises, ten were state-owned, five collectively owned and two were privately owned and managed independently of
government supervision. The firms were located in Beijing (eight), Guangdong
Province including the Special Economic Zones (eight) and Shanghai (one).
Some checking of the reliability of the information collected was possible
through further interviews and personal observation during visits to the organizations. Chung used questionnaires with follow-up interviews to study the
'motivation' of 76 PRC senior managers located in Beijing, Shanghai and
Guangdong Province who were enterprise directors and 'division chiefs' (the
latter appear to have been vice-directors or equivalent). Some information was
collected on their work activities. Hildebrandt and Liu conducted a survey of
436 Chinese 'middle managers' in a range of specialist areas in thirty-one
manufacturing industries. Their survey touches upon a few aspects of work
activity.

Working time and its distribution

Chinese managers have an official 48-hour, 6-day work week, but in practice
they tend to work longer. The Hildebrandt–Liu survey concluded that middle
managers put in an average of 52.3 hours per week, or 8.72 hours each day. The

more senior managers studied by Boisot–Xing and Stewart had longer working hours still, with averages of 9.67 hours and 11.7 hours per day respectively. Boisot and Xing found a substantial difference in the average hours worked by the directors of large and small enterprises. Those in large firms worked an average of 11.35 hours each day, which contrasts with 8.1 hours in the smaller firms. These averages are based on very few cases, and must therefore be treated with caution. Nevertheless, what they suggest is interesting, namely that the additional burden of coping with competing expectations from above and below is quite considerable for the heads of larger enterprises. The larger Chinese firm is normally more closely coupled to higher governmental authorities which, as was evident in the case of decision making, retain an interventionist stance that takes up extra managerial time and effort. The burden will be correspondingly greater in the larger enterprise if, as evidence presented in chapters 4 and 5 suggests, Chinese directors do not readily delegate. The reluctance to delegate is reinforced by the fact that, in keeping with Chinese paternalistic tradition, those working in an enterprise (and, indeed, their family members) often insist on access to the director for advice or assistance in personal problems, and in the larger enterprise there will obviously tend to be more such cases to deal with.

Although American top managers are noted for their long working hours (cf Child and Macmillan 1972), comparisons by Boisot–Xing with Mintzberg and by Hildebrandt–Liu with survey findings indicate that Chinese senior managers tend to work longer hours still. Even so, as Boisot and Xing note, their working day may not really be over when they leave the office because it is quite likely that an employee or two will be waiting for them at home to discuss personal matters in private.

Mintzberg reported a high degree of brevity and variety in the work of his American chief executives which fragmented their typical working day. Stewart (1992) concluded from her 'general observations' that the Chinese managers were in a better position than the American ones to focus on one job at a time. 'Most of them seemed to concentrate on their desk work or on personal improvement for a solid period during the day, and apparently with few disturbances' (p. 178). However, the detailed direct observations of Boisot and Xing led to the contrasting finding that their Chinese enterprise directors dealt with a large number of separate issues during the working day. They averaged twenty-eight different activities every day, each lasting an average of twenty-one minutes, and this comes close to the activity time-profile of Mintzberg's senior managers. In the larger enterprises, the directors tended to deal with over 50 per cent more activities than did Mintzberg's managers, each of somewhat shorter duration. This divergence in findings beteen the two samples of Chinese managers is quite possibly a reflection of their methodologies and as such it indicates the need for caution with interview-based descriptions in which top managers can present themselves as having an undisturbed reflective control of the situation, whereas the reality might be otherwise.

One of the problems in reaching any conclusions about Chinese managers lies in the great size and diversity of the country. For example, the hand of higher administration and the Communist Party is likely to bear more heavily upon enterprises located in Beijing than in other cities located away from the capital, particularly in the south. For the latter the old Chinese saying still applies: 'Heaven is high and the Emperor is far away'. Some light is thrown on the impact of regional location for the balance of managerial activities by Chung's findings (1990). He asked how managers distributed their weekly working hours between three areas of activity: political affairs, administrative and personnel matters, and 'basic business activities'. He found that managers working in Beijing and Shanghai tended to spend more time on political activities and administration/personnel matters than did those from Guangdong. Guangdong managers therefore devoted more time to getting on with running the business, with apparently more freedom from political and administrative obligations imposed by external governmental and political bodies.

Chung's sample was also drawn from different types of organization: trading and service companies, manufacturing firms and R&D institutes. It emerged that the managers in trading/service companies spent most time on basic business activities and those in the manufacturing companies the least time. He notes that 'during discussions it was suggested that trading companies in Guangdong were more like Hong Kong firms. Business and profits had become the manager's major task. The company's structure was much simpler than the normal organization inside China. The party secretary's role was not of major importance . . .' (p. 30). Managers in these Guangdong trading companies also tended to work the most hours over and above the standard 48-hour week – on average 20 hours overtime per week. The managers of manufacturing enterprises in all three locations spent appreciably more time than in the other enterprises on administration and personnel matters, reflecting the fact that factories remain social communities and impose a paternalistic role upon their directors.

Mintzberg (1973) broke down the activities of the managers he sampled into a typology based on the form of work: desk work, scheduled meetings, unscheduled meetings, telephone calls and tours. Desk work refers to periods when the managers worked alone, or with their secretaries, in the confines of their offices. Tours refers to time spent walking around the organization, greeting people in the lobby, and so forth. His findings compare with those from the two equivalent studies of Chinese managers as shown in table 8.1.

Unfortunately, the two available studies of Chinese managers again do not provide us with a consistent picture. It would seem that top managerial involvement in scheduled meetings may be substantially less than in America. Since

Table 8.1. *Comparison of the working day of Chinese senior managers with that of American senior managers studied by Mintzberg*

Activity	Percentage of total time		
	Mintzberg	Boisot–Xing	Stewart
Desk work	20	9	23
Scheduled meetings	59	22	39
Unscheduled meetings	10	n.a.	31
Telephone	6	2.5	} 7
Tours	3	n.a.	

they do not spend any more time on desk work (indeed, much less according to Boisot–Xing), a considerable amount of the top Chinese manager's time would typically appear to be spent on informal personal contacts. Stewart and Chong recorded that unscheduled meetings took up three times the proportion of managers' time than in Mintzberg's sample. Boisot and Xing draw attention to the personalized style of the Chinese executives they studied. They found that these managers spent an average 91 per cent of their working day in verbal contact with others in contrast to 78 per cent among Mintzberg's managers.

Stewart suggests two reasons for the Chinese managers' preference for informal contacts and communication as opposed to scheduled meetings. The first reflects the hitherto limited experience and competence of Chinese managers in the use of formal scheduled meetings, one of the problems that we shall later see is highlighted when they work together with foreign managers in joint ventures:

in the western world scheduled meetings as a communication medium have been fully developed and practised with sets of structured, formal and commonly accepted meeting procedures, and their actions in information dissemination and problem-solving are well exploited. However, these procedures and functions are still somewhat lacking in China. Instead, the PRC managers tend to attach different values to attending scheduled meetings – cultivating interpersonal relationships, showing one's commitment, diligence, and fishing for unsystematic information – but these aims are more easily achieved in unscheduled meetings. (1992: 176)

Secondly, Chinese managers rely heavily on the cultivation of personal relationships to cope with the exigencies of their situation, and this is moreover a traditional way of so doing:

the value of unscheduled meetings in the PRC is due to another factor. The importance of guanxi, or personal connections, in China is well known . . . The unscheduled meetings provide ways in which to cultivate valuable interpersonal relationships more easily than during formal occasions. Most managers interviewed stressed the need to develop and maintain good working relationships with colleagues and environmental contacts: they saw this as the chief factor in their career success. (ibid: 178).

The way that senior managers in China allocate their time between different forms of activity thus begins to point towards the relationships in which they are most engaged and the style of managing they adopt. These features are now considered in turn.

Relationships

All managers operate within a web of relationships, though these are particularly complex in the structure of Chinese industry because managers there have to negotiate the combined arenas of bureaucracy, market, polity and community. The upward relation of enterprises to their controlling bureaux is particularly important, above all for state-owned ones, and has been formalized in the contract responsibility system and other provisions for the institutional approval of managerial conduct and distribution of economic resources.

Boisot and Xing's detailed investigation throws some interesting light on the relationships which enterprise directors have to manage and how they go about this. Out of the time the directors spent on verbal contacts, getting on for half involved interactions with their subordinates (42.2 per cent), a proportion which is only marginally less than that for the chief executives Mintzberg studied. The big contrast arose in the balance of their other verbal contacts. The Chinese managers spent four times as long in contact with their superiors (27.4 per cent of total contact time) than did the American managers and only half the time of the Americans (23.5 per cent compared with 44 per cent) in contacts with outsiders and peers. The time they gave to people in relevant markets was extraordinarily limited: customers (1.5 per cent), suppliers (1.3 per cent) and bankers (nil). This contrast between the attention enterprise directors gave to upward relationships with the governmental bureaucracy and to those with the market is remarkable. As Boisot and Xing comment, 'the figures show that the directors spend the same amount of time looking down the administrative pyramid as do their Western counterparts, but four times as much looking up and only half as much time looking outward . . . there is no evidence here of the rugged risk-taking individualist going out on his own to confront his external environment.' (1992: 171–2).[1]

Further contrasts between the Chinese and American managers are provided by an analysis of mail received and sent. The Chinese managers received under half the number of items of mail and sent out only a little more than half the items of their American counterparts. Written postal communication features far less in their work. The sources of mail confirm the indications provided by an analysis of contact time. Almost 30 per cent originates from government departments or supervisory bureaux, compared with the 6 per cent that Mintzberg's managers received from higher levels. Under 1 per cent originates from customers, suppliers or bankers, compared with Mintzberg's 13 per cent from these sources. A similarly tiny proportion of the mail sent out goes to these groups. This means that while Chinese enterprise directors engage far less than their American equivalents in market-based relationships, when they do this is on the basis of personal rather than impersonal contact. The fact that they spend under half the time of the Americans on the telephone also indicates that such contact, when it takes place, is person-to-person in China.

Under 1 per cent of outgoing mail goes upward to higher authorities. So while the Chinese enterprise directors were experiencing a steady flow of written communication downwards, almost certainly instructions and regulations for the most part, they were reluctant to use formal means in communication back to the same authorities which could both appear stand-offish and pin them down to a particular position before they could ascertain what was really in the minds of their superiors. They chose instead to handle the relationship in a personal way which permitted the exercise of influence in accord with cultural norms of due deference to authority.

Style

We have noted how Chinese managers tend to personalize communications and relationships. In a system where enterprise directors are at the same time seeking to gain a space within which to manage their businesses and to avoid placing themselves in fixed positions which could attract subsequent opprobrium, personal verbal communication offers them clear advantages. Less is committed to the record and there is more scope for attaching personal trust and obligation to any arrangements that are made, especially with resource providers. So the Chinese enterprise director becomes a master of handling multiple informal and unscheduled interactions. As Boisot and Xing note, he does not keep a diary, is constantly interrupted in his office and often runs several conversations simultaneously.

The conduct even of high-level scheduled meetings in China is relatively unstructured and does little to avoid the need for personalized follow-up. The writer draws here on his own experience when, as director of the CEMI, he took part in such meetings within Chinese enterprises and a government ministry; this experience is corroborated by the reports of foreign managers participating in joint ventures with Chinese firms (cf. Child et al. 1990). It is rare for such meetings to have a formal agenda or for papers to be presented to members in advance. Discussion defers very much to the most senior person present, who is generally more concerned to establish a climate of consensus around general principles or directions of policy than to raise specific issues. His or her approach looks to securing agreement on these general lines, which can then serve as the justification for arrangements and deals that are later struck through informal personal discussions. The outcome of these meetings is sometimes left so vague that it is not even clear what has been agreed. Normally, no minutes are taken though various clerks will take copious notes which are then filed away primarily to protect the heads of their departments or units should any dispute or criticism later arise. This means that follow-up action has to be initiated personally by the senior manager and that the next meeting does not necessarily review progress on any systematic basis. It all reinforces the ever-continuing need of Chinese senior managers, and directors in particular, to deal with matters on a personal basis.

This heavy, personal engagement is encouraged by the reluctance to delegate which emerged from studies of decision making (see chapter 5 and Laaksonen 1988: chapter 6), and which is further indicated by the long hours that enterprise directors work in China. The evidence is that Chinese managers suffer from considerable overload and that the problem tends to become worse the larger the firm.

While the heavy involvement of enterprise directors in what is going on is itself a concomitant of a personalized management style, Boisot and Xing (1992) suggest two further reasons for their lack of delegation. First, the director does not trust his own organization to implement decisions. The administrative system within enterprises was originally conceived as an instrument to control him and his workforce in the not-too-far-off days when enterprises came under the control of the party committee. The specialized departments within enterprises still have direct lines to corresponding departments within industrial and functional bureaux and so the director is placed in a position of competing for control of the firm with this administrative system rather than being able to rely on it to support him and to extend his managerial power through delegation. Second, directors could not delegate even if they wanted to because everyone both within the enterprise and above it wants to deal with them personally: 'Both employees and external stakeholders look to him for personal guarantees that their own particular interests will be properly attended to. If the director does not trust his organization to deliver, others do not either.' (p. 175)

Conclusion

Different interpretations can be offered for the conclusion that Chinese senior managers are inclined to handle matters personally and are reluctant to delegate, and indeed for the patterning of their activities in general. Which one is favoured comes down basically to whether the behaviour of these managers is viewed primarily as a response to the system of industrial governance within which they operate (particularly the informational environment and the power structure), to their cultural context, or to the competences at their disposal.

Boisot and Xing (1992) conclude that 'personalization and centralization are ... responses to an information environment that is essentially uncodifiable or, to use Perrow's terminology [Perrow 1970], a task environment that is neither analysable nor routinizable' (p. 177). We saw, for example, that Chinese managers continue to rely primarily on market information that is transmitted personally through salespeople and/or their own personal contacts rather than on information secured through market research. In a context where frequent amendments to governmental policies and regulations can overturn assumptions about the conditions of trade, personal contact offers some chance of obtaining prior knowledge about these and even negotiating a partial exemption from the provisions of new regulations. The reliance on personal information channels encourages centralization because in Chinese society information is likely to be withheld from more junior managers, especially information coming from higher authorities which often insist on dealing with the enterprise director.

Information required for business decisions in China is not only relatively uncodified and with a limited time-span of validity; it is also highly impacted in the hands of bureaux and ministries. Here one returns to the power structure within which the managers of state-owned enterprises work and the significant role of higher authorities in this. The skew of top managerial activity towards these authorities is very clear when compared with that of Western counterparts. Under a system in which enterprises are highly dependent for their critical resources upon administrative allocators and redistributors, directors have to give considerable attention to their upward relations. Indeed, in China, the directors of state-owned enterprises owe their four-year terms of appointment to their supervisory ministries or bureaux. It is not surprising that they devote so much more of their working time to contacts with their superiors than do American managers. Note that they do this on a personal basis which gives them an opportunity to re-affirm their institutional loyalty and to press the case for their own enterprise's needs while at the same time avoiding the trap of tying their hands in an uncertain environment by committing themselves on paper.

The disproportionately greater contact that Chinese enterprise directors had with their administrative superiors compared with agents in the marketplace (customers, suppliers and bankers) is consistent with the finding that the strategic business decisions of state enterprises remain heavily under bureaucratic influence. We found that operational transactions with the market are now largely handled by specialist purchasing managers, product marketeers, or recruiters of personnel, rather than by directors. On the other hand, directors are not normally granted the right to deal directly with external agencies on more strategic matters, such as raising funds from banks, without the mediation of the supervisory bureau. Management is still highly constrained in taking action on issues where enterprises are dependent on higher authorities to approve the allocation of new resources (as with investment) or to give approval to changes which have an institutional and political significance (as with changes to enterprise organization). It is, of course, the case that Western top managers also tend to give some of their time to relations with relevant government departments, and sometime a more active lobbying of politicians, in order to promote their companies' interests (cf. Fidler 1980), but not to anywhere near the same extent as appears to be the case in China. In other words, the nature of the system and its inherent power structure is a major determinant of Chinese top managers' work activities.

The father-figure role of Chinese directors within their enterprises accords with the expectations of traditional culture and is indeed reflected among Chinese businesses outside the People's Republic (Redding 1990). Leadership is a term often employed with reference to the Chinese enterprise. It is instructive that when that leadership was officially collective, residing in factory management committees in the early period after 1949 and later in the factory party committee after 1956 and 1978, it tended in practice to evolve into a focus on one role such as that of the party secretary. This suggests that cultural leanings towards paternalism do of themselves help to shape the personalized and centralized style of present-day enterprise directors and to legitimate its continuity despite the cost in overload and inefficiency.

Finally, the fear of all managers when contemplating the prospect of delegating some of their decision authority is that their subordinates do not have the competence and capacity to make such good decisions as they can. Despite the large efforts which have been made to provide management training during the past ten years or so (reviewed in the next chapter), many managers in China are still not familiar either with business conditions or with the necessary technical substructure for running an efficient firm. This, together with the poor coordination between departments which is characteristic of many enterprises, cannot give top managers much confidence that decisions other than those of limited scope and a routine nature will be made effectively if they delegate them. Moreover, successful delegation also depends on the introduction of systems to guide and provide feedback on decisions taken lower down the hierarchy. These are not well established in the general run of Chinese firms, and we note later how one of the initial contributions of foreign management in joint ventures is to provide a systematic framework within which management can take place. If the top manager favours a personalized and centralized style, the development of a systematic framework and approach will not be encouraged; this is a problem experienced by many Western firms started by entrepreneurs when they grow to a size at which a more professional management is required.

In short, the work activities of top Chinese managers are adapted to the circumstances in which they have learned to operate and the competences at their disposal. These are at present reinforced by institutional and cultural factors. The different, more open and competitive environment towards which the economic reform is leading Chinese industry will require some significant re-orientation on the part of senior managers towards spending more time on accessing markets, on evaluating market information and on strategic activities in general if the reform is to be successfully implemented.

9   The management of personnel

Some have argued that the winds of economic change in China, and the accompanying interest in Western management practices, open the door to the introduction there of 'human resource management' (e.g. Cyr and Frost 1991; Specter and Solomon 1991). Management training programmes offered in China by Western institutions normally contain courses on the subject in an attempt to make up for its apparent neglect in that country. The United States Congress Office of Technology Assessment published a report in 1987 on functional management knowledge that was lacking in the Chinese economy. It listed the following wide range of areas of deficient knowledge under the heading of 'human resources': motivation and incentives, the concept of directorship, the role of the manager, executive compensation, organizational design, and leadership styles (Warner 1992a: 40).

Although definitions of personnel management and human resource management vary considerably, modern Western thinking tends to be predicated upon assumptions such as the primary contribution of competent and motivated people to a firm's success, the compatibility of individual and corporate interests, the importance of developing a corporate culture which is in tune with top management's strategy for the firm, and the responsibility of senior management rather than employees' own representative bodies for determining personnel practices. It attaches importance to systematic recruitment and selection, training and development (including socialization into the corporate culture), close attention to motivation through personal involvement and participation in work and its organization, appraisal and progression procedures and incentive schemes.

This concept of human resource management is not found in Chinese enterprises. It is represented neither in the structures of management nor, by and large, in its practices. Within enterprises, particularly state-owned ones, administrative functions related to employment are organized into several areas, namely personnel, labour, salaries and training. Other tasks, such as personnel appointments, communication with workers and political education, are mostly undertaken or supervised by the enterprise party organization. Western human resource management practices are also alien to the Chinese scene, even

157

in Chinese companies outside the PRC. Redding (1990), for instance, concluded that among overseas Chinese family businesses, 'the management of personnel has a distinctly harder edge to it in the Chinese case than in the Western' (p. 170). The use of control and penalties is universally stronger, and while recruitment and appraisal are given relatively high importance, they are not backed by sophisticated systems for selection and development. The notion of personnel management as a quasi-professional activity is absent.

It would be naive to think that in this culturally and politically sensitive area of management, Chinese organizations can readily adopt Western, or even Japanese, approaches. They would require a substantial change in cultural norms which, for example, favour equality of rewards and respect for age more than for competence. They would also require a major change in the institutional structures within which personnel practices are formed in PRC industry, particularly the continuing restriction of managerial initiative in this area by governmental bureaux for labour and personnel and by the party organization within enterprises. As we shall note in chapter 13, foreign managers working in Sino-foreign joint ventures have found the personnel area to be the most difficult of all in which to introduce their preferred approach.

On the other hand, some conditions favouring change in this area of management are now coming into play. We noted that many personnel decisions have been decentralized down to enterprise managers, even in state-owned firms. A more highly educated younger generation of employees is emerging which is more receptive to foreign values and may therefore accept many aspects of the Western approach to personnel management. Moreover, companies with foreign involvement have in many cases succeeded in introducing changes in this area, despite initial opposition. In view of their economic success and the favourable employment conditions they offer, their example is likely over time to have some influence within Chinese industry more generally.

Overall, then, as Warner (1993) concludes, while China is changing rapidly, it would still be realistic to 'think more than twice' before perceiving recognizable human resource management practices in most Chinese enterprises. The aim of this chapter is to examine how a number of aspects of the management of personnel are handled in Chinese enterprises, with particular reference to state-owned ones. Chapters 12 and 13 will refer to human resource management in Sino-foreign joint ventures. This chapter begins by considering the institutional context of managing personnel in China. It then reviews labour and personnel employment systems as defined by Chinese regulations. Following that, recruitment, dismissal and training are examined. The chapter finishes with the question of motivation, concentrating on its intrinsic sources. Material motivators, in the form of monetary earnings, form the subject of the following chapter.

The institutional context of managing personnel

Figure 9.1 outlines the complex of institutional authorities which have an influence over personnel management policies within Chinese enterprises.[1] Although the National People's Congress is the supreme law-making body in China, most regulations on personnel matters carrying the force of law are issued by the State Council. The State Council has a number of state commissions subordinate to it, of which the State Planning Commission is the most important in national economic affairs. The State Planning Commission draws up long-term national plans and approves the national budget, including the overall budget for remuneration in employment. Below the level of state commissions are state ministries which can be categorized into two groups. One contains ministries having direct administrative authority over enterprises, for instance the industrial ministries. The other has regulatory authority and issues general instructions to enterprises. The Ministries of Labour and of Personnel come into this second category.

In China, a distinction is made between labour management and personnel management and they are organized into separate systems. The former covers manual employees and those whose jobs are closely related to physical activities. The personnel system covers managers, technicians, political staff, office and clerical employees. The Ministries of Labour and Personnel take responsibility for labour and personnel policies through their detailed regulations covering working conditions, recruitment procedures and standards, personnel selection and appointments, salary and bonus levels, and on-the-job training.[2] In addition to these two Ministries, other governmental authorities contribute to the process of policy determination in this field on issues falling within their purview. For example, regulations about salaries and bonuses must be approved by the central bank and the Finance Ministry, and if necessary by the State Planning Commission.

Parallel to the administrative hierarchy connecting the State Council to enterprise management, the party forms the other important chain in the management of personnel. At the top, the Party Central Committee formulates the policy agendas for party development. Down the chain, every organization from a ministry to an enterprise has its own party committee and branches. These organize and monitor the party members working in the organizations. The party system within a work organization consists of the party committee, branches, and functional offices. In a large enterprise there might be two or three offices undertaking personnel development, working on party propaganda and dealing with party discipline, though we noted in chapter 4 how the scope of enterprise party offices and the number of staff they employed had tended to reduce. The party organization is independent of the management hierarchy within enterprises.

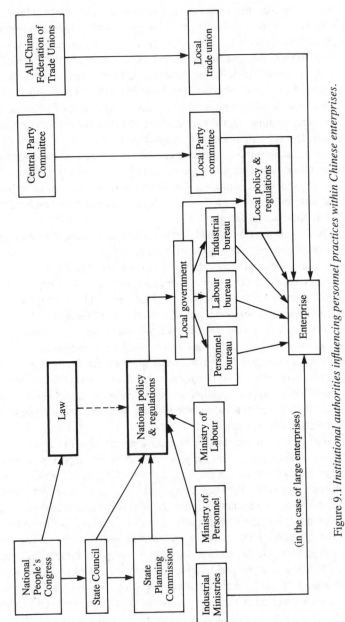

Figure 9.1 *Institutional authorities influencing personnel practices within Chinese enterprises.*

Source: adapted from Lu 1992.

Although the enterprise director's role strengthened during the 1980s, the party never abandoned its control over personnel. First, most managers are also party members. Political loyalty is still a necessary requirement for their promotion and they are subject to party discipline. Second, the power of the party was strengthened for a while after 1989, with enterprise party committees regaining a collective influence but leaving directors their authority over the conduct of business and over technical issues such as those involved in production. All important matters, especially those relating to employment and incentives, were in this period generally decided within the enterprise party committee, of which the director and some other senior managers would normally be members. It will be seen that a study conducted in 1991 in some large, state-owned enterprises found that all decisions on the promotion of middle and senior managers were now made by the party committee rather than by directors themselves.

The role of the trade union was discussed briefly in chapter 4. Each enterprise has a branch of the All-China Federation of Trade Unions (ACFTU). At the time of writing, official policy is for the trade union to assist the party, and the union chairperson is in most cases a member of the enterprise party committee. The union is not an independent political force acting on behalf of employees, despite the formal role that union officials play in representing the workers' congress. The focus of union activities is on welfare and entertainment for workers, though it is likely that trade union officials would also be consulted over an issue such as the dismissal of a worker.

In theory, decisions on labour and personnel management are framed by co-operative relations between enterprise directors and their counterparts in the party and the union. In practice, as the examination of relations between directors and party secretaries in chapter 4 indicated, much depends on the experience and influence enjoyed by the persons concerned. In enterprises where the directors have greater experience and influence, the party and union would have less effective say over personnel decisions. In effect, there is a 'game' of power dynamics here, the exact outcomes of which are likely to vary according to the issue and situation.

One of the most important channels of influence is, of course, from municipal and provincial governments which have their own bureaux of labour and personnel. With statutory powers to intervene directly within enterprises located within their boundaries, local authorities, for instance, normally limit the ability of employers to recruit from outside their areas in order to protect local employment levels. The supervision of recruitment by local authorities adds to the considerable rigidity of labour mobilization. The high immobility of labour in China is reinforced by the underdevelopment of social security systems which places a major onus and burden upon employers to retain employees.

The following section looks at labour immobility and the attempts to deal with it under the reform.

The system of employment

As White (1987) noted, there is not much resembling a labour market in the state-owned sector of enterprise. In the non-state sector of the urban economy, the flow of labour and the status of workers come closer to the concept of a labour market. In smaller collective enterprises and in private firms, workers do not generally enjoy permanent status, their position and rewards depend on the profitability of the firm and they are more likely to move to better jobs elsewhere. Outside the urban areas, the success of the rural responsibility systems has thrown up a large pool of surplus labour which has become available to work in township enterprises and as temporary labour in the cities (though the flow into urban areas is officially restricted). Even more of a labour market now exists in the rural economy, with movement across provincial boundaries and the rural–urban divide. In the discussion of state enterprise employment which follows, it is important to bear in mind these differences from other sectors of employment.

Most people working for Chinese state-owned enterprises enjoy permanent, 'lifetime' employment. There are two employment systems. Workers are in the 'labour employment' system. Clerical, technical and managerial employees count as cadres (*gan bu*), and their appointment, salaries and promotions are determined by the 'personnel system'. The labour employment system has been reformed since the mid-1980s, with new forms of employment being introduced such as the contractual system. There has, however, been little change in the personnel system.

Labour employment system

In the early 1950s, the government introduced the 'fixed' employment system to state-owned enterprises. The term 'fixed' refers to the arrangement whereby an enterprise received a fixed quota of labour allocated by a local labour bureau and a worker was then permanently attached to the organization. Under this system, enterprises were not permitted to discharge workers, even if they had over-employment and even if particular employees were habitually absent, lazy or negligent (World Bank 1985: 131).

A number of proposals to adopt a more flexible labour employment system were advanced even as early as the 1950s. In 1956, a delegation visited the Soviet Union to learn about labour management there, and this led to a proposal for a 'contractual labour system'. This initiative was interrupted by the Great Leap Forward. In the early 1960s, Liu Shaoqi proposed a 'Two Labours

System', involving the co-existence of permanent and temporary labour, but this was terminated by the Cultural Revolution. In 1980, the Communist Party organized a conference to discuss reform in labour employment. The State Council published its 'Decisions of Open Ways to Activate Economics and Resolve the Employment Problem in Cities and Towns'. This allowed the children of employees to replace them or to work in labour service companies organized by the enterprises. It was designed primarily to relieve urban unemployment and did not add to labour mobility or productivity. The immobility of labour and low productivity remained serious problems. The wage budget became a heavy burden for the government. Low labour productivity and a waste of human resources co-existed with a short supply of qualified skilled labour. An enterprise was responsible for the whole life of its employees. It not only paid them salaries, but also provided accommodation, social welfare, medicine and children's education. The Chinese enterprise was therefore regarded as a community. Production was only one of its tasks, alongside a range of social and political obligations. In the absence of a social security system, the job provided welfare benefits and security.

Moreover, almost all persons with any post-secondary training and some skilled workers as well were assigned by labour and personnel bureaux to enterprises, which meant that the latter had to accept packages containing both wanted and unwanted recruits. They could not readily recruit badly needed skilled workers from other enterprises where their skills might be less valuable; nor could they discharge surplus workers or easily dismiss unsatisfactory ones (World Bank 1985: 131).

These serious and comprehensive problems contributed to low labour productivity as well as to an imbalance in the whole social and economic structure. Because of the extreme social sensitivity of the matter, progress in reform of the employment system has been very slow. Although the director responsibility system introduced between 1985 and 1987 gave enterprise directors delegated powers to manage personnel, the authorization of the local labour authorities was still required to hire or fire workers. Directors avoided firing a worker in order to preserve harmony in labour relations.

In 1986 the State Council published a set of four regulations which:

1. placed new recruits into a contractual rather than the previous permanent system of employment. An employer and employee were to sign a contract, normally of four years' maximum duration.
2. encouraged the 'open' recruitment of new employees. The labour authorities were no longer responsible for allocating workers; this was to be accomplished through the decisions of employers and workers themselves.
3. encouraged workers to receive training before they took up their posts.
4. accorded greater powers in labour management to enterprise directors, particularly over the hiring and dismissal of workers.

There was in practice only a slow growth in the numbers of contractual workers. In Beijing industry, for example, there were only 42,000 contractual workers by September 1988 compared with 1.96 million permanent workers. The Beijing local government in 1987 launched a campaign to raise labour productivity by adopting the 'two guarantees and one linkage' variant of the contract responsibility system, whereby an increase in the fund available to pay salaries and bonuses was linked to the growth of the enterprise's profit (a target for which was one of the two contractual 'guarantees'). Enterprises could enlarge or reduce the size of their labour forces, but no increase in the contracted labour budget would be allowed unless profits rose.

This expansion of enterprise autonomy in labour management failed to achieve the improvement in labour productivity expected of it. According to a survey conducted by the Beijing Municipal Economic Commission (BMEC), productive working hours in most enterprises were less than half of the total. In Automotive, for example, average productive time was only 1.7 hours per day. In other words, a worker stayed in the enterprise for 8 hours a day, 6.3 of which were wasted. Labour productivity could be low even in foreign joint ventures. For example, average productive time in the Beijing Jeep Corporation was only 5.5 hours per person per day according to a 1988 report of the BMEC (Lu 1991: 228) and labour productivity was only about 60–70 per cent of the foreign parent's facilities in Toledo, Ohio (Aiello 1991: 58).

Personnel employment system

There has been little change in this system under the economic reform. It covers cadres, a term that includes managers, technicians and engineers, secretaries and other clerical staff, and trade union staff. Cadres are normally recruited from the graduates of universities, colleges and institutes; also from former military officers. Cadres are expected to perform managerial or clerical jobs as opposed to workers who carry out physical tasks. The appointment of a worker to a post within the personnel system officially requires authorization from the local personnel bureau. In practice, it has been common for enterprises to use workers to perform office-based tasks such as planning and the preparation of statistics, when there is a shortage of qualified staff.

The proportion of administrative and clerical staff in the workforce has been increasing. More and more workers are employed in office and support positions and fewer in direct production jobs. While this trend is a normal accompaniment of economic development, a further specific reason for it in China stems from the insistence of the enterprise's superior authorities that it establish a structure of departments to reflect the organization of those authorities rather than the requirements of the business. For example, in 1985 the Beijing Municipal Economic Commission ordered enterprises to set up Total Quality Control Offices, and their directors were ordered to head them up. These TQC offices directly corresponded to the TQC office in each industrial bureau, to which they were instructed to report on the quality performance achieved by the enterprises. When staff from a bureau's TQC office visited an enterprise, they expected to be received formally by the enterprise's TQC office. It was not surprising that staff numbers in enterprises increased under this system.

Categories within the employment system

By the end of 1988, the employment system in our focal group of six Beijing state enterprises consisted of four main component categories: three covering workers and the fourth covering cadres. They are summarized in table 9.1. The first category was that of 'fixed labour employment'. These were workers who enjoyed permanent employment status. Their basic salaries were determined according to a government eight-point scale. Their recruitment and dismissal had to be authorized by the municipal labour bureau, and they enjoyed medical and welfare benefits set by the state. Workers in this category had always enjoyed permanent status or had been recruited from the ranks of redeployed soldiers who had an urban residence[3] or by transfer from other organizations which had a quota of permanent employees.

The second employment category was that of 'contractual employment'. The workers in this category were employed on a limited-term contract, the renewal of which depended on their performance and/or the enterprise's need for their services. Their salaries were determined by the enterprise in terms of eight grades. The enterprise covered their medical and welfare benefits and also had the right to hire and fire them. School leavers since 1987 and other contractual labour provided the source of people coming into this category.

The third category was that of temporary employment. Employment conditions for people in this category were similar to those of contractual workers except that they were hired for a limited time or for a specific task. Enterprise management could hire and fire temporary workers, though this had to be registered with the local labour bureau. Temporary workers were recruited mainly from the agricultural sector or from workers who had retired.

Cadres, who comprised the fourth employment category, were paid according to a state-defined seventeen-point scale. They enjoyed permanent employment with medical and welfare benefits guaranteed by the state. The recruitment and (on very rare occasions) discharge of such employees were

Table 9.1. *The employment system in the Beijing enterprises*

	Employment system	Sources of labour
1.	*Fixed labour employment*	
	Wages set by the state (8 wage grades)	Current fixed employees
	Permanent employment	College graduates
	Medical & social welfare benefits set by the state	Retired soldiers
		Movement of personnel from other
	Hiring and firing authorized by labour bureau	organizations with a fixed employment quota
2.	*Contractual employment*	
	Wages set by enterprise (8 wage grades)	Recruitment of young school graduates since 1987
	Contract-term employment	Other contractual labour
	Medical & social welfare costs covered by the enterprise	
	Hiring and firing by enterprise	
3.	*Temporary workers*	
	Wages set by enterprise (grades regulated by the state)	Retired workers
		Workers from agricultural sector
	Contract-term employment	
	Medical & social welfare costs covered by the enterprise	
	Hiring and firing by enterprise but registered in labour bureau	
4.	*Personnel system* (cadres, technicians, engineers)	
	Salary set by the state (17 grades)	University/college graduates
	Permanent employment	Retired army officers
	Medical benefit covered by the state	Current cadres
	Managed by personnel bureau	

Source: Lu (1991).

controlled by the municipal personnel bureau. People in this category were recruited from university and college graduates, retired army officers and those already enjoying the status of cadres.

Recruitment, promotion and dismissal

Recruitment and promotion

This section deals first with the recruitment of non-managerial employees and then considers the selection and promotion of managers.

The contractual management system was introduced in Beijing during 1987 together with the contract labour system. From then on, a state enterprise's plans for employment and its budget for salaries and bonuses had to be approved by three bureaux of the municipal government. The industrial bureau was responsible for checking both the enterprise's level of employment, and for approving the enterprise's profit targets according to its historical data. The labour bureau fixed the enterprise's employment establishment and its budget for salaries and bonuses. The municipal finance bureau then checked this budget and approved it. The enterprise could not subsequently change its employment budget without securing the further authorization of the labour and finance bureaux. This system meant that the local authorities controlled the employment budget, while enterprise management determined how the budget was allocated and how the labour force was utilized. This included freedom to hire and fire in the case of contract and temporary workers.

The system also left three ways by which management could increase employees' incomes. The first was to reduce the size of its labour force. The second was to increase profits since, under the contract responsibility system, an enterprise was permitted to increase its employment budget by 0.7 per cent for every 1 per cent rise in the level of profits. The third way was, if it was necessary to take on more people, to employ university graduates or former military personnel whose salaries were allocated from the local personnel bureau.

Following the signing of contracts with the three local bureaux in 1987, all the six focal Beijing enterprises stopped increasing their employment. They encouraged people with low qualifications or skills, and temporary workers, to leave. They tried to attract younger skilled or qualified workers, but found this difficult because of the low payment, poor welfare benefits and inadequate housing they could offer compared with collective, private and foreign-funded enterprises. Another effect of the new system was that the orientation of labour managers in the enterprises changed. Previously, their major responsibility had been to draw up an annual recruitment plan to be submitted to the labour bureau which then made an allocation of new recruits to the enterprise. Now labour managers concentrated on identifying labour needs and seeking suitable people for the positions concerned. In practice, workshop managers or managers in charge of technical departments initiated requests to fill vacancies created by people leaving jobs. Normally, labour managers then put together a number of recruitment needs in the form of a proposal which was discussed with the vice-director in charge of personnel and often with the supervisory labour bureau. The bureau offered comments and information about the availability of recruits, especially university and college graduates. The final decision to recruit was usually authorized by the enterprise director or relevant vice-director. If the matter was purely routine and did not involve any increase in the size of the employment establishment, the decision was also often delegated to the labour manager. Compared to the situation in 1985 before the contract responsibility system was introduced, recruitment had clearly become decentralized down to the enterprise. For in 1985, all recruitment had to be authorized by government agencies.

The information sources used in the recruitment process indicate that an efficient labour market had not yet developed. Recommendation of a candidate through personal relations (*guanxi*) was perceived to be more reliable than information from the labour market, particularly for categories of employee in short supply.[4] As the labour manager in Heavy Electrical explained:

We seldom contact the local labour market. As a labour manager, I know that highly qualified people, such as skilled workers, do not go there to find jobs. Such people are tied down strongly by their organization not allowing them to leave. It requires strong personal influence to enable them to leave. In the case we are discussing, the reason for the driver wanting to take up our post was that he wanted to work closer to his family. We learned that his performance had been very good through his factory director. That director had a long-term relationship with us and we trust each other. So we believed what he told us.

The labour manager in Audio-visual indicated that the effects of an introduction to employment based on *guanxi* often carried over into the new job with beneficial effects for management:

If a person is introduced by your acquaintance, a friend or relative whom you trust or know well, it will help their future management. The sponsor will later help you to supervise the new recruit's behaviour. Often he or she will perform well because he/she has in mind your relations with his/her sponsor.

Labour and personnel managers also formed their own networks between enterprises to exchange information on the availability of labour. In the case of new school and university graduates, the local labour and personnel bureaux normally possessed better information than any individual enterprise. Enterprises sometimes established their own direct connections with local technical schools and sometimes individual graduates took their own initiative in contacting possible employers. By and large, however, enterprises relied on personnel bureaux for information on the availability of technical school, college and university graduates and for their personal profiles. There were still occasions when the enterprise agreed to take on a graduate whom it did not really want in order to maintain good relations with the local bureau.

By the end of the 1980s, enterprise management had gained more autonomy in determining the recruitment process for non-managerial employees. They still tended to bunch their needs into an annual recruitment plan, as they had been required to do under the older centralized system, but the role of local industrial and labour bureaux had changed from being the source of final approval to that of agents providing enterprises with services. Personnel (cadre) recruitment remained more dependent on the local bureau, both for information and through the continued practice of allocating highly qualified graduates. Moreover, despite the presence of regulations which now indicated that labour recruitment was to be decided by the enterprise, the framework for structuring those decisions administratively remained in existence and could be used by the local government authorities. They had, in effect, the power to determine whether the new regulations were to be applied or not.

Enterprise directors do not, however, enjoy the same degree of initiative and autonomy in the case of recruitment or promotion to managerial appointments. Evidence gathered in 1991 from three large, state-owned enterprises in the chemicals, petro-chemicals and iron and steel industries indicated that a standardized formal procedure was followed in the selection or promotion of middle and senior managers at the level of department head and above. The criteria applied were reported in identical terms and they were regulated by the party. They included moral and political attitudes, education, competence, relations with others, record of performance and physical attributes such as age and health. They were consolidated into four principles: 'good moral practice' (*de*), 'adequate competence' (*neng*), 'positive working attitude' (*qin*), and 'strong performance record' (*ji*). Among these four principles, priority appeared to be given to political loyalty and moral standards. Importance was also attached to a prospective manager's ability to sustain harmonious relations with other people.

When a managerial position is available, candidates may be proposed by various sources and posts are also increasingly being advertised. The personnel staff in the party system then talk to people who work with and/or know the candidate in order to gain a general impression. These discussions are summarized and reported directly to the enterprise party secretary and the director. They will then decide whether to proceed further and shortlist the candidate or not. This is the first stage in managerial selection. A more formal investigation is then conducted into the shortlisted candidates. Party personnel staff inquire systematically among middle managers and senior office staff through face-to-face talks or questionnaires in order to ascertain the attitudes and views they have towards the candidates. Workers may also be consulted. The personnel managers interviewed in the 1991 study stressed the importance of the principle of what they termed 'democracy' in the selection of managers, by which they meant collecting the opinions of staff and workers as to the performance and qualities of the persons being considered. This process is a more focused and predictable procedure than the election of senior managers by workers' congresses which had been envisaged for state-owned enterprises by provisional regulations issued in 1981.

The final decision is usually taken in an enlarged party committee meeting which includes all the enterprise party officers, senior managers and some important administrative staff. In this meeting, participants are asked to express their opinions about the candidates and then to vote on a final choice. After this collective decision, the director signs the letter of appointment on behalf of the enterprise. Evidence from the 1991 study suggests that the powers to give final approval to managerial appointments can vary in specific cases, with the enterprise director sometimes exercising them and in other cases the party committee doing so. Before appointees take up their new managerial posts party staff normally brief them on the decision and on the opinions about them uncovered in the process (Lu 1992).

Dismissal

The dismissal of personnel remains a delicate matter in China. Although the State Council published a temporary regulation in July 1986 permitting the dismissal from state-owned enterprises of workers who had committed disciplinary offences, enterprise managers were very reluctant in practice to sack workers. Sacking someone means not only cutting off his or her income, but welfare and social life as well. The Chinese government is aware that unemployment will be a growing problem in China as the economic reform places increasing pressure on firms to ensure their own survival, but the scope and funding of unemployment at present is acknowledged to be wholly inadequate (*Beijing Review* 1992b).

The work unit was, and usually remains, the Chinese worker's social and community unit as well. Workers and staff who insist on retaining their accommodation, even if performing badly or having become redundant, gain considerable sympathy from their colleagues in such circumstances. The enterprise party organization and labour union might well support their case, and directors are careful to consult with these organs first if a serious disciplinary problem arises. When the Beijing Municipal Government organized a campaign of labour rationalization ('Optimizing Labour Organization') in the middle of 1988, it at the same time required redundant employees to stay within the enterprise by opening up a new business, constituting themselves into service units and so forth. Enterprise managers were extremely reluctant to create even this level of threat to jobs for fear of the harm it would cause to the quality of human relations within their organizations. Despite this campaign, any dismissal of an employee, even for gross negligence or violation of work rules, still required the authorization of the municipal labour authority.

The problem of who should assume responsibility for a discharged employee remains an acute one in a country where everyone is supposed to belong to a social unit. Errant individualism is in this respect certainly not permitted in China. A system of local labour and personnel exchanges has now been established, and these hold the personal files of redundant or dismissed employees. Although the system is intended to facilitate labour mobility, many Chinese who find themselves on the books of the employment exchanges are very uneasy about this, especially if they previously enjoyed or expected to attain permanent status. They experience a sense of personal devaluation, even betrayal by their employer. This is, of course, a reaction shared to some extent with their counterparts in the West, but it is felt more strongly by those who have been reared on socialist ideology.

Kohut (1992) cites cases where cuts in payment because of poor work performance, let alone redundancies, have aroused violent reactions among Chinese workers against their reform-minded managers. For instance, when half the workers at the Tianjin watch enterprise were sent home on partial wages: 'One man is said to have found it so difficult to accept dismissal that he killed himself and his wife and child. Other workers smashed machinery at the factory until security forces were called in' (p. 16). Kohut comments that until an efficient national social security system is established, outbreaks of worker revenge are likely to continue. Because of the practical problems arising from the lack of an adequate social support system for unemployed people, managers in state enterprises have evolved various ways of coping with redundancy and even poor work discipline. One is to tolerate the problem and to bear its cost. One enterprise, for example, declared a labour establishment in its official returns to the Beijing government that was only 75 per cent of the actual numbers on its payroll. Another way, which has been condoned by the local authorities, is to transfer surplus employees to a service company that works on a sub-contractual basis for the enterprise. In cases which the writer was able to investigate, it appeared that such employees had little real value to contribute to the enterprise and that this was in practice another approach to covering up redundancy. While there has been an increase in the number of dismissals for disciplinary offences, this remains very small and a step that is not taken lightly. There is, in other words, still a considerable tolerance of poor discipline and poor work performance in state enterprises.

The problem of redundancy, and the challenge to the 'iron rice bowl', takes a particularly acute form when an ailing state-owned enterprise is declared bankrupt. As the official journal *Beijing Review* put it, 'the placement of personnel in bankrupt enterprises has a close bearing on social stability and is also instrumental in determining whether socialist enterprises can effectively handle bankruptcy.' (*Beijing Review* 1992d: 23). China promulgated a Bankruptcy Law on State-Owned Enterprises in December 1986 and it has subsequently been applied selectively to both state and collective enterprises, with the North-Eastern city of Shenyang being a focus for learning how to deal with the consequences. By the end of 1991, there had been 252 cases of enterprise bankruptcy in China and the first half of 1992 saw another 66 cases, 15 of which were state-owned enterprises (*Beijing Review* 1992d; 1992h).

In Shenyang, 18 enterprises went bankrupt between August 1986 – the first case in China – and July 1992. This is a small number in relation to the total of over 300 large and medium size state enterprises and over 3,000 collective enterprises in the city, but institutionally it represents a major development in the economic reform both symbolically and in the new structural arrangements it calls forth. The first bankruptcy created major shock waves and gave considerable psychological teeth to the concept of contractual enterprise responsibility then being introduced into the state enterprise system. The employees made redundant faced substantial income reductions; in fact payments due to them dropped to zero after two years. It took 27 months before all the employees of the first bankrupt enterprise found new jobs. As of mid-1992, about 90 per cent of the 3,330 workers who had been actively working in Shenyang's 18 bankrupt enterprises had been re-employed and the other 2,670 persons on the payroll had been retired with pensions.

The local government authorities in Shenyang have had to play a key role in redeploying redundant employees. The first bankruptcy was declared at a time when the local institutional framework was not ready to handle it. It drew in a range of departments concerned with insurance, banking, industrial and commercial affairs, tax and auditing which exhibited 'inter-departmental wrangles and . . . [a] tardy pace of work' (*Beijing Review* 1992d: 24). Subsequently the Shenyang municipal authorities established an Office for Handling Enterprise Bankruptcy, the first of its kind in China, which co-ordinates the work of the relevant departments. The municipal authority has also learned to take a more proactive role in two other respects: firstly, by brokering the absorption of bankrupt firms' personnel and assets by viable concerns; secondly, by establishing 'labour service markets' (job centres) in each trade where there have been redundant workers.

Training

Warner (1992) discusses China's industrial training and development needs, the enormous scale of which stems from a conjunction of two factors. The first is the depredation of the Cultural Revolution when formal education was greatly disrupted. This led to a shortfall of the highly educated technical and managerial personnel capable of running sophisticated technology and managing modern enterprises. The second factor lies in the ambitious programme of the four modernizations which the economic reform is dedicated to achieving. This calls for the successful exploitation of technology transfer and the shouldering of considerably more responsibility by enterprise management. It is not surprising, therefore, that the reformers have called for the training and building up of managerial and technical cadres to lead the modernization process (e.g. CPC 1984).

Warner (1986) found from visits to six large state enterprises in 1984 that their training investment had grown to account in the main for about 2 per cent of their total budgets. This effort was encouraged and given some direction by a Higher Educational Commission and a Vocational Education Commission which operated both at national and provincial levels. Factory directors decided who should attend a training course below the level of workshop heads; above that level the corporate head office (industrial bureau) decided. Each of the enterprises Warner visited supported a number of internal training departments. These ran three main types of course. Firstly, remedial general education for employees who were disadvantaged by the Cultural Revolution, including those who had lost some years of university study. Secondly, technical education. Thirdly, 'economic management' training in accounting, planning, personnel and so forth. At the time, there were also the beginnings of training in computer applications.

Chinese enterprises had by 1984 re-introduced extensive apprenticeship programmes on a large scale. Apprenticeships were normally directed towards specialized training according to each workshop's production requirements. Their length varied from between one and three years depending on the job and at the end of the period there was an examination.

However, China continued to experience a chronic shortage of trained personnel in the area of new technology. There was, for instance, a virtual absence of applications engineers in the manufacturing sector. Science and technology graduates continue to be needed, as do trained technicians and skilled workers in the high technology fields. Warner visited six high technology production sites in the summer of 1987 which were engaged in the production of computers, consumer electronics, electrical goods and in development work on new computers and software. All of the organizations had systematic training programmes except for one which was wholly Hong Kong-owned and made telephones and speaker-phones. In that organization, workers learned on the job and technical staff were recruited from outside. However, even in this case, managers and supervisors were sent to Hong Kong for training at the end of the year when the factory was less busy (Warner 1992).

In three of the other enterprises, managers and/or senior technical staff had been sent abroad for training. Use was generally made of relevant Chinese university courses (including the TV University, an equivalent of the Open University) and other management and technical programmes. Outside experts were in several cases invited in and in-house training was usually given to skilled workers. Several of the enterprises hired graduates directly from university science and technology departments. Nevertheless, Warner concludes that despite this effort devoted towards training, the level of human resource expertise in these companies did not match the level of inward technology transfer in hardware that they had achieved. The effective use of high technology equipment, often imported or copied from abroad, therefore remains a serious problem in Chinese industry.

As Warner (1992) details in his book on the subject, the Chinese authorities attempted to establish a national institutional framework for management training, once the initial post-1978 expansion had highlighted the relative lack of trained management as a major bottleneck in achieving modernization. In March 1979 the China Enterprise Management Association (CEMA) was set up by the State Economic Commission to co-ordinate management education in China. This national association brings together leading experts in industry, government, research institutes and universities. It is headquartered in Beijing with local associations in major urban centres around the country. It has established a network of training activities involving universities and institutes, state-owned enterprises, TV and correspondence schools. CEMA entered into partnership with foreign institutions to run both MBA and executive programmes. MBA programmes were established in Beijing (1984 with the European Community), Dalian (1984 with the US Department of Commerce) and Xian (with the British Council and Lancaster University). Executive programmes were established in Shanghai (West Germany), Chengdu (Canada) and Tianjin (Japan). Many Chinese universities were twinned with Canadian universities by the Canadian International Development Agency (CIDA) to develop their management education capabilities. The State Education Commission oversaw managerial and technical training for senior managers and technicians in factories until 1987, and after the mid-1980s worked with fifteen universities to establish new MBA programmes, most of which by Western standards remained oriented towards Management Science.

The scale of China's management education and training effort is impressive and is a clear manifestation of the regime's determination to modernize the economy. It is claimed that, during the period 1979 to 1985, over 8 million managers and supervisors underwent some kind of management training course (Wang 1990). In 1988 the total number of students in a wide variety of management-related programmes, excluding the many correspondence and evening courses, exceeded 100,000. This number amounted to 5.5 per cent of the total number in higher education at the time (Warner 1992: 60).

The major weakness which persists in the system lies on the employer's side of things. Very few enterprises have drawn up systematic programmes for the training and development of their managers and employees, based on anything like an audit of future needs and personal potentials. Too frequently the choice of whom to send on a training programme is treated as a matter of status and/or reward rather than one of finding an appropriate match between organizational needs, personal abilities and experience, and the content of the training available. Nor do many Chinese enterprises appraise managers on a systematic basis, despite the claim by the three large firms studied in 1991 periodically to survey opinion among workers and co-managers on the performance of managers. However, these surveys did not apparently extend to senior managers who had been appointed by the director or the superior authority (in this case the industrial ministry).

Our experience at the China–European Community Management Institute (CEMI) points to another aspect of this lack of personnel planning within Chinese enterprises. The Institute's MBA programme drew able young recruits from Chinese state enterprises and the intention was that they should return to them and help to improve the quality of their management. When the first graduates did return to their employers they found themselves slotted into their old jobs, or used as interpreters and technical translators, as though nothing had happened. There was no appreciation that the graduates had been through a major development experience, integrating class and practical project work, and had acquired an understanding of business and complementary technical skills which could be put to good use. Even when staff of the Institute subsequently endeavoured to explain the nature of the MBA programme to enterprise managers, graduates still found that they were being placed back onto an established career ladder in which progression was primarily related to age and length of service.[5] The consequence was that MBA graduates increasingly moved over to join foreign joint ventures or representative offices, much to their personal gain and the benefit of such enterprises in which their contribution was highly valued.

Motivation

Tung (1991) argues that the ways Chinese enterprises motivate their employees can be analyzed according to the Katz and Kahn (1978) paradigm of rule enforcement, external rewards and internalized motivation. Rule enforcement refers to the acceptance of role prescriptions and organizational directives because of their legitimacy. External rewards attach incentives to desired behavioural or other performance outcomes. Tung refers with the term 'internalized motivation' to the internalization of political and organizational cultures, regarding it as 'almost synonymous with moral encouragement' (p. 348). We shall extend its scope to include also motivation which comes from the intrinsic attractiveness of the work or job itself.

Rule enforcement in terms of adherence to administrative regulations remains a real force in the governance of Chinese state enterprises as we have seen when discussing different aspects of their management. At the same time, and because of the significance of regulations and the sanctions that the authorities retain to enforce them, there is a considerable incentive to find ways of getting around regulations in order to facilitate the actual running of an enterprise. The forms taken by rules as they impinge on individual workers or their work groups include regulations relating to political correctness (including prohibitions on disclosing certain categories of information to foreigners), contracts of employment for non-permanent workers and job descriptions. Judging from the writer's own experience, job descriptions carry little motivational impact for

Chinese employees. Office workers in particular look to job descriptions as protective devices. They are an insurance against being called upon to assume a new and potentially threatening responsibility and against being overworked. They are not regarded as instruments for goal-setting and motivation towards goal-attainment.

In the case of external rewards, as the following chapter notes, much emphasis has been placed by China's economic reformers on the use of material incentives to stimulate productivity. In practice, a relatively egalitarian distribution of bonuses and other incentive payments continues to prevail, especially in the state sector. More progress appears to have been made towards linking payment to a person's level of responsibility, education and training, and to the profit performance of the enterprise.

Internalized motivation is the third type identified by Katz and Kahn. One source is political indoctrination and campaigning, and this has been relied upon greatly in certain periods since 1949, most notably the Great Leap Forward and the Cultural Revolution. Since the crushing of the Democracy Movement in June 1989, the credence placed by urban staff and workers in this ideological approach has been next to zero. Their response to the post-Tiananmen attempts at political indoctrination, which amounted to passive mental resistance on a massive scale, provided ample evidence of this frame of mind.[6]

Another source of internalized motivation is the building of an organizational culture. The potential for doing this in Chinese enterprises is very strong. The organization there is a comprehensive social unit in which the majority of people remain throughout their working lives and indeed beyond. However, as we have seen, the Chinese enterprise typically contains entrenched barriers between different departments and functional areas, which themselves have inherited strong vertical linkages that pass over and above the enterprise itself. This sub-unit identity has limited people's sense of allegiance to the work unit as a whole, though the latter is a real force as well. In the state-owned sector, the lack of pressures to secure economic survival through its own achievement has reduced management's incentive to attach to this identity a keen sense of corporate striving to win. The social organization and corporate thinking in people's minds are in place for Chinese management to embark on conscious efforts at organizational culture-building (Barnowe 1990). The contract responsibility system now encourages organizational cultures to be oriented towards profit and investment performance.

A third aspect of internal personal motivation concerns the commitment to doing a good job which may arise from the intrinsic characteristics of the work and the extent to which appreciation for it and for the views of employees are built into the processes and style of management. An insight into this aspect is provided by our investigations in the Beijing state-owned enterprises.

In October 1985 and then again in March 1990, Chinese MBA students at CEMI working under the writer's direction collected information from 144 job-holders in the six enterprises. Within each enterprise, data were collected on a sample of 24 jobs: 4 managerial, 4 technical staff, 4 office and 12 production. The production jobs were sub-divided into 6 assembly and 6 machining or preparatory. The samples at the two points in time were carefully matched by job type, age and gender. Further information on the type of jobs included in each category is provided in Appendix 9.1.

Each job-holder was, as part of this study, asked to complete a schedule of structured questions which included twelve scaled items on the content of their jobs, the changes they perceived (if any) in those same items of content over the previous twelve months and their level of satisfaction with those items plus others of a contextual and extrinsic nature.[7] Figure 9.2 compares the extent to which members of the 1985 and 1990 samples perceived that their jobs contained the twelve features listed. The results are striking in several ways. First, there is relatively little difference between the profiles which emerge for 1985 and 1990. In other words, five years of economic reform appear not to have made a major difference to the intrinsic content of people's jobs. Second, there are sharp differences in the extent to which people perceived different features to characterize their jobs. Most people tended to think that their chance of promotion was very small. By contrast, a large majority also thought that they were given quite high levels of responsibility, that they were able to tell how well they had done their work, that they were doing something worthwhile, and that they had the satisfaction of completing a whole piece of work. Overall, this suggests that these Chinese employees generally perceived that they had an intrinsically meaningful job, but that they were stuck in it for a long time to come.

If one breaks the sample down into its four main groups, rather greater contrasts emerge. The managerial group registered an increase, on average, in their intrinsic job content over the five years, whereas members of the other three groups recorded average decreases. The items on which managers recorded the greatest increase were recognition, immediate knowledge of results, and attention to suggestions. They recorded average decreases in their ability to control time and physical movement. These shifts suggest that enterprise managers were now working in a more results-oriented context following the extension of the responsibility system, but that their personal 'slack' had diminished – they were working under more pressure.

There were systematic differences between the four groups along many of the perceived job characteristics, both in 1985 and 1990. The level of personal autonomy enjoyed by managers was quite clearly greater than that enjoyed by technical and clerical workers, who in turn perceived that they had more autonomy than production workers. This was the case with the freedom to choose

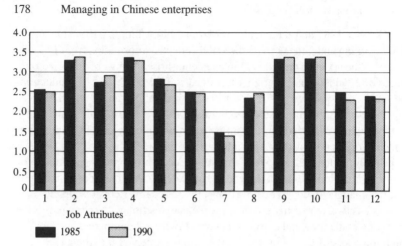

Figure 9.2   Comparison of perceived job attributes, 1985 and 1990. Mean scores (N=144 job holders). Higher score=more the attribute is perceived to be present in the job (scale: 1–5). *Key to items:* 1=freedom to choose your own method of working; 2=responsibility given to you; 3=recognition for good work; 4=being able to know right away in your own mind how well you have done your work; 5=the opportunity to use your abilities; 6=variety in your job; 7=the chance of promotion; 8=attention paid to suggestions you make; 9=the feeling of doing something which is not trivial, but really worthwhile; 10=the satisfaction of completing a whole piece of work; 11=the ability to decide how much time you are going to spend on different activities; 12=the opportunity to move around to different parts of the building.

their own methods of working, responsibility, attention to suggestions, ability to determine time allocation between activities, and freedom to move around the premises – in all these instances the differences in inter-group averages were highly unlikely to have occurred by chance. The office group, however, registered somewhat more autonomy overall than did the technical staff. This pattern also emerged in the case of variety in the job and attention to suggestions: the rank order between groups being managers, office workers, technical staff and production workers. The four groups also rated their promotion chances differently, though all were pessimistic. Managers tended to think that they had the greatest chance of promotion, followed in order by technical, clerical and production workers.

Although the overall scores only registered a slight decline in perceived chances of promotion between 1985 and 1990, it was apparent that in both years the general pessimism attached to this motivator carried over to the way people evaluated changes in their jobs over the previous twelve months. The only items for which in both two years the samples registered declines over the previous year were promotion chances, and level of personal control over time allocation and physical movement. The samples registered an increase over the previous twelve months for every other job attribute.

It is not surprising, therefore, that, again in both years, the level of satisfaction with promotion chances was one of the lowest of all the sixteen items questioned (see figure 9.3). Only two aspects of the job attracted lower satisfaction, namely physical working conditions and level of pay, both of which tend to be very poor in state-owned enterprises. The intrinsic content of the work itself generated, on average, the highest job satisfaction: people were most satisfied with knowledge of results, doing something worthwhile, and completing a whole piece of work. They also tended to be satisfied with the opportunities they had to relate socially to colleagues and fellow workers. The overall sample profiles presented in figure 9.3. conform to a two-factor picture of motivation of the kind identified by Herzberg and his colleagues (1959) in which intrinsic job attributes are positive motivators while extrinsic features tend to be objects of dissatisfaction. This pattern was not appreciably different between the four job groups.

The comparison between 1985 and 1990 points to an improvement in satisfaction over opportunities to participate in decisions and the attention paid to suggestions. This was a general trend since the differences in these satisfaction scores between the job groups were not large. Unfortunately, questions were not put directly about the level of opportunity for participation and the attention paid to suggestions, but the data on satisfaction suggest that opportunities for personal involvement in discussions and in the decision process had improved somewhat during the reform period.

These findings, if they were found to apply to larger populations of Chinese employees, imply that considerable motivational potential could be generated from the opening up of opportunities for advancement, so long as these were clearly tied to demonstrated performance. By and large, the Chinese managers and employees we studied perceive that they enjoy quite a high level of intrinsic job content and challenge, and good opportunities to enjoy social relationships in the workplace. They are not satisfied, however, with their chances of advancement, their level of earnings and their physical working conditions. On the basis of an objective comparison with conditions offered abroad and indeed in many Sino-foreign joint ventures, they are justified in their assessment.

It is interesting in this respect to note the findings reached by Shenkar and Ronen (1987b) from a questionnaire study of 163 PRC managers participating in a management training programme delivered by scholars from the United States in China in 1982. They elicited the work goals of these managers in the form of questions about the importance to them of various job and employment attributes. They compared the results of this exercise with those from essentially the same questionnaire obtained in studies of managers from other

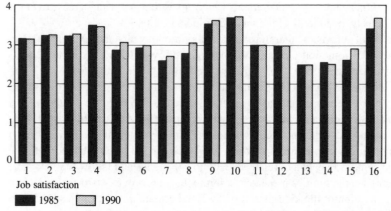

Job satisfaction

■ 1985   ▦ 1990

Figure 9.3 Comparison of job satisfaction, 1985 and 1990. Mean scores (N=144 job holders). Higher score=more satisfied with the aspect of the job (scale: 1–5). *Key to items 1–12:* as for figure 9.2. *Key to items 13–16:* 13=physical working conditions (noise, heat, comfort, etc.); 14=level of pay for job; 15=opportunity to participate in decisions; 16=opportunities for relating to colleagues.

Chinese cultural areas – Hong Kong, Taiwan and Singapore. This comparison identified three work goals on which managers from the PRC and other Chinese societies differed significantly. The PRC managers attached significantly more importance than the other groups to (1) autonomy to adopt their own approach to their job and (2) having co-workers who co-operate well with each other. They attached significantly less importance to having the opportunity for promotion to higher level jobs. Shenkar and Ronen explain these differences by reference to 'Maoist ideology' and its consequences. Our investigations suggest that the PRC managers were being quite realistic since the contrasts in their professed work goals with those expressed by other managers from Chinese cultures are certainly consistent with the evidence of job attributes and job satisfaction which we have presented. Shenkar and Ronen suggest that PRC managers have experienced ideological pressure against personal advancement. Our findings indicate that managers (and other employees) have little chance of personal advancement in the 'dead man's shoes' system which has characterized state-owned industry, and that this is an area where reform would offer major motivational gains.

The following chapter notes how the 'dead man's shoes' system manifests itself in the area of extrinsic rewards as well, with age and length of service playing an important role. At the same time, there is evidence that these factors are beginning to give way to criteria related to qualification and level of contribution.

Conclusion

This chapter opened by expressing doubts as to how far the concept of human resource management could be applied to China. HRM is culturally laden in a way that does not necessarily chime well with Chinese traditions and has not been wholeheartedly adopted even by non-mainland Chinese business. In the case of the People's Republic, the expectations attached to the management of personnel are of quite a different order. Even more than with other facets of management in China, heavy institutional pressures continue to bear upon the personnel sphere. Personnel management remains to an important extent an extension of political control, especially over people at the higher levels of organization. The *quid pro quo* is that management is constrained to maintain social welfare objectives among its priorities, even where these constitute a serious additional cost to the enterprise. When this social employment contract breaks down, as in the case of bankruptcy, government agencies have been mobilized to ensure a redeployment of the displaced labour, or at least that acceptable terms are achieved for retirement.

The economic reform is nevertheless introducing more pressures for enterprises to improve their economic performance, and these are changing the management of personnel in several ways. The introduction of the contract labour system and the decentralization of labour recruitment to enterprise management are effecting improvements in the matching of employment to economic requirements. The authorities have also instituted various forms of training on a very substantial and relatively systematic scale.

Progress is being made towards greater labour mobility. More workers are going on to the contract system and provisions are also in place permitting employees to leave their units and lodge their personal files in a community labour exchange during the interim. A more adequate system of unemployment benefit and social security is being devised, and a widespread system of employment exchanges has now been established. Apart from the availability of training, somewhat less progress is being made towards realizing the full potential of those who are in work. The notion of appraisal and career progression procedures is largely absent. Implying as it does the identification of merit by reference to objective performance criteria and the encouragement of personal ambition, this is the side of personnel management furthest removed from the collective norms of Chinese tradition and socialist ideology.

Innovations in this sensitive area are proceeding on an experimental and incremental basis so as to preserve a continuity with cultural and socialist traditions. This contrasts with the recent discontinuity in some post-socialist economies. The Chinese are searching for ways which meet the economy's human resource requirements but with less wastage of key manpower resources and less human misery than one is seeing in the newly de-regulated labour markets of Eastern Europe or in many Western capitalist economies. The obverse of the coin is the maintenance of a high degree of administrative and political regulation over this particular field of management.

Appendix 9.1   Examples of jobs by category (levels)

Job category 1: Managerial
Director; vice-director (production); head of financial department; head of design section; workshop manager.

Job category 2:Technical
Design engineer; section chief engineer; quality control engineer; computer programmer.

Job category 3: Office
Accountant; statistician; clerk; factory planner; salesman; secretary.

Job category 4: Production
(1) machining or preparation; punch operator; silicon sheet cutter; lathe operator; drill operator; grinder; compounder (pharmaceuticals); machine cutter; planer.
(2) assembly.

Appendix 9.2   Explanation of scales employed

Reported job content
Respondents were asked to indicate the extent to which they perceived their jobs had each of a set of twelve features. They indicated this in terms of a Likert-type five-point scale for each feature, with the scale ranging from extremes of 'there's none of that in my job' to 'there's a great deal of that in my job'. The features of job content are as follows:
1. freedom to choose your own method of working
2. responsibility given to you
3. recognition for good work
4. being able to know right away in your own mind how well you have done your work
5. the opportunity to use your abilities
6. variety in your job
7. the chance of promotion
8. attention paid to suggestions you make
9. the feeling of doing something which is not trivial, but really worthwhile

10. the satisfaction of completing a whole piece of work
11. the ability to decide how much time you are going to spend on different
    activities
12. the opportunity to move around to different parts of the building

Changes perceived in job content over the previous twelve months
Respondents were asked whether there had been an increase or decrease in the
above twelve job features during the previous twelve months, or whether there
had been no noticeable change.

Job satisfaction
Respondents were asked to indicate their level of satisfaction with their job in
terms of each of the above twelve features, plus the additional four listed below,
along a Likert-type five-point scale ranging from 'very satisfied' to 'very dis-
atisfied'.
The additional items were:
3. physical working conditions (noise, heat, comfort, etc.)
4. level of pay for the job
5. opportunity to participate in decisions
6. opportunities for relating to colleagues

10   The structure and system of earnings

The mobilization and motivation of an effective workforce is an essential requirement for any successful economy. It presents a particular challenge for a country such as China which has embarked on an ambitious programme of economic growth based on modernization and requiring substantial increases in productivity. The socialist transformation of industry should in principle create the conditions for a collective interest in the success of enterprises and therefore give efficacy to non-material motivation supported by moral and ideological encouragement. In practice, however socialist countries have combined material with non-material incentives, the balance between them often varying markedly over time (cf. Lane 1986 Wood 1987).

This chapter focuses on the structures of material rewards, specifically monetary earnings, in place at two points in time within the six state-owned Beijing enterprises. The first date, October 1985, represents an early stage in the extension of the Chinese economic reform to urban industry as a whole, and came shortly after new basic guidelines had been announced for payment reform in state-owned enterprises. The second was March 1990 by which time the reform had substantially advanced and many enterprises had introduced new payment systems ostensibly linking earnings more closely to criteria of contribution and performance.[1] The chapter begins with a brief review of policy towards earnings and incentives under the Communist regime, and how this compares with the likely impact of Chinese tradition in the area. This discussion serves to identify two models that contain different sets of predictors of variation in the earnings enjoyed by Chinese employees. The first model refers to traditional thinking drawn both from Chinese culture and socialist principles; the second refers to the functional criteria advanced by Chinese economic reformers. Our findings from 1985 and 1990 permit some conclusions to be drawn on the predictive power of each model and they also serve as an indication of whether the criteria for allocating earnings had actually changed under the reform.

Changing policies on earnings and incentives

The Chinese leadership has at different times since 1949 attempted to utilize both material and moral incentives to encourage productivity in support of economic growth (Henley and Nyaw 1987; Jackson 1992). As Henley and Nyaw observe:

Material incentives have been developed according to the socialist principle of 'from each according to his ability and to each according to his work.' In practice this means payment of a basic wage according to national scales plus an incentive bonus, developed at plant level. Moral encouragement has relied on a variety of different campaigns designed to strengthen the political and ideological education of workers so that they recognise their moral obligations to work hard for the benefit of the nation for under socialism they are 'the masters of the house'. (p. 128)

In China the authorities brought moral incentives to the fore during periods of ideological intensity characterized by low growth, notably the Great Leap Forward and the Cultural Revolution, while they have emphasized material incentives during periods of more moderate policy characterized by rapid industrial growth. During the years of socialist modernization according to the Soviet model up to 1957, output-linked individual bonuses were introduced for many production workers (especially in the larger factories) as well as bonus payments to managers and technical staff when targets were reached or exceeded. As the Great Leap Forward got underway during 1958, there was a trend towards the abolition of workers' individual piece-related bonuses in favour of a workgroup contribution to collective goals. Bonus payments for cadres, which had helped to widen income differentials, were also abolished. As Andors comments (1977: 125), 'what distinguished the Great Leap Forward incentive policy was the emphasis on political dedication to the building of socialism'.

Following the severe drop in industrial production and real wages in 1960–1, interest in piece-rate payments or hourly payments plus incentive rewards revived and they were reintroduced in many factories, but alongside various schemes appealing to moral motivation and aimed towards securing commitment through participation. Piecework and bonuses began to be eliminated entirely with the onset of the Cultural Revolution. Competitive, individual, material incentive was rejected in favour of co-operative, collective, moral incentive (Prybyla 1976). Direct worker participation in discussions of factory policy and in technical project teams was seen as an essential condition for realizing this incentive.

The years of economic reform since 1978, identified with pursuit of the 'Four Modernizations', have seen a renewed emphasis on material incentives coupled with rising real incomes. Earnings increases had been virtually frozen from 1963 to 1977, and by 1977 average real earnings were lower than in 1952

(Walder 1987: 23). The first widespread application of economic reform was in agriculture, which incorporated various incentive policies linked to permitting higher levels of commodity production for the market. In industry, bonus systems were revived from 1978 such that by 1984 incentive pay had increased to 24 per cent of the industrial payments bill. Starting in 1979, enterprises were able to generate larger bonus funds based on their overfulfilment of profit targets (Walder 1987: 24–5). There was also a move at the beginning of the reform period to break the government monopoly in job assignment by allowing people to seek jobs in private firms and foreign joint ventures; this encouraged the offering of higher payments, particularly by joint ventures, to attract good staff (Jackson 1992: 143–6).

In October 1984 the Communist Party of China's Central Committee adopted the major policy document on 'China's Economic Structure Reform' which sought to build upon experience with the economic reform programme and to expound a 'systematic' and 'all-round' policy to be applied generally throughout the industrial sector. The document articulated a clear expectation that industrial performance would benefit when personal contribution was reflected in the level of material reward:

The well-spring of vitality of the enterprise lies in the initiative, wisdom and creativeness of its workers by hand and brain . . . when their labour is closely linked with their own material benefits, their initiative, wisdom and creativeness can be brought into full play. This has been vividly and convincingly proved by our experience in rural reform. (CPC 1984: 11)

The so-called 'enterprise responsibility system' lies at the the heart of the Chinese industrial reform. One of this system's three 'basic principles' is stated by the same policy document to be 'the linking of the income of workers and staff members with their job performance' (p. 24). In mid-1984 it was announced that workers and managers in all state enterprises would receive payments above their basic salaries to reward hard work, efficiency and special responsibilities.[2] Deng Xiaoping (1984: 117) had called for 'distribution according to the quantity and quality of an individual's work' such that 'a person's grade on the pay scale is determined mainly by his peformance on the job, his technical level and his actual contribution'.

Enterprises were given more opportunity to reflect these policy aspirations when the fiscal reform of 1984 replaced profit remittance to the state by taxes on profits. They could henceforth decide on the bonuses to be paid to their workers and staff within the constraints of a centrally determined norm for the annual total, beyond which the state would levy a punitive tax. Managements were also enjoined at the time not only to use the bonus for 'rewarding the diligent and good and punishing the lazy and bad' (CPC 1984: 26) but also to widen differentials between mental and manual work and work of different skill, complexity and 'heaviness'.

Secondly, the 'floating salary' system became widely adopted in state enterprises after the mid-1980s. It was easy to implement, neither requiring drastic changes to the existing payment structure nor a long preparation time. This system was intended to replace bonuses (at least in part) which were by then increasingly recognized to have failed to link pay directly to performance. The first form of floating salary introduces a variable element into the salary, often fluctuating according to attainment of production norms for workers and according to degree of responsibility, workload and/or enterprise profit levels for managerial and non-production workers. The second form of floating system is one that links the total enterprise payroll to the fulfilment of a predetermined enterprise performance indicator such as profit, sales or a measure of output. This system involves payroll contracts with the government specifying the linkage and ratio involved. The floating element in salaries is quite often adjusted on a monthly basis, though it can also vary less frequently (Jackson 1992: 185–90).

The introduction of the contract responsibility system encouraged enterprise managements further to reform their payment systems. The State Council and central government departments responsible to it in 1985 issued several documents providing guidelines and regulations on payment system reform. These were followed up by more detailed regulations from the Beijing Municipal Government. By 1987, about 80 per cent of state-owned enterprises had 'reformed' their payment systems in one respect or another (Jackson 1992: 183).

Three of the six Beijing enterprises introduced a floating salary in addition to the basic salary. This varied according to the level of profit earned by the enterprise. Four of the enterprises had introduced additional payments for length of service and for employees having higher levels of technical skill. Overall, judging by the situation in Beijing, enterprises after 1987 were introducing more components into their payment systems in an attempt to bind monetary reward more closely to variations in (1) responsibility, (2) technical expertise, (3) enterprise performance and (4) individual performance. Attempts were usually made to effect these linkages through quite complex formulae.

The economic reform policy therefore called for the level of earnings to be related to a number of criteria. According to the reform's principles, salaries would reflect the level of work undertaken, of qualification and of training (as indicators of contribution and expertise). The campaign accompanying the reform, to promote younger and qualified persons to senior positions, might also be expected to strengthen a correspondence (once other factors had been taken into account) of higher salaries with both relative youth and newness in the job, especially among higher job categories. A floating element would often be added to the salary and reflect individual or collective performance. The total payroll available for distribution should reflect the enterprise's capacity to pay as indicated by its profitablility. Individual bonus payments, particularly for production workers, should reflect personal motivation and performance.

In practice, the nationwide application of economic reform to state-owned enterprises was still relatively recent in October 1985 when the first study reported here was undertaken. Measures such as a harsh tax on above-norm bonus funds constrained the extent to which bonus levels could reflect enterprise profitabilility. The virtual absence of any competence in job evaluation or work measurement limited the ability to relate either basic salary to the intrinsic content of individual jobs or bonuses to individual performance. The reform's policy on earnings, and indeed on other matters, also challenged the established status-order and ran counter to several existing ideological and cultural tenets.

The underlying rationality of the reform policy on material rewards is based on recognizing differential performance both of the enterprise and of the individual. While as Henley and Nyaw (1987) state, this appears to be compatible with the socialist principle of 'from each according to his ability, to each according to his work', it is in reality an implantation within soil that harbours contrary antecedents stemming both from Chinese socialism and cultural tradition.

One of the declared objectives of the reform movement is to overturn the culture of egalitarianism. Some, however, maintain that this is more than just a recent phenomenon associated with the Yan'an and Cultural Revolution periods; it is, rather, a deeply-rooted traditional value closely associated in the popular mind with that of equity (e.g. Qian 1986). Insofar as it continues to underlie people's expectations, egalitarianism constitutes a force working against the movement toward greater differentiation in earnings advocated by the economic reformers. Walder (1987) comments that egalitarianism has been the motive behind an indiscriminate distribution of bonus payments to workers with little regard to their performance.

Chinese culture also manifests a deep respect for age and for the father-figure within a tradition of paternalistic authority (Pye 1985; Lockett 1988). This implies a strong expectation that the grades on which workers and staff are placed, and hence their basic salaries, will honour their age and that, other things being equal, men will enjoy a higher grading than women. Lockett and Littler (1983) comment that available statistics suggest there are differences in wages associated with gender, despite laws regulating equal pay. Finally, the inclusive social nature of the work unit (*danwei*) is consistent with the group orientation in Chinese tradition (where it was primarily directed toward the family unit) and which was particularly encouraged during the first three decades of communist government. On this basis, one would expect long service with the work unit to be recognized in superior pay, and to be a factor reinforcing the postulated influence of age.

The drive within China's industrial reform movement toward relating earnings to economic contribution is therefore not only handicapped by fiscal restrictions and limited competence in the necessary measurement techniques, but it has also been initiated within a context of socialistic and traditional values. These values are likely to lessen the differentiation of material rewards by criteria relating to work level, qualification, youthfulness and performance. Such values are expected to operate instead in favour of granting higher rewards to those who are older, male and longer serving.

These various strands in the situation may be summarized in terms of the two models shown in figure 10.1. They represent respectively the contrast between socially embedded values and the functional requirements for modernization expressed by the reformers. The 'traditional model' predicts that earnings will be higher for people who are older, loyal to their unit (i.e. longer serving) and male. This model also recognizes that the cultural and socialist value of egalitarianism will militate against wide differentials in earnings, and encourage what the Chinese themselves call 'eating from the same big pot'. By contrast, the 'reform model' predicts that earnings will be higher for people who have formal qualifications, who have received training relevant to their job, who hold positions of greater responsibility and who are performing well and/or belong to a successful enterprise. The postulates of the two models are now examined in the light of our data.

Scope and method of the investigations

The writer, assisted by his Chinese faculty colleagues, visited the six enterprises on several occasions in the period 1985 to 1990 and obtained general information on their payment systems as well as managers' comments on them. The focused investigations reported here were undertaken in October 1985 and in March 1990. For this purpose, Chinese students studying for the Master of Business Administration (MBA) degree at the China–European Community Management Institute in Beijing collected information from 144 job-holders in the six enterprises. They were trained by the author and worked under his direction. All the students had previous working experience and they were mature with an average age of thirty-one. They had previously conducted other projects in the same enterprises and had become accepted by them.

As described in chapter 9, data were collected within each enterprise on a sample of 24 jobs: 4 managerial, 4 technical staff, 4 office and 12 production. The production jobs were sub-divided into 6 assembly and 6 machining or preparatory. Examples of jobs falling within these categories were provided in Appendix 9.1. The samples at the two points in time were carefully matched by job type, age and gender.

Identical methods of investigation were employed on both occasions. The data obtained relating to earnings included salary and its components, average

The traditional model

Earnings will be higher for people who are:

★ older
★ longer serving and 'loyal'
★ male

(Egalitarianism is a strong ideological and cultural value in this model, which discourages high differentials in earnings)

The reform model

Earnings will be higher for people who are:

★ qualified
★ have relevant training
★ hold positions of responsibility
★ are performing well or are part of a successful enterprise

(The reward of merit and achievement is a value underlying this model, which favours differentials in earnings)

Figure 10.1 Two models predicting the level of earnings in Chinese enterprises.

bonus over the previous three months, welfare and subsidy payments, and any other special payments. Information was also collected on each person's age, education, training received and career history, as well as the assessments they made of their job content and job satisfaction. The medium of communication for obtaining this information was relatively informal, direct, personal questioning in the enterprise, though non-production employees completed a written schedule of questions on their perceived job content and job satisfaction. Appendix 9.2 explained the scales used for job content and job satisfaction, and Appendix 10.1 indicates how information on educational level and experience of training was coded.[3]

The structure and level of earnings

By 1985, when the first of the two studies was conducted, earnings in the enterprises studied normally consisted of four main elements. The first was basic salary based on an eight-grade system for workers and a seventeen-grade system for cadres. The salary was intended to provide for the employee's minimum living costs and it was therefore adjusted according to the cost of living index. The second was a bonus which was paid from a fund linked to each enterprise's total annual salary bill, the allocation of which was intended to reflect individual performance. The third element was a position salary linked to the special skills and/or working conditions required in a job. This was often at the time called a 'special payment' and was just being introduced into enterprises. The fourth element in the payment structure consisted of welfare and subsidy allowances.

In October 1985, the norm for an enterprise's annual total of bonus payments was raised to four months of the year's salary bill – beyond that the enterprise was subject to a punitive progressive 'bonus tax'. Within this restriction on the total allocation to the bonus, management enjoyed some discretion over its distribution to production workers. In principle, workshop managers awarded individual bonuses each month to workers fulfilling their quotas according to a system of points relating to different performance criteria such as output, quality, timekeeping and cleanliness. In practice, a monthly bonus of between ten and twenty Yuan was becoming accepted as a norm, thus attenuating its relation to individual performance.[4] Cadres automatically received a bonus subject to an upper limit on absenteeism, and this was determined as a percentage of their basic salary depending on the job they were occupying.

Two supplementary payments were also being made. Nearly all workers and staff received welfare and subsidy payments, often a standard flat rate for the enterprise, which at the time ranged up to around twenty Yuan per month. In certain factories welfare payments could be higher than bonuses. Secondly, a few employees (mainly managers) were receiving a special payment introduced in 1985 for those holding posts of particular responsibility, the maximum being twenty-five Yuan per month for an enterprise director.

Finally, all members of an enterprise received extensive fringe benefits in forms such as pension, low-rent housing, free medical facilities and subsidised family health-care, maternity leave and free child-care. These were less closely controlled than basic salaries and bonuses, a fact that often led to complaints by workers against self-interested allocations by management. Cadres generally enjoyed superior fringe benefits; in the heavy electrical enterprise, for example, fringe benefits accounted for 17 per cent of cadres' personal income in 1984 in contrast to only 8 per cent of workers'.

Since the mid-1980s, enterprise managements enjoyed much greater discretion in the structuring of their salary and incentive systems, with the result that by early 1990 considerable variety had developed between the six enterprises. Each of them offered a salary, often called a 'structural salary'. Its components now varied. It included a basic salary in the case of every enterprise, plus a floating element (in three cases), a seniority element (four cases) and an element recognizing responsibility or skills in the job (four cases). All the enterprises offered a bonus in some form, sometimes based upon internal contracts with different groups in the enterprise. In addition, total earnings always included welfare payments and/or various subsidies, the definition and level of which varied considerably between the enterprises. Many Chinese enterprises were increasing the number and content of these subsidies during the late 1980s to offset the erosion of urban real incomes through high inflation. This elaboration of earnings' structures was ostensibly an attempt towards combining a more functionally and performance-related system with the enterprise's continuing role as provider of social welfare. It means that a precisely matched comparison between 1985 and 1990 of the various components in earnings is not possible. In particular, salaries were comprised of additional elements by 1990 while welfare payments were generally accompanied by a greater range of sub sidies.

The stratified sample of jobs was chosen to afford comparability between the six enterprises and over time; it is therefore not precisely representative of the specific employment structures in the enterprises themselves. Hence, the overall average monthly earnings of the sample members – 90 Yuan in October 1985 and 191 Yuan in March 1990 – is of only academic interest, although it is close to the 1985 and 1990 averages of 95.7 Yuan and 190.3 Yuan respec tively for employees in all state-owned enterprises given in official Chinese statistics (*Beijing Review*, 22 December 1986: 16; State Statistical Bureau 1991: table 4–34).[5]

The jobs sampled in each enterprise spanned from the director or deputy director down to young recently recruited assembly workers. In 1985, the total monthly earnings of these job-holders ranged from 217 Yuan to 40 Yuan. Among the enterprises, the differential of total earnings between the director and lowest-paid, non-apprentice worker varied between approximately 5:1 and 3:1. The ratio of earnings among non-apprentice production workers ranged between a high of 2.23:1 in the audio enterprise and a low of 1.38:1 in the elec trical switchgear enterprise.

In 1990, the total monthly earnings of the same categories of job-holders ranged from 398 Yuan to 98 Yuan. Among the same enterprises, the differen tial of total earnings between the director and the lowest-paid non-apprentice worker samples varied between approximately 3.5:1 and 1.6:1. This suggests a considerable narrowing of overall differentials compared with 1985. This could, of course, be a sampling artifact since the comparison here is only between two jobs per enterprise, although the jobs were matched closely by content, age and gender between the two points in time. If in fact we examine the differentials between average total earnings for the four categories of employee sampled, the picture is modified. (These job categories approximate to a hierarchical ordering and are henceforth referred to collectively as 'job level'.) Table 10.1 compares both average total earnings and average salaries for managerial, technical and office employees as a percentage of those for pro duction workers in 1985 and 1990. This calculation indicates that as a group managers had tended to improve their differentials compared to production workers, whereas (in terms of overall earnings) technical and office employees had not. The differential between office and production workers' total earning had in fact tended to decline. Among non-apprentice production workers the ratio of earnings varied almost identically to the pattern of 1985: there was again a high of 2.24:1 in the audio enterprise and a low of 1.33:1 in the electri cal switchgear enterprise.

Table 10.1. *Average total earnings and average salaries for office, technical and managerial employees as a percentage of those for production workers*

Job level	1985		1990	
	Average total earnings	Average salary	Average total earnings	Average salary
Office	119.27	124.86	114.13	129.65
Technical	127.23	136.59	126.66	147.90
Managerial	156.73	169.30	162.06	187.81

These earnings differentials are considerably less than would be normal in Western enterprises and the comparison might therefore appear to support the rationale of Chinese reformers for widening them. Whether the reformers' intentions to widen differentials are actually being achieved is, however, more doubtful, judging by our data. These suggest that up to 1985 differentials had widened compared with 1981, judging by survey data for that year cited by Lockett and Littler (1983). Between 1985 and 1990, differentials between managers and other categories of employee had increased in line with the reform policies, but they had not widened within the rest of the enterprise employment structure.

It is interesting to note in this connection that, while in 1985 there were no significant differences in the satisfaction expressed with levels of pay by people in the different job categories, managers' satisfaction with their pay had by 1990 pulled ahead of the other groups by a now statistically significant margin. Nor in 1985 was there any relation between earnings and the degree of satisfaction expressed with pay by any group of job-holders, whereas in 1990 this relation had emerged among managers and probably denotes that pay had become in their minds more of a mark of personal worth within the enterprise.

Table 10.2 compares the percentage make-up of total earnings by their main components for 1985 and for 1990. The data are presented both for the whole samples and for the four job levels. Between the two dates the percentage of earnings contributed by salary dropped by an average of 10 per cent, while the proportion contributed by welfare and subsidy payments more than doubled to almost 24 per cent. The proportion of earnings made up of bonuses declined slightly. The net result is that, while the ratio of bonus payment to salary had increased, and while the formulae for salaries in 1990 ostensibly included a link with enterprise performance, much of this incentive element was being offset by the considerable rise in welfare and subsidy payments. The latter, however, were intended to be a short-term response to declines in urban real living standards occasioned by inflation rather than a permanent feature.

Table 10.2. *Composition of earnings 1985 and 1990 by job level (sample: 1985 N=143, 1990 N=144 matched job-holders in six Beijing enterprises)*

Job level	Salary		Bonus		Welfare and subsidy payments	
	1985	1990	1985	1990	1985	1990
Managerial (N=24)	72.94	64.20	14.36	16.22	8.71	19.52
Technical (1985 N=23 1990 N=24	72.49	64.69	16.67	14.18	10.74	21.40
Office (N=24)	70.69	62.93	17.55	13.57	11.76	23.28
Production (N=72)	67.53	55.40	18.65	17.66	13.73	27.00
Total sample	70.15	60.32	17.15	16.03	11.74	23.66

Percentage of total earnings

The proportions of earnings accounted for by salary, bonus and welfare/subsidy payments were in both years rather similar for managers, technical staff and clerical workers. Production workers at both points in time tended to receive a lower percentage of earnings in the form of salary (although this was generally over half even in 1990), a somewhat higher proportion as bonus and a rather more markedly higher proportion as welfare or subsidy payment. The contribution to their pay in 1990 from welfare or subsidy payments considerably exceeded that from bonuses, partly due to the weak profit position of some enterprises. The real incentive power of earnings' structures among these six enterprises in early 1990 was therefore rather doubtful, though this point in time will probably prove to have been rather exceptional economically and politically and an aberration from the longer-term trend.

Predictors of variation in earnings

It is to be expected from the logic of the Chinese salary system that employees' total earnings would vary both according to their job level and to the enterprise in which they work. The grading system that determines the base part of salaries formally relates to job level. The size of the fund from which bonuses can be paid depends upon enterprise profits which are subject to competing claims for funding investment, welfare facilities and so on. The introduction of a floating element into salaries, often linked to enterprise performance, should by 1990 have given rise to further differences in earnings between enterprises for a given level or type of job. The six Beijing enterprises, moreover, belong to different sectors and in China 'heavier' industries (including automotive) have tended to pay somewhat more per basic salary grade (cf. Wang 1978; Henley and Nyaw 1987). In fact, as tables 10.3 and 10.4 indicate, these expectations were largely borne out both in 1985 and 1990, though changes had also occurred between the two points in time.

Tables 10.3a and b report the average levels of total earnings and their components for job level. Total earnings tended to rise with each higher job level chiefly due to the fact that job level accounted for respectively 35 per cent (1985) and 57 per cent (1990) of the variation in salaries. It bore no significant relation to the level of bonus or welfare payments which people received. The considerable strengthening of the relationship between job level and size of salary by 1990 indicates that changes in payment arrangements since 1985 had enhanced the extent to which the core element of earnings reflected levels of responsibility.

Tables 10.4a and b report the same data in terms of averages for the jobs sampled in each of the six enterprises. The average of total earnings varies between the enterprises in a non-random manner, but now primarily due to differences in enterprise bonus levels. The average monthly bonus payment contrasted markedly between the enterprises such that a large part of this variation could be accounted for by membership of a given enterprise – almost 50 per cent in 1985 and 60 per cent in 1990. With only six enterprises, it is not possible to demonstrate statistically whether particular aspects of their performance bore a predictive relationship to the level of bonus. In 1985, the closest rank ordering with average bonus levels was that of the enterprise's percentage rate of sales growth. The connection of bonus level with sales growth appeared at the time to be stronger than that with profit retained after tax. In 1990, however, bonus levels showed a closer relation to retained profit, with Pharmaceutical actually paying zero bonus over the three-month period surveyed because of a collapse in its profit level. This shift suggests that the linkage of enterprise payrolls to their profits under the contract responsibility system had become a strong motivator towards raising performance through its effect on employees' pockets.

Salary levels tended to vary between enterprises as well, but to only a modest degree, in both years. It is rather surprising that there was not significantly more variation in average salary levels between the enterprises in 1990 considering that three of the enterprises had by then included a 'floating' element in salaries which officially varied according to each enterprise's level of profit. It is also noticeable that welfare and subsidy payments had not only risen appreciably by 1990 but that their average level now tended to vary significantly between the enterprises chiefly because two (Automotive and Pharmaceutical) were paying high sums in that category.

Table 10.3a. *Total earnings and their components by job level: 1985*
(N=143 jobholders in six Beijing enterprises)

	Average earnings (Yuan/month) for each job level				Value of		Per cent variance accounted for by job level
	Managerial (N=24)	Technical (N=23)	Office (N=24)	Production (N=72)	F	P	
Total earnings	120.13	97.52	91.42	76.65	25.10	<.001	34
Salary	87.63	70.70	64.63	51.76	26.76	<.001	35
Bonus	17.25	16.26	16.04	14.29	1.19	n.s.	—
Special payments[1]	4.79	0.09	0.00	0.07	*	—	—
Welfare and subsidy payments	10.46	10.48	10.75	10.53	*	—	—

Notes:
[1] Special payments attached to seven managerial jobs, one technical job, one production job.
* Statistics cannot be computed because values are constant for at least 1 job level.
n.s. not statistically significant.

Table 10.3b. *Total earnings and their components by job level: 1990* (*N=144 jobholders in six Beijing enterprises*)

| | Average earnings (Yuan/month) for each job level | | | | Value of | | Per cent variance accounted for by job level |
	Managerial (N=24)	Technical (N=23)	Office (N=24)	Production (N=72)	F	P	
Total earnings	265.13	207.21	186.71	163.60	42.29	<.001	48
Salary	170.21	134.04	117.50	90.63	61.24	<.001	57
Bonus	43.00	29.38	25.33	28.89	1.84	n.s.	—
Welfare and subsidy payments	51.75	44.33	43.46	44.17	1.20	n.s.	—

Table 10.4a. *Total earnings and their components by enterprise: 1985*
(N=143 job-holders in six Beijing enterprises)

	Average earnings (Yuan/month) for each enterprise						Value of		Per cent variance accounted for by enterprise
	Audio (N=24)	Audio-visual (N=24)	Automotive (N=24)	Electrical switchgear (N=24)	Heavy electrical (N=23)	Pharmaceutical (N=24)	F	P	
Total earnings	108.88	83.63	93.46	92.00	71.48	88.50	5.79	<.001	17
Salary	68.00	58.63	73.79	57.75	60.22	59.42	2.16	0.06	7
Bonus	21.71	19.17	16.33	13.29	5.13	16.33	26.49	<.001	49
Special payments[1]	0.00	0.83	0.00	1.46	2.91	0.00	*	—	—
Welfare and subsidy payments	19.17	5.00	3.33	19.50	3.22	12.75	*	—	—

Notes:
[1] Special payments attached to: Heavy-electrical enterprise (4 managerial, 1 technical, 1 production worker)
    Electrical switchgear enterprise (2 managerial jobs)
    Audio-visual enterprise (1 managerial job).

* Statistics cannot be computed because values are constant for at least 1 enterprise

Table 10.4b. *Total earnings and their components by enterprise: 1990* (N=144 job-holders in six Beijing enterprises)

	Average earnings (Yuan/month) for each enterprise						Value of		Per cent variance accounted for by enterprise
	Audio (N=24)	Audio-visual (N=24)	Automotive (N=24)	Electrical switchgear (N=24)	Heavy electrical (N=24)	Pharmaceutical (N=24)	F	P	
Total earnings	196.13	182.92	230.08	173.67	193.46	173.58	4.19	< .01	13
Salary	122.08	119.17	97.63	121.92	128.13	104.71	2.26	.05	8
Bonus	43.96	24.46	71.50	16.83	27.83	0.00	41.16 [26.80]	< .001 < .001	60 48][1]
Welfare and subsidy payments	31.46	39.58	61.38	35.42	37.13	67.08	35.65	< .001	56

Note:
[1] Values when Pharmaceutical is omitted. No bonus had been paid in this enterprise during the three-month criterion period due to economic difficulties.

When taken into account together, job level and the identity of the employing enterprise independently predicted the levels of total earnings (p <0.001 in both cases in 1985 and 1990, with job level being the stronger predictor). The two factors together predicted 52 per cent of the variation in total earnings in 1985, and by 1990 they predicted 61 per cent. Job level was also in both years the stronger predictor of variations in salary, though the enterprise had a significant effect (p <0.01 in 1985 and p <0.001 in 1990) once job level was taken into account. While in 1985 the two factors only accounted for 44 per cent of the variation in salaries, by 1990 they accounted for as much as 64 per cent.

In 1985, the enterprise was the only predictor of bonus level when examined in conjunction with job level: taken together, the two variables then accounted for 52 per cent of the variation in bonus levels. By 1990, both factors predicted variations in bonus level when considered together, though enterprise was by far the stronger; together they accounted for 64 per cent of the overall variation in bonus levels.

These comparative figures indicate some shift further away from the characteristics of the traditional model which favoured egalitarianism (at least within social categories) rather than relating earnings and their components to performance and contribution. The payment systems in the enterprises studied had moved towards the reform model. By 1990, both the level of personal responsibility exercised by job-holders and the enterprise in which they worked had strengthened as predictors of variations in payment. In some respects payment levels had become more closely linked to the economic health of enterprises (for instance in the case of bonuses), though not apparently in others (as in the case of welfare and subsidy payments). Salaries tended more to reflect the general hierarchical ordering of job categories, which is to be expected from their formal relation to grades and responsibility allowances. Bonus levels reflected to a large extent the capacity of enterprises to pay through the size of the salary and bonus fund they could command by virtue of their profit levels.

Both the traditional and reform models suggest that there is scope for other factors to influence salary levels either through their bearing on job and grade allocation or independently. With this in mind, multiple regression analyses were performed with total earnings and salary level as the dependent variables respectively. Predictors ('independent variables') were derived from both the traditional and reform models, namely the jobholder's age, gender, educational level, experience of training, length of time in the job, length of employment in the enterprise, and job level as an indicator of responsibility held. The results are set out in tables 10.5a and b and 10.6a and b.[6]

Tables 10.5a and b indicate that at both points in time about 60 per cent of the variation in total earnings could be predicted from a knowledge of only three factors. In 1985, a person's age was by far the most powerful of these predictors accounting alone for over half (54 per cent) of the variation in earnings.

Table 10.5a. *Multiple regression of total earnings on postulated predictors: 1985 (stepwise procedure, N=143 jobholders)*

Postulated predictors	Beta coefficient	Cumulative multiple R^2	Level of confidence (p)	Zero order correlation
Age	0.80	0.54	<.001	0.74
Job level	-0.19[1]	0.59	<.05	-0.58
Length of service in enterprise	-0.23[2]	0.60	<.05	0.53
Gender	-0.09[3]	0.61	n.s.	-0.22
Educational level	0.04	0.61	n.s.	0.25
Training[4]	0.03	0.61	n.s.	0.01

Notes:

[1] Higher job level predicts higher total earnings.
[2] Shorter length of service predicts higher total earnings.
[3] Being male predicts higher total earnings.
[4] In contrast to the analysis presented in Child (1990), this variable indicates whether or not any job-relevant training had been received, rather than its level.

The contribution of the variable 'length of time in the job' to the prediction equation was too insignificant for it to be entered into the analysis, once the above variables had been taken into account.

Table 10.5b. *Multiple regression of total earnings on postulated predictors: 1990 (stepwise procedure, N=144 jobholders)*

Postulated predictors	Beta coefficient	Cumulative multiple R^2	Level of confidence (p)	Zero order correlation
Job level	-0.36[1]	0.45	<.001	-0.67
Age	0.42	0.57	<.001	0.67
Training	0.15	0.59	<.01	0.21
Educational level	0.09	0.60	n.s.	0.42
Gender	-0.05	0.60	n.s.	-0.19
Length of service in enterprise	0.04	0.60	n.s.	0.53

Notes:

[1] Higher job level predicts higher total earnings.

The contribution of the variable 'length of time in the job' to the prediction equation was too insignificant for it to be entered into the analysis, once the above variables had been taken into account.

Job level added some 5 per cent to the prediction, while once other factors had been taken into account *shorter* length of service in the enterprise marginally added still more to the prediction. This last result (which, as we shall see, strengthened in the prediction of salary levels) suggests that for a given age newer recruits to the enterprise tended to command higher pay. It points to differential rates of upward mobility within the enterprises, and these were due partly to the presence of some higher salary earners whose tenure in the organization had been shortened by banishment during the Cultural Revolution.

In 1990 job level had (just) replaced age as the strongest predictor of a person's total earnings. Age, while still important, now accounted for only 45 per cent of the variation in earnings. The nexus between age and length of service had also weakened, the common variance between the two declining from 71 per cent to 55 per cent. The influence of job level had strengthened, and having received job-relevant training also emerged as a modest predictor of higher earnings. Overall, then, there appeared to have been a shift away from age and towards level of responsibility and training as determinants of total earnings. This represents a strengthening of some criteria within the reform model.

The comparable analysis for salary levels is given in tables 10.6a and b. In 1985 it was possible, by reference to the selected independent variables, to predict two-thirds of the variation in salary levels within the sample. The strongest single predictor was an employee's age: older people tended to enjoy higher salaries and their age accounted for fully 60 per cent of the variation in salary levels. Job level on its own accounted for 35 per cent of salary variation, while length of service in the enterprise accounted for 30 per cent .

Once the influence of age was taken into account, other predictors of higher salary which enjoyed an acceptable level of statistical confidence (regression coefficient at least 1.5 times standard error) were in descending order of confidence: shorter service in the enterprise, higher job level, and being male. Higher educational level only became a significant predictor of larger salaries when job level was left out of account.

The profile which emerged in 1985 of the higher salary earner in these Chinese state enterprises was an older man who had spent many years in the enterprise and worked his way up to a higher category of job. This sounds like a rather typical bureaucratic type of progression, an observation which is particularly strengthened by the fact that this profile characterized the staff (cadre) half of the sample rather than production workers. Some 65 per cent of the variation in staff members' salaries was predictable from a knowledge of their age (which predicted 57 per cent alone), job level and length of service in the enterprise. By contrast, among production workers only their age predicted variations in salary and to a much lesser extent (33 per cent of variation predicted). Overall, then, the pattern of predictors of salary levels conformed more closely in 1985 to the traditional than to the reform model.

Table 10.6a. *Multiple regression of salary level on postulated predictors: 1985 (stepwise procedure, N=143 jobholders)*

Postulated predictors	Beta coefficient	Cumulative multiple R^2	Level of confidence (p)	Zero order correlation
Age	0.88	0.60	<.001	0.77
Job level	-0.16[1]	0.64	<.001	-0.59
Length of service in enterprise	-0.26[2]	0.66	<.001	0.55
Gender	-0.11[3]	0.67	<.001	-0.23
Educational level	0.07	0.67	n.s.	0.31
Training	0.03	0.67	n.s.	0.01

Notes:
[1] Higher job level predicts higher basic salary.
[2] Shorter length of service predicts higher basic salary.
[3] Being male predicts higher basic salary.
The contribution of the variable 'length of time in the job' to the prediction equation was too insignificant for it to be entered into the analysis, once the above variables had been taken into account.

Table 10.6b. *Multiple regression of salary level on postulated predictors: 1990 (stepwise procedure, N=144 jobholders)*

Postulated predictors	Beta coefficient	Cumulative multiple R^2	Level of confidence (p)	Zero order correlation
Age	0.46	0.60	<.001	0.77
Job level	−0.41[1]	0.74	<.001	−0.75
Educational level	0.08	0.75	.10	0.48
Gender	0.06	0.75	n.s.	−0.07
Length of service in enterprise	0.08	0.75	n.s.	0.63
Training	−0.06	0.76	n.s.	0.05

Notes:
[1] Higher job level predicts higher basic salary.
The contribution of the variable 'length of time in the job' to the prediction equation was too insignificant for it to be entered into the analysis, once the above variables had been taken into account.

Analysis of the equivalent 1990 data points to a more complicated picture. Even when the floating element is included in salaries, the result is that age remains as strong a predictor as in 1985 but now with job level only marginally behind. Age also remains a much stronger predictor of non-production workers' salaries (53 per cent) than those of production workers (34 per cent). Although educational level and length of service in the enterprises are positively correlated with salary levels, their effect is largely subsumed within that of job level. Taken together greater age and higher job level predict a very substantial 74 per cent of the variation in salary levels. If the floating element is not included in salaries, age and job level remain the main predictors, but higher levels of education and training now predict higher salaries as well. In this latter analysis, however, only 53 per cent of the variation in salaries is accounted for.

The increasing part played between 1985 and 1990 by education and training in the determination of earnings is clarified by table 10.7 which focuses on personal characteristics rather than those related to the job. The effect of age is again shown to have weakened, though remaining a dominant factor, while those of education and training strengthen. Gender, the advantage of being male, which was of marginal significance in 1985, had by 1990 become of no real consequence.

Taken together, these findings lend qualified support to the view that a shift has occurred from the traditional to the reform model. While people's age clearly remains a potent influence on their salary level, being a man had lost any impact by 1990. The level of job that people held had become very much more closely tied to salary level (especially compared to other predictors), while the role of education and training was now more significant for levels of pay as a whole and of salary when the floating element is excluded.

The level of average bonus payments was seen to vary considerably between enterprises. Bonus payments to production workers are in principle linked to their personal performance, but it was impossible to obtain data on job holders' performance which would test the strength of this link. There is some reason to doubt its consistency since there was relatively little variation among production workers' bonus levels within each enterprise either in 1985 or 1990. The greatest variation in bonuses among production workers was in the automotive enterprise which had in 1988 entered into a joint venture with foreign partners and was adopting a foreign approach towards linking incentives to measured performance.

The bonus given to staff members is formally not related to individual performance but is supposedly geared to their basic salary in relation to the job they hold. In this sample of staff employees, however, bonus and basic salary levels were not related. Nor were the bonuses given to higher-level job holders consistently higher either for the whole sample or when examined enterprise by

Table 10.7. *Multiple regression of total earnings level on personal characteristics*

Postulated predictors	Beta coefficient	Cumulative multiple R^2	Level of confidence (p)	Zero order correlation
		1985 data		
Age	0.70	0.54	<.001	0.74
Educational level	0.16	0.56	<.10	0.25
Gender	-0.10	0.57	<.10	-0.22
Level of training	0.04	0.58	n.s.	0.01
R^2=0.58				
		1990 data		
Age	0.60	0.44	<.001	0.67
Educational level	0.25	0.50	<.001	0.42
Level of training	0.17	0.53	.001	0.21
Gender	-0.06	0.54	n.s.	-0.19
R^2=0.54				

Table 10.8. *Product-moment correlations of reported intrinsic job content with total earnings for four job categories: 1985 and 1990[1]*

Managers	
1985 (N=24)	0.75*
1990 (N=24)	0.00
Technical staff	
1985 (N=23)	0.61**
1990 (N=24)	0.46
Office staff	
1985 (N=24)	0.50**
1990 (N=24)	–0.17
Production workers	
1985 (N=72)	0.05
1990 (N=72)	0.24

Notes:
[1] Intrinsic job content is the aggregate of scores of ten Likert-type scales where a higher score=more of the intrinsic feature was reported in the job (see note 7 for further details).
  * p<.01 (one-tail)
 ** p<.05 (one-tail)

enterprise. The only predictors of higher staff bonus levels were in 1985 being a man rather than a woman and in 1990 having higher educational qualifications and relevant training. This shift in predictors is again consistent with a shift from the traditional to the reform model.

All-in-all, then, there must be some doubt over whether bonus payments are being related to the officially desired criteria at an individual level. On the other hand, their apparent reflection of enterprise growth performance should serve to reinforce the identity of employees with the success of their organization, which is now being encouraged through the enterprise contract responsibility system. A collective basis for the bonus will in any case become steadily more appropriate as advanced technology is introduced and productive systems consequently become more integrated on a 'team' basis.

Another of the economic reform's principles is that differentials in basic earnings should reflect 'contribution'. One way of assessing contribution is in terms of intrinsic job variables that indicate the discretion and control delegated to employees, their responsibility, and the scope and variety of the tasks they undertake. With this in mind, the strength of the connection between jobholders' earnings and self-reported job characteristics was examined for each of the four job categories in the sample. The results are presented in table 10.8 using a composite measure of intrinsic job content which covers ten items.[7]

In 1985, there was a connection between the level of contribution assessed in this manner and earnings for each job category except production workers. By 1990, the connection had disappeared. It is not clear what lies behind this unexpected change. Taken together with the other developments we have reported, especially the growing association between job level and salary, one possible interpretation is that over the five-year period there had been a shift in emphasis towards formalistic and away from substantive payment criteria. In other words, differential payment was possibly coming to be tied more closely to *formal responsibility* as denoted by hierarchical job level and less to actual *job content.* If so, the implication is that the elaboration of components within earnings, some of which were designed to recognize intrinsic job requirements, was not having the intended result. Many people working in the six enterprises expressed the view that pay was not in practice being linked to either the intrinsic challenge of the job or to how well it was performed, and even that traditional norms of 'eating from the same pot' still had currency. A major problem was that managements had not become familiar with techniques of work measurement which would provide systematic data for effecting the links. To that extent, the conceptual elaboration of the payment systems could not be supported in practice.

Moreover, the absence already noted of a relationship between the levels of total earnings or salaries or bonuses and the degree of satisfaction expressed with pay by job-holders other than managers raises the general question of the extent to which material rewards were serving as effective motivators in the work situations studied. Managers had benefited from the reforms in payment, and seemed to be aware of this, but the same cannot be said of other groups in the enterprise.

Conclusion

China's economic reformers have staked the success of their drive toward modernization upon raising levels of technical expertise, training and promoting younger people, and linking rewards to contribution and achievement. To succeed through this route they have to negotiate the obstacles which arise from previously established interpretations of the socialist value system, from traditional Chinese culture, from the system of centralized economic administration, and from a limited supply of the management expertise necessary for the design and control of reward systems.

The first study reported in this chapter was conducted at a relatively early stage in the programme of transforming enterprise reform from an experimental status to one of general adoption, and so one would not expect it to reveal a strong application of reform principles. Nor did it do so. Earnings were not significantly related to level of attested expertise. Their modest association with formal educational level was primarily mediated by job level, but job level itself much more strongly reflected an employee's age and length of service. Of the sample, 70 per cent had received no training, and experience of training was not at all reflected in the level of earnings within a job category. There was some evidence of a male bias in salary allocation.

Among cadres, salary differentials were in 1985 related to the perceived level of intrinsic job content which suggests a link between salary and contribution of the kind sought under the reform. Among production workers, however, the link between salary and job content was missing on the evidence available, while that between bonus and individual performance appeared quite tenuous. By contrast, those linkages reflecting established social expectations were mostly still in place, especially that between higher pay and more advanced years. The overwhelming significance of age for salary level among all categories of job-holders points to the continued influence of a strongly embedded traditional Chinese value, and this has of course been evident in the political arena as well as the industrial.

By 1990 in the same enterprises, hierarchical job level had become much more important as a basis for differentials in salaries and, in the case of managers, for the differential they enjoyed in total earnings as well. The experience of more advanced education, and of training, was beginning to make a difference to people's levels of pay, though education level continued to be associated with job level. The role of gender had effectively disappeared and, relative to other predictors, length of service also played less part. The average levels of bonus paid continued to vary considerably between enterprises and by 1990 reflected the profit levels they achieved.

These were all signs that a shift was underway towards the reform model for payment. Qualifying this was the continuing influence of age on earnings, particularly on salaries, and the apparent weakening of the connection between pay and the intrinsic content of people's jobs in terms of perceived responsibility, challenge, variety and control.

The enterprises studied had inherited a system of age-related earnings' progression through accumulating length of service. Although the common variance between age and length of service had reduced between 1985 and 1990, the connection still remained an important one. Despite the emphasis placed by the reformers on education and training, these factors still played a minor role in determining payment levels compared to that of age. This conclusion closely matches that reached by Henley and Ereisha (1987) from their study of the textile industry in another (largely) state-socialist modernizing economy, Egypt. Henley has suggested in subsequent correspondence with the writer that socialist wage systems reflect a 'dictatorship of the gerontocracy'.[8]

The public statements of Chinese economic reformers imply that this age and service-related system of material rewards is not functional for performance-oriented competitive business. They would rather see earnings reflect the intrinsic value of the employee (indicated *inter alia* by education and training), the responsibility and contribution required by the job, and indicators of performance both in the job and for the enterprise as a whole. Comparison of 1985 and 1990 data from closely matched samples has suggested that the structures and systems of earnings in state-owned enterprises had moved closer to this reform model, but that there is still a long way to go.

It remains an open question as to how far this apparent progress has been a formal rather than a substantive adjustment in view of the minimal link between earnings and intrinsic job content and the relatively small variation in individual bonus earnings. Formulae are now widely applied in state enterprises to allow earnings to reflect individual competence and performance as well as that of the whole enterprise. The result, however, is sometimes an extremely complex system which one suspects is beyond the capacity of management to operate as intended and, possibly, beyond the full comprehension of many of the individuals it is intended to motivate. In other words, the endeavour to incorporate into payment systems all of the criteria developed by the reformers may at present be counter-productive. There was certainly a good deal of evidence that the variable performance-related elements in pay were failing to discriminate as intended. Thus not only were individual bonuses not permitted to diverge appreciably, but the floating element in salaries had in some cases become transformed into an annual increment that everyone could expect to receive so long as at least some profit had been earned by the firm, rather than being an accurate reflection of the actual level of its economic performance.

Appendix 10.1 Coding of educational level and training

Educational level
This was coded as follows with reference to the highest level of formal education completed:
1=primary school
2=junior middle school or vocational school
3=senior middle school or secondary technical school
4=college or polytechnic
5=university.

Training
This was coded as follows:
0=none
1=some training relevant to the job or enterprise.

Part III

Joint ventures in China

11 Establishing joint ventures

The background

In December 1978, the post-Mao Chinese leadership announced that the country would 'open to the outside world'. An important part of this policy, and one which provided its direct link with the goal of modernization, was to invite foreign direct investment. The authorities expected that by attracting foreign investment, China would secure access to new sources of capital, to advanced technology and to management skills. They also believed that partnership with foreign companies would provide access to international markets which would take China's exports and furnish the foreign exchange to finance its needs for imports.

This was a dramatic shift away from the policy of self-reliance which had been pursued in the belief that foreign involvement in the economy would lead to exploitation of a neo-colonialist type and the corruption of traditional and socialist values. For this reason, the opening to foreign capital after 1978 was combined with an attempt to control its use and impact through the mechanism of joint ventures in which the Chinese partner would normally be a state-owned and state-regulated enterprise (Pearson 1991).

Just some thirteen years later, by 1991, joint ventures and other foreign-funded enterprises in China had grown in economic significance to contribute 5 per cent of the gross national product (*Beijing Review* 1992a: 4). By mid-1993, these enterprises were accounting for 25.1 per cent of the country's total exports (*Beijing Review* 1993: 28). Table 11.1 provides statistics on the numbers of foreign-funded enterprises and the value of foreign investment involved. It can be seen that the rate of foreign investment in China has fluctuated, with a particularly marked decline in 1986. Despite an initial falling away immediately after the Tiananmen Square incident in June 1989, there has been a recent acceleration of foreign investment. Between 1989 and the first half of 1991, the number of approved foreign-funded enterprises totalled 18,000, and this exceeded the total of the ten previous years. The negotiated funds pledged in that period reached 64 per cent of the previous ten-year total (Yang 1992: 20). The following two years saw a veritable explosion of foreign direct

Table 11.1 *Pledged and disbursed foreign direct investment (all forms) 1979–1992[1]*

Year	Number of projects pledged	Value of investment pledged (US$bn)	Value of funds actually invested (US$bn)
1979–82	922	6.01	1.17
1983	470	1.73	0.64
1984	1856	2.65	1.26
1985	3073	5.93	1.66
1986	1498	2.83	1.87
1987	2233	3.71	2.31
1988	5945	5.30	3.19
1989	5779	5.60	3.39
1990	7273	6.60	3.49
1991	12978	11.98	4.37
1992	48764	58.12	11.0

Sources: tables 15–9 and 15–10; *Statistical Yearbook of China* 1993: Beijing: State Statistical Bureau.

investment into China with US$169 billion of newly pledged funds and a total of 167,500 foreign-funded enterprises registered by end – 1993.

The Chinese authorities distinguish four main types of foreign direct investment: (1) equity joint ventures; (2) 'co-operative enterprises', namely contractual joint ventures; (3) wholly foreign-owned enterprises; and (4) offshore oil development projects. Equity joint ventures have a separate legal status and take the form of a limited liability company. The Chinese and foreign partners contribute to the registered capital and take profits, risks and losses in proportion to that contribution. They are usually managed jointly. Prominent examples of Sino-foreign equity joint ventures are the Beijing Jeep Corporation and China Hewlett-Packard (US partners), Shanghai Volkswagen (German), Beijing-Matsushita Color Picture Tube (Japanese), and the Shenzhen Konka Electronics Group (Hong Kong). As table 11.2 indicates, the equity joint venture remains by far the most numerous type and also accounts for the greater portion of pledged investment.

Contractual joint ventures are akin to partnerships in that no separate 'legal person' is formed. However, they share many characteristics with equity joint ventures since with most contracts the partners contribute capital in a variety of forms (such as cash, buildings, equipment and know-how) towards a project which runs for a specified number of years. The partners also negotiate rights and obligations and often manage the ventures jointly (Pearson 1991: 232). The

Table 11.2. *Breakdown of foreign-funded enterprises in China (end June 1991)*

Type	Number	Pledged investment (US$bn)	Funds actually invested (US$bn)
Equity joint venture	19,524	17.78	10.01
Co-operative enterprise (contractual joint venture)	9,984	16.95	5.73
Wholly foreign-owned enterprise	4,513	6.81	1.88
Offshore oil project	69	3.37	3.00

Source: Yang (1992: 20).

McDonnell-Douglas Corporation's co-operation with the Shanghai Aircraft Manufacturing Plant and the Occidental Antaibao coal project are examples of major contractual joint ventures.

The third type of foreign-funded enterprise is that wholly owned by the foreign party. Wholly foreign-owned enterprises have become much more important since 1988, when the Chinese government began making a special effort to attract them. The greater number of them are owned by investors from Hong Kong and Macau and are located in the Special Economic Zones. They are typically manufacturing plants which their owners have established for reasons of land availability and cheaper labour and over which the owners have full management rights.

The last type of direct foreign investment is the offshore oil development project, which accounts for small numbers of highly capitalized ventures. These are governed by a special set of laws.

Teagarden and Von Glinow (1991) have suggested a fourfold categorization of business alliances between Chinese and foreign firms according to two dimensions (see figure 11.1). The first dimension is that of *obligation* and the second is *involvement*. The obligation dimension defines the structure of profit allocation and the extent of rights and obligations. The wholly foreign-owned enterprise can be placed at one end of this dimension insofar as the right to profit clearly accrues to the one owner. Some business alliances between partners are also built upon explicit reciprocity, as when the distribution of profits and benefits in equity joint ventures is made in accordance with equity shares. The notion of explicit reciprocity can be extended to any business alliance in which the partners extract benefit in direct proportion to their contribution to that alliance. It covers not only equity joint ventures but also arrangements such as countertrade, process/assembly and buyback agreements and long-term licensing deals.

Towards the other end of the obligation dimension come arrangements

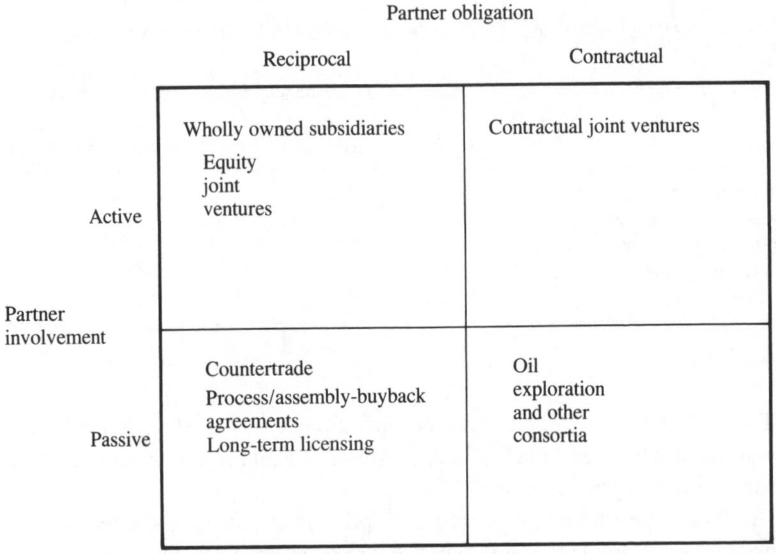

Partner obligation

	Reciprocal	Contractual
Active	Wholly owned subsidiaries Equity joint ventures	Contractual joint ventures
Passive	Countertrade Process/assembly-buyback agreements Long-term licensing	Oil exploration and other consortia

Partner
involvement

Figure 11.1 Typology of Sino-foreign business alliances. *Source:* adapted from Teagarden and Von Glinow (1991: figure 1)

whereby the distribution of profit and other benefits is not made in proportion to contribution. For example, in contractual joint ventures and oil exploration consortia the structure of profit distribution, and other rights and obligations, are negotiated and embodied in a contract and are not necessarily in proportion to value of contribution. Teagarden and Von Glinow (1991) note that in many Sino-foreign coproduction (joint manufacturing) agreements, the foreign partner has accepted disproportionately low returns in the expectation of cementing future business relationships in China through the contract – in other words, the foreign partner is deferring its expectation of reciprocity.

The dimension of involvement distinguishes between an alliance that is fully 'operating', in that each partner takes an active role in its strategic business decisions, and the passive alliance in which any partner does not take part in such decisions. In China, both equity and contractual joint ventures are normally active in this sense, while arrangements such as technology licensing and oil exploration often involve passivity of the foreign and Chinese partner respectively.

This two-dimensional analytical scheme can be used to distinguish between the main forms of foreign investment in China and the managerial challenge they are likely to present. Equity joint ventures have actively operating partners and entail reciprocal obligations. These features identify the fact that equity joint ventures have a high level of interdependence between the partners but that at the same time they leave each partner with low strategic flexibility. The more interdependent the partners, the more they share control of decision making and the more intensive will be their joint managerial relationship. At the same time, their strategic flexibility is low because with an equity stake the partners cannot easily withdraw from or modify the arrangement between them. These considerations point to the particularly difficult nature of equity joint venture management.

Contractual joint ventures also have actively operating partners but do not necessarily involve reciprocal partner obligations. The interdependence between partners tends to be lower and their strategic flexibility higher. Those which Teagarden and Von Glinow (1991) call 'Passive Contractual Alliances', such as oil exploration consortia, have passive involvement by one or more partners and non-reciprocal obligations. Partner interdependence is relatively low and strategic flexibility quite high. The fourth type they call 'Passive Reciprocal Alliances', such as process buyback, licensing and countertrade arrangements. These have the lowest partner interdependence and the highest strategic flexibility. An example in this category is Nike sportsware which had process buyback arrangements with several Chinese manufacturers. When Nike came up against quality and delivery problems from some of these suppliers, it was quickly able to retrench to two manufacturers who could meet its specification and delivery requirements. This ordering of categories approximates to a reduction of risk and uncertainty facing the foreign investor and to a corresponding reduction in the level of direct engagement between foreign and Chinese managements.

The wholly foreign-owned enterprise, which Teagarden and Von Glinow do not consider in detail, is usually characterized by very intensive relations with its Chinese management and a low level of strategic flexibility. Indeed, the difference in these respects between the foreign majority-owned equity joint venture and the wholly owned subsidiary is only a matter of minor degree.

Foreign-funded enterprises in general, and joint ventures in particular, therefore constitute an important and fast growing area of management in China. Jointly owned and jointly managed enterprises present additional challenges to those facing management in the unitary firm (cf. Contractor and Lorange 1988). The challenge is considerably accentuated in a context like China when local managers join a co-operative venture with foreign managers whose approach bears the mark of a different culture and political economy. Both the peculiar nature of Sino-foreign joint management and the growing importance of foreign involvement in the Chinese economy warrant some attention to the subject within the compass of this book.

The present chapter concentrates on the establishment of joint ventures while the following two chapters are concerned with their management. The next section of this chapter outlines the legal framework within which joint ventures are formed and operate in China. The following section then examines the objectives which Chinese and foreign partners typically have for entering into business co-operation. This then raises the question of the basis on which a viable joint venture can be established even if there remain elements of conflict between partner objectives. A final section addresses the process of negotiation to establish joint ventures in China.

Legal framework [1]

A number of guides are available on the laws and regulations governing joint ventures in China, and the official bodies which administer them. An excellent example is *China Perspectives* published by Arthur Andersen and Company (1993). All that can be presented here is an overview of features which bear particularly on the structure and process of joint venture management. Separate laws governing wholly foreign-owned enterprises and contractual joint ventures were established only in April 1986 and April 1988 respectively. Prior to that legislation, the laws drafted for equity joint ventures were either applied directly to, or were used as guides for, other forms of foreign investment.

It is important to note at the outset that in China there are two separate legal systems which govern foreign investment. In most countries endeavouring to encourage foreign investment, there are special regulations which set out the procedures under which a foreign company can apply to invest in the host country and which specify the forms and types of investment, special incentives and so forth. Once approved, however, the joint venture will be regulated by the general laws of the host country which apply equally to domestic enterprises. In China, foreign investment laws not only set out the conditions and procedures under which foreign investment is permitted, they also lay down the form of the enterprise thereby created and include special laws pertaining to joint ventures on matters of foreign exchange, tax, accounting and labour. The scope of laws and regulations specific to joint ventures and other foreign-funded enterprises is therefore greater than that found in most other countries. Domestic laws are applied when there are no specific regulations in China laying down how a joint venture is to handle a legal problem. These domestic laws have, however, been designed to regulate transactions within a state planned socialist system, whereas those specific to foreign-funded enterprises have been designed to approximate the legal relationships found in 'Western' market economies, often with foreign investor expectations in mind.

If a legal issue arises, joint venture managements must therefore first ascertain whether there is a law or regulation on that issue which relates specifically to foreign-funded enterprises. Houben and Nee (n.d.) give the example of supply transactions. When a joint venture contracts with a foreign company for the supply of goods, the supply contract will be governed by China's Law on

Foreign Economic Contracts which is generally similar to accepted international contract law principles. If there is a breach of contract, the defaulting party should pay damages to the non-defaulting party so that the latter receives the benefit of the original agreement. If the same joint venture contracts with a Chinese enterprise, that domestic contract will be governed by the Law on Economic Contracts which was drafted to regulate the transactions between two state-owned enterprises. Under this law, if the default of contract is caused by an administrative intervention, such as an order from a local industrial bureau to the Chinese enterprise to supply its goods to an enterprise other than the joint venture, then no damages can be paid and the contract must be amended or cancelled.

The legal status of equity joint ventures is defined by four major sets of laws: the 1979 Joint Venture Law, the 1983 Implementing Regulations, the 1986 State Council Provisions and the Amendments to the Joint Venture Law of 1990. China's legal system prior to 1979 did not recognize the possibility of foreign investment. It recognized only state and collective ownership. *The Law of the People's Republic of China on Joint Ventures Using Chinese and Foreign Investment*, adopted on 1 July, 1979, created an entity called the 'joint venture' and gave this new form its own distinct and separate status.

The 1979 Joint Venture Law contained only fifteen articles. These set out the general principles governing the establishment and operation of joint venture enterprises. They dealt with approval procedures, capital structure, forms of equity contribution, profit distribution, general management structure, foreign exchange and remittance of funds abroad, action in the case of losses, labour relations and settlement of disputes. The Law referred to the incorporation of foreign companies into joint ventures with Chinese enterprises 'on the principle of equality and mutual benefit and subject to authorization by the Chinese government' (Article 1). It protected the resources invested by a foreign participant and 'the profits due to him'. Each joint venture was to have a board of directors with a chairman appointed by the Chinese side and one or two vice-chairmen appointed by the foreign side. Managerial autonomy was granted to the board on issues of business programmes, expansion, financial and personnel policy and procedures, and the hiring and remuneration of senior officers. However, at the same time Article 2 stated that 'all the activities of a joint venture shall be governed by the laws, decrees and pertinent rules and regulations of the People's Republic of China'. This clearly stated the general principle that joint venture activity would be dominated by Chinese laws.

The 1979 articles themselves were relatively short and vague. Given that it would take time and experience to draft a complete legal framework for joint ventures yet at the same time wishing to make progress with its foreign investment programme, the Chinese authorities adopted a three-pronged approach:

1 formulating new laws and regulations in an incremental fashion, correcting mistakes and elaborating as they went along;

2 trying out new proposed laws and regulations through internal (*neibu*) guidelines that are made available only to Chinese officials and enterprise managers, or occasionally experimenting with such new laws in the Special Economic Zones;

3 adopting model forms of foreign investment contracts that can be used with minor variations for many different investments. The Ministry of Foreign Economic Relations and Trade (MOFERT), for example, at the end of 1984 issued a Sample Contract and Articles of Association for 'Joint Ventures Using Chinese and Foreign Investment'.

Although they are not legally binding, given the bureaucratic nature of the Chinese state-sector industrial governance system, the internal guidelines and model forms of contract have been treated by Chinese negotiators and joint venture partners in much the same terms as law. Confining attention to China's published laws and regulations would mislead foreign investors into thinking that there is more flexibility than there really is.

The *Regulations for the Implementation of the Law on Joint Ventures Using Chinese and Foreign Investment* were promulgated by the State Council in September 1983. They were designed to improve the investment climate by clarifying the legal position so as to give foreign investors greater confidence and also to guide joint venture negotiators. They provided greater detail on questions of profit repatriation, technology transfer, foreign exchange and labour management. As Pearson (1991: 257) notes, these Implementing Regulations had a dual character. On the one hand, they clarified many controls over joint ventures to which the 1979 articles had alluded and added even further controls. On the other hand, they began a process of liberalization.

The Implementing Regulations re-affirmed that the board of directors was the highest authority of a joint venture and that joint ventures carry out their business independently within the scope of Chinese law. The regulations stipulated that government departments should not interfere in the production and operating plans of joint ventures. They indicated that once a joint venture had been approved the role both of the Ministry of Foreign Economic Relations and Trade (MOFERT) and the industrial bureau ('department in charge') should shift towards a facilitating one, with the bureau giving priority to meeting the venture's needs for raw materials, fuel and labour. The authority to approve the establishment of small joint ventures, with a total investment of $5 million or less, was now decentralized to municipal, provincial or autonomous regional governments, or the local branch of the relevant ministry. Generally speaking the quality of co-operation with government authorities was perceived by foreign investors to be better at these local levels (as well as in the south of the country).

The limits on the sectors in which joint ventures were permitted to operate were clarified in the Implementing Regulations. These were sectors where technology, advanced management, natural resources and products for export were urgently required. They were not normally permitted in most military fields, though in practice these restrictions tended to relax over the years. Moreover, joint ventures were now allowed to sell primarily on the domestic market if the authorities considered there was an urgent need for their products or if these were imported in large quantities. The Bank of China or foreign banks were also now allowed to lend foreign exchange to joint ventures, while those with permission to sell on the domestic market for part payment in non-convertible *renminbi* (RMB) under import substitution provisions were to be compensated for any resulting foreign exchange imbalance from government foreign currency reserves.

The Implementing Regulations also specified, *inter alia*, the provision of documentation and exchange of information under technology transfer agreements, the rules of accounting and fiscal reporting from joint ventures, and allocations to expansion funds, reserve funds and bonus/welfare funds before profits were distributed between partners. These allocations often amounted to 10–15 per cent of after-tax profits. There were additional provisions on the role of labour organizations and personnel policy which are examined more closely in the next chapter.

The Foreign Economic Contract Law was promulgated in March 1985, and contained forty-three articles. This law further clarified the rights of the parties to economic contracts involving foreign interests, a clarification that was intended to improve the environment for foreign investment. The law allowed arbitration in the foreign partner's home country and reiterated the validity of third-country arbitration. It went into detail on the formation, amendment and termination of contracts.

Nevertheless, from 1985 to 1986 the growth rate of foreign direct investment and of new equity joint ventures fell sharply and, in the case of investment pledged in equity joint ventures and other forms, even became negative. This decline reflected 'a growing wariness on the part of foreign investors about the problems in China's overall economy and the effect of these problems on joint ventures' (Pearson 1991: 74). China had sustained a very large expansion in imports during 1985 and 1986 which led the authorities to curtail severely domestic spending on foreign exchange. This had an immediate impact on joint ventures. Fewer domestic customers could afford to pay for joint venture goods in foreign currency, and this added to the difficulties they faced in earning the foreign exchange required both to import materials or parts and to repatriate profits. Some smaller joint ventures were forced to close when their Chinese partners were suddenly confronted with the new restrictions.

The Beijing Jeep joint venture became a highly publicized example of the problem. After restrictions on foreign exchange were imposed in mid-1985, the purchasers of the joint venture's jeeps (mostly the army and government bureaux) did not have the foreign currency to cover the cost of imported component kits which made up about two-thirds of the sale price. The venture was no longer able to secure import licences, or letters of credit from the Bank of China, to pay for new kits. An additional motivation for these restrictions on Beijing Jeep appears to have been the Chinese authorities' realization of how the foreign partner was making profits from the knock-down kit imports and their consequent desire to renegotiate the original joint venture agreement (Aiello 1991). In the event, the joint venture halted production and the American partner threatened to withdraw from it (Mann 1989).

The Beijing Jeep case attracted particular publicity to the problems which many joint ventures were facing at this time. A survey of seventy manufacturing equity joint ventures involving fifty parent companies, conducted by consultants A. T. Kearney in collaboration with the International Trade Research Institute of the PRC in 1986, found that the foreign exchange balance featured second only to the lack of suitable quality or type of raw material and local components among their major concerns in day-to-day operations. Lack of autonomy was a further concern mentioned by over half of the joint ventures in the survey. The problems being experienced gave rise to considerable complaint and lobbying by foreign business interests. The unfavourable publicity came at a time when competition for foreign investment within Asia was growing, fostered by the liberalization of conditions by other governments offering alternative locations that were attractive especially for investors seeking low-cost labour.

By the middle of 1986, the reformist central authorities were quite aware of these factors and this led the State Council in October to issue twenty-two further *Provisions for the Encouragement of Foreign Investment*. An official from the Investment Working Group of the State Council commented at the time on the 'spirit' of the Provisions:

Briefly, it is a determined, down-to-earth effort to improve China's investment environment . . . Some ventures involving foreign investment have experienced difficulties. These were due partly to our lack of experience, our failure to make certain arrangements for absorption and utilization of foreign investment, deficiencies in our management system and bureaucratic wrangling. This has been the subject of much talk outside China. We do not deny these problems and realize that we need to study them seriously and make efforts to solve them. (*Beijing Review* 1986a: 28)

Article 1 of the 1986 Provisions stated that they were formulated in order to improve the investment environment, facilitate the absorption of foreign investment, introduce advanced technology, improve product quality, expand exports to generate foreign exchange and develop the Chinese economy. They offered special incentives for export-oriented and technologically advanced enterprises, thus targeting the government's priority areas. These enterprises were to now to pay reduced fees for labour and for land use. They were to be given priority in the allocation of infrastructural services and also in the granting of funds for working capital. Profits remitted abroad by such enterprises were now exempt from income tax and enterprises exporting 70 per cent or more of their turnover were to continue to be awarded tax reductions after the normal period for tax incentives on foreign investment. The Provisions also offered further tax exemptions for profits that were reinvested to establish or expand export or advanced technology enterprises. They further guaranteed the autonomy of enterprises with foreign investment from external bureaucratic interference and promised that they would receive more positive support from government departments. The Provisions permitted foreign and joint enterprises mutually to adjust foreign exchange surpluses and deficits among themselves. Enterprises with foreign investment could also henceforth refuse to pay 'unreasonable' local charges and appeal against them.

The economic retrenchment programme initiated in the autumn of 1988 adversely affected joint venture operations. In particular, the credit squeeze made it difficult for them to collect bills. Then, in the months after the Tiananmen crackdown, joint ventures were subject to increased political interference. There was a revival of political study groups, the exercise of more authority by party secretaries and labour union representatives (including attempts to veto personnel appointments and promotions and demands to attend board meetings), and some harassment of joint ventures by government agencies (Leung 1989; Pearson 1991).

For approximately a year after the Tiananmen incident, there was a reduction in the growth of foreign investment, especially from Western and Japanese sources among which an absolute decline was registered in 1989. Partly as a response to this foreign reaction to the prevailing environment, the Chinese government in April 1990 enacted four amendments to the 1979 Joint Venture Law. The assurance given to wholly foreign-owned enterprises that they would not be nationalized was now extended to joint ventures as well. Secondly, the chair of joint venture boards was to be chosen through consultation between the parties to a joint venture or elected by the board, and could now be occupied by a foreigner. Thirdly, the time limit applied to the operation of some joint ventures was now to become indefinite in line with the principle of varying the treatment of contract time in different lines of business. In the summer of 1991, a Sino-Japanese joint venture, the Nantong Himo Company which primarily manufactures garment lining material, became the first joint venture to be given permission to operate in China for an indefinite period (*Beijing Review* 1991: 31). Fourthly, the emergence of a range of banks offering foreign exchange services in China led to an amendment permitting joint ventures to open foreign exchange accounts with any bank officially approved to handle foreign exchange transactions.

Despite the considerable growth of foreign direct investment into China over the relatively short period since 1979, the proportion of gross domestic product accounted for by the foreign-invested sector remains small compared to both its East Asian neighbours of Singapore, Hong Kong and Taiwan and to larger developing countries such as Indonesia and Brazil. It was officially recognized that 'China's investment environment is weak' (Yang 1992: 22) and that it is vital for the authorities to maintain stability in the policies, laws and regulations which affect foreign investors. More laws have been promulgated in the early 1990s, including a Copyright Law and provisions for strengthening the property rights of foreign businessmen, and regulations concerning land-use rights in urban areas and the development and management of land by foreign investors.[2]

Objectives of Chinese and foreign partners

Joint ventures generally have built into them elements both of a mutually beneficial 'win-win' relationship between the partners and of a conflictual 'win-lose' relationship. The partners establish the joint venture because each expects to derive some economic benefit from so doing. Although the process of selecting partners and negotiation of terms for the joint venture has as a major aim the search for complementarity between their respective goals, this does not guarantee that conflicts of interest will be avoided or that misunderstandings will not arise. It is therefore important to consider the objectives held by the Chinese and foreign parties when they undertake joint ventures or similar forms of business collaboration.

Objectives of Chinese partners

Insofar as most foreign joint ventures in China are with state-owned enterprises and joint venture contracts require the approval of MOFERT or local government authorities, the objectives of their Chinese partners are those of the state. While Chinese managers have often been motivated to seek a foreign joint venture for specific local advantages of greater managerial autonomy, higher salaries and operating privileges, the fundamental Chinese criteria for entering foreign joint ventures are (1) to absorb foreign capital, advanced technology and management skills and (2) to gain better access to export markets. The favourable terms granted to foreign-funded enterprises with advanced technology and a high export capability clearly reflect these objectives.

The senior Chinese managers of four Sino-foreign joint ventures investigated by the writer and Tony Cheung in 1991–2 each expressed goals for establishing them which fall within the range of objectives just mentioned. In one case, a Chinese government ministry initiated the venture and was said to have been attracted by the international standing of the American partner's unique photo-imaging technology. In the second case, the American soft drinks partner was seen to offer the means for achieving considerable improvements in production technology and product quality, as well as being willing to export from a China-based joint venture. In the third case, a joint venture with a Japanese construction materials manufacturer, the Chinese partner's main goal was to achieve greater efficiency through acquiring a good management system from its partner. In the fourth case, a joint venture hotel, the Chinese partner's objective was to generate foreign earnings through gaining acceptance by an international clientele, via the reputation and know-how of its Swiss partner.

It has also been evident in these and many other joint ventures that the Chinese partner has a strong interest in achieving short-term profits, in contrast to the longer-term orientation of the foreign partners. As Pearson notes (1991: 204), local government officials have been keen to show quick results from joint ventures within their purview, since profitable projects bring in tax revenues and prestige to the municipality. Many state-owned enterprises which became partners in foreign joint ventures were not in sound financial health and a speedy attainment of profitability was also welcomed by the Chinese side as a means of underwriting such enterprises. These local pressures for quick returns from foreign investment encouraged the levying of charges which many joint ventures regarded as quite unreasonable, a problem which the 1986 Provisions endeavoured to mitigate.

Daniels, Krug and Nigh (1985) investigated eleven Sino-US joint ventures established between 1979 and 1983. They noted that in some cases foreign firms were unwilling to transfer technology to China without securing some control through an equity holding in the operation. From the Chinese point of view, technology transfer through a joint venture as opposed to, say, a licensing agreement, offered assistance in the use and management of the technology and also the prospect of further learning if a joint research and development unit were established as part of the joint venture. The handling of export marketing by a foreign partner could also facilitate access to overseas markets and so build further on the advantages which a joint venture might bring.

Objectives of foreign partners

Companies engage in foreign direct investment for a variety of reasons which generally concern either (1) accessing foreign markets, or (2) securing a resource or basis for production not found elsewhere under the same favourable conditions. The former constellation of reasons includes expansion into new markets, avoidance of protectionist barriers around markets, and pre-empting entrance to new markets by competitors. The latter includes gaining access to new or cheaper labour, materials or transportation routes, and responding to attractive host country investment incentives. In the case of China, both sets of motives apply, though they tend to vary somewhat in degree according to the source of foreign investment and the sector in question.

The dominant motive for Western and Japanese corporations to invest in China has been the prospect of gaining access to what they perceive as a huge domestic market. There was some early euphoria following the declaration of the open-door policy which then gave way to a more realistic appreciation of the technical difficulties of operating in China and the determination of the governmental authorities to protect their own local industry and to avoid a drain on foreign exchange. However, most Western investors have taken a long-term view that an early presence in China's market might lay the basis for a substantial market share and at the same time prevent international rivals from squeezing them out. Moreover, the protection of domestic industry and avoidance of imports did not apply equally to all foreign firms. Some introduced products or services which were new to China and/or also used local materials; examples are hair cosmetics and express document delivery.

Surveys of US firms investing in China (Daniels et al. 1985; A. T. Kearney/ITRI 1987) found that the great majority wanted to establish a long-run position in China as a potentially strong growth market and as a base within the Asian region. They did not see short-term profit as a major objective and even less emphasis was placed on low-cost sourcing. Even firms such as Nike footwear, which invested in China primarily as a lowest-cost supplier, could not but help note at the same time the potential market of 'two billion feet'. By contrast, many investors from Hong Kong and Macau, together with some Japanese firms, have looked for more immediate profits through low-cost unskilled labour and (in the case of Hong Kong and Macau) land which had become a scarce resource in their own territories. Much of the investment from Hong Kong and Macau has been in small, low technology processing and assembly plants catering for simple goods such as television antennas, toys, textiles and porcelain figurines. In keeping with the greater emphasis of these foreign investors on short-term profits and their limited technological commitment, the average contract term of joint ventures with Hong Kong/Macau partners tends to be less than that for those with Western and Japanese investment (cf. Child et al. 1990: 16).

Sino-foreign joint ventures are generally among the most successful firms in China and many of them have been able to match their partners' objectives to the satisfaction of all concerned. The willingness of foreign investors to commit capital and transfer technology to China, and to use local resources, is quite compatible with Chinese objectives. The foreign desire to produce for the Chinese market may present few problems if the joint venture's products are new to the country and/or if the market is growing rapidly. Equally, many foreign companies are happy to use China as a production base from which to export, particularly to developing countries and those of the former Soviet Union.

On the other hand, the foreign partner's intention to safeguard its proprietary technology, to control the management of its investment and to import components or materials (whether for reasons of quality or profiting from transfer pricing) could clearly be in conflict with Chinese interests. Access to markets can also be the cause of serious dispute when this threatens the position either of Chinese producers or of the foreign partner's existing pattern of international business. The foreign wish to have access to China's domestic market and the Chinese wish for joint ventures to facilitate the access of their Chinese partners to international markets has in practice been the most fundamental difference of interest between Sino-foreign joint venture partners. Disputes about the quality standards offered by local suppliers and achieved by the joint venture as a potential export producer, and about the foreign restriction of access to proprietary technology which had therefore to be imported or paid for through royalties, are also endemic to this issue. In addition to intrinsic conflicts of this kind, other difficulties arise because of the mix of Chinese and foreign management traditions and the dynamics of adjustment and learning between the joint venture partners – these are considered further in the following two chapters.

Sometimes it is not so much the maximization of economic returns from the operations of the joint venture *per se* as associated benefits or even the fulfilment of political objectives which primarily motivate the formation of a Sino-foreign joint venture. We mentioned the advantages of tax concessions and increased autonomy which Chinese managers enjoy if they enter a joint venture with a foreign partner. Aiello (1991: 50–1) concludes from his analysis of Beijing Jeep that this particular joint venture does not conform to the normal assumption in international business economics that the partners have chosen to enter into this organizational form because it offers an attractive transactions governance structure for revenue-enhancing and cost-reducing activities. Rather, he argues, the maximization of dividend income from the venture was not a top priority for either partner. The American partner, while seeking an adequate return from its capital invested, was actually reaping much richer rewards from selling knockdown kits as well as spare parts and manufacturing equipment to China for payment in hard currency. The Chinese partner, in effect the Beijing Municipal Government, appears to have entered into the joint venture for reasons that were to do with politics as well as economics. It wished to prevent Beijing from being excluded from the national automotive market, in response to the central government's plan to make plants elsewhere into China's primary automotive producers. The development of modern productive capacity with the aid of American capital and know-how was also seen by the Beijing municipal authorities as a basis for building up local suppliers and an export base. The joint venture was, moreover, expected to bring in advanced manufacturing technologies and Western management techniques.

The Beijing Jeep joint venture, in Aiello's view, served therefore to provide a 'platform' from which both partners can extract what they want from the other party. In this case, the foreign partner was not necessarily all that interested in developing the joint venture as a self-standing successful economic unit, while the Chinese partner was not interested in retaining a foreign connection once it has outlived its usefulness.[3]

Other joint ventures have also been established on this basis; Gordon (1990) in effect concludes that Volkswagen includes a similar scenario within its range of possibilities in China. He comments that Beijing Jeep and Shanghai-Volkswagen together are

assembly operations, in which there has been little foreign capital, little technology transfer, no saving in foreign exchange by comparison with importing the finished product, and no exports in the foreseeable future to cover the cost of imports and the foreign investment. (p. 8)

There may be a number of instances where one or both partners use a joint venture primarily as a platform from which to extract gains rather than looking necessarily to its long-term development as a viable enterprise in its own right. In the case of a glass manufacturing joint venture, for example, the foreign minority investor is receiving a return primarily through sales royalties, levied as a fee for its closely guarded proprietary technology, rather than from the operating profits of the venture. It would like the venture to earn good returns on its capital, but it does not regard these as its main source of profit and has therefore been reluctant to inject further capital even when good investment returns were in prospect. The platform approach is obviously a perspective that foreign investors can adopt towards establishing a joint venture in China, though it is not one which promises a long life for the partnership. It may also be the case that the foreign investor acquires doubts about Chinese intentions to continue the joint venture over the long term and it must then decide whether to go along with this approach.

Factors to consider in establishing a joint venture in China

It is clearly of the utmost importance for prospective foreign investors in China to be certain of their own objectives and to examine whether (1) the general situation and (2) potential partners are likely to permit the realization of those objectives. Many Chinese enterprises are seeking foreign partners, sometimes more for the benefits of tax breaks and increased managerial autonomy which joint ventures offer than for longer-term and more fundamental economic advantages. The scope for mismatch and misunderstanding at this stage is considerable, and this points to the wisdom of allowing sufficient time for mutual expectations to be discussed and any problems to surface.

If a complementarity or compatibility of objectives emerges between the potential Chinese and foreign partners, there are also a number of more specific considerations to take into account in deciding whether or not to invest in China through the establishment of a joint venture. Geringer's (1991) distinction between 'task-related' and 'partner-related' criteria for partner selection identifies several of these considerations. Task-related criteria concern the quality of the market opportunities, productive skills, resources and other factors which bear directly upon the economic viability of the proposed venture's operations. Examples include access to marketing and distribution systems, the availability of skilled labour and experienced managers, and the quality of local supply. Partner-related criteria refer to factors which assume relevance because the success of the joint venture also depends on the ability of local partners to work together. The variables here include the compatibility of and trust between the Chinese and foreign top management teams, and the ease with which their respective systems and structures can be matched.

It is essential to establish task-related complementarities for the proposed joint venture which are economically viable. Disparities in partner-related features, emanating from the partners' different national and organizational cultures and from differences in their economic and institutional systems, can often be accommodated and indeed built upon constructively through a process of mutual learning, once the collaborative venture has been established. In particular, cultural differences which appear quite daunting at first do not generally constitute a serious long-term problem (cf. Punnett and Yu 1991).

Underlying both sets of criteria, but more closely dependent on task-related items, is the strategic question of whether the Chinese and foreign partners can define a basis for co-operation on which they can achieve their different objectives and thus be motivated to work for the continuing success of the joint venture. The task and strategic bases for establishing a joint venture are considered in this section. The negotiation of a relationship between partners is considered in the following section and its subsequent development as a managerial partnership is discussed in chapters 12 and 13.

Information on the quality of task-related factors in a prospective joint venture match is now more readily available in China. Consultants, trade associations, embassy commercial sections and chambers of commerce can all be of assistance. Indeed, one China analyst recently concluded that 'any foreign company approaching China for the first time should not be able to plead ignorance if it does something wrong. There are enough sources of information and advice available.' (*Financial Times*, Survey on China, 16 June 1992: 6).

De Bruijn and Jia (1992) advance a useful set of guidelines to assist a potential foreign corporate investor to assess the quality of task-related and strategic factors in China. To be more precise, these writers cast their discussion in terms of selecting products that are suitable for the Chinese environment, but their framework can also be helpful for determining whether the Chinese context and potential Chinese partners offer a basis for meeting foreign expectations. They categorize task-related criteria under the headings of (1) environmental factors, (2) key internal factors of the Chinese partner, and (3) operational criteria.

Environmental factors sub-divide into (i) the market situation, (ii) the local supply situation and (iii) government policies. With regard to the Chinese market, De Bruijn and Jia point out a number of potential pitfalls. Firstly, the products of some foreign investors are still too advanced for Chinese customers, an example being powder coatings for building construction materials in a context where liquid paint is still widely used for protection. Secondly, certain markets are still subject to bureaucratic control; in particular those for many large industrial projects. They cite the case of industrial computer control equipment which the Chinese authorities still continued to import in 1986 and 1987, using up scarce foreign currency, even though the Shanghai–Foxboro joint venture had been established and was producing such equipment to world-quality standards and at a competitive price. Thirdly, the Chinese market is fragmented between different municipalities, provinces and regions. Different local governments compete with each other and strive to protect the local enterprises under their purview (cf. Nee 1992). This means that a foreign investor going into partnership with a Chinese enterprise cannot necessarily expect to be able to sell its products in local markets outside the area in which its partner is located and enjoys established connections.

The second aspect of the Chinese environment concerns the supply situation where there are official pressures on joint ventures to achieve certain targets for localization. Localization is the process in which a joint venture works with local suppliers to locate and improve components and materials. It serves both to develop the standards of domestic Chinese producers and to save foreign exchange. Since companies with foreign ownership are encouraged to manufacture products with advanced technology and to export a high proportion of their output, they are often willing to make considerable efforts via technical and other advice to enhance the performance of Chinese suppliers.

Successful localization is, however, not an easy task and the targets set out in many joint venture contracts have proved much too optimistic. It is advisable for prospective joint venture partners to examine the possibilities for localization carefully, since a number of problems often arise, some of which were noted in chapter 7. Local suppliers may be unwilling to switch to the relatively small quantities and exacting quality standards required by joint ventures. Despite relatively cheap labour, the costs of Chinese-produced components can be higher than those of imported ones. Higher Chinese prices may also result from the absence of a fully competitive price system. In addition, the relevant infrastructure is underdeveloped. While telephone and fax communications are now quite good, problems can arise in the transportation of materials and in energy supply.

The problem has been highlighted by the experience of automotive joint ventures such as the Beijing Jeep Corporation (BJC) and the Shanghai Volkswagen Automotive Company (Gordon 1990). For example, when the BJC began to assemble Cherokee jeeps in 1985, the American partner (AMC/Chrysler) agreed to help the Chinese in a localization programme which envisaged that over 80 per cent of the jeep's components would be manufactured in China by the end of 1990. In the event, the level of localization achieved by the end of 1989 was only 40 per cent and the goal for 1990 was clearly unattainable (Aiello 1991: 56). This shortfall was due to problems of both quality and cost. The regional fragmentation and local protectionism that characterize Chinese production militate against the attainment of economies of scale. Foreign investors have been reluctant to join forces with suppliers because of insufficient volumes and fears that Chinese manufacturers with improved technology and quality standards could become formidable competitors. The investment required to produce some components, such as auto engines, is very large and the risks render this scale of commitment unattractive.

Government policies comprise a third aspect of the Chinese environment. The extent to which the success of a joint venture depends on governmental agencies is indicated by the fact that every aspect of a foreign investment project needs a licence from the government. As De Bruijn and Xia state: 'to create a joint venture a licence is required; to manufacture each product/ component and to import some necessary machines/components, separate licences are also necessary; to sell the JV's products in the local market requires a licence as well' (p. 7). The policies of the Chinese government, expressed through regulations, licences and favourable treatment, shift in response to changing economic circumstances. For example, a previously preferential policy towards the development of the TV industry has now ceased because of the rapid growth of colour TV production in recent years. Therefore, whatever product or service a foreign firm can offer, its success will often depend on whether or not it fits China's economic priorities which are expressed in its state plan. These priorities change and it is incumbent on foreign investors to anticipate such shifts in policy as far as they can.

Key internal factors are the second set of task-related criteria which De Bruijn and Jia identify. These include the technological and market capabilities of the Chinese partner. Its technological capability rests upon the quality of the existing Chinese production technology, the development of its manufacturing systems and R&D, and the availability of trained and educated personnel. The gap between Chinese technological capabilities and the level suited to the production or service intentions of the foreign partner will point to the resources and time needed to attain a satisfactory level of performance. The Chinese part-ner's market capability rests on whether it sells on a national scale, the distrib-ution channels it can offer and the experience it has of the Chinese market. The market share of many state-owned enterprises is usually below 10 per cent and this may well inhibit the scope it can offer to a joint venture partner even for products which are officially approved for domestic sale.

De Bruijn and Jia single out as key operational criteria, their third task-related category, the localization of supply (which we have just discussed) and the foreign exchange balance. There are various ways of achieving a forex balance and an intending foreign investor should investigate their feasibility in its particular case. Firstly, subject to approval from the State Administration for Exchange Control (SAEC), foreign-funded firms are allowed to trade non-convertible RMB for foreign exchange among themselves at certain currency 'swap centres'. Secondly, goods that substitute for imports can be sold in China for hard currency; it has, however, proved difficult in practice to obtain the required official approval for this arrangement. Thirdly, foreign investment enterprises may use their RMB to purchase domestic products not subject to state planning to export them through their own sales outlets. This method is officially intended only to meet temporary shortfalls of foreign exchange; it is again difficult in practice to obtain approval and to find a Chinese counterpart which is willing to give up the prospect of direct exporting for foreign exchange. Fourthly, subject to approval from the SAEC, foreign-funded enter-prises are able to sell certain goods on the domestic market for hard currency. Finally, it is possible for foreign-funded enterprises to re-invest their RMB profit in another enterprise that generates foreign exchange, though the practi-cal difficulties of arranging this mean that few joint ventures have put it into practice.

Negotiation of joint ventures

There is now quite a substantial literature on commercial negotiations with the Chinese, including those involved in establishing joint ventures. Most of this literature emphasizes the cultural basis of problems which can arise (e.g. Pye 1982; Tung 1982; Knutsson 1986; Shenkar and Ronen 1987a; Seligman 1990). This literature is helpful in detailing the practical problems which stem from different norms between the Chinese and foreign parties to negotiations, over matters such as etiquette, the appropriate speed and overall duration of a nego-tiation, the amount of detail that should be gone into, and the form of the process itself.

However, while cultural sensitivity is necessary for negotiations with the Chinese to succeed, it is not a sufficient or even the primary determinant of being able to establish a Sino-foreign joint venture contract successfully. A

more fundamental requirement is to identify a set of economic benefits sufficiently attractive to both parties which can be realized within China's regulations and practices for foreign-funded ventures. This point is consistent with
the earlier argument that while both task-oriented and partner-oriented factors
are important for the success of a joint venture, finding sufficient complementarity between the prospective partners in task-oriented features is the fundamental requirement.

Hakam and Chan (1990), for example, studied two different negotiations
with Chinese counterparts in which the same Singaporean firm was involved.
Although a relatively high level of cultural affinity exists between (Chinese)
Singaporeans and those from mainland China, the fact that one negotiation was
a success while the other failed has to be ascribed to economic factors. In the
case of the failed negotiation, each participant perceived that the other firm was
not contributing sufficiently in terms of complementary resources and sharing
the functions of the proposed joint venture. As the investigators put it, 'shared
cultural traditions, such as language, was [sic] not sufficient to overcome fundamental economic differences' (p. 261). The other negotiation owed its success to the fact that both sides were able to identify a non-equity co-operative
arrangement from which they stood to benefit.

Campbell and Yee (1991) also stress that a high level of task-related complementarity of the parties is vital both for the outcome of negotiations and for
the subsequent prospects of building up the joint venture. They conclude from
six case studies of Sino-British joint ventures that:

The ideal seems to be where the Chinese supply raw material, of the necessary quality,
and management and labor capable of efficient production. The foreign partner provides
the technology and the export markets. In this way the objectives of both sides are met.
The Chinese earn foreign currency and gain new technology and the foreign company
gets low-cost production, which helps it to compete in markets outside China. (p. 225)

Another precondition for the successful negotiation of a joint venture is for the
foreign side to do its homework on the pertinent features of the Chinese industrial and regulatory systems with sufficient thoroughness. This requires investigation of the quality of task-related and strategic factors bearing on those
products which the foreign side seeks to introduce into production and/or to
market in China. The previous section identified these in terms of environmental factors, key internal characteristics of the Chinese partner, operational
criteria and partner goals. It also requires research into the regulations and
administrative structures which operate in the area of economic activity to be
negotiated. It is essential to check whether prevailing regulations single out the
activity as one of sufficient priority so as to minimize the problem of securing
any necessary foreign exchange and indeed of securing the approval of the
Chinese higher authorities for a new venture in the first place. It is important to
understand the relevant Chinese administrative structures so as to identify who

on the Chinese side is likely to have authority to take decisions in the negotiation. One of the more frequently expressed frustrations of foreign negotiators in China is that those on the other side of the table who do most of the talking are usually not the persons with authority to take the relevant decisions. It is therefore incumbent on the foreign party to find out who can take those decisions.

Decentralization under the economic reform process now means that rather more discretion has been granted in most industries to enterprise management, although all new ventures still require the approval of higher local or central authorities. Gaining privileged access to these decision makers is difficult but not impossible. If it cannot be secured directly, it may be possible to approach them by working through their systems of *guanxi* or family connections. Even if these are established, however, the nature of the Chinese governance system still has to be borne in mind. Chinese government officials have grown used to exercising caution, especially in making agreements with foreigners, lest they be blamed afterwards for having given away too much and so creating the conditions for foreign exploitation. As we noted in the case of two automotive joint ventures, some agreements have resulted in provisions which are very costly in foreign exchange to the Chinese and which so far have transferred limited technological or other benefits.

Once these preliminary investigations have been undertaken, the would-be foreign investor can enter into the process of negotiation with some expectation that both sides will perceive mutual benefit from reaching an agreed basis for co-operation. It becomes highly relevant to appreciate the particular nature of Chinese negotiating behaviour and a distillation of expert opinion (plus the writer's own experience in negotiating Sino-foreign academic collaboration) is now offered as a bridge to the extended analyses available in the literature recently cited.

The Chinese are very hospitable within the bounds of official relationships, and normally offer a warm welcome, even extending to flattery, to the foreign team. Their practice is to seek initial agreement quite quickly on very general principles, without clarifying the details. This gives the foreign party a gratifying sense that the Chinese desire to reach an agreement quickly and on 'reasonable' terms. As Pye (1982) points out, what is happening is that the Chinese side is taking the opportunity at this stage to size up the foreign party and to determine how vulnerable it may be, and especially to see if it lacks patience. In this way, the foreign party may easily be placed into a disadvantageous position if it is psychologically unprepared for the hard road which still lies ahead. To quote Pye (1982: ix–x) 'For Chinese officials, displaying impatience is a major sin, and they are masters of the art of stalling while keeping alive the other party's hopes.'

Another common characteristic of Chinese negotiating behaviour which soon becomes apparent is that they keep their interests and priorities obscure. The Chinese will insist that the other party reveals its proposals first. This allows the Chinese side to gather information from 'presentations' by the foreign party. It probably needs this information because its understanding of what precisely a co-operative venture could offer is likely to be vague at this point. This behaviour may, additionally, reflect the diverse number of interest groups present in the Chinese party and problems of communication and reaching agreement that result (and which may become apparent later in the negotiating process). The Chinese party may not be in a good position to reveal its intentions first, because it does not have sufficiently detailed knowledge of what the foreign side could provide in a co-operative venture and because it may lack internal agreement on its priorities. Having said this, insistence on the foreign party revealing its intentions first is also a conscious ploy which makes it easier to play off competing foreigners against each other during the negotiations.

Negotiating with the Chinese usually generates considerable uncertainty among the foreign party, which can easily turn into anxiety if the foreign negotiators do not appreciate what is going on. While much of this uncertainty generation is intended by the Chinese, and forms part of a tradition prefigured in classics such as Sun Tzu's *The Art of War*, some of it stems from organizational problems and a lack of information. Chinese negotiating teams tend to be large and their lines of authority somewhat vague. They will usually include administrators and technical specialists from different government offices and institutes, in addition to enterprise managers. Chinese negotiators are therefore often uncertain about their mandates and about the decisions which their superiors will eventually take. The latter usually take a back seat in the negotiating process and may even be absent from it for most of the time, partly to avoid direct involvement in inter-personal conflict and hence the risk of losing face. These organizational ambiguities can give rise to disconcerting features in negotiations with the Chinese. If relatively junior officials are fronting the discussions with the foreign side, apparent progress in a warm atmosphere can be followed by a disappointing outcome. There may also be long periods of no movement for reasons which the other side is not prepared to explain.

A further unpremeditated cause of uncertainty is a lack of appreciation of the realities outside China. This can lead to unrealistic expectations on the part of the Chinese, which once put on the table take time and patience to bring down to reality. For example, in a negotiation which the writer conducted to establish an academic exchange agreement with a major university in Beijing, the Chinese side argued that the British partner should endow a personal computer laboratory. The Chinese negotiators claimed that this was straightforward because in Britain PCs had become almost as common and cheap as pocket radios, and that in any case their prospective foreign partner was rich. In reality, the British university had been subject to savage budgetary cuts at the beginning of the 1980s and was certainly in no position to endow a computer laboratory. In this case, it was necessary to go into the British partner's situation in considerable detail to convince the Chinese side that the situation simply did not allow for their expectations to be realized.

Students of Chinese negotiating behaviour point out that this also encompasses tactics to unsettle the other side through deliberately creating uncertainty. The Chinese may put forward extreme demands and use extreme language from time to time in order to try to extract further concessions. Believing that people can be devastated by a sense of shame, they can make an issue over minor mis-statements and errors. At the same time, they will hint of future opportunities for the foreigner which may be jeopardized by his present unreasonable behaviour. They often try to play upon sentiments of friendship, the genuineness of which has to be shown by concessions by the foreigner, not by the Chinese. Indeed, it will be frequently implied that Chinese friendship is being shown by 'inviting' the foreigner to their country and giving him so much time, overlooking the fact that this hospitality is at great expense to the foreigner's pocket and is usually accompanied by considerable difficulties over basic arrangements such as securing visas, planning itineraries and finding the right Chinese officials to talk to.

The process of negotiation, taken as a whole over a period of time, tends to follow a sequence in which the Chinese side takes uncertainty generation to a knife-edge. This is particularly likely if they know that the foreign party faces a time-limit and is keen to secure an agreement. The normally rapid initial move towards agreement on general principles engenders a sense of progress on the foreign side. The natural tendency is to believe that only details now remain to be worked out. During the subsequent days or weeks, as each detail is addressed, the Chinese side will demand something extra attempting to build up what can become a formidable overhead on what the foreigner first calculated. Meanwhile, time is passing and the foreign negotiators, having early on reported success back to their home base, now wonder whether they should concede each point in order to retain the chance of a deal. This can become a quite nerve-racking stage of the proceedings, just when a cool head must be retained. Indeed, there is a consensus among experts that it is essential in negotiating with the Chinese to preserve emotional restraint and not to display what would be interpreted as serious weakness. For this reason, it is a good idea for the senior member of the foreign team to withdraw from the fray just as his Chinese counterpart has almost certainly done. For at a certain point, the foreign side may simply have to say 'no deal' and it can afford to do this if in doing its homework it has concluded that the Chinese need the deal at least as much as it does.

In the inter-university negotiations this had to be said after a week during which each day new 'little problems' were one by one brought to the table by the Chinese. At this stage the negotiations were being handled on a delegated basis by one British colleague, who by the Thursday evening was under considerable psychological pressure despite being a trained lawyer with extensive experience of East Asia. He came to the writer in some desperation feeling that he was about to lose the whole deal. We decided to explain on the following morning that all the additional Chinese demands bar one were unrealizable and that if they insisted on them no agreement was possible. This was done courteously; by that same afternoon the deal was concluded on terms acceptable to the British side and formally celebrated by a banquet on the Saturday!

This particular academic exchange agreement was subsequently a great success for everyone concerned and has led to personal friendships, joint work and further mutually beneficial projects. This chimes in well with a Chinese cultural expectation that a formal contract at the conclusion of negotiations does not signal the end of the process. The Chinese attach more importance to the long-term relationship which should follow and this loyalty can be both productive and gratifying. It does mean, however, that the Chinese partner will not hesitate to suggest modifications to the agreement almost before the ink is dry and that negotiation will be a continuing feature of the joint venture relationship (cf. Frankenstein 1991: 140). Moreover, while contracts are honoured, others like suppliers may be blamed for operational problems which are actually the fault of the Chinese partner. Much the same advice therefore continues to apply: be prepared to combine patient explanation with necessary firmness, avoiding personal aggression and pique at all cost.

Pye (1982:xii) offers an excellent conclusion to this brief review of the negotiating process likely to be involved in establishing a joint venture in China when he sums up the lessons of his study of Chinese commercial negotiating behaviour:

The most elementary rules for negotiating with the Chinese are: (1) practice patience; (2) accept as normal prolonged periods of no movement; (3) control against exaggerated expectations, and discount Chinese rhetoric about future prospects; (4) expect that the Chinese will try to influence by shaming; (5) resist the temptation to believe that difficulties may have been caused by one's own mistakes; and (6) try to understand Chinese cultural traits, but never believe that a foreigner can practice them better than the Chinese.

Conclusion

China has successfully attracted a rapidly rising level of foreign direct investment in conditions where the competition among developing countries for such investment has become intense. Foreign firms now play a major role in one of the world's most dynamic economies. The Chinese authorities have welcomed foreign involvement in their industry and commerce but on terms of their own choosing. They have been determined to avoid becoming victims of foreign economic colonialism. With this in mind, they have normally directed foreign investment to state-owned enterprises which remain under their close control. Foreign investment, with the technology and managerial know-how that accompanies it, has additionally been regarded as an important means for revitalizing state enterprises in line with one of the main objectives of the economic reform.

The expectations of foreign investors have been disappointed from time to time, particularly in the mid-1980s and after the Tiananmen incident. Much of the problem lies in the slow process of adjustment from a system of ostensibly bureaucratic governance in which resources were administratively allocated, a process in which patronage and special connections played a large role, to one based upon market transactions regulated on the basis of law. Largely in response to pressures from foreign investors, more specific and comprehensive legal provisions have been brought into play since the early and very limited law of 1979. The inducements offered to foreign investors have been made more attractive and foreign management control, including 100 per cent ownership, is now an accepted option.

There is today a much wider availability of information and advice on potential Chinese joint venture partners and on the supply and demand parameters of different sectors; this permits reasonably valid analyses on task-related complementarities with foreign firms. Moreover, experience has provided guidelines on the conduct of negotiations with Chinese counterparts which can facilitate the process of arriving at a sound basis for partnership. What remains far less understood is how to achieve the partner-related matching that is necessary if managerial synergies are to be achieved in the subsequent operation of a Sino-foreign joint venture or other enterprise with mixed Chinese and foreign management. It is also through such synergies that foreign companies can contribute to the development of Chinese management practice. The management of Sino-foreign joint ventures is therefore an issue of great importance and challenge, and is the subject of the two chapters that follow.

12 Management of joint ventures

While the parties to a joint venture in China want it to be a success and to be founded on good long-term relationships, there are a number of substantial problems which have to be managed in order to realize those intentions. Some of these are inherent in all co-operative ventures, such as conflicts between the goals which the partners hold for the venture and tensions between them concerning the control they exercise over its policies and practices. Other problems, which are more specific to international co-operative ventures especially between companies from developed and developing countries, stem from differences in the culture, formative experience, business understanding and technical expertise of the collaborating partners. In the case of China, there is the further complication that foreign companies are working within a fundamentally different political-economic system and with partners who have grown up with the norms of that system. These differences create problems of mutual comprehension and present both sides with the need for considerable adjustment and learning.

The previous chapter described the objectives which foreign firms and the Chinese authorities seek to pursue through the establishment of joint ventures, and the potential for conflict between these. Earlier sections of the book, especially chapter 2, analysed the location of Chinese managers in their cultural and political-economic context and how this helped to form practices and outlooks which contrast markedly with those of foreign managers, even from places like Hong Kong which draw upon the same Chinese cultural tradition. Foreign involvement in Chinese management is extremely important for policy – both China's policy to strive for rapid modernization and the policies of international business towards such a large potential market and business partner. The dynamics of the Sino-foreign relationships also bring into sharp relief ways in which Chinese management differs from its counterpart in other industrial countries.

The present and following chapters examine the management of Sino-foreign joint ventures. This chapter focuses on the key issue of control. It also examines conflicts between partners which both occasion and arise from the question of control, and it reviews the problems that foreign managers have experienced in China. Chapter 13 focuses more on the dynamic properties of the Sino-foreign business relationship in considering changes that have resulted from foreign involvement and the process of adjustment between the partners. Information on these issues is available from several sources, two being studies in which the writer was involved. The first of these was conducted by the writer with European and Chinese colleagues in 1989 in thirty equity joint ventures with foreign partners from Western European countries (eleven cases), the United States (seven cases), Japan (seven cases) and Hong Kong (five cases). The joint ventures were mostly located in northern China, they ranged widely in size and in industry, and all had been in operation for at least a year. Further details of this sample are given in Child et al. (1990). A second investigation was undertaken in 1991–2 by the writer and Tony Cheung of four joint ventures, two with partners from the USA, one from Japan and one from Switzerland. This study addressed change and learning in more detail. Both investigations covered a mixture of manufacturing and service companies and were conducted through interviews with the senior foreign and Chinese managers in each venture. Those interviewed were all men and their interviewers were fluent in the appropriate language except in Japanese where an interpreter was used when necessary. Appendix 12.1 provides an outline of these two samples which, for convenience, will henceforth be called 'China 1' and 'China 2' respectively.

The heterogeneity of the China 1 sample was intended to provide clues as to whether features such as scale, sector or nationality of foreign partner made any difference to the management approach being adopted in joint ventures or to problems of co-operation between the partners. For example, we were aware from previous research (e.g. Pugh and Hickson 1976) that features such as the extent of formalization and other changes introduced into the joint ventures could reflect their size or that of their parent companies; also that it might be relevant to take account of the time that had elapsed to allow for adaptation between the partners since the date the joint venture was founded.

Another consideration was that many of the foreign partners in the two samples came from what Hofstede (1991) concludes are three distinct cultural regions – Anglo-Saxon, Germanic and Japanese – which tend to have different approaches to management and organization (cf. Smith 1992). The foreign partners not only differ among themselves culturally but, with the exception of the five joint ventures with Hong Kong partners, they also hail from cultural regions which contrast to local Chinese traditions and all the foreign partners bring an approach to management developed within different, capitalist and market-based, business systems. Considerable prominence has been given to stereotypes of management said to characterize these cultural regions (cf. Lawrence 1980; Alston 1986; Redding 1990) and it was therefore expected that the approaches and priorities adopted by foreign managers in the joint ventures would contrast in predictable ways and engender different reactions from their local counterparts. The main contrasts expected were, briefly, that the American approach would display a somewhat inflexible insistence on the adoption of home-grown formalized management techniques; that the Germanic approach would emphasize the professional competence and technical training of employees; and that the Japanese approach would stress normative control through enveloping local personnel within a culture of high personal commitment and loyalty to the company.

Several significant studies of joint ventures in China have been conducted by other researchers. A particularly insightful study of the control of foreign investment in China is that by Pearson (1991) whose analysis extends to national and regional levels as well as that of the enterprise, and who locates her discussion within the historical development of the Chinese outlook on foreign investment. She was able through interviews, primarily with foreign managers, and supplemented by printed sources, to build up full and comparable information for twenty-eight equity joint ventures covering the first half of the 1980s. The consulting firm of A.T. Kearney in partnership with the International Trade Research Institute of MOFERT in 1986 surveyed the experience of seventy manufacturing equity joint ventures from Europe, Japan, the USA and Hong Kong, but excluded the sixteen with Hong Kong partners from its report (A.T. Kearney/ITRI 1987). The US–China Business Council (formerly the National Council for US–China Trade) produced a comprehensive data base on American joint ventures in China and a detailed examination of their experience in 1987 (NCUSCT 1987) which was followed by an updating report (USCBC 1991) based partly on surveys conducted in 1989 and 1990. Several other surveys of Sino-foreign joint ventures are reported and/or referenced in Campbell and Henley (1990), Wang and Wedley (1990) and Shenkar (1991).

Control as an issue

Joint ventures are often regarded as second-best forms of investment compared with wholly owned subsidiaries because there is a concern over the limits to the control that a parent company can exercise. They have all the control problems of subsidiaries plus those which arise from joint ownership (Schaan 1988). Since both partners are bringing complementary strengths to the joint ventures, the full realization of which depends on finding an agreed basis of co-operation between them, even the holding of a majority equity position cannot be used to enforce control over the venture without jeopardizing the basis for its success. Some limitation of control is therefore a price that has to be paid for securing the advantages of a joint venture or similar co-operative agreement for a company's internal development and/or its strategic positioning. Internal advantages include access to new technology, managerial competences and economies of scale, sharing risks and costs, and obtaining new resources. Advantages for strategic positioning include co-opting or blocking competition, overcoming governmental trade or investment barriers, and the facilitation of initial international expansion (Harrigan 1986; Contractor and Lorange 1988).

In China, culture, history and ideology make the control of foreign investment a particularly sensitive issue. Historically, the cultural isolation of the Chinese and their remarkable artistic, organizational and technical advances up to the fifteenth century bred a reluctance to admit any relevance or value in foreign ways. When the foreign powers forced open China's economy in the last century, the shock was made the more bitter by the exploitation which accompanied the inward investment and control over economic transactions. Following the 1949 revolution, there was a strong ideological aversion to Western influence. China's Communist leaders viewed private foreign capital as incompatible with goals of socialist development and since the early-1960s, after the break with the Soviet Union, they pursued a policy of self-reliance. As Pearson (1991:3) notes:

The policy of self-reliance had been rooted in the historically and ideologically grounded belief that private direct investment in China would lead to a number of negative results. China's leaders doubted China's ability to capture its share of the economic benefits generated by foreign investment. They also feared loss of state control over the country's development path, loss of political independence, and the potential for foreign influences to contaminate traditional and socialist values.

These fears led to a determination to control the effects of foreign investment, which since 1979 has been permitted under the 'open door' policy, in order to combat what were seen to be the dangers of 'unhealthy' cultural and political tendencies. This was to be done by applying to joint ventures and other foreign-funded enterprises both external government economic regulation and control through the Chinese management partner. These two channels of control, external and internal, and their impact on Sino-foreign joint venture management, are now considered in turn.

External channels of control over joint ventures

The Chinese authorities have channelled foreign co-operation towards state-owned or larger collective enterprises over which they exercise the closest regulatory control. The continuing endeavours of government authorities to exercise control over joint ventures are a feature of the Chinese investment context which now sets it apart from most countries of Eastern Europe. These authorities will expect the joint venture to pursue policies which benefit the local (if not national) economy rather than the foreign partner or even the venture itself. The areas of economic regulation where control over strategic decisions is most likely to be contested in Sino-foreign joint ventures are those where the goals of the partners tend to conflict. They concern the joint venture's contribution to exports, the competitive threat it poses for domestic enterprises, the allocation of profit and the transfer of technology.

In addition to the various regulations formally limiting the decision powers of foreign investors, the Chinese system provides for three external organs to influence and control the management of enterprises. These are the labour union, the Communist Party and the economic bureaucracy. We have already seen that while all three organs tended to draw back under the economic reform from active involvement in the management of state enterprises, the party and the bureaucracy have retained a potent influence in certain areas.

The 1983 'Regulations for the Implementation of the Law on Joint Ventures' state that labour unions have the right to represent staff and workers in signing labour contracts and supervising their execution. They can also participate in board meetings as non-voting members. Trade unions are not mandatory in joint ventures though they have been formed in most of them. In practice, however, neither joint venture managers nor local trade union officials enforced the implementation of these provisions. For example, union officials rarely if ever attended joint venture board meetings and the extent of worker participation in management is much less than in state-owned enterprises. Instead, the labour unions have tended to assist the Chinese management in encouraging labour discipline and to organize staff recreational activities. Nyaw (1991) asked eighteen high-ranking union officials from joint ventures in the Shenzhen Special Economic Zone about the importance of different roles played by the union. Overall, they attached great importance to the union's role in being consulted on staff dismissals and penalties, in inculcating employees with the virtues of hard work and discipline, and in organizing cultural and recreational activities. They attached little importance to union involvement in major operational and strategic decisions. As Nyaw concludes, 'analyses of the significance and roles of trade unions demonstrate that the Chinese are not inclined to take drastic measures that may jeopardize the confidence of foreign investors' (1991:120).

There has been official silence about the party's role in joint ventures, though its function in them was discussed in internal regulations not officially available to foreigners. Pearson (1991: 187) notes that in the early years the party was intended to play a role completely independent from foreign management in order to monitor the implementation of joint venture policy and to lead the fight against 'unhealthy tendencies' among Chinese who were in frequent contact with foreigners. The organizational strength of the party was stronger in the North, especially in Beijing, than in Shanghai and Guangdong. However, as chapter 4 noted, there was a general decline of the party's role in Chinese

Table 12.1. *Role of the economic bureaucracy: Chinese government agencies of particular significance to the operation of Sino-foreign joint ventures*

Agency	Significance
Ministry of Foreign Economic Relations and Trade (MOFERT)	Screens proposed joint venture projects; grants them final approval
State Administration for Exchange Control	Regulates foreign currency transactions
Customs Authority	Regulates imports and exports
Local government agencies:	
1. Planning Commissions	Give permission and facilities for expansion
2. Economic or Industrial Committees	Give advance information on domestic business opportunities
3. Labour and Personnel Bureaux	Establish Chinese salary levels
4. Foreign Investment Committees	Give permission to export; allocate transport

management with the introduction of the factory director responsibility system in 1984 and the contract responsibility system in 1986. There was from the beginning resistance to party activity from some foreign managements and it had virtually no formal organization in a significant portion of joint ventures.

The role of the economic bureaucracy has remained more significant and manifests itself in several key areas, which are summarized in table 12.1. MOFERT has the primary responsibility for screening joint venture projects and for granting final approval to their implementation. The State Administration for Exchange Control regulates the foreign currency trans- actions of joint ventures, mainly through monitoring their balancing of foreign exchange income and expenditure. The Chinese joint venture partner, nor- mally a state-owned enterprise, retains a reporting relationship to its 'Department in Charge' which is usually the local (municipal or provincial) branch of the relevant central ministry. As was seen in chapter 5, higher admin- istrative authorities continue to retain an active involvement in state enterprise decision making even in areas which have been officially decentralized to enterprise management under the economic reform. Similarly, despite the fact that the 1979 law on joint ventures granted authority to their boards of direc- tors, central and local bureaux continued to issue formal directives or to inter- vene in decisions especially on matters of foreign exchange, technology and personnel (Pearson 1991: 192).

Complaints by foreign investors of poor co-ordination between, and restric- tions by, bureaucratic agencies led the Chinese authorities to introduce further regulations in 1983 and 1986, in the latter case following a significant down- turn in new foreign investment. The 1983 'Implementing Regulations' clarified

Chinese policy on the important issues of profit repatriation, technology transfer and foreign exchange, and so to some extent promised a basis for containing the arbitrary aspect of bureaucratic intervention in these areas. The 1986 articles, as well as offering economic improvements to foreign investors with regard to the availability of foreign exchange, profit remittance and local costs, also expressed an intention to provide enterprises having foreign investment with greater support from government agencies. Article 15 included the following statement: 'The people's governments at all levels and relevant departments in charge shall guarantee the right of autonomy of enterprises with foreign investment and shall support enterprises with foreign investment in managing themselves in accordance with international scientific advanced methods.' Article 17 stated that government departments 'shall strengthen the co-ordination of their work, improve efficiency in handling matters and shall promptly examine and approve matters reported by enterprises with foreign investment that require response and resolution.' Pearson concludes that in the light of these provisions, and the perceived Chinese need to improve the climate for foreign investment which lay behind them, both MOFERT at the national level and the supervisory bureaux at the local levels 'came to be facilitators of joint venture operations. They reserved "supervisory" powers, but their role was less one of supervision than of defenders of the interests of joint ventures as carved out in the laws' (Pearson 1991: 194). In some places, Fuzhou and Shanghai for example, the city governments introduced a 'one-stop' service in which a single government office had authority to deal with all necessary official matters for enterprises with foreign investment. Nevertheless, constraints imposed by bureaucratic agencies remained the item of complaint mentioned most frequently by the senior Chinese managers of the joint ventures in the China 1 sample (nineteen out of thirty) and the second most frequently mentioned by foreign managers (fourteen joint ventures out of thirty). They were also stressed in two of the four China 2 joint ventures. This suggests that, whatever assistance government agencies had come to afford joint ventures by the late 1980s and early 1990s, they were also frequently still regarded as a problem. This was particularly true of American partners: foreign managers in seven out of the nine Sino-American joint ventures cited dealing with the external bureaucracy as among their main difficulties. It is worth noting in this connection Aiello's conclusion from his study of the Beijing Jeep Corporation joint venture with Chrysler that 'despite rhetoric to the contrary, many joint ventures like BJC are under Chinese government control. They are state enterprises with temporary foreign management' (Aiello 1991: 62).

It was still proving necessary, even in places like Shanghai which had tried to introduce the 'one-stop' government office for enterprises with foreign investment, to expend time and energy dealing with different government offices, though it was also generally commented that the situation was

improving. Given the existence of internal rules which were not readily dis-
closed to foreigners, considerable time could be required just to find out what
the regulations bearing on a particular matter actually were. Among the various government departments, the Customs office was often singled out as a
source of particular difficulty, and as an agency in which officials exercised
apparently arbitrary powers.

Another source of frustration was the continued control over salary levels
paid to Chinese staff being exercised by local government labour and personnel bureaux, despite the stipulation of the law governing joint ventures that their
boards of directors could decide on this matter. This control was felt to inhibit
the joint venture management's ability to pay appropriate rewards for responsibility and performance, and it caused at least as much dissatisfaction among
Chinese managers as among their foreign colleagues. A third item of complaint,
which was by the late 1980s attracting the attention of the central authorities,
concerned the expectation of many local government officials that bribes and
lavish perks were preconditions for any assistance they might afford. Indeed,
there were several complaints that in any case government officials were more
forthcoming with restrictions and demands than with any real assistance.

Such assistance, or approval, nevertheless remained essential. The four joint
ventures in the China 2 study were questioned in some detail on the outside
connections they considered important and all gave primacy to various governmental agencies. The common perception is that a joint venture cannot take
important action without the support of these agencies. For example, a Sino-
Japanese joint venture producing building materials required the support of the
city's foreign investment committee in order to have permission to export and
to be able to have the necessary transportation arranged. It was also in this
company's field of operation to develop a close relationship with the city's
building committee so as to have advance information on forthcoming major
construction projects which enabled the joint venture to secure a privileged
position in the arranged market. The senior manager representing the American
partner in a soft drinks joint venture summed up his reasons why the Ministry
of Light Industry, the Provincial Planning Commission and the Customs Office
are of particular importance to the success of his company:

For doing business in China, basically two ministries: the Planning Commission and the
Ministry of Light Industry. These two are a must. China is a planned economy.
Everything is planned. For example, if you want to expand your factory, to expand your
capacity, or to buy more sugar, you need so much water, so much electricity. All that
must be planned in advance, otherwise you will run out of water or electricity. The
Ministry of Planning is very important – they approve . . . The Ministries are a good
source of information. The Light Industry [officials] . . . tell us the trend of the soft
drinks industry, what their plans are and how they propose to do things. We can base
our plans on that . . . Of course, the third very important department is the Customs
people. They can create a lot of problems for importing and exporting. They can say

'this truck is not one of yours. I don't believe you, open all the cans!' That's why it is very important to keep good relations with the Customs.

The ability of government officials to exercise a degree of arbitrary power over facets of joint venture operation, in a context of regulations that are often vague and only partially revealed to the foreign party, clearly renders it important for managers to cultivate good relations with them. As we have noted in earlier parts of this book, and as Pearson (1991) and other analysts (e.g. Lockett 1988) all agree, the use of *guanxi* and 'the back door' in order to secure approval, benefits and resources is a culturally-embedded feature of economic and political life in China. *Guanxi* is a reciprocating relationship built on trust and mutual identity. (This is at the very least an identity of interest and among the Chinese it is often based on shared social membership as well, such as being a classmate at school.) While its necessity for joint venture managements arises from the persistence of areas where bureaucratic officials can exercise control over the fortunes of their companies, at the same time the relationship can develop only because the authorities and the community for which they are responsible benefit from the success of the joint venture. *Guanxi* ties officials to the joint venture just as their command over permissions, information and resources ties the joint venture to them. Hence, as Pearson has put it, 'the persistence of guanxi competed with the bureaucracy's ability to function as a mechanism to control foreign investment' (1991: 196).

Internal control of joint ventures

Control of internal management policies and practices is often a contentious issue in joint ventures and this is certainly true of those located in China. Internal conflicts can arise between the desire of foreign investors to manage their overseas operations according to their norms of good practice and the Chinese desire to avoid ideological contamination and to be treated as equals even while they are learning foreign management skills. The avoidance of 'unhealthy tendencies' often leads Chinese managers, supported by their higher authorities, to resist Western human resource management practices such as differential payment levels and the attachment of job security to performance, and generally to strive to retain control over personnel matters. The desire to be treated as equals often manifests itself in unease with foreign supervision and with the much higher salaries received by foreign managers.

Geringer and Hebert (1989) point out that while there are formal mechanisms of control over an international joint venture, the actual extent of control achieved will depend also on the informal dynamics of the collaboration. Schaan (1988), for example, argues that a joint venture partner, even with only a minority equity holding, can enhance its likelihood of exercising effective control through a conscious attempt to fashion the process of management. We now examine formal control mechanisms applying to Sino-foreign joint ventures, returning to the more informal dynamics of control in the following chapter.

In contrast to many developing countries, China's Joint Venture Law does not lay down a maximum limit on the percentage foreign ownership of a joint venture, though the foreign party is normally required to hold a minimum of 25 per cent. Most joint ventures in China have foreign holdings of between 40 and 60 per cent. Nevertheless, Pearson reports (1991: 165) that the potential link between majority ownership and control was a salient issue for government officials in the early years and that as a result Chinese majority or equal ownership was the most common arrangement for joint ventures formed in the first half of the 1980s. Campbell (1989) in a sample of 496 equity Sino-foreign joint ventures taken in 1986 found that the foreign equity holding averaged 43.4 per cent. The average share for the thirty joint ventures in the China 1 study was 46.6 per cent; American partners tended to hold the largest share with an average of 55.4 per cent.

The normal expectation that representation on joint venture boards of directors will reflect the division of equity between the partners was met in the great majority of companies in both the Pearson (1991) and China 1 studies. The 1979 Joint Venture Law, until it was amended in April 1990, required the Chinese side to appoint the chair of the board of directors. This was seen explicitly as a means of ensuring Chinese control regardless of the foreign investor's proportion of equity. However, this requirement had already been abandoned in Guangdong's Special Economic Zones from the beginning of 1987, and the foreign side claimed to have determined the choice of the Chinese chair of the board in as many as nineteen (63 per cent) of the China 1 joint ventures. In any case, the right to make this appointment was of limited value as a control device since it carried no special powers such as a veto or an extra vote.

In the early joint ventures, the Chinese side most usually negotiated into the agreement management structures which divided responsibilities evenly between the partners, so that each side's appointees 'shadowed' the other's. Under this system, every Chinese or foreign head of a department was matched with either a deputy in the same department or with a counterpart of equal rank in another department – in each case appointed by the other partner. When Chinese staff acted as deputies to foreign managers this was intended to let them participate in decisions and to learn about foreign decision-making processes and techniques, with the eventual intention of taking over full responsibility. When the reverse arrangement applied, this enabled Chinese managers to maintain formal authority and at the same time benefit from foreign expert advice. In every case in Pearson's sample and in all but three of the China 1 joint ventures, the positions of general manager and deputy general manager were split between the two partners. Most (61 per cent) of Pearson's cases also maintained a rough shadow management system at lower levels of management (Pearson 1991: 169).

In the China 1 sample, the somewhat higher equity share taken out by American partners was reflected in the occupancy of key managerial positions, but this was not the case with partners of other nationalities. The American-partnered joint ventures had the highest proportion of foreign managers heading major departments which reported to the general management level. None of these ventures had all their departments headed by Chinese managers, whereas, by contrast, nine of the eleven European-partnered ones did. Foreign involvement in the management of the American-partnered joint ventures was further strengthened by the fact that in six out of seven of them the general manager was not Chinese or even overseas Chinese.

The particular managerial positions held by non-Chinese varied considerably and did not on the whole describe a distinct pattern. In the engineering and automobile joint ventures it was quite common for a foreigner to occupy the position(s) of technical and/or manufacturing manager. Sales back to the foreign partner's domestic market tended to be handled by a member of that partner's management. With only two exceptions (both American joint ventures), personnel was in the hands of Chinese management. Personnel and social welfare, as Pearson (1991) points out, are two areas in which the authorities in the early days were careful to try to maintain Chinese dominance in order to protect workers and to retain their ideological commitment to socialist principles.

Detailed rules dealing with the employment of workers in joint ventures or foreign-owned enterprises were included in regulations issued by the State Council in July 1980. These regulations covered recruitment, wage levels, bonus and welfare funds, insurance, worker discipline, dismissals and resignations. Further so-called 'Joint Venture Implementing Regulations' were issued in September 1983. These regulations *inter alia* specified that the Ministries of Labour and Personnel, through local labour and personnel bureaux, should oversee employment; that employment terms for joint ventures should be set out in a labour contract approved by the labour bureau, that the joint venture's salary level should be between 120 and 150 per cent of that of equivalent workers in state-owned enterprises, and that bonus and welfare funds should be set aside for the benefit of staff. Following complaints from foreign investors and a significant downturn in the level of new foreign investment in 1986, the State Council in October of that year promulgated twenty-two 'Articles for the Encouragement of Foreign Investment' which liberalized the investment environment for inward foreign capital and offered incentives for investment in the advanced technology and export-potential sectors (*Beijing Review*, 27 October, 1986: 26–8). Article 15 included the following: 'Enterprises with foreign investment may, in accordance with their production and operational requirements, determine by themselves their organizational structure and personnel system, employ or dismiss senior management personnel, increase or dismiss staff and workers.' In that same year, the government removed the salary ceiling of 150 per cent, encouraged the use of bonuses and incentives, indicated that labour bureaux should support joint ventures by facilitating the transfer of qualified staff from other work units, and eased the dismissal of workers though this was still subject to approval by the labour bureau (Arthur Andersen 1993).

An assessment of the balance of formal control between Chinese and foreign partners was made for the thirty-four cases in the China 1 and China 2 studies on the basis of three control mechanisms: (1) the balance of equity holding; (2) the balance between the partners of board of director memberships; and (3) occupancy of the chief executive officer (general manager) position. When at least two of these indicators pointed to foreign control, the balance of formal control was estimated to lie with the foreign partner and vice versa. If two or three indicators pointed to an equal division between the partners, then control was estimated to be balanced (control through the CEO position was taken to be balanced when there were joint CEOs). This method of assessment enables a comparison to be made with a recent study of fifteen foreign joint ventures in Hungary (Child, Markoczy and Cheung 1994).

According to this indicator, foreign partners held the balance of formal control in only six of the thirty-four joint ventures. There were thirteen cases of joint control and fifteen cases of Chinese control. As already noted, American foreign partners held the balance of formal control more often than those from other countries; they also tended to take higher shares of the equity and were more likely to have one of their own nationals in the CEO position. While foreign partners held the balance of control in relatively more of the Hungarian joint ventures (7/15), the same distinctive tendencies were evident among those with American partners.

Formal control had implications for the opportunities which local managers were granted to acquire more commercially and market-oriented ways of thinking by participating in decisions on strategic issues for their company. In the China 1 sample, foreign control gave rise to more extensive foreign occupancy of senior management positions below that of CEO. In other words, it tended to squeeze Chinese managers out of the senior management team among whom strategic decisions were formulated. Among the China 2 ventures, the only case in which Chinese managers participated in decisions on strategic issues for the company had a Chinese majority equity holding and board membership. A high level of formal control appears to be a necessary condition for participation by that partner's managers in strategic decisions, at least in the earlier years of joint venture life, and a similar association was evident among the Hungarian joint ventures studied.

In China at least, it appears that until joint ventures have progressed along a learning path whereby mutual confidence is established, new outlooks and techniques acquired and a systematic framework for delegation and participation established, decision making will remain centralized. High centralization of decision making will, by definition, tie the process to whichever partner possesses greater formal control through holding the CEO position and a majority on the board of directors. Chinese managers in two-thirds of the China 1 joint ventures reported that these were highly centralized to the extent that the general manager was involved in virtually every decision, and their foreign counterparts agreed with this assessment in most cases. In other words, within the management structure, control was often centralized and this reinforced the link between managerial decisions and the holding of formal control over the venture as a whole.

Although some foreign partners were investing heavily in training for their Chinese managers as well as other employees, the situation prevailing at the time points to a serious tension between a foreign desire for control and the need which all foreign partners endorse for local joint venture managers to develop to a position where they can manage the business. Their opportunity to acquire new strategic paradigms, in other words higher-level cognitive learning (cf. Fiol and Lyles 1985), was severely constrained in those cases where they were not permitted even to share in the strategic management process – and these tended to be predominantly ventures with American partners. This is consistent with a point to emerge later, namely that American partners tended to be more forceful than the others in introducing their foreign national approaches to management.

Problems experienced by foreign managers

We noted in chapter 11 that foreign companies have invested in China for different reasons. Those from Hong Kong and Macau have usually been motivated to locate in China, normally the southern coastal provinces, by the attraction of low cost labour as a manufacturing base and export platform for products ranging from clothing and sports shoes to television aerials. These are low technology products requiring relatively simple production processes. Both the level of investment and time-scale of the foreign partner tends to be limited. The foreign partner has therefore generally not felt the need to intervene a great deal in the Chinese management process, except to ensure productivity and quality standards. The Chinese operation is primarily a sub-contracting one, with wider commercial, financial and product development matters being retained by the foreign company. Managers from both sides in the five Hong Kong partnered joint ventures in the China 1 sample mentioned appreciably fewer problems than did managers in the other companies, and these centred on issues of external bureaucracy and quality standards rather than the managerial process itself.

By contrast, American, European and in recent years Japanese investors have been mainly motivated by the prospect of access to the growing Chinese domestic market. Once the potential in that market for their products has been established and the possibilities of supplying it through direct imports clearly closed off, they have often invested on a considerable scale and entered into long-term joint venture contracts. Import substitution and maintaining a forex balance are requirements placed upon them by the Chinese authorities and this has meant that considerable attention has had to be given to bringing standards of joint venture products, and those of local suppliers, up to international levels. While, in some cases, foreign investors have built in high returns from their ventures on the basis of technology royalties or the need to import key components and ingredients, on the whole they have been looking to secure a good return from the actual operation of the venture, at least over the longer term. They have therefore been quite concerned to introduce what are in their eyes advanced management practices and to secure control over the planning of operations. This concern in many cases stems from the desire to manage the Chinese venture as a subsidiary within the overall network of the foreign company's global operations. It also arises because it is important to maintain the good name of the foreign company: the brand image of its products (soft drinks, consumer electronics and so forth) and the reputation of its services (as with an international hotel chain).

Joint ventures with American, European or Japanese partners often utilize relatively high technology. In these cases, the foreign partner may well seek to retain control over proprietary know-how, not only to ensure the maintenance of quality standards but also to retain a strategic advantage. Since it usually charges quite heavily for the use of such know-how, this can become a point of conflict with its Chinese partners and a source of problems in the relationship. A number of managers mentioned how conflict had arisen when one partner attempted to appropriate advantages as it learned from its experience in the joint venture (cf. Hamel 1991). In one case, foreign staff established their own direct contacts with market outlets in other parts of the country to overcome the dependence on customers in their Chinese partner's own local network, while, in another example, the Chinese side were keenly seeking ways of acquiring information on their partner's secret product ingredients.

Foreign investors from non-Chinese backgrounds are much more likely to perceive problems in the management of their China joint ventures. They come from different cultural backgrounds, and these shape their perception of problems. As we note later, foreign partners coming from different cultural regions tend to view working with the Chinese somewhat differently and consequently to adopt their own responses to managing their joint ventures. For example,

Japanese managers are frequently frustrated at the fact that the Chinese do not display the same pride in membership of the joint venture and sense of belonging to it as they are used to in Japanese companies. Nevertheless, there are certain problems which are mentioned fairly consistently by a broad spectrum of foreign managers working in China. Most fall into two categories. The first concerns problems arising from the character of the Chinese state-owned enterprises with which the great majority of joint ventures have been formed, and from the system under which those enterprises have been operating. A second major problem area concerns human resource management.

Problems arising from state industrial ownership and control

Many of the problems expressed by foreign managers in the thirty-four joint ventures covered by the China 1 and China 2 samples reflect a frustration with the characteristics of state-owned enterprises, and they have indeed also been articulated in much the same form by foreign partners in recently socialist countries such as Hungary which have many enterprises still remaining in state hands (Child and Markoczy 1993). The managers of Chinese state-owned enterprises are accustomed to looking for top-down initiative and approval. This vertical emphasis carries over into the organization of such firms which usually have many hierarchical levels, functional structures and a high degree of specialization, albeit with overlapping responsibilities. This kind of establishment is not conducive to a willingness by managers and employees to accept responsibilities outside a narrowly prescribed field, let alone to take initiatives. Nor does it encourage good communications or a broad corporate perspective. Moreover, Chinese enterprises have offered very limited rewards for additional responsibility, effort or risk, despite the evidence of change noted in chapter 10. There has been little systematic evaluation of individual performance or planning of personal development and progression. Managerial skills remain rather limited, despite large-scale training efforts in recent years, and this also fosters a reluctance to accept personal responsibility.

Overall, then, the fundamental problem with Chinese state enterprises lies in their poorly developed orientation towards corporate performance. Together with the acquisition of technical knowledge and skills, a change in this orientation is what the reformers anticipate to be one of the main benefits of participating in joint ventures. Paradoxically, a fundamental change in outlook is much the more difficult to bring about, particularly when existing ways of thinking are reinforced by institutional arrangements and their attendant ideology and when managers therefore must seriously consider the acceptability of new thinking to those in more powerful positions. A Japanese general manager of a Shanghai joint venture, for example, said that the greatest difficulty he had encountered in the development of his joint venture was 'To change their [Chinese] mind. They have state enterprise thinking, with no responsibility.' While problems continued to arise from dealing with the external bureaucracy, from restrictions on imports and foreign exchange dealing and from high charges for accommodation and other services, internal difficulties were also frequently mentioned. In the China 1 sample, almost two-thirds of the problems cited by foreign managers concerned decision making, achieving a systematic approach, communication and information dissemination, or human resource management (Child 1991).

It was a common complaint that Chinese staff were reluctant to accept personal responsibility and preferred the foreign partner to shoulder the risk of blame. For example, one company reported that Chinese departmental managers would not implement decisions reached at a formal meeting unless the general manager provided them with written authorization. In meetings many Chinese staff prefer to listen rather than to contribute actively to reaching a decision. They are particularly reluctant to assume a public responsibility for taking action, especially if this involves the risk of personal blame as in the use of discretion or the need to place obligations on others. This passivity could impede learning in that it makes it difficult to assess whether or not Chinese managers or workers have understood and accepted a new concept or technique. As one frustrated American put it, 'it is difficult to make them understand because the Chinese listen to you, they say they understand but forget it afterwards.'

Some commentators see this behaviour as rooted in traditional Chinese culture (e.g. Smith 1894). It was noted over fifty years ago that 'what he [the Chinese person] would like to do would be to . . . obey specific orders, so that if the job he is supposed to do is hopelessly bungled he will be able to say that he did what he was told and is in no way to blame for the failure which resulted' (Crow 1937, cited in Reeder 1987: 5). However, similar complaints have been voiced by foreign managers of their counterparts in Hungary. A reluctance to assume responsibility appears to be more a product of the top-down bureaucratic socialist system under which many managers in both countries learned their trade, and which stressed conformity rather than the individual's contribution to profit performance (Child and Markoczy 1993).

The Western approach to operational management continues to rest heavily upon a scientific management philosophy with respect to the use of systematic, usually formalized practices. Even Japanese management, which has been so often contrasted to the Western (especially American) model, rests on this foundation in areas such as quality control, operational planning and industrial engineering (Warner 1994). China had an injection of scientific management under the influence of Russian experts during the 1950s but this was confined to the heavy industrial sector largely in the north-east of the country.

Whereas foreign systems and formal management practices are normally designed to meet operational needs for control, information and the like, a great deal of Chinese formalization is oriented towards the maintenance of personal position and control. For example, Chinese staff working in foreign managers' offices are often required to provide someone in the Chinese hierarchy with a summary of what they do each week. The intention is not to assess and improve their efficiency but to monitor what the foreigners are doing. Chinese joint venture partners also favour job descriptions. These are not, however, used as a guide to action and a basis for appraisal so much as devices to control the behaviour of job-holders by placing limits on it. The latter in fact generally welcome job descriptions as devices to protect them from having to perform personally risky tasks that can be argued to fall outside the strict limits of their jobs.

These differences in approach frequently give rise to the complaint that Chinese management is unsystematic and not geared towards performance. For example, it takes foreign managers time and patience to get their Chinese staff to appreciate the value of conducting meetings in a systematic and action-oriented manner – such as starting on time; using agendas, minutes, action points and reviews of previous action items; preparing relevant documents beforehand; and conducting proceedings through a chairperson with full attention and participation from members.

Differences also arise over quantification. Foreign quality standards, for instance, are normally precise and fixed. In foreign eyes, 100 per cent means just that, whereas many Chinese managers would consider that such a standard should be tempered by other considerations. The foreign management of a winery joint venture rejected large quantities of grapes supplied locally because they did not meet its quality standards. The Chinese partner was reluctant to accept this decision, regarding it as wasteful. It eventually established another plant nearby to produce from the substandard supplies and at the same time to generate more employment. Disagreements about the precision of quantification also arise over matters such as delivery dates, other deadlines and costings.

Language poses obvious problems for communication between foreign managers and Chinese staff. In some joint ventures, three languages are in use: Chinese, English (which is the foreign language most Chinese have studied) and the foreign partner's language. Even though the language barrier can be reduced by using good and trusted interpreters and working with other support staff possessing a language capability, it does reinforce the isolation of the foreign manager from informal communication with his Chinese staff. It also means that foreign managers depend heavily on Chinese staff for communicating information both up and down the organization, at least on a day-to-day basis. The isolation of foreign managers is reinforced when, as so often still happens in China, social contact with Chinese colleagues is discouraged by the Chinese partner or by higher authorities.

This is one aspect of a wider problem of communication and information flow within Chinese organizations which foreign managers confront when they enter into collaboration with them. Because the jobs and units within them are highly specialized, people working there tend to take a narrow view of their roles. Add to that the vertical orientation which has been acquired from a centralized system and the Chinese tendency to regard information as a personal privilege, then one has the seeds of a major problem.

For example, in the educational joint venture, CEMI, which the writer directed, it took much time and effort to change the behaviour of the Chinese staff from one based on the premise that 'if s/he wants some information let them come and get it' to one based on the realization that 'I have some information of use to a colleague so I will pass it onto him/her immediately'. Foreign managers in the China 1 joint ventures found that there was no predisposition towards the free distribution of information. Staff members sent abroad for experience or training were on their return reluctant to share what they had learned. As a result, foreign managers had to take extraordinary measures to ensure that this dissemination of information occurred. One company, for instance, calls together all employees and asks returnees from abroad to pass on what they have learned. Another joint venture was attempting to increase awareness and concern among its Chinese staff about its loss-making situation by leaving financial reports out on tables.[1]

It is difficult to develop a view of the total corporate purpose among Chinese workers and managers because they have never had to think in such terms before. One food-manufacturing joint venture, for example, introduced an output-related bonus scheme in its biscuit-packing department with the result that, despite emphasizing the paramount need for careful handling, breakages mounted rapidly as workers speeded up. The scheme had to be withdrawn. This narrow view of work life affects attitudes towards the dissemination of information, especially laterally. Foreign managers in almost half the China 1 joint ventures spontaneously mentioned this as a difficulty. Departments are not only reluctant to share information but fail to communicate with each other even when this is the only possible way to keep production going and to overcome problems. As Lockett (1988) pointed out, poor lateral communication is a major problem in Chinese organizations. It is partly a result of the vertical authority chains which the Chinese have been used to in the state bureaucratic governance system – where everything has to be referred to the top. It has also partly to do with the absence of a concept of 'inter-dependence' between departments and units, and of interest among employees in how they fit into an overall organizational process. This is reinforced by the cultural tendency of the Chinese to identify with relatively small inter-personal groups rather than with larger formal entities, noted in chapter 2.

Problems of human resource management

In all but one of the thirty China 1 joint ventures, foreign managers observed a large difference between human resource management practices in their home company and those they were obliged to accept in China. As we noted earlier in the book, the personnel area is where the power of Chinese authorities over employees is the most concentrated. This is where the personal file that dogs every Chinese employee's life is kept. As we saw in chapters 4 and 9, it is the aspect of management in which the company party organization is most involved, and it is where the Chinese are usually most reluctant to allow significant foreign influence. At the same time, the Chinese conception of the personnel management role is quite at variance with that normally held by foreign managers today. The personnel management role in Chinese organizations is geared towards the maintenance of control and conformity, supplemented by an ideological appeal to the virtues of work. This clearly contrasts with the foreign concept that the personnel function exists to provide a service to management through assisting the selection, training, assessment, motivation and organization of employees, doing this systematically with reference to their contribution to organizational effectiveness.

Differences between foreign and Chinese personnel practices appear in a number of areas within joint ventures. A combination of the control over staff just mentioned with traditional attitudes means that Chinese managers tend to emphasize negative discipline: punishment, restrictions and personal loss of face. By contrast, many foreign managers today favour positive (or self-) discipline: motivation through praise and reward, and encouragement of initiative (Shore et al. 1993).

Foreign personnel management tends to rely on standard practices for selection, appraisal, time-keeping, assessment of attitudes and discipline. In the thirty joint ventures, there had been various attempts to introduce Western personnel tools with varying, but never very significant, degrees of success. One firm attempting to introduce employee appraisal was constrained by the three-year limitation written into job contracts. Another firm, wishing to introduce rules for time-keeping and time off for domestic reasons, found itself confounded by lax practices within the Chinese mother company. Foreign management in another joint venture was attempting to establish a rule that employees could not be penalized at work for transgressions committed outside working hours which had nothing to do with their employment.

Foreign managers also found it difficult to persuade Chinese staff to accept promotions – especially if these would entail supervising their previous fellow workers. There was a strong impulse towards keeping everybody at the same level in terms of both authority and pay. Many firms experienced strong pressures from the local labour and personnel bureaux against introducing differential base salaries which reflected responsibility levels and/or job content. There was also resistance against introducing performance-related incentives: internal resistance against the differentiation these would generate and external resistance against the higher levels of earnings that were implied.

Although most joint ventures were originally assigned new Chinese employees, since the change in regulations in 1984 permitting open recruitment, some companies have found it possible to recruit in this way. Others, in contrast, have continued to experience pressures and restrictions from local labour bureaux to engage unsuitable applicants (often relatives of existing employees) or to take on larger numbers than required. On the whole, though, foreign joint venture managements are succeeding in gaining control over the selection process, as the following chapter shows.

The other side of the equation – disengagement of employees – was problematic for the China 1 joint ventures sampled in 1989, but less so for the China 2 ones studied in 1991–2. Only three of the China 1 companies stated that the firing of unsatisfactory workers was easy. Chinese managers tended to be highly protective of their employees, a protection which was in many cases cemented by a strong sense of close personal relationship and obligation. In their eyes, some foreign managers had wilfully dismissed employees without adequate reason. As an American manager put it, 'loyalty is appreciated [by the Chinese] even in the face of incompetence.' None of the four China 2 joint venture foreign partners regarded firing to be a problem so long as there was a good reason for so doing. They all happened to be expanding their workforces rather than seeking to contract them, which made the position much easier, so that they cannot really serve as an indicator of whether there is now greater flexibility in this area of personnel practice or not.

Pearson (1991: 211) concludes that during the 1980s reformers at the centre became convinced that foreign personnel management practices, especially the autonomy of enterprises to hire and fire workers and to institute sophisticated salary and incentive systems, were beneficial and that they somewhat relaxed their efforts to maintain personnel policy as an area under strict Chinese management control. At the same time, she points out that such relaxation was frequently obstructed by Chinese personnel managers and local labour bureaux.

In the establishment of joint ventures between partners from industrially developed countries and a less developed country, training plays a crucial role. Chinese official sources (cf. CPC 1984) and enterprise managers ostensibly accept this point, but the reality is rather different. For Chinese employees tend to regard attendance at a training course as a perk rather than as an investment which should take account of the potential of the person in relation to the needs of the organization. This is especially the case when the training is abroad. Chinese candidates for training have therefore often been selected by their compatriate superiors on the basis of seniority rather than of capacity and promise. In recent years, joint ventures have begun to favour conducting their training in China to minimize this problem as well as to link the process more closely to local conditions.

The problems experienced by foreign managers in China are intimately linked to their role as agents for the introduction of new managerial approaches and methods. Practices viewed as problematic through foreign eyes become candidates for change, whereas an *a priori* disposition on the foreigners' part towards introducing change will necessarily lead to existing Chinese practices being defined as problematic. The changes that foreign partners are bringing into Chinese management through the medium of joint ventures and other forms of collaboration, and the process of adjustment to the Chinese situation that is involved, are considered in the following chapter.

Conclusion

The legacy of historical isolation, the fear of neo-colonialism and a concern to defend socialist values all helped to make control over foreign industrial involvement a major issue when China embarked on its open door policy. In the early days of the economic reform, the prime question in the eyes of conservative 'leftist' politicians was how to enforce this control so as to minimize the transfer of undesirable foreign ideas and practices – they were prepared to accept 'hard' technology from abroad but not 'soft' technology. Various regulations were put into place to limit the decision powers of foreign investors. In addition, further constraints were placed upon foreign managers through the labour union, the enterprise organization of the Communist Party, and the economic bureaucracy. Later on, as the reform progressed and more features of a competitive market economy were introduced, management techniques and practices from abroad became increasingly acceptable so long as they were applied in ways that did not offend the values of Chinese staff or undermine their loyalty to the system.

Nevertheless, the Chinese partner quite frequently retained formal control within the joint ventures the writer investigated, and this was highlighted through a comparison with the greater level of foreign dominance in Hungarian joint ventures. Where they were present, high levels of foreign control tended to exclude Chinese managers from the strategy formulation process and this denied them a good opportunity to engage in learning at this level of business. The joint ventures studied were tightly controlled in another respect since their decision making was generally highly centralized. As we shall note in the following chapter, it was the intention of many foreign partners to introduce systems designed to permit delegation down the managerial structure, and a centralized approach with elements of foreign control may turn out to be features characterizing the early phase of Sino-foreign joint venture operation rather than a more mature phase. Again, the next chapter provides some examples of movement from the one phase to the other.

Some of the problems mentioned by foreign joint venture managers reflected a struggle for control over areas such as human resource management. Many others arose from the dependence of Chinese joint venture partners on the external bureaucracy, which was seen to be sustaining the reluctance among local managers to adopt economic performance criteria single-mindedly and to accept responsibility for such performance. This difficulty is, however, reducing as the official attitude towards enterprise performance hardens. Current policies are placing increasing pressure on state-owned enterprises to achieve profitability through the reduction of subsidies and special dispensations, and through the movement towards market-level prices in basic industries.

Yet other problems which came to light could be said to reflect the contrast between practices embedded in the Chinese industrial system and those which foreign partners sought to introduce. Both traditional culture and the ideological priorities established since 1949 played their part in sustaining Chinese practices.

Appendix 12.1 Outline of Sino-Foreign joint ventures studied

Appendix 12.1   *Outline of Sino-foreign joint ventures studied*

Company	Total employees	Main product(s)	Nationality of foreign management
China 1			
American partners			
1	4,307	Cars	American
2	2,509	Boilers	American
3	1,750	Hotel	American
4	387	Computers, instruments	American
5	200	Computers	American
6	154	Air express carrier	American
7	74	Glass engineering	American
German/Swiss partners			
1	2,289	Cars	German
2	1,454	Elevators	Swiss
3	936	Hotel	Swiss
4	88	Clothing	German
5	81	Dental materials	German

Appendix 12.1   (*cont.*)

Company	Total employees	Main product(s)	Nationality of foreign management
Other European partners			
1	953	Float glass	British
2	503	Radios, recorders	Dutch
3	69	Heating wire	Swedish
4	50	Food	French
5	35	Wine	French
6	14	Wine	French
Japanese partners			
1	1,036	Elevators	Japanese
2	206	Medical products	Japanese
3	202	Clothing	Japanese
4	133	Furniture	Japanese
5	101	Financial leasing	Japanese
6	92	Calculators	Japanese
7	62	Photography	Japanese
Hong Kong partners			
1	1,370	Hotel	Hong Kong/German
2	541	Air catering	Hong Kong/German
3	90	Illumination	None foreign
4	54	Printing	Hong Kong
5	32	Interior design	Hong Kong
China 2			
American partners			
1	201	Photography	American
2	160	Soft drinks	American
Swiss partner			
1	580	Hotel	Swiss
Japanese partner			
1	26	Building products	Japanese

13 Dynamics of the Sino-foreign management relationship

The reformers in China regard foreign managers and technical personnel working in the country as agents of modernization. In this chapter we look at the
changes in management techniques, practices and policies that have come
about through foreign involvement in joint ventures. We note any differences
in approach or emphasis between American, European and Japanese foreign
partners. We then examine how that process of introducing change and dealing
with problems has been accommodated within the Sino-foreign management
relationship.

Changes resulting from foreign involvement

There are three levels of change in Chinese management that could arise as a
result of foreign involvement. The first level is the technical and refers to the
introduction of new techniques. While these usually require some modification
to the content of people's jobs, they do not necessarily involve a major change
either to their behaviour or to the pattern of relationships between them. The
second level is the systemic. This refers to the introduction of new procedures
and systems which are likely to have behavioural consequences. Systemic
changes generally affect large numbers of people within the enterprise, their
ways of working and inter-relating, and the formal obligations placed upon
them by which their performance is judged. The third level of change is the
strategic and refers primarily to a new pattern of thinking about business objectives and how they can be realized through interaction with the environment. It
is essentially a cognitive level of change and learning.

Despite its importance, there is little information on the impact of foreign
management on Chinese managers' strategic thinking and policy-making. This
section therefore concentrates on technical and system level changes. It begins
with new techniques, continues with system level change in terms of formalization, responsibility systems and human resource management, and then
turns briefly to the strategic level.

New techniques

A variety of foreign management techniques and operating technologies were introduced in all of the joint ventures studied, through the agency of their foreign partner. The categories of foreign managerial techniques and technologies which were most often singled out were marketing and market research, new quality controls, production planning, new technology, IT software, and techniques of managerial accounting and financial control.

American partners attached particular importance to the introduction of a marketing approach and the use of associated techniques. This was often an extension of the partner company's approach worldwide and one which it believed to be the best practice. A good example of this view was provided by a Sino-American soft drinks joint venture, whose foreign general manager stated:

China has always been production oriented. They produce, then sit down and wait for you to come and buy. We took two and a half years to convince them that this is not the way to do business. That they should make money for themselves by cutting off the middleman, cutting off the dealers and sell direct to the customers. Right now we have a very good distribution system going in China. We supply training and the local guy then runs the business. [The foreign partner company] has direct distribution all over the world and we do this everywhere . . . if we want to do business long term, we have got to do it properly. That's why we insist . . . and that's why we try to distribute directly in China.

Although it took time to train and persuade Chinese managers to adopt a marketing orientation, there were no signs of any fundamental resistance to this process. This is possibly because this was a new area of attention for most state enterprise managers in which the burden of previous outlooks and practices did not have to be jettisoned first through a process of 'unlearning'. Opening to the market is, of course, a watchword of the economic reform and thus ideologically quite acceptable too.

More resistance was reported to the adoption of Western accounting techniques. This involved an additional burden on Chinese accounting staff, who were sometimes still using manual procedures, because the Chinese authorities insisted that accounting data were still prepared using their conventions as well. Another more problematic area concerned quality control, an area of continuing complaint for foreign managers in half of the China 1 joint ventures. The improvement of production standards was usually a particularly uphill struggle in those joint ventures which utilized existing Chinese production facilities and staff, and was far less difficult in cases where new facilities had been installed and new staff recruited and trained.

On the whole, foreign investors in this collection of joint ventures transferred state-of-the-art production technology to support the manufacturing of worldwide branded products or, in some cases, locally adapted products bearing the company's worldwide name. The tendency to transfer standard foreign partner techniques was thus complemented by the use of standard technology with the result that production processes were often the same in the Chinese joint ventures as in the foreign partner's other plants, a feature which Barnowe, Yager and Wu (1992) also observed. The transfer of a completely standard international approach was also evident in all the four hotels studied, which followed written operating procedures common to the foreign chain throughout the world.

In several companies visited, the management were proud of the fact that the joint venture's productivity or quality already matched the best in the foreign partner's worldwide operations. Moreover, the introduction of new technically related practices was, in principle at least, welcomed by Chinese partners as an important learning experience and did not normally give rise to any complaints about a foreign reluctance to 'understand' the Chinese situation.

Formalization and responsibility systems

One of the most important consequences of foreign involvement in Chinese joint ventures is the introduction of a more systematic management approach. The means of achieving this favoured by American and European companies are to introduce formalized systems for transmitting key information and for defining the framework of managerial authority and responsibility. Formalized in this context means that the systems are defined in writing, are standardized and are operated on a regular basis. Systems of this type were introduced in eighteen of the thirty-four Chinese joint ventures studied. As would be expected from investigations into organizational structuring (cf. Pugh and Hickson 1976), it was the larger joint ventures, employing more capital and people, which tended to have developed formal systems more comprehensively, as table 13.1 shows.

At the same time, there were differences in this respect between categories of foreign partner. As table 13.2 shows, the highest proportion of formalized joint ventures was those partnered by international American companies which generally introduced the systems they operated in other parts of the world. Formalization was somewhat less prevalent in ventures with European partners. It was far less developed in the Japanese and Hong Kong-partnered ventures. Instead, the Japanese attempted (but did not wholly succeed) to fashion Chinese work behaviour through creating organizational cultures with strong collective norms, while the approach among generally small Hong Kong-partnered joint ventures was to control through personal intervention. As one senior Chinese manager commented on his Hong Kong general manager's style, 'he operates by shouting'. In fact, the single Hong Kong venture to have

Table 13.1. *Level of formalization and scale of investment among thirty-four Sino-foreign joint ventures*

	Formalization		
Scale of investment	High	Medium	Low
Under US$1 million	0	2	9
US$1–5 million	0	5	4
US$5–20 million	2	4	3
Over US$20 million	3	2	0
Total	5	13	16

Notes:
'High' formalization: a wide range of meetings, activities and communications on a formal basis;
'Medium' formalization: some of the above formalized, or a wide range of meetings, etc. partly formalized;
'Low' formalization: formal reporting and recording only in connection with finance.

a high level of formalization was a hotel, and apart from the fact that this company was by far the largest among the Hong Kong group (with 1,370 employees), this tends to be a characteristic of all international hotel chains.

The introduction of formal systems not only clarified managerial roles and obligations, but in so doing established a framework within which operational decisions could potentially be delegated. This delegation of decision making was intended to encourage local managers to make decisions in their designated areas and formalization enabled their responsibility for decisions to be clearly identified. The new responsibility systems were introduced with the idea of overcoming the problem which foreign managers have reported in many socialist, and former socialist, countries, namely the unwillingness of host country managers to assume individual responsibility (Child and Markoczy 1993; Markoczy 1992). Indeed, problems of delegation and decision making have been reported for strategic alliances between Western firms as well (Shenkar and Zeira 1987).

It is again American joint venture partners who have been introducing a formalized approach to management with the greatest vigour. Seven of the nine American partnered joint ventures studied had brought in systems which covered a range of activities in addition to the formal systems for financial reporting which all the strategic alliances operated. Only a minority of the joint ventures with foreign partners from other countries had introduced a formalized approach to this degree. It is not necessarily easy to increase the formalization of Chinese management and the American strategic alliances had incurred conflict in so doing. Some other companies had abandoned their

Table 13.2. *Level of formalization and nationality of foreign partner among thirty-four Sino-foreign joint ventures*

	Formalization		
Foreign Partner Nationality	High	Medium	Low
Europe	0	6	6
USA	3	4	2
Japan	1	2	5
Hong Kong	1	1	3
Total	5	13	16

attempts to introduce specific aspects of formalization. One had attempted to introduce a formal reporting system and had given up as the Chinese staff never produced any reports. Another had attempted to institute formal meetings but abandoned the project as these were constantly interrupted by people answering phone calls (Chinese managers rarely have secretaries) or having something else to do at the time of the meeting. Nevertheless, the experience of the Sino-American joint ventures does suggest that foreign partners can introduce some formalized and systematic management and that their apparent determination to do so reflects a distinctive characteristic of their national management approach.

As table 13.1 indicated, there was a clear tendency for the larger joint ventures to have introduced more developed and extensively applied formalized systems, including ones for communication of information as well as for the definition of responsibility and action. While this size effect has been widely reported elsewhere, in the Chinese samples the companies with American partners also tended to be the larger ones and it is not, therefore, possible to separate out the relationship with size from that with foreign partner cultural region.

Starbuck (1965) and Inkson et al. (1970) have noted how managements learn over the course of time and tend to capture that learning in the form of new rules and systems – a view endorsed more recently by many students of organizational learning (cf. Levitt and March 1988). The joint venture which is under mixed international management requires a considerable managerial learning process both because it is a new organization and because of the phases of mutual accommodation through which it must pass. This gives rise to the expectation that longer-established joint ventures will tend to have adopted formalized systems to a greater extent than younger ones. There was however, only a slight tendency for this among the Sino-foreign joint ventures studied.[1]

In practice, the intention behind attempts to introduce more formalized systems, namely to provide a framework which would facilitate delegation, had been realized in only very few of the joint ventures. In general, decision making remained centralized around the CEO and with no participation in the process below the level of departmental head. Those companies which had introduced formalization had not on the whole decentralized their managerial decision making, though it remains to be seen whether or not this is a question of the time it takes to develop the capacity of local staff to take on greater responsibility.

The experience of three longer-established joint ventures in fact suggests that the introduction of formalized procedures combined with a substantial management training programme does after a while develop local managers to the point where the foreign partner feels confident about delegating responsibility to them. It is relevant to note that as well as being relatively long-standing, all three joint ventures had large and highly formalized foreign parent companies. Two are Sino-American joint ventures formed in 1981 and 1984, while the third is a Sino-British joint venture formed in 1984.

The American parent of the first company had originally sent four of its managers to take charge of general management, finance, sales and marketing, and engineering. Now it only retains one joint general manager. The second joint venture had reduced its expatriate employment from 52 in 1986 to 17 in 1990, while increasing total employment from 260 to 387 over the same time period. It had steadily transferred responsibility from expatriate to Chinese managers. The companies had built up a formalized and systematic framework for both their operations and their managerial responsibilities. They also devoted considerable resources to training. The first company runs four or five management training programmes each year in China which follow the standard international format developed by the American parent in New York. These programmes cover marketing, production and quality control, financial analysis, and the conduct of meetings (including board meetings). The second company had invested some $20 million in training and development for managers and employees between 1985 and 1990, albeit that much of this was spent on the overseas training of technical personnel. In the American joint ventures, training was regarded as vital not merely for its technical content but also as a mechanism for socializing Chinese managers into the American corporate approach to business.

While the third joint venture only has a small British equity holding and involves the foreign partner in a primarily technical role (the main source of income for the foreign partner being royalties earned on its production process), it engaged senior Chinese managerial and technical staff in a major training programme both in China and the UK, which focused on technical and system development. The joint venture is now staffed entirely by Chinese personnel and is expanding rapidly on a level of performance far exceeding original expectations.

Systems of human resource management

There had been various attempts among the joint ventures to introduce foreign approaches to human resource management, such as systematic schemes for appraisal, promotion and career development. These are the aspects of human resource management which touch upon loyalties – in this case tying these to a foreign conception of good corporate conduct – and are therefore sensitive areas in the social and political context of the Chinese enterprise. The attempts to introduce them had not been really successful in any of the companies. Somewhat more success had attended efforts to introduce a more systematic approach in other areas, notably in payment, selection and disengagement.

All the joint ventures paid earnings above the average of the locality. This was an important factor in securing a willingness to accept change and the ability to hire people of superior quality (see also Cheng 1992). Among the two groups of Chinese companies, 40 per cent had a differential salary system which endeavoured to reflect responsibility, a principle which is also endorsed in recent Chinese regulations governing state-owned enterprises. Half of these companies were operating incentive bonus schemes. American partners generally attached more importance to having a systematic reward policy and they were marginally more likely to have succeeded in combining a salary based on responsibility and/or contribution with a performance-linked incentive. Nevertheless, in all joint ventures investigated, the local partner insisted that whatever system was agreed they would allocate salaries. Indeed, they were officially prohibited from divulging to the foreign partner information on the salaries actually paid to Chinese staff, and the Chinese authorities also tried to set upper limits on incentive payments to their nationals.

We expected that the cultural origin of foreign joint venture partners would show itself in the extent to which non-financial incentives were offered, such as having the chance to work or be trained abroad, opportunities for employees to develop their potential, public praise of exceptional workers through ceremonies and notices, good working conditions and secure jobs, personal and informal discussions between senior managers and employees about problems, promotion of sporting activities associated with the company image, and fringe benefits. In particular, we anticipated that the strategic alliances with Japanese partners would employ these non-financial incentives the most, in keeping with Japanese community values, but this was not in fact the case.

While all the Japanese-partnered joint ventures offered the chance for selected Chinese managers and employees to be trained abroad (which is regarded as a considerable perk for most Chinese), held informal discussions and fostered a corporate identity through events, newsletters and the like, this approach was by no means unique to them. Most of the American and European (especially German) companies did the same, with one or two going to considerable lengths to claim that they had developed a distinctive and commonly held corporate culture for their organizations. There was a widely held view that Chinese staff would be responsive to non-financial incentives which chimed in with the paternalistic Confucian aspects of their culture and socialist education, so long as they were offered good financial rewards in the first place. In practice, however, some foreign partners were more sparing with fringe benefits than their words might suggest. Training abroad, for instance, was treated as a functional necessity rather than as a perk, especially by American partners. Many foreign partners also resisted the Chinese expectation that they should provide accommodation for their employees.

We had also expected to find German-partnered joint ventures to be undertaking training on the largest scale and there are certainly some impressive examples of German-funded technical training centres now to be found in China. However, among the companies studied, a higher proportion of the American-partnered joint ventures provided management training and recurrent (largely technical) training abroad than was the norm for the other companies. The American-partnered companies tended to have recruited the most highly educated workforce as well. Two factors appear to contribute to this pattern, namely that there were more large American joint ventures where size spreads the training overhead, and that a number of them were in high technology sectors. Virtually every joint venture was providing some technical training and this constitutes one of the most significant contributions to long-term Chinese economic development that foreign companies are making.

Originally most joint ventures operating in China were assigned employees, either from the Chinese partner's company or from Middle Schools or Universities. A change of regulations in 1984 permitted open recruitment and most companies were able to recruit new staff and supervisors from external sources, the usual method being advertisement followed by selection through interviews and examination. They found it considerably more difficult to recruit managers in this way because there is a tradition of appointment to this level from within the work unit, with such appointments being closely controlled by the party and higher administrative authorities. Virtually all the companies reported that they came under pressure to accept, or at least consider, friends and relatives of existing Chinese employees; some refused this while others regarded it as a useful additional channel for attracting job applicants.

Joint ventures operating in China continue to rely on the goodwill of higher authorities for the recruitment of employees from outside, particularly those at technical and managerial levels. Such recruits are unlikely to come from a local labour pool but will be already fully employed members of another work unit which can make their release extremely difficult. The assistance of the local government personnel bureau is often essential to remove this barrier. In this respect, China contrasts markedly with a former socialist country such as

Hungary which now enjoys a totally open employment market. As a result, joint ventures in Hungary almost all recruit through advertisement, with personal recommendations as a supplement in some cases. It was apparent that a high proportion of American managers claimed that firing was a straightforward matter, whereas opinion among the other foreign groups was evenly divided.

Overall, the experience of the joint ventures studied suggests that American partners are more vigorous in introducing standardized techniques and procedures. They generally place considerable emphasis on the use of marketing techniques and on the establishment of a formal system for managerial responsibility and reporting. They have usually tried to establish a systematic approach to recruitment and a rationalized reward policy. This approach, which of course varied in its details, is not inconsistent with expectations generated by the literature on, and conventional wisdom of, the American 'style' of management.

More surprising was the observation that Japanese strategic alliance partners do not so often introduce management according to their national stereotype, particularly in view of the fact that several Japanese managers said that they wished to change the prevailing cultures of Chinese organizations. They often expressed frustration at what they had not been able to achieve in that respect. This may be due in part to limitations imposed by the situation. For example, it was mentioned in interviews and personal communication that poorly trained Chinese workers and managers were unable or unwilling to contribute to quality circles and other group discussions where Japanese managers are present. All the Japanese respondents pointed to externally imposed barriers to the introduction of the Japanese style of management in Chinese companies in which, because of dependence on higher authorities, initiatives remained highly centralized and in which informal after-hours interaction was officially discouraged. Another likely reason for the cautious approach to introducing change adopted in practice by the Japanese is their awareness of Chinese sensitivities in view of events earlier this century, though our evidence here is purely anecdotal.

Change at the strategic level

The main area of adaptation and new learning for enterprise managers who are experiencing the transformation towards a market economy is that of developing a strategic understanding. They have to learn to function without the protective paternalism of the state and instead to understand the nature of doing business competitively in a relevant domain (Child 1993).

In the joint ventures we investigated, it was this higher-level strategic learning that caused most problems. Where conflict had become endemic, it was usually over strategic matters such as where to apply annual surpluses, sourcing, and the priority between home and export markets. In itself the strategic level constitutes a greater learning challenge for Chinese managers, who have generally been working for state-owned enterprises. The fact that strategic learning can easily become embroiled with competition and conflict between the partners does not make it any easier to encourage.

We noted in the previous chapter how the opportunity for Chinese managers to participate in strategic discussions and decisions was caught up with the question of which partner dominated in a joint venture, and that some foreign managements (particularly American) were not giving their local colleagues much opportunity to get involved in the strategic process. It is therefore a paradox that foreign involvement in transforming economies through joint ventures offers a direct channel for transferring strategic understanding to local management, and yet this is just the area of managerial discussion and decision making from which these local managers may be excluded.

Change and the process of adjustment

As would be expected from the problems which foreign managers have experienced, the process of adjustment between them and the Chinese, both outside and inside the joint venture, is not without its difficulties. Nevertheless, there was considerable determination to find solutions to them and it was widely agreed that the conditions for operating a business in China were becoming more favourable as the years passed.

External adjustment

We have seen that external constraints on bringing about change and development in joint ventures stemmed primarily from the central and local government bureaucracies. Problems of dealing with the Chinese bureaucratic system were mentioned in many companies, and these included restrictions on the import of materials or parts, and constraints imposed on payment levels. For example, the production of one American soft drinks joint venture was restricted by the fact that the Chinese government had to approve on an annual basis the quota of concentrate which it was allowed to import. Even where imports were approved, a great deal of time could be spent negotiating with the Chinese customs authorities. Frustration was expressed in many joint ventures by both foreign and Chinese managers at the continued control exercised by local government labour and personnel bureaux over the salaries and bonuses paid to Chinese staff, despite the stipulation of the law governing joint ventures that their boards of directors can decide on this matter. Such control was felt to inhibit the joint venture's ability to pay appropriate rewards for responsibility and performance.

Another rather common complaint, which has been publicized and which the government claims to be tackling, concerns the expectation of many local government officials that gifts and lavish entertainment are preconditions for any assistance they might afford. Even then, it was sometimes observed that government officials were more forthcoming with restrictions and demands than with any real assistance. While corruption certainly has strong antecedents in China's pre-socialist history, it is not discouraged by the concentration of powers into the hands of officials under state socialism.

The problems stemming from the external system were actually mentioned more often by local managers than by their foreign counterparts. It is likely that working in a partly foreign business culture served to heighten their awareness of these lags in the adjustment of Chinese social behaviour. Among the foreign managers, those in American joint ventures tended to complain the most about the external bureaucracy.

The nature of the Chinese polity, the way its economic institutions are regulated, and the continued concentration of much relevant business information in government hands, give government officials the ability to exercise considerable influence over the conditions in which joint ventures operate. It is therefore not surprising that central and local government agencies are regarded uniformly as the most important external connections for joint ventures located there. The importance for managers to cultivate good relations with government officials was stressed in the previous chapter.

Progress has been achieved in dealing with external constraints through a mixture of foreign and indigenous approaches. Sometimes, when their collective frustration has come to a head, foreign managements have adopted the approach familiar to them of public complaint and political lobbying. This has usually led the Chinese authorities to acknowledge the problem and to its often quite rapid amelioration. In one important development, the authorities in a number of cities have established bodies through which foreign business leaders and local officials can meet to discuss issues and find agreed solutions to them. An example is the International Business Leaders' Advisory Council established by Zhu Rongi when he was Mayor of Shanghai. We noted how, at the national level, a downturn in incoming foreign direct investment coupled with loud complaints from abroad about unfavourable conditions for operating in China, led in 1986 and again in 1990 to new regulations granting better terms for foreign-funded enterprises.

The high-profile confrontational approach towards external problems is, however, not consistent with the Chinese way of doing things and always runs the risk of intransigence because of the question of losing face. It is appropriate only when a serious and widespread sense of crisis has arisen. The indigenous Chinese approach is much better suited to dealing with ongoing matters and to ensure the steady incremental development of a joint venture.

Many foreign managers have learned that the use of *guanxi* to secure the external support they need is a culturally embedded feature of Chinese economic and political life. They seek to identify the key centres of influence in their localities and domains of operation, and then patiently to build up relationships and trust with those concerned. This means taking the time to interact with Chinese decision makers socially and to indicate to them through both practical and symbolic means the goodwill of the foreign partner towards Chinese aspirations. It does not mean compromising the quest for improved standards of performance, but rather demonstrating how success in that regard can be used to mutual benefit. It is difficult to understate the importance of working to establish sound relationships with Chinese counterparts. The process also involves the staff of the joint venture itself, who can in so many ways give sound advice and effect important arrangements and introductions to key persons outside the enterprise.

Internal adjustment

Internally, a certain amount of tension, even conflict, between local and foreign personnel is to be expected within joint ventures located in transforming economies because the foreign partner is introducing pressures for systemic change over and above the normal problems that arise due to divergence in the partners' objectives, and strains in culture and mutual perception.

Foreign partners were not, however, aiming to introduce the same type of change, nor did they appear to be equally pressing. The Japanese talked about the most fundamental type of change in the sense that it would import a new set of values which they wished local managers to accept, over and above the adoption of new techniques and systems. As one Japanese vice-chairman of a Shanghai joint venture put it: 'We want to change their minds.' In practice, American partners generally pushed for change more aggressively than did the Japanese, but what they required was not so much a re-culturation as an understanding of how to conduct business and to use the modern techniques associated with this. As one said:

One of the difficulties we encountered in China is that the Chinese have no concept of quality control, no concept of marketing principles and things like that . . . It is a problem to make them understand that they need to clean the factory every day, to make them understand they need to keep the correct amount of inventory.

German partners placed more emphasis on the transfer of technical expertise as well as of market-related skills. They often committed considerable resources to technical training of their own determination, but in several cases professed themselves eager to move at a more paradigmatic level towards an integrated form of strategic alliance management in which foreign and Chinese elements are blended. While not necessarily approving of Chinese behavioural norms, they neither dismissed them nor expressed disappointment, as did most Japanese managers, that they could not readily transfer their home-grown management system to the Chinese context.

The more recent study (China 2) explored the perceptions which foreign and local managers held of each other in order to afford further clues as to the problems which might attend their mutual adaptation. Both foreign and Chinese sides expressed qualified satisfaction with their partner managers. On the foreign side a distinction was drawn between younger, better educated Chinese managers who are willing to learn and are good candidates for further development and promotion, and older ones who do not readily accept foreigners, show little initiative and are politically oriented. The main change they wished for among their Chinese counterparts was a cognitive one which may be summarized as greater strategic business awareness – in other words, that they would come to understand the concept of running a competitive business and the requirements for its success.

On the Chinese side, the main qualification lay in a perception that foreign managers did not sufficiently 'understand' the Chinese system of state enterprise or Chinese cultural attitudes. The thrust of foreign intervention as an agency of change in socialist-trained management shows through these comments. With only four cases, it is not possible to discern any systematic differences in these perceptions according to the culture of the foreign partner, though the one case where the Chinese manager complained of inadequate respect from the foreign side was in the Japanese joint venture.

Among the joint ventures in the China 1 study, those with American partners reported about a 50 per cent higher incidence of difficulties than was the case with either of the other foreign groups. This points to a greater degree of resistance on the part of Chinese management to the changes which the Americans were rather forcefully endeavouring to introduce. They backed this effort by a higher proportion of expatriate managers than in most other joint ventures, especially in departmental head positions and, as we have noted, they succeeded in introducing a greater amount of formalization according to traditional American management principles. A graphic illustration of the kind of conflict that could arise is given by the Chinese chairman of one of the two Sino-American joint ventures in the China 2 sample:

I have to say that originally there was a lot of upset among our staff in working with the foreigners. They don't understand that in China the workers are the masters of the country. When the [American partner] managers first came, they always shouted at our staff and tried to fire workers who they thought didn't perform. Our workers were very angry. They said they had been ill-treated by Westerners fifty years ago, and they didn't want to experience the same things again in the new China.

Conflicts also arose over economic issues. The Chinese partner usually pressed for a high level of short-term profit and profit distribution. It was under pressure to secure short-term returns usually as a means of providing immediate financial support for its state-owned operation which was underperforming. Foreign partners were on the whole concerned to build up the joint venture's position in the Chinese market which often required re-investment plus market and human resource development costs, and thus entailed a sacrifice of short-term profit. The Chinese also frequently sought to have the joint venture offer more employment than was economically justifiable, in this way applying to it the social role undertaken by the state enterprise.

Modes of adjustment

There is not sufficient evidence from our studies, or from others currently available, to identify the forms of Sino-foreign management relationship which are most conducive to the successful development of joint ventures. It is, however, possible to discern four modes by which foreign and Chinese managers relate and adjust to each other in the process of introducing change. Although requiring further research, it appears that the mode which is adopted might depend on two factors, namely the relative power of the partners and the attractiveness of one to the other, in terms of approach and what it can offer to the venture. Despite their tentative status, it is worth outlining the four modes since they provide an indication of the range of practical possibilities for achieving adjustment between foreign and Chinese personnel.

The first mode of adjustment is 'forced' in the sense that through their control of know-how or other resources, staff from one partner oblige those from another to accept their techniques, systems or strategic priorities. When this dominant approach is not attractive to the other partner's personnel, perhaps because of its challenge to existing practices or the way it is introduced, the recipients of the new inputs are likely to experience resentment. The probable consequence is that, while they may modify their behaviour, this is not done willingly and they resist internalizing the reasoning behind the changes they are obliged to accept.

The forced mode of adjustment will not therefore provide a sound basis for the longer-term development of a joint venture. If the dominant partner in such cases is the foreign investor, it cannot rely on host-country personnel to take over the eventual running of the organization along lines it believes to be necessary to ensure sound performance. If the dominant partner is that of the host country, then forcing its approach on foreign personnel may destroy its chances of successfully utilizing knowledge and techniques from abroad. Some American joint venture partners adopted this mode of adjustment, and it could give rise to considerable conflict.

It was noticeable, however, that when foreign joint venture partners brought with them an internationally respected product, new technology and extensive training, a forceful approach to introducing change became somewhat more acceptable to the Chinese side because what the foreign partner offered held considerable attraction. In these circumstances, a second 'dependent' mode of adjustment came into play.

Dependent adjustment, unlike the forced mode, involves a willingness to change behaviour on the part of those undergoing change. It can have two outcomes. When the new ways are accepted as legitimate but without fully understanding the rationale behind them, then 'imitation' takes place. The rather wooden and sometimes inappropriate utterance of courtesies to guests which the writer has encountered in some Sino-foreign hotels presents an example of how imported practices have become imitated. If, on the other hand, its recipients comprehend the rationale behind the new approach, then it has become 'internalized' and learning has also been achieved. The notion of dependence signifies that the development involves a one-way transfer of knowledge, which in China is likely to be from foreign to local personnel.

Dependent adjustment seems likely to occur when there is an asymmetrical balance of power between the partners, but when at the same time the non-dominant partner finds the inputs of the other to be attractive. This may be because it seeks to acquire new techniques from the dominant partner or accepts that it can benefit from new systems and/or strategic acumen.

A third form of adjustment within joint ventures may be called the 'segmented' mode. This is more likely to arise in circumstances where the partners' power is relatively balanced, and their mutual attractiveness in terms of their management style and practice is low. The segmented solution is usually manifested by the partners taking responsibility for the organization and conduct of different areas of joint venture activity. This is seen in those frequent instances where the Chinese partner retains managerial responsibility for personnel and administration, while the foreign partner takes responsibility for other functions. In this way, a balance of managerial control is preserved and there is little or no attempt to integrate practices from either of the partners.

There is an obvious danger of sub-optimization, if not disintegration, under this arrangement, and the transfer of knowledge and competences between the partners is limited. Its encouragement of separate channels of upward communication to representatives of the respective partners could readily jeopardize the quality of strategic decisions made on behalf of joint ventures. Segmentation does not, therefore, offer a good basis for the long-term development of joint ventures or for them to be effective agents of modernization for developing economies.

A fourth mode of adjustment found within Sino-foreign joint ventures is 'mutual' in the sense that managers appointed by both partners endeavour to address each others' experience and knowledge in a receptive and sensitive manner. In so doing they increase the probability of learning from each other and working out an approach that is both mutually acceptable and suited to the joint venture's specific situation. This mode of adjustment is integrative in the sense noted by Mary Parker Follett; that is, it enables differences between the parties to be accommodated through a process of mutual problem-solving which usually gives rise to an innovative solution (Metcalf and Urwick 1941). Mutual adjustment is the mode most likely to offer a basis for the long-term development of a joint venture as an organization with its own identity and sense of purpose. Some European and Japanese partners claimed that they were trying through mutual discussions to integrate foreign and Chinese approaches creatively into a specific approach for their joint venture, but we did not have clear evidence of how far they had succeeded in travelling down this road. Indeed, it is necessary to look behind the attractive facade which the concept of mutual adjustment can present. For example, projects conducted within one automobile joint venture whose public relations stressed that it had developed its own integrated way of management through mutual discussions, revealed that on the contrary it was rift by an internal power struggle between Chinese and foreign managers. To place Sino-foreign management relationships onto a basis of willing mutual adjustment and learning is a worthwhile aim when the partners foresee a long-term future for their joint venture, but it is the most difficult mode to achieve and maintain.

Conclusion

The process of managing Sino-foreign joint ventures, and indeed international strategic alliances in general, remains one of the least understood aspects of international management. The presence of foreign collaborators serves to highlight, through contrast, the endemic features of Chinese management, and it raises the question of how constructive accommodation can be reached between foreign and Chinese management traditions.

In China's present situation as a modernizing developing country, much of the adjustment that has to be achieved in collaborative ventures with foreign investors lies on the Chinese side, simply because it is Chinese management that is being exhorted to make the major transition from working within a regulated and closed economic environment to facing the rigours of a market-ed open economy. This chapter has indicated that such adjustment becomes increasingly difficult to achieve as the level of the change rises from the technical level, through to systemic change and then strategic re-orientation. This progression entails an increase in social and cognitive re-adjustment, both of which tend to meet with resistance in any society. The inference is that foreign managements have to work hardest at achieving changes in the mind-sets of

Chinese managers and officials where these have been moulded by careers within the state system. It implies equally that they have to work hard at adjusting their own mind-sets to take account of the Chinese realities within which they work.

New techniques were being introduced into joint ventures with relatively little problem. In many areas, new systems were also in place, though difficulties often arose in the areas of human resource management. The main difficulty, and source of frustration expressed by foreign managers, came at the level of strategic learning. Here, though, the problem lay at least in part with foreign managements. The dilemma was that they might not have felt confident in permitting their Chinese counterparts access to the learning process offered by participation in strategic decision making while the two groups' orientations varied significantly. For when Chinese managers hold a different orientation, this is not necessarily born out of a poor strategic understanding; is may also be founded on a realistic perception of different interests between the partners. So the question of learning in Sino-foreign joint ventures becomes bound up with the issue of control. The two are fundamental to the nature of strategic alliances, and joint ventures in particular, and the problem lies in their inherent conflict.

Joint ventures displayed different ways of adjusting to this problem in the context of relations between Chinese and foreign managements. Although these deserve closer investigation in the future, each appeared to have different consequences for the organizational learning process of the venture and for whether it was likely to develop its own approach and identity rather than becoming a *de facto* subsidiary of one parent or threatened by internal division. The mode of adjustment adopted for a joint venture is clearly of significance in the light of the aspirations which its parent companies hold for it. It also appeared likely that the conditions by which a joint venture is established may have a bearing upon the mode of adjustment that emerges, particularly the relative power of the partners and the degree of task-related and partner-related attractiveness that is inherent in the relationship between them and their respective staff.

Expectations that the foreign partners of joint ventures would adopt a different approach and emphasis consistent with their regional cultural stereotypes gained some support and also deserve further study. There were relatively few differences in the techniques and operational changes that foreign partners introduced – these varied at least as much according to the product area and technology of the company as they did according to the category of foreign partner – though American partners were the most forceful in the way they attempted to bring them in. At the strategic level, however, American partners were more likely to withhold opportunities for local managers to share in the strategic decision process, whereas Japanese and European partners were more prepared to involve senior Chinese managers at this level.

Overall, there was a clear difference of emphasis in the changes foreign partners said they wished to pursue. The Japanese would have liked to see changes in attitudes and behaviour directed towards building up a strong identification with the company. The Americans emphasized a change in the view of business held by their Chinese counterparts, especially their understanding of the market. Germanic partners emphasized the development of professional and technical competence.

The cultural distinctiveness of joint venture foreign partners manifested itself in these differences of emphasis concerning the changes they desired. This implies that the mutual attractiveness of the partners will depend to a significant extent on their cultural compatibility. A comparison with information collected from foreign joint ventures in Hungary (Child, Markoczy and Cheung 1994) indicates that the immediate response to the initiatives introduced by foreign partners depends not just on how forcefully they are applied but also on their compatibility with local cultures. The further exploration of managerial adjustment in international joint ventures would, with these considerations in mind, profit from attention to *both* the balance of power and the mutual attractiveness (including cultural compatibility) between the partners. The former will bear upon the way change is introduced (though this may also reflect sensitivity to other cultures), while the latter will bear upon its perceived legitimacy. Both are likely to be important influences on the mode of managerial learning that ensues.

In contrast, the assessment of what changes have taken place, not only in organizational practices but also in managers' cognitive frames, would benefit from methods that can provide a more quantifiable basis for comparison and also lend themselves to larger samples through which one might hope to tease out the effects of different potential influences. The investigations on which this and the previous chapter have drawn also suggest that task-contingent factors such as size and sector have some influence on the practices adopted. Although we did not find evidence that the age of the joint venture was closely related to the development that had taken place, age clearly remains potentially relevant insofar as time is required for learning and adaptation between the partners. The relevance of these latter factors will need to be clarified through comparative studies based on larger samples.

Part IV

Conclusion

It is impossible to encompass an understanding of China within the bounds of any single perspective: there are always aspects of the country which require a different focus. China is a particularly complex society, by virtue of its deeply embedded and multi-layered cultural heritage, the vicissitudes of its socio-political development (especially during this century), its rapid rate of recent modernization and its vast scale which encompasses strong local identities and traditions as well as distinctive languages. This complexity, combined with the present rate at which the country is changing, makes it extremely difficult to reach anything like an adequate understanding of contemporary developments, even in a specific field of activity such as industrial management. The foreigner finds it a difficult-enough challenge to secure valid descriptions; comprehension is yet more elusive.

China has survived as a society for so long largely through resistance to foreign influence behind walls, deserts and sea and, where this was not possible, through absorbing and adapting external values. It has incorporated several creeds and philosophies, survived many disasters and maintained its way of life under various foreign political masters – both Asiatic and Western. The result is a subtle culture of layers and nuances in which the explicit and formal have come to serve as symbolic marks of outward conformity behind which the people get on with their own lives on the basis of implicit understandings and long-standing relationships of personal trust. It is difficult for the foreigner to penetrate the mysteries of this informal system, and indeed many Chinese themselves have to devote considerable energies to interpreting the meaning of the discourse and social situations in which they are engaged. Chinese culture does not embrace a black-and-white view of the world; rather it is characterized by a holistic view which contains ambiguities, contradictions and multiple meanings, all of which are intrinsically difficult for the Westerner to understand.

There are also a number of reasons why it is hazardous to generalize about China, one of them being the country's considerable diversity. Certain aspects of this diversity have been present throughout China's history. Even the core Han population is divided by different spoken languages and has suffered periodic political fractures, especially between the North and the South. Large areas of the country are populated by 'minorities' of different ethnicity. The balance between central and local control within this social plurality has always constituted a major policy issue. The economic reform has added to the range of variation within the country with the release of local initiative. Under the economic reform, there has been a shift from centralized industrial governance towards greater provincial initiative. This has stimulated divergences in rates of growth between different parts of the country and has encouraged political resistance among the more prosperous provinces, most notably Guangdong, to central economic controls.

The reform has created an economy in transition, which inevitably carries social and political development in its train, despite bureaucratic inertia and sometimes violent resistance to political change. The economic reform is therefore a force for social de-stabilization, at least in the shorter term, and this creates further uncertainty for the external analyst. The fact that the reformers have proceeded on an experimental basis adds to the difficulty of generalizing about the situation as a whole. For example, at the time of writing, initiatives are underway with regard to private corporate stock-holding (extending even to the foreign majority ownership of state firms), the bankruptcy of state enterprises, elimination of the two-tier pricing system and the establishment of new, special economic regions. Going by past experience, some of these initiatives will emerge as models for future application to the economy as a whole, while others will be dropped or modified.

The economic and political development of the country since 1949 has proceeded through severe oscillations. This has continued to be the pattern, albeit on a more restrained scale, since 1979, illustrating Deng Xiaoping's nostrum that China will develop through taking 'two steps forward, one step back'. So while a year like 1993 has proved to be a time of economic boom and new reforms, over-heating could subsequently engender a reversal with the risk of socio-political tension and renewed central control as happened during 1988 and 1989. Further uncertainty is generated by China's failure so far to establish a normal procedure for political succession – again, an event of crucial importance which is conducted entirely behind the scenes.

The attempt to reach conclusions about China must, nevertheless, be made because the country is so significant. Apart from being the most populous society in the world, China is rapidly moving towards the status of an economic superpower and a major world trader, as chapter 2 indicated. An understanding of how China manages its economic activities is crucial to the prospects of success in doing business with it. From a more academic point of view, the differences about China point up certain limitations in currently influential, Western theories of management and organization. They therefore have the potential to contribute importantly to a refinement of those theories.

This concluding chapter takes some tentative steps towards placing the subject-matter of this book into a comparative perspective. It first reconsiders the Chinese road to economic reform, giving particular attention to the question of how far this has now given rise to a fully fledged business system of firms relating with each other as economic actors through markets. A comparison in these terms with other countries, especially those of East Asia, will also help to define the context within which Chinese industrial management currently operates. The second task of the chapter is to offer a framework by which the character of Chinese enterprise management operating within this context might be better understood. The third and last section of this chapter is the most general. It considers how well 'Western' tools for analysing organization and management can be applied to the Chinese case, and what comments can be offered to Western perspectives from a knowledge of Chinese management.

Reform and the development of a business system in China

Chapter 3 grouped the various complementary strands within the economic reform into two main developments: (1) the restructuring of industrial management and (2) the opening of economic relations with the outside world. The key objective in the restructuring has been to change fundamentally the role of the state in economic management and to establish a new relationship between the state and enterprises achieved through decentralization. The purposes of opening economic relations with the outside world have been to import foreign investment and technology, and to fund desirable imports through an expansion of export trade. It has also been intended that the redefinition of the government's economic role and the open-door policy would contribute to the development of market forces within the Chinese economy, under the continuing overall regulation of the state.

The Chinese authorities have endeavoured to proceed with economic reform in a controlled and incremental manner. They have eschewed the 'big bang' policy advocated for Eastern Europe by Jeffrey Sachs and others. Their approach has been one of experiment and learning designed to find a distinctively Chinese and socialist path to modernization rather than accepting the idea of a massive once-for-all economic and political transformation into the Western model of a liberal market system. Despite the many specific problems of implementation discussed in the previous chapters of this book, the Chinese have so far succeeded remarkably well in combining economic restructuring with high levels of economic growth. This economic progress in turn sustains the rising living standards that are offered as the main compensation for the repression of political reform. Indeed, at the time of writing, the question is more frequently being raised as to whether China's path to reform furnishes a better model for Eastern Europe than that associated with the thinking of

Western governments and the International Monetary Fund (e.g. Fan and Nolan 1994).

There are a number of special factors which lend important advantages to China's economic reform and which cannot readily be replicated elsewhere. One is the worldwide 'diaspora' of overseas Chinese who form what Kao (1993) calls the 'Chinese Commonwealth'. These Chinese are distinguished by their conspicuous success in business. They operate within a set of clan and family-based networks of business relations which are bound together by a shared tradition. These networks are rapidly becoming more connected with business in the PRC and offer mainland Chinese entrepreneurs potentially valuable access routes to world markets. Moreover, overseas Chinese from Hong Kong, Macao, Singapore and Taiwan in particular have become collectively by far the largest foreign investors in the PRC, contributing both funds and know-how.

Another attraction for foreign investment is, of course, the lure of a huge potential market based on the world's largest population that is enjoying fairly consistent annual increases in real income. The high level of social and political discipline, which has permitted economically beneficial policies such as non-migration from rural to urban areas and population control, has been a further advantage. This discipline has been maintained throughout society by a comprehensive system of state and party leadership which, though it has become discredited in many citizens' eyes, nevertheless remains an effective force with all its structures in place. The high degree of state control, combined with the attractiveness of the economy to foreign investment, has enabled the authorities to pursue a relatively independent road towards economic development without surrendering economic initiative to agencies or corporations outside the country.

There has been a longstanding political debate in China over how far the economy should move to a free market with a complete decentralization of business decision making, so that firms (or more precisely their managers) become the prime economic actors. Many liberals are again pushing for a free market economy, with conservatives continuing to argue for the co-existence of the market and state planning. It appears that the debate is becoming resolved in favour of a steady extension of market forces. Deng Xiaoping's much publicized visit in January 1992 to Guangdong Province was interpreted as a symbolic act which opened the gate to further reform. An alternative interpretation is that the dynamic business forces which have emerged in the south of China have now become so strong and evidently successful that accommodating to them is the only political response offering any prospect of maintaining the unity of the country under the leadership of the Communist Party.

Now that economic reform is firmly back on the political agenda, the guiding principle of the Chinese authorities is again the establishment of a 'socialist market economy', in which 'market forces, under the macroeconomic control of the state, serve as the basic means of regulating the allocation of resources' (Jiang 1992: 18). This implies that China will continue to develop a business system, where this is understood as a distinctive way of organizing economic activities and resources in a market economy, but along its own lines.

Whitley (1991; 1992; 1994) argues that business systems vary internationally in terms of three main sets of characteristics: (1) the nature of firms as economic actors, especially their autonomy; (2) the way relations between firms are structured to form markets, and (3) the logic which governs managerial systems of co-ordination and control within the firms. His analysis of these three constituents is applied to 'market economies' in which 'control over economic resources is decentralised to private owners' (1994: mss p. 5). This definition would still exclude the bulk of China's economic activity. Nevertheless, Whitley employs his framework to compare the business systems of post-war Japan, South Korea, Taiwan and Hong Kong and it should be instructive to add China to this comparison, both because it has a broad cultural affinity with these countries and because the exercise can help to clarify how far China has moved towards establishing a market-based business system *per se*.

China has always had a significant amount of small-scale commercial and industrial activity outside the centrally planned command economy, but since 1979 the industrial system has become considerably more diversified with the transition towards marketization. Indeed, an outstanding feature of China's economic reform has been the steady and substantial growth in the share of the non-state sector in the total economy. Today, there is a free market for most consumer goods, while the market remains supplementary to planning in the production and supply of some industrial goods and materials especially those considered to be of strategic significance. Moreover, several different forms of industrial property rights have now emerged alongside a diversification in the forms of enterprise ownership and of relationships with the organs of government, including different types of contract for the management of state-owned enterprises.

It is necessary, therefore, to employ a framework for analysis within which the spread of markets and changing structure of property rights in China can be taken into account. As noted in chapter 7, Nee (1992) has made a useful contribution to this end by identifying three categories of Chinese enterprise according to the predominant mode through which their transactions are co-ordinated and the rights over industrial property they embody. He calls the three types the 'non-marketized firm', the 'marketized firm' and the 'private firm'.

To recapitulate briefly, non-marketized firms form part of a centralized structure of economic transactions in which state agencies control the circulation of goods and services through their redistributive mechanisms; indeed, to a large extent they also redistribute income between the firms. Those goods for which the state still sets fixed plan prices come within this category.

The marketized firm, according to Nee, falls outside the bounds of central planning, though it often relies to some extent on local government to secure access to resources allocated through the plan. He regards the collectively owned enterprise as the stereotypical marketized firm, though we argued earlier that some state enterprises also fall within the category. As chapter 2 noted, the economic contribution of collective enterprises has grown considerably under the reform.

Many collective enterprises, especially smaller ones, today operate entirely in the market and with considerable freedom from government control. Together with purely privately owned firms, which also deal wholly through market channels, they constitute Nee's third 'private firm' category. Foreign-funded firms also enjoy a private status, albeit usually with state-owned partners, and operate in the market.

The distinctions which Nee draws have to be borne in mind when assessing how far a business system has now developed in China. Not only is the situation a mixed one, but it is changing quite rapidly. The general direction of the change is indicated by the fact that marketized and private firms constitute the most rapidly growing part of the Chinese economy, and that this growth suffered only a short-term set-back because of the political reaction after the Tiananmen incident. A potentially very significant factor behind the shift towards the marketized and private sectors is the 'hollowing out' of state-owned enterprises through the growth in their sub-contracting to non-state (primarily collective) firms.

Whitley (1994) distinguishes five types of business system that have become established in East Asia, Europe and North America. His three sets of criterion characteristics – nature of economic agents, organization of economic relations between them, internal co-ordination and control – point up the distinctions between the private, marketized and non-marketized sectors in China. They indicate that the country at present contains two business systems and one non-business system.

The characteristics of the Chinese private sector bear several similarities to those of Whitley's 'centrifugal' business system. Indeed, he cites the non-PRC Chinese family business as an example of this type. Within this system, economic power is decentralized to firms only to a limited extent partly because there is a lack of stable institutional procedures (especially laws) governing economic relations. A salient example of the arbitrary regulation to which private business in China remains subject was illustrated by the discrimination exercised against it for a time after 1989 for political reasons. Whitley suggests that this insecurity encourages dependence in this system on personal relationships and a strong preference for skills, products and processes which restrict commitments to particular markets and technologies: 'Thus, strong owner control, a reluctance to invest in capital intensive industries and highly personal connections with employees, customers and suppliers are likely to be distinctive characteristics of business systems in this context.' (1994 mss p. 29). There are several features of the Chinese private firm sector which appear to coincide with Whitley's centrifugal type of business system. Firms in this sector cannot expect much support from intermediaries like banks.[1] They operate under hard budget constraints and have to be self-reliant; as a result they remain small and undercapitalized. Many private firms attempt to compensate for these disadvantages by seeking close ties with local government, but they cannot take support from that quarter for granted. Thus they often have to pay a 'management fee' to the local authority for assistance in securing access to resources and political protection, or they have to register as collective enterprises (Nee 1992: 9-10). This mode of compensation parallels a characteristic of the centrifugal business system posited by Whitley, namely that in the absence of well-developed private intermediaries the managers of firms have to seek and utilize personal connections. A difference is that the key personal connections in China lie with local government officials rather than with other firms.

While there are some similarities between the PRC private sector and Whitley's centrifugal type of business system, they nevertheless diverge in two main respects. The first is that private firms in China are normally still small-scale organizations. Thus the diversity of their operations is limited (which Whitley suggests is not the case when centrifugal systems contain large firms), and they achieve a relatively high level of internal integration under the close personal control of their owners. The second stems from the fact that in China the ownership of property does not furnish legal property rights as it normally does in business systems – these rights continue to depend importantly on the sanction of government and its officials.

The marketized non-private sector of the Chinese economy, comprising many collective firms and most state enterprises responsible to local authorities, fits much of the profile of Whitley's 'state-dependent' type of business system. Firms in this sector do not enjoy the same degree of formal autonomy as do private ones, although their effective freedom of economic action is usually greater because of the support they enjoy from local institutional intermediaries. The growth and profitability of marketized firms have a larger and more direct impact on the income of local government than those of either private or non-marketized firms (Nee 1992: 11). This encourages local authorities to help such firms by providing them with valuable networks and assistance in access to capital, raw materials and labour. Thus local agencies of the state fill many of the roles which in other business systems are played by private intermediary institutions. The isolation of firms in this sector from supporting institutions, at least those within the local economy, is therefore relatively low. The localized nature of 'state-dependency' for firms in this sector supports the development of their personal inter-organizational connections, which are of greater importance than appears to be the norm for this type of business system, according to Whitley. These connections are often arranged by local officials and they may be a continuation of arrangements previously made under the planning system, as Solinger (1989) has illustrated through her study of 'relational contracting' in Wuhan.

It is not so clear how far the internal management of non-private marketized firms in China fits Whitley's state-dependent type. Much depends on specific factors such as the size of the firm, the standing and experience of the director and the relations he and his immediate colleagues enjoy with the supervisory bureau, the local party organization and the trade union. The managers, at least of the larger firms falling within this category, find themselves within the web of interests which Walder (1989) identifies. The way this web is handled can have a significant effect not only on external resourcing of the enterprise but also on the quality of its internal operation.

The non-private marketized sector in China can be said to be a business system in Whitley's terms because it constitutes a mode of organizing market transactions, even though this organization relies a great deal upon local government intervention. However, the third major sector comprising state-owned non-marketized firms remains at least as much an administrative as a business system. Despite the formal decentralization of decision making to their managements under the responsibility system, state enterprises in this category continue to depend on vertical ties to higher level agencies which transfer resources of materials and capital to them according to central plans. They can produce only for the market once they have satisfied the requirements of the plan, and in many cases the prices of both inputs and outputs under the plan are fixed administratively. Their performance is judged more in the light of plan fulfilment than of hard budget criteria. One may recall that one-third of state enterprises are overtly loss-making while another third have so-called 'hidden' (unpaid) debts; these firms rely on subsidies to keep them afloat. This undermines the decentralization of responsibility to enterprises as economic actors, since it is not clear under a non-market system who should bear the responsibility for losses and under soft budget constraints it is effectively government that does so.

The declared policy of the Chinese government is to convert the non-marketized sector into a business system through a number of measures including the abolition of administered prices over the next five years in favour of market regulation for industrial materials (*Beijing Review* 1992c: 9); the granting of autonomy to state enterprises to determine their own production, imports and exports, investment and employment through engaging in market transactions for these (*Beijing Review* 1992f: 4); making these enterprises accountable for their own performance and eliminating subsidies to them even at the cost of bankruptcies (*Beijing Review* 1992f: 4: 1992h: 8); and decentralizing ownership through experiments in stockholding (*Beijing Review* 1992e: 21; 1992g: 14-17). If these measures are carried out across the non-marketized sector, and most commentators regard them as ultimately inevitable, China's economy will have transformed into a market-based business system, albeit one that will almost certainly continue to depend on government agencies as intermediaries and be subject to the overall coordination of a state development plan.

The implementation of the reform programme depends on changes in China's system of industrial governance and on the creation of appropriate financial, legal, auditing and other systems. This illustrates the proposition that business systems develop interdependently with dominant social institutions (Whitley 1994: mss p. 36). In China's case the power to effect institutional change is highly concentrated and, when held by the reformers, can be exercised with remarkable speed.

The extent of economic reform already achieved has given rise to a fundamental change in the context of state enterprise management. Only in joint ventures and other companies in which there has been major foreign investment have even more comprehensive and mould-breaking changes been implemented, and these have often occasioned serious difficulties as chapter 12 noted. These contextual changes inevitably reshape the character of Chinese enterprise management, in ways which the following section analyses.

The changing character of enterprise management[2]

The purpose of this section is to offer an analysis of the structures and transactional patterns that characterize management in Chinese state enterprises, with two objectives in mind. The first is to highlight this character and then to examine the changes which the economic reform seeks to bring about in it. The second and complementary objective is to relate the character of Chinese management to the forces which have given rise to it and which may therefore impede the intentions of the reformers.

Two complementary analytical schemes are useful for identifying respectively the structural and transactional patterns of Chinese state enterprises. The first derives from the so-called Aston Programme of organizational studies. These studies identified two major dimensions of organization: the extent to which activities in organizations are structured and the extent to which authority is concentrated at the organization's apex or even in authorities above it (Pugh and Hickson 1976). The second analytical scheme has been developed by Boisot (1986) with reference to two dimensions of information. Boisot called these dimensions the 'codification' of information and its 'diffusion'.

Information is inherent in transactions because it is a prerequisite for their initiation and completion.

The structuring of activities refers to the degree that work and responsibilities in organizations are formally laid down according to standard procedures and allocated to designated specialties. A high structuring of activities relies upon and constitutes high formalization. Similarly, the codification of information refers to the extent to which information is compressed into a specific and standardized expression to be used as a vehicle for, and referent in, transactions. Codification is therefore part and parcel of formalization. The concentration of authority refers to the degree to which decision-making powers are centralized within the enterprise and/or retained by higher authorities above it. Highly concentrated powers with little participation in decision making imply a low diffusion of information. The concept of information diffusion refers to the extent of information-sharing within a given population and the scope of the transactional net which accompanies this. High information diffusion is therefore indicative of decentralized transactions. These complementary two-dimensional analytical frameworks are illustrated in figure 14.1.

The frameworks are themselves obviously formalized and they are not exhaustive of all relevant dimensions. They can, however, serve to typify the management and operation of the Chinese state-owned enterprise and the direction in which the reform calls for it to change. The structure of this enterprise has up to now approximated to what the Aston researchers termed an 'implicitly structured organization'. Its authority is highly concentrated through vertical dependency relations, while the structuring of its activities is limited and imprecise in terms of procedures, definitions of responsibility and the like. If it has the appearance of bureaucracy, this is somewhat of a 'mock' character (Gouldner 1954) since it actually functions to a great extent through informal sponsorship, personal obligation and a good deal of political control. The implicit and personalized nature of this management system has been thrown into sharp relief within many Sino-foreign joint ventures where it contrasts markedly with the conventions now followed by many foreign companies, especially American multinationals.

In terms of transactional patterns, the Chinese enterprise has operated within a restricted network with information that is neither highly codified nor widely diffused. We noted, for example, in chapters 6 and 8 that its management depends for much of its external information upon the supervising bureau and that even this information tends to be focused upon the immediate city or provincial domain. Codified information on matters such as market structures, customer preferences and profiles, input prices or wage levels is sparse. A widening of the enterprise's trading domain through a broad range of transactional links is inhibited by the lack of codified information and of legal codes

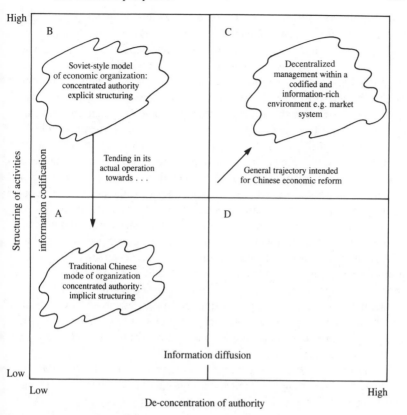

Figure 14.1 A framework for analysing the structuring of Chinese enterprises and the informational nature of their transactions

to guarantee the terms of contracts entered into impersonally and at a distance.
In short, Chinese state enterprises have tended to operate in box A of figure 14.1.

The economic reform is seeking to revitalize and modernize Chinese enterprises by moving their structures and transactional modes closer to box C of the
figure. The transactional modes depicted by that box are those of a market-
based business system. Information on prices and commodities is codified, and
hence readily comparable, and it is widely available. The structural concomitant is that of decentralized management which can organize its responsibilities
and activities in the light of the greater consistency of external expectations and
information. Thus the stated intention of the reform is to de-concentrate
authority, structure the scope of managerial responsibilities more clearly and
encourage managements to enter into a wider range of market transactions
which they will search out and then contract for on their own initiative and
at prices negotiated directly between the transactors. The 'enterprise

responsibility system' envisages the decentralization of planning to enterprises and the delegation of decisions in the areas of marketing, purchasing, investment, personnel and internal organization. Under this system, the enhanced autonomy and responsibility of enterprise directors are at the same time becoming formalized through various types of contract with the higher authorities. Within the enterprise, the 'director responsibility system' is intended to identify and hence structure the distinctive executive powers of management and to disinguish these from the rights and functions of state ownership and of the party. The substitution of profit targets for mandatory output quotas, the open door policy and the delegation of boundary functions (such as purchasing and marketing) to enterprise management are intended to broaden its transactional net. In so doing, the expectation is expressed that enterprises will become increasingly subject to the market test of economic performance.

The reform programme, in short, aims to increase structuring and decentralization in tandem at the enterprise level as well as to increase the availability (diffusion) of systematic (codified) information at the contextual level so as to promote a more effective operation of market indicators. As well as measures bearing directly upon enterprise management, strenuous efforts are being made to facilitate industrial development through improvements to physical infrastructure and telecommunications, through the formulation of legal codes including the protection of patents and copyright, the import of advanced technology and the development of specialist expertise.

The reform is officially legitimated as the means for achieving the 'Four Modernizations'. As chapter 2 noted, the concept of modernization is a controversial one, particularly if it is taken to imply that there is a universal or convergent path of economic development. It is quite possible that China will create its own version of a modern society, which its present leadership insists will remain a socialist one. Be this as it may, it is interesting to note that the concomitants of modernization or industrialization which are hypothesized by some writers (e.g. Kerr 1983; Berger 1987) are generally consistent with the thesis that the impulse of China's economic reforms is towards box C of figure 14.1. For they also point towards high levels of structuring and information codification combined with decentralized economic initiative and information diffusion.

In addition to the model of efficient markets, other examples of structuring and codification in a 'modern' society include an advanced level of occupational specialization based on certified knowledge and a comprehensive system of contracts and common rights enshrined in elaborated legal codes. The wide diffusion of information, both formal knowledge and information about events and opportunities, is made possible in modern societies by its codification and transmission through advanced communication systems. This provides the potential for considerable social and geographical mobility and for decentralized economic initiative.

The gap between this vision of a modern industrial society and the present reality in China is still substantial. It would, however, be an oversimplification to view this challenge merely as one of moving from an economy planned and regulated by bureaucracy to one which permits the bracing freedom of the market. There are two considerations here. Firstly, many of the legal-rational provisions designed to ensure that markets work according to acceptable rules of the game are still lacking in China, as is the expertise to operate in this mode. This is recognized today by the Chinese authorities. This means the country will have to strengthen its substantive formalization and structuring in these areas of box B in figure 14.1 before it can accomplish the transformation into a social-market economy (located in box C of the figure) which is envisaged by the reformers.

Secondly, the underlying logic that has sustained Chinese social and industrial organization for many centuries is based on patrimonial values and personal obligation, giving rise to networks of fief-like relations with implicit structuring and concentrated authority. This is a system for governing transactions that is *sui generis*, distinct from both bureaucracy or markets. This system reflects the norms of traditional Chinese culture, and therefore underpins non-PRC Chinese enterprise as well (Redding 1990; Kao 1993). It has been functionally well adapted to a society in which local social cohesion has carried communities through many natural and man-made disasters. It continues today as the product of a condition of legal-rational under-development where the bounded rationality and information impactedness that result conspire to keep transactional numbers small and relationships personalized (Boisot and Child 1988). This mode of organization stands as a socially embedded obstacle to movement from box A to box C in figure 14.1 and the question arises, to which we shortly return, whether it has necessarily to give way to a market system based on universalistic values as a condition for achieving modernization.

Consideration of the forces which currently sustain the distinctive characteristics of Chinese enterprise management point to the substantial difficulties that lie in the way of this transformation. In chapter 2, it was suggested that three phenomena acting together have an important bearing upon the nature of Chinese management: the system of industrial governance, traditional Chinese culture and the constraints imposed by the country's condition as a developing economy. The impact of these influences can be delineated within the formal framework that has been set out here.

The top-down command structure established in the early days of China's transition to socialism remains in place, and it is unlikely to be amended in any fundamental way for some time to come so far as the state sector of industry is concerned. Its vertical organization embodies a matrix of channels of downward influence bearing upon the enterprise. This ties many state enterprises (especially the larger ones) into a dual administrative dependency – on the channels from industrial ministries and on those operating through the local government – which constrain their opportunities for product or geographical diversification. Moreover, the party resumed a more active engagement within enterprises after 1989 in the area of managerial appointments and personnel policy. Previous chapters have illustrated how these multiple lines of control and influence continue to carry weight despite the formal autonomy accorded to the enterprise by the director and contractual responsibility systems. They are reflected in actions and structures within enterprises which tend to be highly segmented, akin to the 'flower pot configuration' depicted for state-owned enterprises by Hafsi et al. (1987).

A fundamental question is how much of a transition there can be away from the regulatory apparatus of state socialism towards market regulation without this posing a terminal threat to socialism itself. The operation of markets is not conducive to meeting socialist principles of social solidarity, priority of the general interest over the particular, reward sharing and economic security. Insofar as socialism remains the official ideology, it is difficult to envisage the dismantling in China of the centrally administered system for setting socio-economic priorities and regulating transactions within major economic sectors to ensure the implementation of those priorities. The key question, then, for the achievement of a 'socialist market economy' is how to ensure that the state maintains an arm's-length relationship with enterprise management and is sufficiently disciplined to make the new system work. Concern that a totalitarian state could not exercise such economic self-restraint led Kornai (1986) to criticise what he called the 'naive reformers' who advocated a socialist market system in Eastern Europe.

However, as is always the case, one cannot simply translate the failure of the market socialism which prevailed during the 1980s in countries such as Hungary and Poland to the situation in China. Although there have been notable exceptions in recent times, over the longer stretch of history the Chinese have become accustomed to leaders who, while authoritarian, nevertheless operated at a sufficient geographical and administrative distance to avoid too much interference with people's daily lives. The combination of central autocracy with local flexibility is taken for granted in China far more than it was in Hungary or Poland, and it is in any case more natural to a huge diverse country than to a small one. Moreover, the economic reform has demonstrated that the central authorities are prepared to make much more fundamental moves towards an open market system than was ever the case in Eastern Europe before 1989.

So while the system of state socialism that remains in place in China relies on a degree of formalization which impinges on non-marketized state enterprises in the form of plans and regulations, and issues many regulations which are intended to apply to other enterprises as well, these top-down formulations are normally quite general in content and often require considerable specification and interpretation at a local level. Their very ambiguity encourages the adoption of a liberal attitude towards them locally, although requiring that the intentions behind them are checked out just in case. In practice, regulations may be treated ritualistically or even ignored, with considerable discretionary power being exercised by local officials.

There have been many examples cited in this book to show how the Chinese system of industrial governance operates to an important extent through personal contacts, loyalties and obligations. These personal relations, and the access to information, priority allocations and other economic advantages they convey, are for most enterprises localized through controlling provincial, municipal or county agencies which become important gatekeepers between enterprise managers and the higher authorities.

The Chinese structure of industrial governance, in short, constrains enterprise management to the left-hand side of figure 14.1, characterized by a concentration of authority and limited information diffusion. There is some tension between the official formalization of planning and commercial regulations (box B in the figure) and the tendency for the system to operate behind the scenes through informal, personalized modes focused on relations with and through key governmental intermediaries (box A in the figure).

The resource allocation dependencies and the limited efficiency of administered economic transactions gave rise to the informal lobbying, bargaining, *ad hoc* arrangements and other behaviour patterns which characterized the former state socialist systems in Eastern Europe as well (cf. Grancelli 1988; Child and Markoczy 1993). They are therefore products of a particular system of industrial governance, illustrating how organizational behaviour is influenced by the institutional arrangements of a given society which determine the channels through which power and influence are exercised and the rules of conduct which obtain.

At the same time, the conduct of Chinese management is in harmony with important traditional Chinese values. As we noted in chapter 2, these include a collective orientation towards the family and, to an important extent, the work unit, a respect for age, moral leadership and authority (all tending to be equated with hierarchical superiority), and informal relationships based on trust and mutual obligation. Fairbank (1987: 367) concluded that tradition deriving from long history continues to exercise a pervasive influence and poses 'severe problems' for the country's modernization. In terms of the figure 14.1 framework, it anchors transactions in the space designated by box A. The Chinese appear to be most at ease culturally with non-codified transactions that are arranged through informal trust-based channels of a localized face-to-face kind and they accept the governance of such transactions by older respected superiors with whom they can identify through work units and/or communities of which they are long-term members. This configuration of cultural preferences appears at first sight to be at variance with the conditions required for open-market transacting and with other attributes that have been associated with modernization, such as the mobility of people between social and workplace communities.

However, as has become apparent in the case of Japan, strong local collective identities and reciprocal social obligations can also be economic strengths promoting, for example, the rapid and harmonious adoption of technological innovation and allowing for mobility of both capital and labour within the protective umbrella of paternal organizations. Chinese and similar cultural values have not inhibited the rapid development of the 'Little Dragons' of the Pacific Rim. If China were able to link its local economic units effectively into a national, and indeed international, system of information exchange and coordination comparable to that provided by MITI and other central agencies in Japan, or even to follow a more sector-focused policy of state assistance for export-led development such as that pursued by South Korea (Whitley 1991), it could also take a culturally acceptable route to modernization of a distinctively oriental character. Another significant oriental linkage that is already developing rapidly is through partnerships with overseas Chinese businesses which can offer investment funds and access to world markets.

These possibilities would approximate not so much to a Western model of open-market transacting as to a form of transacting for which Chinese enterprises would receive market information plus financial and technical support from units with which they had close and continuing relationships. In terms of figure 14.1, this approach would retains its roots in box A, but it would at the same time enrich the informational environment of enterprises more to the level of box C. It still leaves the question, however, of how much strengthening of institutional (and especially legal) capacities at the centre of the system would be required for this model to work effectively in China.

The passing comparison with Japan also serves to highlight the significance for enterprise management in China of the latter's relatively limited level of economic development. This has a number of consequences for management in terms of our framework. Firstly, the shortage of managerial and professional expertise constrains the de-concentration of authority and delegation of decision making within industrial and other structures. Secondly, the limited communications and information infrastructures constrain the diffusion of information which would otherwise assist enterprise managers to take initiatives in the market. There is still the lack of an adequate physical infrastructure to assist the integration of markets across the economy as a whole. Thirdly, the underdevelopment of codified statistical information, systematic technical knowledge, legal codification and the formalization of organizational roles serves to hamper managerial action and to increase the dependence of managers upon official approval – both because the consequent uncertainties increase the risk of taking initiatives and also because the knowledge that is available tends to be confined to official sources.[3]

China's modest level of economic development is therefore another feature tending to confine the managers of its enterprises to the transactional space depicted by box A in figure 14.1. The shortage of human, informational and physical infrastructural capital raises transaction costs and favours localism and transacting within limited numbers (what Williamson 1975 has called 'small-numbers bargaining'). Nee (1992) has pointed out that, under the conditions of partial reform in China, the marketized firm operating primarily within a local government co-ordinated economic network gains privileged access to factor markets and can, if it chooses, dispose of its outputs through state domestic and export marketing channels.

Chinese management and Western perspectives

China presents a challenge to students of management and organization because it is so different from the situations they have normally encountered. It is therefore not surprising to find that Chinese modes of management and organization do not match Western patterns, or that China's path to modernization is quite distinctive. The fact that our present analyses of management and organization derive so much from Western theories and experience therefore becomes problematic. In particular, the special nature and context of Chinese management raise two questions in relation to Western thinking about management and organization. Firstly, does the West offer concepts that can be applied to the Chinese case? Secondly, what comment can be offered on the different perspectives contained within Western thinking from a knowledge of Chinese management?

To a considerable extent, Western thinking does offer concepts and theoretical perspectives which can be used to analyse Chinese management and organization, and to draw out its distinctive features. After all, many of the founding fathers of Western social science adopted an internationally comparative approach in their attempts to construct general social theories or to trace the distinctive development of Western civilization. This was particularly true of Max Weber, who is one of the progenitors of modern organization theory, and of Emile Durkheim and Karl Marx from whom organization studies has also drawn many concepts and lines of analysis.

The conceptual tools for analysing organizational fundamentals such as authority, control, structures of governance, normative systems, property rights, and constituent economic and technical relations have all been articulated in the literature sufficiently to permit their application to a very wide range of cases and situations. We would argue that they supply the bricks from which a reasonably adequate representation of the Chinese case can be constructed.

For example, the discussion of management in China offered in some of the preceding chapters has been concerned with the nature of managerial authority there and with the basis for eliciting compliance and motivation from organizational members. Analysis of these issues has been informed by existing Western concepts of authority and compliance familiar to the writer, particularly Weber's (1968) distinction between the charismatic, traditional and legal-rational foundations of authority and Etzioni's (1961) identification of the normative, instrumental and coercive grounds for compliance with organizational leadership. The often painful development of a civic social order in China since 1949 and its ramifications for industrial governance can be usefully treated within the framework provided by Weber's three categories, while Etzioni's distinction between normative and instrumental compliance very closely represents the main parameters of shifting policies and practices on moral and material rewards. While it is left to readers to form their own judgement on the matter, this writer concludes that existing concepts and perspectives can be quite helpful when applied to China.

This is not to deny that many concepts may need to be refined to capture certain nuances of the Chinese case or indeed that sometimes new concepts need to be identified. The latter is particularly likely to arise in respect of China's unique cultural heritage. Hofstede (1991), for example, criticizes the Western ethnocentricity of much cultural analysis, including his own previous work, and concludes on the basis of subsequent research that in China a further cultural dimension not found in other cultures – 'Confucian work dynamism' – is likely to have a significant bearing upon people's behaviour within organizations (see also Chinese Culture Connection 1987; Hofstede and Bond 1988). We would argue, nevertheless, that the main challenge to contemporary organization theory posed by the Chinese case does not lie in conceptual development.

It lies, rather, in the need to re-configure into a different social gestalt the features of the Chinese case captured by our existing concepts. China does call for a model of organization *sui generis*. Previous sections of this chapter concluded that Chinese management follows a logic of its own within an economic context that cannot be equated with other economic or business systems. It was possible to support this conclusion and to point up the key features of the Chinese case through using existing comparative concepts and dimensions. The conclusion itself, however, was that China configured in a distinct pattern of its own both along separate dimensions and in terms of the relationship between them. At a subjective level, the writer's own personal encounters in China and his interpretation of the material presented in this book, lead him to conclude that Chinese people attach meanings to, and work with interpretations of, organizational life which are quite their own.

How then might one begin to account for management and organization in

China? A point of departure is one often articulated by the Chinese themselves when they state that they seek modernization with Chinese characteristics. On the one hand, this recognizes that the successful management of a competitive open economy and of its business units does require China to adopt certain management practices and organizational forms used in other countries because they are best suited to the contingencies of scale, technology, available human resource competences and sector conditions. It also recognizes that as Chinese businesses come more frequently to deal directly with non-Chinese corporations and traders – encouraged by the abolition of restrictions such as the monopoly of state import/export corporations – so they will be expected to conform to certain international transactional conventions and legal requirements. On the other hand, the social processes and relationships through which the Chinese system and its constituent business units function within whatever structures and conventions, and the meaning that the people who are involved attach to those processes, will remain peculiarly Chinese.

The question of authority can again illustrate the point which is being advanced. It may be argued, on the one hand, that authority is a functional necessity at least in social units requiring close co-ordination and which are larger than a self-regulating primary group. This functional necessity applies as much to China as it does elsewhere. On the other hand, the way people regard authority is not the same in China as it is in Western societies, with the result that the process of exercising it and the quality of relationships through which it flows is different.

In Western societies, authority tends to be seen as inimical to individual freedom and is consequently more or less regarded as an unfortunate necessity for achieving socially desired ends. In China, such has been the pervasive influence of Confucian thinking at least since the Song Dynasty (from which time it could be propagated throughout the whole nation through the invention of wood-block printing), that authority has come to be accepted virtually as an end in itself – certainly as a social good. Confucianism taught that authority, especially of the father within the family and the ruler within the society, had to be honoured and obeyed. This authority accompanied by correct moral behaviour was regarded as a *sine qua non* for the preservation of the social fabric in a condition of harmony and prosperity (Smith 1974). The authority of the ruler derived from his position as the upholder of this system. The use of authority was to be judged according to its moral quality rather than its accordance with a law setting out abstract and generalized rights. So in effect the ruler decided what was lawful.

This tradition resulted in a disjuncture between ownership and property rights within China. In the West ownership normally confers property rights which are embodied in law. In China, by contrast, the right to acquire, benefit from and dispose of property was always liable to require the approval of the ruler's officials, and the confiscation of property was quite common. Home for the Chinese could never be said to be their castle. The fundamental difference between China and the West in the relationship between ownership and property rights has important consequences for the management of enterprises. In Western countries, the attachment of property rights to the ownership of business assets provides a socially accepted and legally clear basis for the exercise of managerial autonomy, namely that (subject to the general laws of the land) managers can exercise discretion so long as their actions as a whole receive the approval of the owners. In China, the weak link between ownership and property rights, and in particular the mediation of the link by government officials, sets significant limits to managerial discretion. The ambiguous nature of ownership in the so-called 'state-owned' sector of industry only reinforces this situation.

This tendency for officials to act with *de facto* rights of their own remains evident in China today, as we noted in regard to decisions which had according to formal regulations been decentralized to enterprise management under the reform. The property rights which Chinese officials accrue to themselves has, as one might expect, been one of the most difficult features for Western managers to accept.

The issue of ownership and property rights in China can be analysed using a framework derived from the Western literature, and this has the considerable virtue of permitting some comparative observations to be made with the situation in other countries. Available concepts of ownership and property rights are useful for this analysis; what emerges is that it is the nature of the association between the two which distinguishes the Chinese case and which has important implications for management in that context. This is in line with our general response to the first question posed, namely that we can derive a conceptual language from much of Western analysis which elucidates management in China. However, this does not mean that Western assumptions about the interrelationship of variables identified by concepts apply. Hence, the *nature* of the Chinese case could well be different.

The perspectives and schools of thought within a discipline derive their distinctiveness from assumptions as to what is particularly intrinsic or important about the subject of their concern. They therefore compete, but usually from a partial comprehension or representation of that subject. This leads us to the second question, namely what the study of Chinese management has to say on the adequacy and relevance of existing perspectives. Since we are now moving beyond concepts and towards more comprehensive theories (in the sense of systems of explanation), reference to the special gestalt of China can provide a more critical test and should make a useful contribution. The point is now developed by reference to several perspectives which are ostensibly relevant to management in China: the theory of the firm (with particular reference to transaction-costs economics), modernism and the institutional perspective. This latter is considered at some length and compared with the contribution of perspectives which refer to culture and to the level of industrialization.

The theory of the firm in Western economics is predicated on the notion of organizations having clear boundaries. This assumption, for example, underlies the distinction drawn between a hierarchical and a market mode of governing transactions (Williamson 1975). The former is seen to come within the firm while the latter is seen to involve going outside it. This idea of a firm having a definable boundary is essentially a legalistic one based on the definition of the property rights attaching to the ownership of business assets. We have noted how in China this identity between ownership and rights over property has never been so close as in the West. The managements of Chinese firms are beholden to a wide range of stakeholders, each of whom can legitimately bring sanctions to bear on those managements if their interests or opinions are not heeded. These are the 'facts of life' which confront the Chinese manager (Walder 1989).

In spite of attempts under the economic reform to distinguish between ownership and management, and the functions of administration and management, the vertical boundaries between enterprise and higher authorities cannot be sharply drawn. The prevalence of relational contracting, often orchestrated by the agencies of local government, also means that the horizontal boundaries of the Chinese firm cannot be sharply drawn either. The Chinese case therefore suggests that the concept of a firm being the focus of a 'field' of forces might be a better one than any notion of a clearly bounded entity.[4] The forces in operation here include those of transacting, controlling and negotiating within a network of generally long-term relationships which render the boundaries of any one firm quite permeable and changeable.

The important point here is not so much that a different notion of the firm and its boundary conditions needs to be applied to China, but that the limitations in the Western perspective which the comparison highlights also apply to the West as well. Close long-term interconnections between firms have not been uncommon in Western economies and, with the development of industrial districts and the rapid growth in the number of so-called 'strategic alliances' between firms, the concept of a firm having permeable and multiple boundaries within an economic field of closely inter-connected firms is fast becoming more appropriate than the traditional focus on the clearly bounded firm as the economic actor *per se*.

The mode of economic and social organization in China points up a further oversimplification in the Western micro-economics literature. The Chinese case demonstrates that the so-called markets and hierarchies framework of transaction costs economics provides too limited a set of transactional options.

In Williamson's (1975) early analysis, as well as in those of his predecessors such as Commons (1934) and Coase (1937), the choice of how transactions are to be organized was seen to fall between use of the hierarchical structures of formal bureaucracies or the market mechanism. These authors wrote with reference to the United States, a developed capitalist economy, and in the light of further evidence, partly from Western Europe, Williamson has more recently (1985) recognized a number of structures for organizing transactions that fall between the extremes of pure hierarchy and pure market. They are nevertheless conceived of as positions along the single hierarchy-market dimension which, referring back to figure 14.1, is located within the domain of codified information.

It is not possible to accommodate the Chinese system of transactions governance simply along a single bureaucratic-market continuum. Earlier chapters on decision making and on input-output management noted that many transactions are governed in Chinese business through informal groupings of limited scope, exchanging relatively uncodifed information and conforming to the fief as a form of social organization rather than to either bureaucratic hierarchy or the open market. Transaction-costs economics, therefore, requires a significant extension so as to allow for other types of governance structures, such as the fief and the clan.

It is instructive to recall the roots of this Chinese preference for the relatively uncodified and informal mode of transacting. For they point to the fact that the social significance given to what Westerners would regard as economic transactions is not just of an economic nature in China. Such transactions denote long-term relationships which the Chinese value for their own sake and which are subject to systems of regulation based on a preservation of the social respect of the persons involved. The regulation of transactions in China does not rely only, or even primarily, upon financial penalties and rewards, or upon legal sanctions. The philosophical basis for this orientation towards trust and continuity in economic relations derives importantly from the Confucian emphasis on the moral basis of social relations and from the Taoist view of human life as one of continuing flux and process (cf. *I Ching* 1983). The Chinese system for regulating economic relations draws importantly, though not exclusively, from these philosophical foundations and they are deeply engrained in the country's institutional arrangements.

A consideration of the systems of production and transactions which the Chinese have evolved under the reform refutes the 'modernist' thesis popular in Western thinking that economic development gives rise to common forms of economic and social organization, resulting in a convergence between the social structures of industrializing societies. Rather, China's experience supports the view that, while economic development does require certain technical and infrastructural supports to be available, the way in which the economic and industrial systems are organized will reflect national, and to an extent regional, preferences. These preferences are usually assumed to be embedded in cultural and institutional features. Indeed, as some critics of the 'modernist' perspective have argued (e.g. Clegg 1990), there is plenty of evidence of variety among economically viable and socially acceptable forms of organization in different parts of the world, and indeed in different sectors and/or regions of those Western advanced industrial societies themselves which have in the past been taken to conform to the 'modern' model. Clegg calls these other forms 'post-modernist', which, however, for some would imply that their rationale can only be derived by reference to the people who set up and maintain such organizations, rather than to more encompassing contextual factors. If we leave aside the non-marketized state sector, the present diversity of successful business forms within China, each of them with unique features, clearly supports the thesis that there are a number of effective forms of economic organization. The differences between successful business systems suggest a counter hypothesis to that of modernism, namely that, if they did not reflect the key institutions of their respective societies, successful economic development would not take place.

The investigations reported in this book have indeed illustrated how the organization and management of China's enterprises are conditioned by the institutions of that country, prominent among which are the organs of the state. Chinese enterprise management reflects those institutions in ways that are specific to the PRC, and the specificity grows the closer the enterprise is tied by ownership and control into the state institutional structure. Thus the 'business system' in which private PRC firms operate is not dissimilar to that which characterizes small Chinese businesses elsewhere, an important part of which is indeed today directly linked to the Hong Kong business systems, especially in Guangdong Province (cf. Vogel 1989; *The Economist* 1992a). By contrast, the non-marketized part of the state sector remains to a considerable extent incorporated into the state administrative apparatus.

The manifest significance of the institutional context of management in China suggests that the study of Chinese management has potentially much to contribute to the still 'adolescent' (Scott 1987) institutionalist perspective in organizational analysis. As DiMaggio and Powell (1991) point out, this perspective divides into a number of strands and is not by any means unproblematic in its current stage of development. Two questions in particular are raised by the subject matter of this book. Firstly, by what means do institutional forces have an influence over Chinese managerial thinking and behaviour? This bears upon the question of what kind of institutional perspective appears to fit the Chinese case. Secondly, how does the institutional explanation for Chinese management and organization stand comparison with, and relate to, other possible interpretations?

DiMaggio and Powell (1991) draw a contrast between what they call the 'old' and the 'new' institutionalism in organizational analysis. The old institutionalism was developed in studies of industrial companies or public authorities, which emphasized their need to accommodate politically to interest groups in the community such as agricultural lobbies, and those like trade unions which penetrated within the formal bounds of the organization itself. It emphasized informal political processes within organizations in the form of 'influence patterns, coalitions and cliques, particularistic elements in recruitment or promotion' (DiMaggio and Powell 1991: 13). By contrast, the new institutionalism has usually played down conflicts of interest within and between organizations. It has, instead, taken more interest in the stable and taken-for-granted aspects of organizational life, including the role of common understandings and habitual ways of thinking in maintaining these. It emphasizes how institutional bodies outside the organization (such as educational institutions, families, religious bodies and professional associations) penetrate it by 'creating the lenses through which actors view the world and the very categories of structure, action and thought' that constitute the organization (ibid: 13).

The new perspective directs attention to ways that institutions structure people's thinking and programme their actions, ways that may be so taken for granted as to be almost unconscious. It is also consistent with the notion of organizational imprinting, the process whereby organizations acquire structures, programmes, staffing profiles and cultures which reflect characteristics at the time of their founding and which they tend to retain subsequently. These forms of institutional influence are evident in China. One observation widely held among foreign managers working there is that their Chinese counterparts who have a long experience of working within the old political-economic system find it very difficult to discard their attitudes and norms of behaviour which are rooted in notions of the 'iron rice bowl' and 'eating from the same big pot'. Moreover, the structures and systems of state enterprises have clearly continued to reflect those laid down many years beforehand.

On the other hand, these structures and managerial attitudes tend to persist for longer when Chinese managers and employees perceive that there remains a risk in changing them; that is, when they remain sanctioned explicitly or implicitly by the authorities. Managers of the Beijing enterprises initiated changes in their organizational structures once they were confident that their higher authorities and the enterprise party organization would support these. We have noted many instances of how formal and informal political pressures continue to be brought to bear upon state enterprises, which means that external institutional preferences are imposed upon Chinese managers. The system of industrial governance in China hangs very substantial rewards and punishments over the heads of enterprise directors, whose re-appointment lies in its hands. Its agencies continue to control many important channels for allocating material, financial, land and human resources to enterprises. We also noted, through investigations of decision making and resource allocation, how these vertical dependencies create the conditions for active lobbying and other informal processes intended to secure advantage for the enterprise, on the one side, and continued loyalty to (plus sometimes personal gain for) government and party officials on the other.

This indicates that the emphasis which the old institutionalism places on power and political process is highly relevant to an understanding of the situation in which Chinese management finds itself, especially in the state sector. As DiMaggio (1988) has admitted, consideration of power and interest has been rather neglected in recent work within the institutional perspective. No analysis of China can ignore the authoritarian foundation of its present institutions. The institutions of government and party express social-ideological as well as economic criteria for correct managerial conduct. Their control over the dominant ideology and discourse, which Lu (1991) describes in close-up, constitutes a real institutional power (cf. Gramsci 1971; Foucault 1977) that combines with allocative and redistributive powers over material rewards and resources. Managers face high risks from having to satisfy the expectations of superior authorities and their own working communities (both now formalized in responsibility contracts) under conditions of bounded rationality (due to limited information) and the possibility of opportunism on the part of some transactional partners. This sets up a power dynamic because at the same time their institutional counterparts depend on the continued success of enterprises and their good management.

The second question is how well the institutional perspective compares as an explanation for the nature of management and organization in different countries with other approaches, and how it might relate to them. Child and Markoczy (1993) address this question through a comparison of the various explanations that might be offered for the finding that the behaviour of senior Chinese and Hungarian industrial managers shares some striking similarities. They examined explanations for these behaviour patterns offered by reference to national culture, level of industrialization (including the contingencies associated with this) and the system of industrial governance. As we have just noted, the last perspective takes account of the relational and behavioural dynamics encouraged by the institutional framework of state socialism.

They conclude that the institutional is the perspective which can best identify the forces establishing such dynamics. It is the only one which plausibly accounts for similarities between what are otherwise culturally diverse countries at somewhat different stages of industrial development. It is also the only perspective which can account for the sharp differences in managerial behaviour, organizational structures and economic systems between countries that share the same cultural heritage but are institutionally divergent, such as the former two

Germanies and the two Koreas. Child and Markoczy additionally cite various sources which report similarities in organizational behaviour in East European countries during their state socialist period, including the Soviet Union, despite contrasts between them both in culture and level of industrialization.

The same paper also offers some insight into ways in which the institutional, cultural and industrialization perspectives can be mutually informative. For example, comparison between countries such as the former East Germany and Hungary suggests that their cultural inheritance qualitatively affected social relationships and work ethics within similarly institutionalized state socialist systems. Boisot and Child (1988) argue that China illustrates how in the event of both market and bureaucratic failures, the culturally inherited and sanctioned predisposition towards poorly codified, localized transactions of a fief-like nature will fill the gap, and indeed will fashion the ways in which markets and formal organizations operate anyway. Another example is that industrialization, insofar as it requires the growth of a well-educated and qualified sector of society as well as the more widespread diffusion of information, is likely to establish both social expectations and organizational contingencies which eventually reshape a country's institutions. For example, the policy of opening China to the outside world was announced as being a necessity for the country to progress in its modernization, but the input of foreign ideas, norms and people that come with it is having a profound influence on attitudes and awareness, especially those of educated younger Chinese people, and this will over time create pressures to change institutionalized structures and practices.

In short, an emphasis on the analytical power of an institutional perspective on management in China does not imply a total rejection of other approaches, or indeed of a recognition that some of these alternatives can usefully complement institutionalism. It does, however, capture the essence of the economic reform process in China which is an attempt to engineer massive institutional change in the economic sphere, while at the same time limiting any political upheavals that might come in its wake.

The reform is intended to move Chinese management away from operating under externally imposed norms towards working under internally generated norms. The new concepts which reflect this change include market-orientation, responsibility and opening up. The expectation is that Chinese managers will embark on a learning process through which the dynamic for improvement will come from their own actions and those of their employees rather than from direction passed down from above by 'wise old men'. It is vital that all those involved in this bold experiment in China, as well as the foreigners who assist it as channels for new knowledge and techniques, keep a mind as open and informed as possible about the many difficulties which naturally attend such a major programme of national change and development. This book is offered as a contribution to that end.

Notes

1 INTRODUCTION

1 The reform process was halted, though not fundamentally reversed, during the post-Tiananmen reaction from June 1989 to 1991. During the latter year the reform process was resumed cautiously and was then given a marked impetus by Deng Xiaoping's call to speed up the pace of reform during his visit to southern China in January 1992.

2 ECONOMY AND SYSTEM

1 This official figure for per capita income is a very significant underestimate (*The Economist* 1992b) and also masks considerable disparities in income distribution. Thus China had more than one million Yuan millionaires (1m Yuan = £118,000) according to an official report published in March 1993 (*The Independent* 1993).

2 The main source for the statistics cited in this chapter is the *Statistical Yearbook of China 1993*, Beijing: State Statistical Bureau 1993.

3 ECONOMIC REFORM AND OPENING TO THE OUTSIDE WORLD

1 The Boisot/Child scheme is employed in chapter 14 to provide an analysis of the changing nature of Chinese management under the economic reform.

2 For a detailed breakdown of these and related statistics, see chapter 11, tables 11.1 and 11.2.

3 In this respect, transformation of the economy as a whole in China demonstrates a parallel to the combination of change and continuity noted in studies of the successful transformation of large and long-established enterprises in the western context (e.g. Pettigrew 1985).

4 LEADERSHIP IN THE ENTERPRISE

1 This chapter draws extensively from Child and Xu (1991).

2 Many enterprise directors and party secretaries are women, and the male gender is used purely for stylistic convenience.

3 Evidence from other sources on the work activities of senior managers is presented in chapter 8.

5 LEVELS OF DECISION MAKING

1 'Decentralization' is used here to refer to a devolution of powers both to determine organizational goals (or at least to share in goal-setting) and to establish the means by which the goals are realized. 'Delegation' refers to the devolution of decisions on the realization of goals only.

6 THE PROCESS OF DECISION MAKING

1 The author served as supervisor for Lu (1991) and was one of the principal investigators for the project reported by Lu and Heard (1995).

2 The heavy industry investment projects took between just under 2 years to 4.5 years. The shortest decision process was for a considerably less costly investment than in the other two cases. Nevertheless, the petro-chemical investment was a very expensive one that only took 2.5 years to final approval by the State Council in August 1991. In this case the process was considerably shortened by the personal commitment of a minister when he visited the enterprise. As was reported by one of its managers: 'The minister said a decision on the project should be made and there was no need for further discussion. He urged us to submit the proposal as soon as possible and promised that the Ministry would approve it. So, this proposal was approved faster than any other in our history.' This example points again to the continuing importance in China of securing administrative approval for major investment projects and the role of personal relations in facilitating the process. Personal lobbying was also important in facilitating the British investment decisions, but on the whole this took place within the company up to and including its board members (Lu and Heard 1995).

7 INPUT AND OUTPUT TRANSACTIONS

1 The import of branded consumer goods can proceed through several routes, as is illustrated by the case of beverages and spirits. One is through the establishment of a joint venture which usually allows for the import of at least the concentrate or essence of the drink (which foreign companies normally guard jealously as their key product technology). Another is through sale to the China National Duty Free Merchandise Corporation which was set up specially to handle the growing volume of duty free trade. Third, some joint venture hotels have specially approved import licences. Another channel is through consignment sales. The Ministry of Foreign Economic Relations and Trade (MOFERT) each year issues foreign currency quotas for import consignments. These quotas are influenced by annual indications of import need submitted by provinces and municipalities. The companies dealing with different product areas under the Foodstuff Import and Export Corporation of China then negotiate consignment sale contracts with foreign sellers within the limits of the quotas. The purpose of consignment sales is to meet the needs of foreigners in China at deluxe hotels and stores where the convertible Foreign Exchange Certificate is used. The scope of these sales is limited by the insistence of the Chinese authorities on international price levels and on importers bearing the full costs of market promotion, quarantine expenses and damages, purity checks and so forth. Smuggling, especially through the Special Economic Zones where import tariffs are reduced by half, is also an important channel for beverage and spirit imports.

2 Coady, Qiao and Hussain, from whom this summary has been taken, comment that:

> The changes in the vegetable trade are part of wider changes in the SMS [state marketing system], which involve not only farm and sideline products but also industrial products. The main features of the changes have been the removal of government monopoly, the emergence of commercial units specialising in particular commodities and the devolution of authority to the local government. The present system allows for the formation of specialized wholesale companies at the county level. The emphasis is on developing direct links between the areas selling and buying vegetables. In addition, the policy encourages the setting up of wholesale markets in big and medium-sized cities. This is of particular importance because it allows for the proliferation of private traders who themselves are not commodity producers. Also the wholesale trade in vegetables consists predominantly of spot transactions as opposed to being based on long-term contracts. Notwithstanding these important changes, the State Marketing Network still dominates trade in agricultural commodities, and vegetables in particular, especially at the wholesale end. (1990: 16)

3 Whatever the features informing and sustaining the importance attached by the Chinese to the quality of the relationships through which transactions take place, they appear to retain considerable significance. For example, Heap and Campbell (1990) conclude from a study of the conditions for winning large international projects in the Chinese iron and steel industry that two activites were both necessary to success. First, communicating the tangible aspects of technology, price and concessionary funding. Second, effort given to establishing relationships with the relevant Chinese network of ministries, local companies, other associated companies, provincial organizations (banks, import/export agencies, etc.), and the Bank of China. The success of the latter activity coloured the Chinese evaluation of the tangible factors on offer by foreign companies.

8 ACTIVITIES OF SENIOR MANAGERS

1 Chow (1992) found from her questionnaire survey of ninety-seven middle managers in Henan Province during May 1989 that on average they attached most importance to 'maintaining contacts with the Party representative in the organization' and to 'seeing to it that employees have the right political attitude'. This suggests the interesting possibility that whereas senior Chinese managers feel obliged to give most attention to relations with their higher administrative authorities, middle managers are more concerned with maintaining their good standing with the enterprise party secretary who continues to exert influence over personnel matters where the political attitude of employees still counts.

9 THE MANAGEMENT OF PERSONNEL

1 This and the following section draw from the work of Lu (1991:224–58; 1992).
2 Employees in all categories are paid monthly in China and so the general term 'salary' will be used to refer to the periodic relatively fixed element in their pay.
3 This applied to the recruitment of early-retirement soldiers up to 1 October 1987.
4 The term 'labour market' refers here to agencies which offer services such as information on vacancies and which facilitate mobility. These agencies include job agencies, labour mobilization service centres and the labour exchange market organized by the municipal labour bureau.
5 Chapter 10 provides evidence of the extremely strong dependence that earnings have on age and length of service in state enterprises.

6 I witnessed this passive resistance first hand and also received many reports of the same phenomenon from factories and offices. It was not unusual in compulsory workplace political education classes for men to spend the time reading newspapers and for women to do knitting, without entering into any discussion related to the ostensible purpose of the class.

7 Appendix 9.2 gives details of these items. It was also possible in most cases to assess a person's job content through discussion and (in the case of production workers in 1985) through observation. This assessment suggested that the schedule was sufficiently sensitive to discriminate validly. The schedule was normally completed by job-holders on the spot as a questionnaire, but in the case of production workers it was completed through an interview process. The schedule was a translation of one which the writer and colleagues had previously employed in a number of European countries. The translation was accomplished through the following stages. First, two independent translations into Chinese were made by English-speaking Chinese members of the CEMI staff. These were then independently translated back into English. Discrepancies were identified and the whole schedule was then subjected item-by-item to a total of fifteen hours discussion by a group of English-speaking Chinese faculty members and students with the writer's participation. The resulting revised schedule was next piloted on a cross-section of staff working with the Institute and the China Enterprise Management Association (CEMA) whose premises were on the same site. These staff included accountants, secretaries and gatekeepers. Remaining ambiguities were then addressed through discussions with the pilot-study respondents. It may be mentioned that the schedule was subsequently employed by the writer in a study of laboratory technicians within the PUMC Hospital in Beijing accompanied by separate in-depth interviews on the same subject-matter, and it appeared also from this procedure to have acceptable validity.

10 THE STRUCTURE AND SYSTEM OF EARNINGS

1 Many of the findings obtained for 1985 were reported in Child (1990b).

2 Since Chinese employees are normally paid monthly, we shall use the term 'salary' rather than 'wage' to refer to the regular element in payment. Salary is therefore distinguished from bonus, welfare payment or subsidy. The term 'earnings' or 'payment' will normally be used to refer to aggregate remuneration or as adjectives to identify the system or structure as a whole (as in 'payment system').

3 The procedure adopted for constructing and testing the questionnaire and the advantages of mature industrially experienced indigenous students as fieldworkers for this kind of investigation are discussed in Child (1990b: 232–3).

4 At the time 1 Yuan was worth approximately £0.25 Sterling at the official rate.

5 By early 1990, 1 Yuan was worth approximately £0.12 at the official rate.

6 Since several of the predictor variables are not independent of each other, which complicates interpretation, a stepwise regression procedure was employed.

7 These items were selected, with the guidance of factor analysis, from the twelve listed in Appendix 9.2. The two omitted were nos. 4 (being able to know right away in your own mind how well you have done your work) and 10 (satisfaction of completing a whole piece of work). Coefficient Alphas for the aggregated measure were respectively 0.80 and 0.85 for the 1985 and 1990 samples.

8 It would, however, be an oversimplification to account for the system of age-related earnings progression through accumulating length of service simply in terms of the influence of state socialism. Whittaker (1990) among others has pointed to the continuing importance of age and years of service in Japanese payment systems, even though this may now be reducing somewhat in favour of ability and quality of experience criteria. Insofar as China and Japan share some cultural values concerning age and loyalty to the unit, this is consistent with the view that what we have called the traditional model draws from both cultural and socialist values.

11 ESTABLISHING JOINT VENTURES

1 This section draws in part from an unpublished manuscript written by Luc G. Houben and Owen D. Nee, Jr., both Partners in Coudert Brothers. The manuscript, entitled 'The Form of Foreign Investment in China with Case Studies', is not dated but appears to have been written in 1988.
2 Since 1991, China's rapid economic growth in the midst of world recession has dramatically increased the attractiveness of its investment environment.
3 It should be noted that, after a turbulent initial few years, the BJC now appears to have shaken down into an intrinsically profitable operation and that the partners may have modified their goals and expectations in line with this positive experience.

12 MANAGEMENT OF JOINT VENTURES

1 For further examples and a discussion of how foreign joint venture managers were attempting to overcome these communication problems, see Child et al. (1990: 42–54).

13 DYNAMICS OF THE SINO-FOREIGN MANAGEMENT RELATIONSHIP

1 It is interesting to note that both the average size and age of the Chinese joint ventures was generally higher than those we studied in Hungary and yet a higher proportion of the latter had introduced formalized management systems. The implication is that the adoption of this foreign approach to management is less problematic in Hungary, which is consistent with anecdotal evidence provided by the foreign managers interviewed in both countries (Child, Markoczy and Cheung 1992).

14 MANAGEMENT IN CHINA: THE SEARCH FOR PERSPECTIVE

1 Chinese banks have hitherto remained governmental agencies which offer loans as much on the basis of political considerations as economic ones, so favouring state and larger collectively-owned firms. Similar considerations tend to govern the allocation of raw materials and other goods in short supply. The situation will probably change as, for example, foreign banks come to play a more active role in the Chinese economy and with the reforms in banking announced at the end of 1993.
2 This section draws from the author's paper on 'The Character of Enterprise Management' in Child and Lockett (1990).
3 Foreign companies do collect their own market and other business information quite regularly and from direct sources. They often find, however, that they remain dependent for information on government agencies and statistical bureaux.
4 I am indebted to Max Boisot for suggesting that the idea of a 'field of forces captures the essence of the relations between Chinese firms and the units in their immediate context.

References

A.T. Kearney and International Trade Research Institute of the PRC 198' *Manufacturing Equity Joint Ventures in China*. Chicago, Ill: A.T. Kearney.

Aiello, P. 1991. Building a Joint Venture in China: The Case of Chrysler and the Beijing Jeep Corporation. *Journal of General Management*,17: 47–64.

Alston, J.P. 1986. *The American Samurai*. Berlin: De Gruyter.

Anderson, E. 1990. Two Firms, One Frontier: On Assessing Joint Venture Performance *Sloan Management Review*, 31: 19–30.

Andors, S. 1977. *China's Industrial Revolution*. London: Martin Robertson.

Aron, R. 1967. *The Industrial Society*. London: Weidenfeld and Nicolson.

Arthur Andersen 1993. *China Perspectives*. 4th edn. Hong Kong: Arthur Andersen & Co.

Barnowe, J.T. 1990. Paradox Resolution in Chinese Attempts to Reform Organizationa Cultures. In J.Child and M.Lockett (eds.) *Reform Policy and the Chinese Enterprise*. Advances in Chinese Industrial Studies 1A, Greenwich, CN: JAI Press

Barnowe, J.T., Yager, W.F. and Wu Nengquan. 1992. Leaping Forward: Management Experiences of Firms with Foreign Investment in Southern Guangdong, China Paper given to the Conference on Current Developments in Joint Ventures in the PRC, Hong Kong, June.

Behrend, H. 1957. The Effort-Bargain. *Industrial and Labor Relations Review*, 10 503–15.

Beijing Review 1986a. Provisions of the State Council Encouraging Foreign Investment State Council Official Answers Questions. 29/43, 27 October: 26–8.

1986b. Review of Eight Years of Reform. 29/51, 22 December: 14–18.

1988. 'Third Wave' – Enterprise Mergers. 31/42, 17–23 October: 5.

1989a Communique of the Fourth Plenary Session of the 13th CPC Centra Committee. 32/27, 3–9 July: 9–10.

1989b. CPC to Boost Ideological Work. 32/31 31 July–6 August: 5.

1989c. From the Chinese Press: Survey Spotlights Apportionments. 32/3, 16–2: January: 30.

1991. First Indefinite Time Limit Joint Venture. 34/40, 7–13 October: 31.

1992a. Speed up Reform, Open the Doors Wider. 35/10, 9–15 March: 4.

1992b. New Unemployment Programme Launched. 35/22, 1–7 June: 6–7.

1992c. Two-Tier Price System to be Eliminated. 35/28, 13–19 July: 9.

1992d. Shenyang Continues Experiment with Enterprise Bankruptcy. (By staf reporter Zhang Zhiping). 35/28, 13–19 July: 22–4.

1992e. A Multi-Economic Sector Enterprise. (By staff reporter Dai Gang). 35/29 20–6 July: 21–7.

1992f. More Autonomy Given to State Enterprises. 35/32, 10–16 August: 4.

1992g. Stocks: New Excitment in China's Economic Life. (By staff reporter Yao Jianguo). 35/32, 10–16 August: 14–17.

1992h. 66 Enterprises Go Bankrupt. 35/33, 17–23 August: 8.

1993. Foreign Trade Volume of JVs Rises. 36/34, 23–29 August: 28

Berger, P.L. 1987. *The Capitalist Revolution*. Aldershot: Gower.

Berle, A.A. and Means, G.C. 1932. *The Modern Corporation and Private Property*. New York: Macmillan.

Biggart, N.W. 1977. The Creative-Destructive Process of Organizational Change: The Case of the Post Office. *Administrative Science Quarterly*, 22: 410–26.

Blecher, M. 1989. State Administration and Economic Reform. In D.S.G. Goodman and G. Segal (eds.) *China at Forty*, Oxford: Clarendon Press.

Boisot, M.H. 1986. Markets and Hierarchies in a Cultural Perspective. *Organization Studies*, 7: 135–58.

1990. Schumpeterian Learning. Unpublished paper.

Boisot, M.H. and Child, J. 1988. The Iron Law of Fiefs: Bureaucratic Failure and the Problem of Governance in the Chinese Economic Reforms. *Administrative Science Quarterly*, 33: 507–27.

Boisot, M.H. and Xing Guo Liang. 1991. The Nature of Managerial Work in China. In N. Campbell, S.R.F. Plasschaert and D.H. Brown (eds.) *The Changing Nature of Management in China*. Advances in Chinese Industrial Studies, 2. Greenwich, CN: JAI Press.

1992. The Nature of Managerial Work in the Chinese Enterprise Reforms. A Study of Six Directors. *Organization Studies*, 13: 161–84.

Bond, M.H. and Hwang Kwang-kuo. 1986. The Social Psychology of Chinese People. In M.H. Bond (ed.) *The Psychology of the Chinese People*. Hong Kong: Oxford University Press.

Brugger, W. 1976. *Democracy and Organisation in the Chinese Industrial Enterprise*. Cambridge: Cambridge University Press.

Burns, T. (ed.). 1969. *Industrial Man*. Harmondsworth: Penguin.

Byrd, W.A. 1991. Contractual Responsibility Systems in Chinese State-Owned Industry: A Preliminary Assessment. In N. Campbell, S.R.F. Plasschaert and D.H. Brown (eds.) *The Changing Nature of Management in China*. Advances in Chinese Industrial Studies, 2. Greenwich, CN: JAI Press.

Campbell, N. 1987. Enterprise Autonomy in the Beijing Municipality. In M. Warner (ed.) *Management Reforms in China*. London: Frances Pinter.

Campbell, N. 1989. *A Strategic Guide to Equity Joint Ventures in China*. Oxford: Pergamon.

Campbell, N. and Cheng Yee. 1991. Relationship Management in Equity Joint Ventures in China: A Preliminary Exploration. In N. Campbell, S.R.F. Plasschaert and D.H. Brown (eds.) *The Changing Nature of Management in China*. Advances in Chinese Industrial Studies, 2. Greenwich, CN: JAI Press.

Campbell, N. and Henley, J.S. (eds.). 1990. *Joint Ventures and Industrial Change in China*. Advances in Chinese Industrial Studies, 1B. Greenwich, CN: JAI Press.

Campbell, N., Plasschaert, S.R.F., and Brown, D.H. (eds.) 1991. *The Changing Nature of Management in China*. Advances in Chinese Industrial Studies, 2. Greenwich, CN: JAI Press.

Chamberlain, H.B. 1987. Party–Management Relations in Chinese Industries: Some

Political Dimensions of Economic Reform. *The China Quarterly*, no. 112: 631–61

Chen Fuhong 1990. Yige Zhongxing, Yige Renwu [One Target, One Task]. *Chinc Enterprise Daily.* 22 January: 4.

Cheng Gang. 1992. Chinese Employees in Foreign-Funded Ventures. *Beijing Review* 35/46, 16–22 November: 21-23.

Child, J. 1984. *Organization: A Guide to Problems and Practice.* 2nd edn. London Harper & Row.

1987. Enterprise Reform in China: Progress and Problems. In M. Warner (ed. *Management Reforms in China.* London: Frances Pinter.

1989. Transacting the Inputs to Firms in the Context of the Transition from Bureaucratic to Market Co-ordination in China. Paper given at the 9th Colloquium of the European Group for Organizational Studies, Berlin, 11–14 July.

1990a. The Character of Chinese Enterprise Management. In J. Child and M. Locket (eds.) *Reform Policy and the Chinese Enterprise.* Advances in Chinese Industria Studies, 1A. Greenwich, CN: JAI Press.

1990b. The Structure of Earnings in Chinese Enterprises and some Correlates of their Variation. In J. Child and M. Lockett (eds.) *Reform Policy and the Chinese Enterprise.* Advances in Chinese Industrial Studies, 1A. Greenwich, CN: JA Press.

1991. A Foreign Perspective on the Management of People in China. *The International Journal of Human Resource Management,* 2: 93–107.

1993. Society and Enterprise between Hierarchy and Market. In J. Child, M. Crozier R. Mayntz, et al. *Societal Change between Market and Organization.* Aldershot Avebury.

Child, J. et al. 1990. *The Management of Equity Joint Ventures in China.* Beijing China–European Community Management Institute.

Child, J. and Lockett, M. (eds.) 1990. *Reform Policy and the Chinese Enterprise* Advances in Chinese Industrial Studies, 1A. Greenwich, CN: JAI Press

Child, J. and Lu Yuan. 1990. Industrial Decision Making under China's Reform 1985–1988. *Organization Studies,* 11: 321–51.

1992. Institutional Constraints on Economic Reform: The Case of Investment Decisions in China. Research Paper in Management Studies 8/92, University o Cambridge.

Child, J, and Macmillan, B. 1972. Managerial Leisure in British and American Contexts *Journal of Management Studies,* 9: 182–95.

Child, J. and Markoczy, L. 1993. Host-Country Managerial Behaviour and Learning in Chinese and Hungarian Joint Ventures. *Journal of Management Studies,* 30 611–631.

Child, J., Markoczy, L. and Cheung, T. 1994. Managerial Adaptation in Chinese and Hungarian Strategic Alliances with Culturally Distinct Foreign Partners. In S Stewart (ed.) *Joint Ventures in the People's Republic of China.* Advances in Chinese Industrial Studies, 4. Greenwich, CN: JAI Press.

Child, J. and Xu Xinzhong. 1991. The Communist Party's Role in Enterprise Leadership at the High-Water of China's Economic Reform. In N. Campbell, S.R.F Plasschaert and D.H. Brown (eds) *The Changing Nature of Management in China* Advances in Chinese Industrial Studies, 2. Greenwich, CN: JAI Press.

Chinese Culture Connection, The. 1987. Chinese Values and the Search for Culture free Dimensions of Culture. *Journal of Cross-Cultural Psychology,* 18: 143–64.

China Enterprise Daily. 1989. Weihu Changzhang Zhongxing Diwei Jiajiang Qiye Dang De Jianshe [Protect the Central Position of the Factory Director and Strengthen the Construction of the Party Organization in the Enterprise]. 11 September: 1.

1990. Fahui Qiye Dang Zuzhi Zuoyong De Bianzheng Sikao [Dialectical Study of the Party Organization's Role in Enterprises]. 8 February: 3.

Chow, I.H. 1992. Chinese Managerial Work. *Journal of General Management*, 17: 53–67.

Chung Tsui Shun. 1990. Managerial Motivation in the PRC: A Preliminary Look at Senior Managers in the Electronics Industry in the PRC. MBA Dissertation, Newport University, January.

Clegg, S.R. 1989. *Frameworks of Power*. London: Sage.

1990. *Modern Organizations: Organization Studies in the Postmodern World*. London: Sage.

Clegg, S.R. and Dunkerley, D. 1980. *Organization, Class and Control*. London: Routledge.

Coady, D., Qiao Gang and Hussain, A. 1990. The Production, Marketing and Pricing of Vegetables in China's Cities. Research Programme on the Chinese Economy Paper no 6. London School of Economics.

Coase, R.H. 1937. The Nature of the Firm. *Economica*, 4: 386–405.

Commons, J.R. 1934. *Institutional Economics*. Madison: University of Wisconsin Press.

Contractor F.J. and Lorange, P.L. (eds.). 1988. *Cooperative Strategies in International Business*. New York: Lexington Books.

CPC [Communist Party of China]. 1984. *China's Economic Structure Reform: Decision of the CPC Central Committee*. Beijing: Foreign Languages Press.

1986. Three Regulations Governing the Work of the Director, Party Committee and Workers' Congress in State-Owned Enterprises. Issued by the CPC Central Committee and the State Council, 15 September.

1988. Document on the Implementation of the Enterprise Law, issued by the Central Committee of the CPC, 28 April. Beijing.

1989a. Communique of the Fourth Plenary Session of the 13th CPC Central Committee. *Beijing Review*, 32/27 July 3–9: 9–10.

1989b. Discussion Meeting of Older Cadres in the Organization Department of the CPC on Enhancing Party-building. *People's Daily* (Overseas edition), 18 July: 1.

1990. Communique of the Seventh Plenary Session of the 13th Central Committee of the Communist Party of China. *Beijing Review*, 34/1, 7–13 January: 27–9.

Crow, C. 1937. *400 Million Customers*. New York: Harper.

Cyr, D.J. and Frost, P.J. 1991. Human Resource Management Practice in China: A Future Perspective. *Human Resource Management*, 30: 199–216.

Daniels, J.D., Krug, J. and Nigh, D. 1985. US Joint Ventures in China: Motivation and Management of Political Risk. *California Management Review*, 27: 46–58.

De Bruijn, E.J and Jia Xinanfeng. 1992. Transferring Technology to China via Joint Ventures: Product Selection Perspective. Paper given to the Conference on Current Developments in Joint Ventures in the PRC, Hong Kong, June.

Deng Xiaoping. 1984. *Selected Works of Deng Xiaoping 1975–1982*. Beijing: Foreign Languages Press.

1987. On Reform of Political Structure. *Beijing Review*, 18 May: 14–17.

320   References

Denton, N. 1991. A Race Against Time. *Financial Times Survey of Hungary*, 30 Oct VII.

DiMaggio, P.J. 1988. Interest and Agency in Institutional Theory. In L.G. Zucker (ed. *Institutional Patterns and Organizations*. Cambridge, MA: Ballinger.

DiMaggio, P.J. and Powell, W.W. 1991. Introduction. In W.W. Powell and P. DiMaggio (eds.) *The New Institutionalism in Organizational Analysis*. Chicago University of Chicago Press.

ECAM [Euro-China Association for Management Development]. 1986. *Chines Culture and Management*. Brussels: European Foundation for Managemer Development.

Economist, The. 1992a. China Goes for Broke. 25 July: 57–8.

1992b. A Survey of China: When China Wakes. 28 November.

Eisenhardt, K.M. 1989. Agency Theory: An Assessment and Review. *Academy c Management Review*, 14: 57–74.

Etzioni, A. 1961. *A Comparative Analysis of Complex Organizations*. New York: Fre Press.

Fairbank, J.K. 1987. *The Great Chinese Revolution 1800–1985*. London: Chatto an Windus.

Fan, Q. and Nolan, P. (eds.) 1994. *China's Economic Reforms*. London: Macmillan.

Feldman, A.S. and Moore, W.E. 1969. Industrialization and Industrialism: Convergenc and Differentiation. In W.A. Faunce and W.H. Form (eds.) *Comparativ Perspectives on Industrial Society*. Boston: Little, Brown.

Fidler, J. 1980. *The British Business Elite*. London: Routledge and Kegan Paul.

Fiol, C.M. and Lyles, M.A. 1985. Organizational Learning. *Academy of Managemer Review*, 10: 803–13.

Foucault, M. 1977. *Discipline and Punish*. Harmondsworth: Penguin.

Francis, A., Turk, J, and Willman, P. (eds.). 1983. *Power, Efficiency and Institution. London: Heinemann.

Frankenstein, J. 1991. The Chinese Foreign Trade Environment. In O. Shenkar (ed. *Organization and Management in China 1979–1990*. Armonk, NY: M.E. Sharpe

French, J.R.P. and Raven, B. 1959. The Bases of Social Power. In D. Cartwright (ed *Studies in Social Power*. Ann Arbor, Michigan: Institute for Social Research.

Geringer, J.M. 1991. Strategic Determinants of Partner Selection Criteria i International Joint Ventures. *Journal of International Business Studies*, 22: 41–6.

Geringer, J.M. and Hebert, L. 1989. Control and Performance of International Join Ventures. *Journal of International Business Studies*, 20: 235–54.

1991. Measuring Performance of International Joint Ventures. *Journal c International Business Studies*, 22: 249–63.

Gordon, M. 1990. Sino-Western Manufacturing Joint Ventures: The Automotiv Experience. Paper given to the Canada–China International Managemer Conference, Xian, August.

Gouldner, A.W. 1954. *Patterns of Industrial Bureaucracy*. Glencoe, Ill: Free Press.

Gramsci, A. 1971. *Selections from the Prison Notebooks*. New York: Internation; Publishers.

Grancelli, B. 1988. *Soviet Management and Labor Relations*. Boston: Allen and Unwi

Granick, D. 1990. *Chinese State Enterprises: A Regional Property Rights Analysi* Chicago: University of Chicago Press.

Granovetter, M. 1985. Economic Action and Social Structure. The Problem c

Embeddedness. *American Journal of Sociology*, 91: 481–510.

Hackman, B.K. 1989. The Changing Face of Employee Decision-Making Power in China: A Temporal Review of Delegation in Chinese State Owned Enterprises. Australian Graduate School of Management, University of New South Wales. Working Paper 89–029.

Hafsi, T., Kiggundu, M.N. and Jorgensen, J.J. 1987. Strategic Apex Configurations in State-Owned Enterprises. *Academy of Management Review*, 12: 714–30.

Hakam A.N. and Chan Kok Yong. 1990. Negotiations between Singaporeans and Firms in China. In N. Campbell and J.S. Henley (eds.) *Joint Ventures and Industrial Change in China*, Advances in Chinese Industrial Studies, 1B. Greenwich, CN: JAI Press.

Hamel, G. 1991. Competition for Competence and Inter-Partner Learning within International Strategic Alliances. *Strategic Management Journal*, 12: 83–103.

Harbison, F. and Myers, C.A. 1959. *Management in the Industrial World*. New York: McGraw-Hill.

Harrigan, K.R. 1986. *Managing for Joint Venture Success*. New York: Lexington Books.

He Wei and Wei Jie 1992. *Zhongguo Jingji De Fei Juheng Fa Zhang* [The Uneven Development of the Chinese Economy]. Beijing: People's University Press.

Heap, A. and Campbell, N. 1990. Winning Large International Projects in China: A Network Approach. Paper given to the Conference on Management and Economics in China Today: Similarities with Eastern Europe?, Maastricht, November.

Hearn, J.M. 1977. W(h)ither the Trade Unions in China? *Journal of Industrial Relations*, 19: 158–72.

Henley, J.S. and Nyaw, M.-K. 1986. Introducing Market Forces into Managerial Decision Making in Chinese Industrial Enterprises. *Journal of Management Studies*, 23: 635–56.

1987. The Development of Work Incentives in Chinese Industrial Enterprises: Material versus Non-material Incentives. In M. Warner (ed.) *Management Reforms in China*. London: Frances Pinter.

Henley, J.S. and Ereisha, M.M. 1987. State Control and the Labor Productivity Crisis: The Egyptian Textile Industry at Work. *Economic Development and Cultural Change*, 35: 491–521.

Herzberg, F., Mausner, B. and Snyderman, B.B. 1959. *The Motivation to Work*. New York: Wiley.

Hickson, D., Butler, R., Cray, D., Mallory, G. and Wilson, D. 1986. *Top Decisions*. Oxford: Blackwell.

Hildebrandt, H.W. and Liu Jinyun. 1988. Career and Education Patterns of Chinese Managers. *The China Business Review*, Nov.–Dec.: 36–8.

Hofstede, G. 1991. *Cultures and Organizations*. London: McGraw-Hill.

Hofstede, G. and Bond, M.H. 1988. The Confucius Connection: From Cultural Roots to Economic Growth. *Organizational Dynamics*, 16: 4–21.

Houben, L.G. and Nee, O.D. Jr n.d. The form of Foreign Investment in China with Case Studies. Unpublished mss. Hong Kong: Coudert Bros.

Huang Xiang. 1985. On Reform of Chinese Economic Structure. *Beijing Review*, 20: 15–19.

Hunt, R.G. and Gao Yang. 1990. Decision Making and Power Relations in the Chinese Enterprise: Managers and Party Secretaries. In J. Child and M. Lockett (eds.)

Reform Policy and the Chinese Enterprise. Advances in Chinese Industrial Studies, 1A. Greenwich, CN: JAI Press.

Hunter, C.S.J. and Keehn, M.M. (eds.). 1985. *Adult Education in China.* Beckenham: Croom Helm.

Hussain, A. 1990. The Chinese Enterprise Reforms. Research Programme on the Chinese Economy, Paper no. 5, June. London School of Economics.

1992. The Chinese Economic Reforms in Retrospect and Prospect. Research Programme on the Chinese Economy, Paper no.24, August. London School of Economics.

I Ching [Book of Changes]. Trans. R. Wilhelm. 1989. London: Arkana.

Inkson, J.H.K., Pugh, D.S. and Hickson, D.J. 1970. Organization Context and Structure: An Abbreviated Replication. *Administrative Science Quarterly,* 15: 318–29.

Jackson, S. 1992. *Chinese Enterprise Management Reforms in Economic Perspective.* Berlin: De Gruyter.

Jacobs, J.B. 1979. A Preliminary Model of Particularistic Ties in Chinese Political Alliances: *Kan-ch'ing* and *Kuan-hsi* in a Rural Taiwanese Township. *The China Quarterly,* no. 78: 232–73.

Jiang Xiaoming. 1992. The Evolution of Property Rights in China: A Long-Run Analysis with Special Reference to Hefeng Textile Mill. Unpublished PhD thesis, University of Cambridge.

Jiang Zemin. 1992. Accelerating the Reform, the Opening to the Outside World and the Drive to Modernization, so as to Achieve Greater Success in Building Socialism with Chinese Characteristics. Report to the 14th National Congress of the Communist Party of China. Printed in full in *Beijing Review,* 35/43, 26 Oct.–1 Nov.: 9–32.

Jin Qi. 1988 Factory Directors' Worries. *Beijing Review,* 31/40: 4–5.

Katz, F. and Kahn, R. 1978. *The Social Psychology of Organizations.* New York: Wiley.

Kao, J. 1993. The Worldwide Web of Chinese Business. *Harvard Business Review,* March–April: 24–36.

Keesing, R.M. 1974. Theories of Culture. *Annual Review of Anthropology,* 3: 73–97.

Kerr, C. 1983. *The Future of Industrial Societies: Convergence or Continued Diversity?* Cambridge, MA: Harvard University Press.

Kerr, C., Dunlop, J.T., Harbison, F. and Myers, C.A. 1960. *Industrialism and Industrial Man.* Cambridge, MA: Harvard University Press.

Knutsson, J. 1986. Chinese Commercial Negotiating Behaviour and its Institutional and Cultural Determinants: A Summary. In *Chinese Culture and Management.* Brussels: Euro-China Association for Management Development.

Kohut, J. 1992. Chinese Fight for Jobs as Capitalism Creeps In. *Sunday Times,* 2 August:16

Kornai, J. 1980. *The Economics of Shortage.* Amsterdam: North Holland.

1986. The Hungarian Reform Process: Visions, Hopes and Reality. *Journal of Economic Literature,* 24: 1687–737.

Kroeber, A.L. and Kluckhohn, C. 1952. Culture – A Critical Review of Concepts and Definitions. Papers of the Peabody Museum of American Archaeology and Ethnology, Harvard University.

Krug, B. 1989. Economic Reform. In B.Krug, S.Long and G.Segal *China in Crisis.* RIIA Discussion Paper 20. London: Royal Institute of International Affairs.

Kumar, K. 1978. *Prophecy and Progress.* Harmondsworth: Penguin.

Laaksonen, O. 1988. *Management in China During and After Mao*. Berlin: De Gruyter.

Lane, D. (ed.). 1986. *Labour and Employment in the USSR*. Brighton: Wheatsheaf.

Lawrence, P. 1980. *Managers and Management in West Germany*. London: Croom Helm.

Lee, P.N.S. 1987. *Industrial Management and Economic Reform in China 1949–1984*. Hong Kong: Oxford University Press.

Leung, J. 1989. Return of 'Big Brother' Irks China's Investors. *Asian Wall Street Journal*, 28 December: 1,4.

Levitt, B. and March, J.G. 1988. Organizational Learning. *Annual Review of Sociology*, 14: 319–40.

Li Rongxia. 1993. Landmark of China's Economic Growth. *Beijing Review*, 36/1: 15–19.

Lieberthal, K. and Oksenberg, M. 1988. *Policy Making in China. Leaders, Structures and Processes*. Princeton, N.J.: Princeton University Press.

Littler, C.R. 1985. Work Outside the Capitalist Framework: The Case of China. In R. Deem and G. Salaman (eds.) *Work, Culture and Society*. Milton Keynes: Open University Press.

Lockett, M. 1983. Organizational Democracy and Politics in China. In C. Crouch and F. Heller (eds.). *Organizational Democracy and Political Processes*. Chichester: Wiley.

1985. Cultural Revolution and Industrial Organization in a Chinese Enterprise: The Beijing General Knitwear Mill 1966–1981. Management Research Paper 85/7. Templeton College, Oxford.

1988. Culture and the Problems of Chinese Management. *Organization Studies*, 9: 475–96.

Lockett, M. and Littler, C.R. 1983. Urban Inequality and Living Standards: A Note on the Staff of Life. [Later published in shortened form in *The China Quarterly*, 1984. no. 97: 91–3.]

Long, S. 1992. *China to 2000: Reform's Last Chance?* London: The Economist Intelligence Unit.

Lu Yuan. 1991. A Longitudinal Study of Chinese Managerial Behaviour: An Inside View of Decision-Making under the Economic Reform. Unpublished PhD thesis, Aston University, May.

1992. Working Note on Human Resource Management in China, Lancaster University, October.

Lu Yuan and Heard, R., 1995. Socialized Economic Action: A Comparison of Strategic Investment Decisions in China and Britain. *Organization Studies*, 16 (forthcoming).

Mann. J. 1989. *Beijing Jeep: The Short Unhappy Romance of American Business in China*. New York: Simon and Schuster.

Markoczy, L. 1990. Case Study of the Inter-Europa Bank. Unpublished Paper, Budapest University of Economics.

1993. Managerial and Organizational Learning in Hungarian-Western Mixed Management Organizations. *International Journal of Human Resource Management*, 4: 277–304.

Metcalf, H.C. and Urwick, L. (eds.) 1941. *Dynamic Administration: The Collected Papers of Mary Parker Follett*. London: Pitman.

Mintzberg, H. 1973. *The Nature of Managerial Work*. New York: Harper and Row.

Montias, J.M. 1988. On Hierarchies and Economic Reforms. *Journal of Institutional and Theoretical Economics*, no. 144: 832–8.

Moore, B. 1967. *The Social Origins of Dictatorship and Democracy*. London: Allen Lane, The Penguin Press.

Moore, W.E. 1962. The Attributes of an Industrial Order. In S. Nosow and Form W. H. *Man, Work and Society*. New York: Atherton.

National Council for US–China Trade [NCUSCT]. 1987. *U.S. Joint Ventures in China: A Progress Report*. Washington, DC: NCUSCT.

Nee, V. 1992. Organizational Dynamics of Market Transition: Hybrid Forms, Property Rights, and Mixed Economy in China. *Administrative Science Quarterly*, 37: 1–27.

Needham, J. 1980. *The Shorter Science and Civilization in China*. Volume 1. Cambridge: Cambridge University Press (paperback edition abridged by C.A. Ronan).

Ng Sek-Hong. 1984. One Brand of Workplace Democracy: The Workers' Congress in the Chinese Enterprise. *Journal of Industrial Relations*, 26: 56–75.

Nolan, P. and Dong Fureng (eds.). 1990. *The Chinese Economy and its Future: Achievements and Problems of Post-Mao Reform*. Oxford: Polity Press.

Nyaw, M.-K. 1991. The Significance and Managerial Roles of Trade Unions in Joint Ventures with China. In O. Shenkar (ed.) *Organization and Management in China 1979–1990*. Armonk, NY: M.E. Sharpe.

O'Leary, G. 1992. Chinese Trade Unions and Economic Reform. In E.K.Y. Chen, R. Lansbury, Ng Sek-Hong and S. Stewart (eds.) *Labour-Management Relations in the Asia-Pacific Region*. Hong Kong: Centre of Asian Studies, University of Hong Kong.

Ouchi, W.G. 1978. The Transmission of Control Through Organizational Hierarchy. *Academy of Management Journal*, 21: 173–92.

Pearson, M.M. 1991. *Joint Ventures in the People's Republic of China: The Control of Foreign Direct Investment under Socialism*. Princeton, NJ: Princeton University Press.

Peng Zheng. 1984. Speech on Drafting the Enterprise Law, 23 March. In *Collected Materials on Experiments into the Director Responsibility System*. Issued by the DRS Experiment Leadership Committee, Changzhou.

Perkins, D.H. 1988. Reforming China's Economic System. *Journal of Economic Literature*, 26: 601–45.

Perrow, C. 1970. *Organizational Analysis: A Sociological View*. London: Tavistock.

1986. Economic Theories of Organization. *Theory and Society*, 15: 11–45.

Pettigrew, A.M. 1973. *The Politics of Organizational Decision-Making*. London: Tavistock.

1985. *The Awakening Giant: Continuity and Change in ICI*. Oxford: Blackwell.

Prybyla, J.S. 1976. Work Incentives in the People's Republic of China. *Weltwirtschaftliches Archiv*, 112: 767–91.

Pugh, D.S. and Hickson, D.J. (eds.). 1976. *Organisational Structure in its Context*. Farnborough: D.C. Heath.

Punnett, B.J. and Ping Yu. 1991. Attitudes toward Doing Business with the PRC. In O. Shenkar (ed.) *Organization and Management in China 1979–1990*. Armonk, NY: M.E. Sharpe.

Pye, L.W. 1982. *Chinese Commercial Negotiating Style*. Cambridge, MA:

Oelgeschlager, Gunn and Hain.
1985. *Asian Power and Politics*. Cambridge, MA: Harvard University Press.

Qian Binghong. 1986. Social Values that Influence Chinese Organisational Behaviour. Unpublished paper, Shanghai Academy of Social Sciences, February.

Qian Yingyi and Xu Chenggang. 1993. Why China's Economic Reforms Differ: The M-Form Hierarchy and Entry/Expansion of the Non-State Sector. Research Programme on the Chinese Economy, Paper no. 25, July, London School of Economics.

Reader, J.A. 1987. Motivating Chinese Employees in Joint Ventures in the PRC. Unpublished paper, Appalachian State University, April.

Redding, S.G. 1990. *The Spirit of Chinese Capitalism*. Berlin: De Gruyter.

Riskin, C. 1987. *China's Political Economy The Quest for Development since 1949*. Oxford: Oxford University Press.

Schaan, J.-L. 1988. How to Control a Joint Venture even as a Minority Partner. *Journal of General Management*, 14: 4–16.

Scott, J. 1985. *Corporations, Classes and Capitalism*. London: Hutchinson, 2nd edn.

Scott, W.R. 1987. The Adolescence of Institutional Theory. *Administrative Science Quarterly*, 32: 493–511.

Seligman, S.D. 1990. *Dealing with the Chinese: A Practical Guide to Business Etiquette*. London: Mercury Books.

Shaw, S.M. and Woetzel, J.R. 1992. A Fresh Look at China. *The McKinsey Quarterly*, 1992/3: 37–51.

Shenkar, O. (ed.). 1991. *Organization and Management in China 1979–1990*. Armonk, NY: M.E. Sharpe.

Shenkar, O. and Ronen, S. 1987a. The Cultural Context of Negotiations: The Implications of Chinese Interpersonal Norms. *The Journal of Applied Behavioral Science*, 23: 263–75.

1987b. Structure and Importance of Work Goals among Managers in the People's Republic of China. *Academy of Management Journal*, 30: 564–76.

1989. Culture, Ideology or Economy: A Comparative Exploration of Work Goal Importance among Managers in Chinese Societies. In *Managing the Global Economy III*. Proceedings of the Third International Conference of the Eastern Academy of Management. Hong Kong, June.

Shenkar, O. and Zeira, Y. 1987. Human Resources Management in International Joint Ventures: Directions for Research. *Academy of Management Review*, 12: 546–57.

Shore, L.M., Eagle, B.W. and Jedel, M.J. 1993. China-United States Joint Ventures: A Typological Model of Goal Congruence and Cultural Understanding and their Importance for Effective Human Resource Management. *International Journal of Human Resource Management*, 4: 67–83.

Smith, A. H. 1894. *Chinese Characteristics*. New York: Fleming H. Revell.

Smith, D.H. 1974. *Confucius and Confucianism*. London: Paladin.

Smith, P.B. 1992. Organizational Behaviour and National Cultures. *British Journal of Management*, 3: 39–51.

Solinger, D.J. 1989. Urban Reform and Relational Contracting in Post-Mao China. An Interpretation of the Transition from Plan to Market. *Studies in Comparative Communism*, 23: 171–85.

Specter, C.N. and Solomon, J.S. 1991. The Human Resource Factor in Chinese Management Reform. In O. Shenkar (ed.) 1991. *Organization and Management in*

China 1979–1990. Armonk, NY: M.E. Sharpe.

Starbuck, W.H. 1965. Organizational Growth and Development. In J.G. March (ed.) *Handbook of Organizations*. Chicago: Rand McNally.

State Council Research Office 1989. The Last Decade: Bridging the Economic Gap. *Beijing Review*, 32/5: 16–23.

State Statistical Bureau. 1988. A Decade of Reform: Facts and Figures. A series of ten articles in *Beijing Review*, 31/39–47, 49.

1993. *Statistical Yearbook of China 1993*. Beijing.

Stewart, S. 1992. China's Managers. *The International Executive*, 34: 165–79.

Stewart, S. and Chong Chung Him. 1990. Chinese Winners: Views of Senior PRC Managers on the Reasons for their Success. *International Studies of Management and Organization*, 20: 57–68.

Stewart, S. and Yeung Yun Choi. 1990. Chinese Decision-making: A Case Study of How the Hexian Paper Pulp Project was Accepted for Possible Inclusion in China's Seventh Five Year Plan. *Public Administration and Development*, 10: 41–51.

Teagarden, M.B. and Von Glinow, M.A. 1991. Sino-Foreign Strategic Alliance Types and Related Operating Characteristics. In O. Shenkar (ed.) *Organization and Management in China 1979–1990*. Armonk, NY: M.E. Sharpe.

Tidrick, G. and Chen Jiyuan (eds.). 1987. *China's Industrial Reform*. New York: Oxford University Press for the World Bank.

Tung, R.L. 1982. *US China Trade Negotiations*. New York: Pergamon.

1991. Motivation in Chinese Industrial Enterprises. In R.M. Steers and L.W. Porter (eds.) *Innovation and Work Behavior*, 5th edn, New York: McGraw-Hill.

US–China Business Council [USCBC]. 1990. *U.S. Investment in China*. Washington, DC: China Business Forum.

Vogel, E. 1989. *One Step Ahead in China: Guangdong under Reform*. Cambridge, MA: Harvard University Press.

Walder, A.G. 1986. *Communist Neo-Traditionalism: Work and Authority in Chinese Industry*. Berkeley, CA: University of California Press.

1987. Wage Reform and the Web of Factory Interests. *The China Quarterly*, no. 109: 22–41.

1989. Factory and Manager in an Era of Reform. *The China Quarterly*, no. 118: 242–64.

Waley, A. (trans.). 1938. *The Analects of Confucius*. London: Allen and Unwin.

Wang Hsiaohsien. 1978. Wage adjustments in communist China. *Issues and Studies*, XIV: 12–21

Wang Jingzhong. 1986. *Speeches on the Director Responsibility System*. Beijing: Enterprise Management Publishing House.

Wang Yingluo and Wedley, W.C. (eds.). 1990. *Proceedings of the Canada–China International Management Conference*. Xian, August.

Wang Zhongming. 1990. Human Resource Management in China: Recent Trends. In R. Pieper (ed.) *Human Resource Management: An International Comparison*. Berlin: De Gruyter.

Warner, M. 1986. 'The Long March' of Chinese Management Education, 1979–84. *The China Quarterly*, no. 106: 326–42

1992. *How Chinese Managers Learn: Management and Industrial Training in China*. London: Macmillan

1993. Human Resources Management 'with Chinese Characteristics'. *International*

Journal of Human Resource Management, 4: 45–65.

1994. Japanese Culture, Western Management: The Impact of Taylorism on Human Resources in Japan. *Organization Studies*, 15 (forthcoming).

Warner, M. (ed.). 1987. *Management Reforms in China*. London: Frances Pinter.

Warwick, D.P. 1975. *A Theory of Public Bureaucracy*. Cambridge, MA: Harvard University Press.

Weber, M. 1964. *The Theory of Social and Economic Organization*. (Trans. A.M. Henderson and T. Parsons). New York: Free Press.

1968. *Economy and Society: An Outline of Interpretative Sociology*. New York: Oxford University Press.

White, G. 1987. Labour Market Reform in Chinese Industry. In M. Warner (ed.) *Management Reforms in China*. London: Frances Pinter.

Whitley, R.D. 1991. The Social Construction of Business Systems in East Asia. *Organization Studies*, 12: 1–28.

1992. *Business Systems in East Asia: Firms, Markets and Societies*. London: Sage.

1994. Varieties of Effective Forms of Economic Organisation: Firms and Markets in Comparative Perspective. *Organization Studies*, 15 (forthcoming).

Whittaker, D.H. 1990. The End of Japanese-Style Employment? *Work, Employment and Society*, 4: 321–47.

Williamson, O.E. 1975. *Markets and Hierarchies*. New York: Free Press.

1985. *The Economic Institutions of Capitalism*. New York: Free Press.

1986. *Economic Organization*. Brighton: Wheatsheaf.

Wood, S. 1987. Towards Socialist-Capitalist Comparisons of the Organisational Problem. In J.Child and P. Bate (eds.) *Organisation of Innovation: East–West Perspectives*. Berlin: De Gruyter.

World Bank. 1985. *China: Long Term Development Issues and Options*. Baltimore: Johns Hopkins University Press.

Wu Shuqing. 1990. Article in People's Daily, 23 January, reported under the title 'Can China Practise Market Economy?' *China Daily*, 25 January: 4.

Xiao Liang. 1986. People's Daily, 17 March. Cited in A. Fujimoto. Progress in China's Enterprise Reform. *China Newsletter*, no. 68, May–June 1987: 3.

Yang, M.MH. 1989. Between State and Society: The Construction of Corporateness in a Chinese Socialist Factory. *The Australian Journal of Chinese Affairs*, no.22: 31–60

Yang Xiaobing. 1988. Enterprise Law: A Milestone for Reform. *Beijing Review*, 31/18: 20–2.

Yang Xiaogong. 1992. Foreign-Funded Enterprises in China. *Beijing Review*, 35/5–6, 3–16 February: 20–2.

Yuan Baohua 1990. Qiye De Dang Zheng Guangxi He Gan Qun Guangxi [The Relationship between the Party and Administration, and the Relationship between Cadres and Workers]. *China Entrepreneur*, 8: 5–6.

Yao, Yilin. 1989. Report on the Draft 1989 Plan for National Economic and Social Development delivered to the 2nd Session of the 7th National People's Congress, 21 March 1989. Printed in *Beijing Review*, 32, 1–7 May, centrefold.

Zhao Ziyang. 1986. Speech of June 1986 quoted by Yuan Baohua in his Address on the Implementation of the Enterprise Law, 5 May 1988. Reported in Nantong Economic Commission, *Study Materials on the Enterprise Law*, Nantong. 1988.

1987. *Report Delivered at the 13th National Congress of the CPC*. Beijing: Foreign Languages Press.

Zheng Guangliang. 1987. The Leadership System. In G. Tidrick and Chen Jiyuan (eds.). *China's Industrial Reform*. New York: Oxford University Press.

Index

Cambridge Studies in Management